BIG ISLAND
OF HAWAII

W9-CFB-013

Portions of this book appear in *Fodor's Hawaii*.

WELCOME TO BIG ISLAND

It takes time to explore the Big Island's stunning landscapes, but the rewards are spectacular. Hawaii's largest island has more than 250 miles of coast from Kona to Hilo and beyond, lined with incredible beaches, elegant resorts, coffee farms, rain forests, and waterfalls. History and culture resonate everywhere, from Kealakekua Bay, Captain Cook's landing site and modern-day snorkeling haven, to the rugged Valley of Kings near Waipio. Above it all, snowcapped Mauna Kea contrasts with fiery Mauna Loa, the centerpiece of popular Hawaii Volcanoes National Park.

TOP REASONS TO GO

★ **Hawaii Volcanoes National Park:** The world's most active volcano is an amazing sight.

★ **Fun Towns:** Humming Kailua-Kona, cowboy country Waimea, rainbow-streaked Hilo.

★ **Stargazing:** Mauna Kea's peak is the best place on Earth to stare out into space.

★ **Beaches:** The Big Island offers sand in many shades—black, white, or even green.

★ **Wildlife:** You can watch sea turtles on the beach or humpback whales in the waves.

★ **Kona Coffee:** Farm tours, smooth sips, and a coffee cultural festival are all memorable.

Fodor's BIG ISLAND OF HAWAII

Publisher: Amanda D'Acierno, *Senior Vice President*

Editorial: Arabella Bowen, *Editor in Chief*; Linda Cabasin, *Editorial Director*

Design: Fabrizio La Rocca, *Vice President, Creative Director*; Tina Malaney, *Associate Art Director*; Chie Ushio, *Senior Designer*; Ann McBride, *Production Designer*

Photography: Melanie Marin, *Associate Director of Photography*; Jessica Parkhill and Jennifer Romains, *Researchers*

Maps: Rebecca Baer, *Senior Map Editor*; Henry Colomb and Mark Stroud, Moon Street Cartography; David Lindroth, Inc. *Cartographers*

Production: Linda Schmidt, *Managing Editor*; Evangelos Vasilakis, *Associate Managing Editor*; Angela L. McLean, *Senior Production Manager*

Sales: Jacqueline Lebow, *Sales Director*

Marketing & Publicity: Heather Dalton, *Marketing Director*; Katherine Fleming, *Senior Publicist*

Business & Operations: Susan Livingston, *Vice President, Strategic Business Planning*; Sue Daulton, *Vice President, Operations*

Fodors.com: Megan Bell, *Executive Director, Revenue & Business Development*; Yasmin Marinaro, *Senior Director, Marketing & Partnerships*

Copyright © 2014 by Fodor's Travel, a division of Random House LLC

Writers: Karen Anderson, Kristina Anderson

Editor: Eric B. Wechter
Editorial Contributor: Andrea Lehman
Production Editor: Evangelos Vasilakis

Fodor's is a registered trademark of Random House LLC. All rights reserved. Published in the United States by Fodor's Travel, a division of Random House LLC, New York, a Penguin Random House Company, and in Canada by Random House of Canada Limited, Toronto. No maps, illustrations, or other portions of this book may be reproduced in any form without written permission from the publisher.

5th Edition

ISBN 978-0-8041-4214-4

ISSN 1934-5542

All details in this book are based on information supplied to us at press time. Always confirm information when it matters, especially if you're making a detour to visit a specific place. Fodor's expressly disclaims any liability, loss, or risk, personal or otherwise, that is incurred as a consequence of the use of any of the contents of this book.

SPECIAL SALES

This book is available at special discounts for bulk purchases for sales promotions or premiums. For more information, e-mail specialmarkets@randomhouse.com

Printed in the United States of America

10 9 8 7 6 5 4 3

CONTENTS

Fodor's Features

MAPS

ABOUT
THIS GUIDE

Fodor's Recommendations

Everything in this guide is worth doing—we don't cover what isn't—but exceptional sights, hotels, and restaurants are recognized with additional accolades. **Fodor's**Choice★ indicates our top recommendations; and **Best Bets** call attention to notable hotels and restaurants in various categories. Care to nominate a new place? Visit Fodors.com/contact-us.

Trip Costs

We list prices wherever possible to help you budget well. Hotel and restaurant price categories from **$** to **$$$$** are noted alongside each recommendation. For hotels, we include the lowest cost of a standard double room in high season. For restaurants, we cite the average price of a main course at dinner or, if dinner isn't served, at lunch. For attractions, we always list adult admission fees; discounts are usually available for children, students, and senior citizens.

Hotels

Our local writers vet every hotel to recommend the best overnights in each price category, from budget to expensive. Unless otherwise specified, you can expect private bath, phone, and TV in your room. For expanded hotel reviews, facilities, and deals visit Fodors.com.

Restaurants

Unless we state otherwise, restaurants are open for lunch and dinner daily. We mention dress code only when there's a specific requirement and reservations only when they're essential or not accepted. To make restaurant reservations, visit Fodors.com.

Credit Cards

The hotels and restaurants in this guide typically accept credit cards. If not, we'll say so.

Top Picks	Hotels &
★ **Fodor's**Choice	**Restaurants**
	⛩ Hotel
Listings	⤶ Number of
✉ Address	rooms
✉ Branch address	ꛛ Meal plans
☎ Telephone	✕ Restaurant
🖷 Fax	⚓ Reservations
⊕ Website	⌂ Dress code
✍ E-mail	▭ No credit cards
▣ Admission fee	Ⓢ Price
⊘ Open/closed	
times	**Other**
Ⓜ Subway	⇨ See also
✛ Directions or	☞ Take note
Map coordinates	🏌 Golf facilities

1

EXPERIENCE
BIG ISLAND

WHAT'S WHERE

1 Kailua-Kona. This seaside town is packed with restaurants, shops, and a busy waterfront bustling with tourists along the main street, Alii Drive.

2 The Kona Coast. This area stretches a bit north of Kailua-Kona and much farther south, including gorgeous Kealakekua Bay. It's the place to take farm tours and taste samples of world-famous Kona Coffee.

3 The Kohala Coast. The sparkling coast is home to all those long, white-sand beaches, and the expensive resorts that go with them.

4 Waimea. Ranches sprawl across the cool, upland meadows of the area, known as *paniolo* (cowboy) country.

5 Mauna Kea. Climb (or drive) this 13,796-foot mountain for what's considered the world's best stargazing, with 13 telescopes perched on top.

6 The Hamakua Coast. Waterfalls, dramatic cliffs, ocean views, ancient hidden valleys, rain forests, and the stunning Waipio Valley are just a few of the treats here.

7 Hilo. Known as the City of Rainbows for all its rain, Hilo is often skipped by tourists in favor of the sunny Kohala Coast. But for what many consider the "real" Hawaii, as well as incredible rain forests, waterfalls, and the island's best farmers' market, Hilo can't be beat.

8 Puna. This is where the most recent lava flows are happening, so it has brand-new jet-black beaches with volcanic hot springs.

9 Hawaii Volcanoes National Park and vicinity. The land around the park is continually expanding, as the active Kilauea Volcano sends lava spilling into the ocean. The nearby town of Volcano Village provides a great base for exploring the park.

10 Kau and Ka Lae (South Point). Round the southernmost part of the island for two of the Big Island's most unusual beaches: Papakolea (Green Sands) Beach, and Punaluu Black Sand Beach.

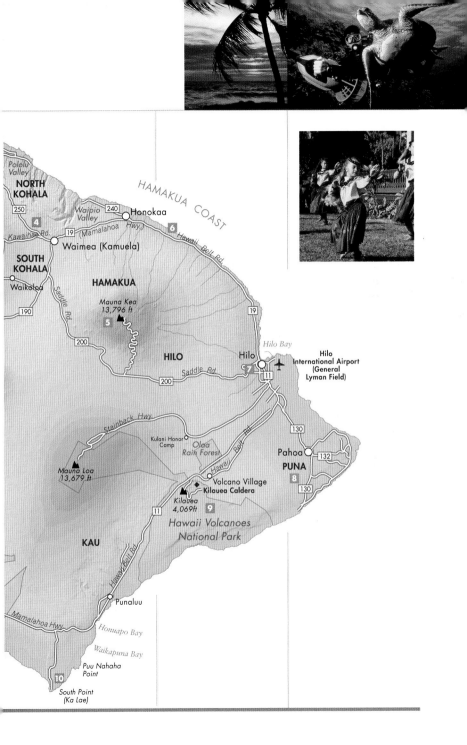

NORTH KOHALA

Pololu Valley

250

4

Kawaihae Rd.

SOUTH KOHALA

Waikoloa

190

200

Saddle Rd.

HAMAKUA COAST

Waipio Valley

240

19 (Mamalahoa Hwy.)

Waimea (Kamuela)

Honokaa

6

Hawaii Belt Rd.

HAMAKUA

Mauna Kea
13,796 ft

5

200

Saddle Rd.

19

HILO

7

11

Hilo Bay

Hilo

Hilo International Airport (General Lyman Field)

Stainback Hwy.

Kulani Honor Camp

Olaa Rain Forest

Hawaii Belt Rd.

130

Pahoa

132

PUNA

8

130

Mauna Loa
13,679 ft

Volcano Village
Kilauea Caldera

Kilauea
4,069ft

9

11

Hawaii Volcanoes National Park

KAU

Hawaii Belt Rd.

Punaluu

Honuapo Bay

Waikapuna Bay

Mamalahoa Hwy

Puu Nahaha Point

10

South Point (Ka Lae)

BIG ISLAND AND HAWAII TODAY

You could fit all the other Hawaiian Islands into the Big Island and still have a little room left over—hence the name. Locals refer to the island by side: the Kona (leeward) side to the west and Hilo side to the east. Most of the resorts, condos, attractions, and restaurants are located along 30 miles of the sunny Kona side, while the rainy, windward Hilo side offers a much more local and "Old Hawaii" experience.

Hawaiian culture and tradition have experienced a renaissance over the last few decades. New developments often have a Hawaiian cultural expert on staff to ensure cultural sensitivity and to educate newcomers.

Nonetheless, development remains an issue for all Islanders—land prices are expensive, putting many areas out of reach for the local population. The cost of living and the cost of doing business make Hawaii one of the more challenging places to live in the United States if you are on a fixed income.

Sustainability

Although sustainability is an effective buzzword and authentic direction for the Islands' dining establishments, 90% of Hawaii's food and energy is imported.

Most of the land was used for mono-cropping of pineapple or sugarcane, both of which have all but vanished. Sugarcane is now only produced on Maui, while pineapple production has dropped precipitously. Dole, once the largest pineapple company in Hawaii, closed its plants in 1991, and after 90 years, Del Monte stopped pineapple production in 2008. The next year, Maui Land and Pineapple Company also ceased its Maui Gold pineapple operation, although in early 2010 a group of executives took over one third of the land and created a new company. The low cost of labor and transportation from Latin American and Southeast Asian pineapple producers are factors contributing to the industry's demise in Hawaii. Although this proves daunting, it also sets the stage for great agricultural change to be explored.

Back-to-Basics Agriculture

Emulating how the Hawaiian ancestors lived and returning to their simple ways of growing and sharing a variety of foods has become a statewide initiative. Hawaii boasts the natural conditions and talent to produce diversity in agriculture, from coffee to flowers. The seed of this movement thrives through various farmers' markets and partnerships between restaurants and local farmers. Localized efforts such as the Hawaii Farm Bureau Federation are collectively leading the organic and sustainable agricultural renaissance. From home-cooked meals to casual plate lunches to fine-dining cuisine, cooks, farmers, and chefs are blazing a trail of sustainability, helping to enrich the culinary tapestry of Hawaii and to uplift the Islands' overall quality of life.

Tourism and the Economy

The over-$14.3-billion tourism industry represents a third of Hawaii's state income. With a record number of visitors coming to the Islands in 2012, tourism is poised to recover from the economic downturn of previous years. Arrivals from Asia, Europe, Latin America, Australia, and New Zealand increased by 21.3 percent from 2011. Visitor spending contributes to at least 167,000 jobs locally.

One way the industry has changed has been to adopt more eco-conscious practices that positively impact local communities and the natural environment.

More companies are also incorporating authentic Hawaiiana into their programs and aim not only to provide a commercially viable tour but also to ensure that the visitor leaves feeling connected to the host culture.

Sovereignty

Political issues of sovereignty continue to divide Native Hawaiians, who have formed myriad organizations, each operating with a separate agenda and lacking one collectively defined goal. Ranging from achieving complete independence to solidifying a nation within a nation, existing sovereignty models remain fractured and their future unresolved.

The introduction of the Native Hawaiian Government Reorganization Act of 2009 (The Akaka Bill) attempted to set up a legal framework in which Native Hawaiians can attain federal recognition and coexist as a self-governed entity. Still held up in Congress, the bill has faced innumerable challenges through the years, including among Native Hawaiians who disagree about its merits and mission.

Rise of Hawaiian Pride

After the overthrow of the monarchy in 1893, a process of Americanization began. Traditions were duly silenced in the name of citizenship. Teaching Hawaiian language was banned from schools and children were distanced from their local customs.

But Hawaiians are resilient people, and with the rise of the civil rights movement they began to reflect on their own national identity, bringing an astonishing renaissance of the Hawaiian culture to fruition.

The people rediscovered language, hula, chanting, and even the traditional Polynesian arts of canoe building and wayfinding (navigation by the stars without use of instruments). This cultural resurrection is now firmly established in today's Hawaiian culture, with a palpable pride that exudes from Hawaiians young and old.

The election of President Barack Obama increased Hawaiian pride. The president's strong connection and commitment to Hawaiian values of diversity, spirituality, family, and conservation have restored confidence that Hawaii can inspire a more peaceful, tolerant, and environmentally conscious world.

The Arts

The Hawaiian Islands have inspired artistic expression from the time they were first inhabited. From ancient hula to digital filmmaking, the arts are alive and well. Honolulu is the artistic hub of the state. The Honolulu Museum of Art has an impressive permanent collection and hosts major exhibitions throughout the year. It comprises four locations including the spectacular Shangri La, the former home of heiress Doris Duke, filled with Islamic treasures. The Hawaii Theater in Honolulu—a restored art deco palace—stages theatrical productions, concerts, and films. The Maui Arts & Cultural Center (MACC) has a 1,200-seat theater for concerts, theatrical productions, and film, as well as an amphitheater and art gallery. Numerous art galleries thrive on the Islands.

BIG ISLAND PLANNER

When You Arrive

The Big Island's two main airports are almost directly across the island from each other. Kona International Airport, on the west side, is about a 10-minute drive from Kailua-Kona and 30 to 45 minutes from the Kohala Coast. On the east side, Hilo International Airport, 2 miles from downtown Hilo, is about 40 minutes from Hawaii Volcanoes National Park. A 2½-hour drive connects Hilo and Kailua-Kona.

Visitor Information

Before you go, contact the Big Island Visitors Bureau to request a free official vacation planner. The Hawaii Island Chamber of Commerce also has links to dozens of museums, attractions, bed-and-breakfasts, and parks on its website. The Kona-Kohala Chamber of Commerce also has resources for the west side of the island.

Big Island Visitors Bureau ☎ *808/961–5797, 800/648–2441* ⊕ *www.bigisland.org.*

Hawaii Island Chamber of Commerce ☎ *808/935–7178* ⊕ *www.hicc.biz.* **Kona-Kohala Chamber of Commerce** ✉ *75-5737 Kuakini Hwy., Suite 208, Kailua-Kona* ☎ *808/329–1758* ⊕ *www.kona-kohala.com.*

Getting Here and Around

It's essential to rent a car when visiting the Big Island. As the name suggests, it's a big island, and it takes a while to get from point A to point B.

For those who want to travel from the west side to the east side, or vice versa, the newly rerouted and repaved Saddle Road creates a nice shortcut across the middle of the island.

See Travel Smart Big Island for more information on renting a car and driving.

Island Driving Times

Before you embark on your day trip, it's a good idea to know how long it will take you to get to your destination. Some areas, like downtown Kailua-Kona and Waimea, can become congested at certain times of day. For those traveling to South Kona, the county has opened a long-awaited bypass road between Keauhou and Kealakekua, which has alleviated congestion considerably during rush hour. In general, you can expect the following average driving times:

Kailua-Kona to Kealakekua Bay	14 miles/25 min
Kailua-Kona to Kohala Coast	32 miles/40 min
Kailua-Kona to Waimea	40 miles/1 hr
Kailua-Kona to Hamakua Coast	53 miles/1 hr, 40 min
Kailua-Kona to Hilo	75 miles/2½ hrs
Kohala Coast to Waimea	16 miles/20 min
Kohala Coast to Hamakua Coast	29 miles/55 min
Hilo to Volcano	30 miles/40 min

Weather-Related Driving Tips

As a result of multiple microclimates and varying elevations, the Big Island experiences its share of diverse weather. On one circle-the-island trip you may experience combinations of the following: intensely heavy tropical downpours; cool, windy conditions; searing heat; and even snow flurries if you happen to be driving up Mauna Kea. Be cautious on the mostly single-lane roads through rural areas, as these can be slick, winding, and poorly lit. Pull over to the side of the road to wait out intense bursts of rain that may obscure vision and create other hazardous conditions. These are usually brief and may even end with a rainbow.

Dining and Lodging on the Big Island

Hawaii is a melting pot of cultures, and nowhere is this more apparent than in its cuisine. From luau and "plate lunches" to sushi and steak, there's no shortage of interesting flavors and presentations. The "grow local, buy local" movement is in full force on the Big Island. This is a welcome shift from years past, in which many foods were imported, and it's a happy trend for visitors, who get to taste juicy, flavorful Waimea tomatoes, handmade Hamakua goat cheese, locally raised beef, or even island-grown wine. Whether you're looking for a quick snack or a multicourse meal, you can find the best that the island has to offer at farmers' markets, restaurants, and cafés.

Consider spending part of your vacation at a resort and part of it at a small inn or bed-and-breakfast. The big resorts sit squarely on some of the best beaches on the Big Island, and they have a lot to offer—spas, golf, and great restaurants for starters. The B&Bs provide a more intimate experience in settings as diverse as an upcountry ranch, a rain-forest tree house, and a Victorian mansion perched on a dramatic sea cliff. Several romantic B&Bs nestle in the rain forest surrounding Hawaii Volcanoes National Park— very convenient (and romantic) after a nighttime lava hike.

Will I See Flowing Lava?

Without question, the best time to see lava is at night. However, you may not know until the day of your visit whether the lava flow will be in an accessible location, or even visible from a distance. Your best bet is to call the visitor center at Hawaii Volcanoes National Park before you head out. No matter what's happening at the active lava flows, there's plenty to see and do inside the national park, where the Halemaumau Crater is located. The nighttime glow of the crater, located below the Jaggar Museum and Halemaumau Overlook, is a jaw-dropping sight and one that should not be missed. Plan your trip to the volcano so that you can be near the crater at dusk. Fortunately, the park is open 24 hours a day, and night visits are allowed.

In recent years, active lava flows have been taking place outside of the park in lower Puna. When lava is flowing outside the park boundaries, hiking is sometimes regulated because trails pass through private land. Pay attention to all warning signs, and take safety advice from park rangers seriously. ■TIP→ **Bring a flashlight, water, and sturdy shoes, and be prepared for some rough going over the lava fields at night.**

For more information about visiting Hawaii Volcanoes National Park, see Chapter 2.

BIG ISLAND OF HAWAII TOP ATTRACTIONS

The Lava Show
(A) Watch as fiery hot lava pours into the sea, creating huge steaming explosions; stare in awe at nighttime lava fireworks; and hike across the floor of a still-steaming crater at Hawaii Volcanoes National Park.

Green Sands Beach
(B) It's a bit off the beaten track, but this is one of the few places in the world to see green sand, which gets its unusual color from the mineral olivine. And it happens to be surrounded by turquoise waters and dramatic cliffs.

Exploring Waipio Valley
(C) Whichever way you choose to get there—on horseback, in a four-wheel drive, or on foot—you'll discover that the Valley of the Kings, on the Hamakua Coast, is full of sky-high waterfalls, lush green cliffs, and a mystical quality that can't quite be described or rivaled.

A Window on the Universe
(D) Teams of astronomers from all over the world come to Mauna Kea for the clearest skies and some of the best conditions anywhere. Head up the mountain in the late afternoon for the prettiest sunset on this island and the best stargazing on this planet.

The Perfect Beach
(E) Whether you drive the paved roads to Hapuna, Kaunaoa (also known as Mauna Kea), Anaehoomalu Bay, or Kua Bay, or walk the rocky route to Makalawena, you'll find that the Big Island abounds with postcard-perfect beaches.

Stunning Waterfalls
(F) Watch rainbows forming in the mist; then take a refreshing dip in cold, deep pools fed by powerful waterfalls spilling over the dramatic cliffs of the Hamakua Coast.

A Snooze with a Sea Turtle

(**G**) Hang out at Punaluu Black Sand Beach, fringed with coconut groves, where sea turtles surf the waves and nap on the black sands.

A Healing Lomilomi Massage

(**H**) The traditional Hawaiian *lomilomi* technique uses a combination of arms, elbows, hands, and breath to impart the overall sense of well-being associated with this ancient healing practice.

A Kona Coffee Farm Tour

(**I**) Spend an afternoon discovering why Kona coffee commands those high prices. Visit a working estate and watch as "cherries" become beans, enjoy the smoky aromas of the roasting process, then indulge in the smoothest cup of coffee you'll ever taste. Did we mention that it's all free? Our favorite: Lions Gate Farms in the heart of Honaunau's coffee belt. The annual 10-day Kona Coffee Cultural Festival in November celebrates coffee with tours, cupping contests, tastings, and special events.

Whale the Day Away

(**J**) From November to late April, you can sit on any beach on the west side of the island and watch breathtaking humpback whales. The sight of their massive bodies, glistening as they move through the water, or the occasional perfect fluke cutting through the surface, is a matchless experience.

A Swim Through Coral Gardens

Diving or snorkeling in the crystal-clear waters off the Kona Coast is like being let loose in your very own ocean-size aquarium. Bright yellow, purple, and rose-colored coral creates surreal kingdoms ruled by octopi, turtles, rays, dolphins, and fish in every color of the rainbow.

GREAT ITINERARIES

Yes, the Big Island is big, and yes, there's a lot to see. If you're short on time, consider flying into one airport and out of the other. That will give you the opportunity to see both sides of the island without ever having to backtrack. Decide what sort of note you'd rather end on to determine your route—if you'd prefer to spend your last few days near the beach, go from east to west; if hiking through rain forests and showering in waterfalls sounds like a better way to wrap up the trip, move from west to east. If you're short on time, head straight for Hawaii Volcanoes National Park and briefly visit Hilo before traveling the Hamakua Coast route and making your new base in Kailua-Kona.

From exploring the shores of green- and black-sand beaches to stargazing atop Mauna Kea, there's no shortage of ways to spend the day immersed in nature on the Big Island. Choose a couple or several of our favorite one-day itineraries to suit your interest and length of stay.

Green Hawaii

Take full advantage of Hawaii's living classroom. Visit one of the island's botanical gardens or take a farm tour in the morning, then head to the Natural Energy Lab, near the Kona International Airport, for a peek at how various enterprises raise shellfish, spirulina, and even seahorses. Wrap it up with an evening spent enjoying the delicious island-grown products at one of Waimea's top restaurants, such as local favorite Merriman's or its nearby neighbor Red Water Cafe.

Black and Green Sand

Check out some of the unusual beaches you'll find only on the Big Island. Start with a hike into Green Sands Beach near South Point and plan to spend some time sitting on the beach, dipping into the bay's turquoise waters, and marveling at the surreal beauty of this spot.

When you've had your fill, hop back in the car and head south about half an hour to Punaluu Black Sand Beach, the favorite nesting place of the endangered Hawaiian hawksbill turtle. Although the surf is often too rough to go swimming with green sea turtles, there are typically at least two or three napping on the beach at any given time.

Sun and Stars

Spend the day lounging on a Kohala Coast beach (Hapuna, Kaunaoa—also known as Mauna Kea—or Kua Bay), but throw jackets and boots in the car because you'll be catching the sunset from Mauna Kea's summit. Bundle up and stick around after darkness falls for some of the world's best stargazing.

For the safest, most comfortable experience, book a summit tour or stop in at the Onizuka Center for International Astronomy, a visitor center located at about 9,000 feet, or join the free summit tour at 1 pm on Saturday or Sunday, and return to the center to use the telescopes for evening stargazing.

Hike Volcanoes

Devote a full day (at least) to exploring Hawaii Volcanoes National Park. Head out on the Kilauea Iki trail—a 4-mile loop near Thurston Lava Tube—by late morning. Leave the park to grab lunch at nearby restaurants in Volcano Village just a few minutes away, or plan ahead and pack your own picnic before you start your morning hike. Later you can take a stroll past the steam vents and sulfur banks, and then hit the Jaggar Museum, which offers great views of Halemaumau Crater's glow at night.

Majestic Waterfalls and Kings' Valleys

Take a day to enjoy the splendors of the Hamakua Coast—any gorge you see on the road is an indication of a waterfall waiting to be explored. For a sure bet, head to beautiful Waipio Valley. Book a horseback, hiking, or four-wheel-drive tour, or walk on in yourself (just keep in mind that it's an arduous hike back up—a 25% grade for a little over a mile).

Once in the valley, take your first right to get to the black-sand beach. Take a moment to sit here—the ancient Hawaiians believed this was where souls crossed over to the afterlife. Whether you believe it or not, there's something unmistakably special about this place.

Waterfalls abound in the valley, depending on the amount of recent rainfall. Your best bet is to follow the river from the beach to the back of the valley, where a waterfall and its lovely pool await.

Underwater Day

Explore the colorful reefs populated with tropical fish off the Big Island's coast. We challenge you to stop thinking about the world beneath the waves when you're back on land. Our favorite spots include easily accessible Kahaluu Beach Park (off Alii Drive), Kealakekua Bay, and the Kapoho Tide Pools.

Early morning or late afternoon is the best time to see pods of Hawaiian spinner dolphins that rest in calm bays, but you're likely to encounter turtles any time of day, along with convict tangs, puffer fish, triggerfish, angelfish, spotted moray eels, trumpet fish, and hundreds of other brightly colored species.

Thermal Springs and Waterfalls

Due to its remote location, many visitors skip Puna. They don't know what they're missing. Venture into this isolated area for a morning, and you'll be rewarded with lava-tube hikes (Kilauea Caverns of Fire), volcanically heated pools (Ahalanui Park), and tide pools brimming with colorful coral, fish, and the occasional turtle (Kapoho Tide Pools).

Head to Hilo in the afternoon to visit Rainbow Falls, located right in town, or Akaka Falls, just outside town. Stroll Banyan Drive and Queen Liliuokalani Gardens before dining at one of Hilo's great restaurants.

Pololu and Paniolo Country

North Kohala is a world away from the resorts of the coast. Visit the quaint artists' community of Hawi; then head to the end of the road at Pololu Valley for amazing views.

A steep ½-mile hike leads to a fantastic black-sand beach surrounded by beautiful, sheer, green cliffs. Back on the road, head up Highway 250 to Waimea and the rolling hills and pastures of *paniolo* country. Indulge in a memorable meal at one of the town's fantastic restaurants.

Venture Off-Road

Book an ATV tour or take your four-wheel drive for a spin to check out some of the Big Island's isolated beaches. There are green beaches (in addition to *the* Green Sands Beach) waiting in the Kau region and ruggedly beautiful white beaches with perfect turquoise water along the Kohala Coast; deal with the tough, four-wheel-drive-only roads into these beaches and you're likely to be rewarded with a pristine tropical beach all to yourself.

THE HAWAIIAN ISLANDS

Oahu. The state's capital, Honolulu, is on Oahu; this is the center of Hawaii's economy and by far the most populated island in the chain—976,000 residents add up to 71% of the state's population. At 597 square miles Oahu is the third largest island in the chain; the majority of residents live in or around Honolulu, so the rest of the island still fits neatly into the tropical, untouched vision of Hawaii. Situated southeast of Kauai and northwest of Maui, Oahu is a central location for island hopping. Pearl Harbor, iconic Waikiki Beach, and surfing contests on the legendary North Shore are all here.

Maui. The second-largest island in the chain, Maui is northwest of the Big Island and close enough to be visible from its beaches on a clear day. The island's 729 square miles are home to only 150,000 people but host more than 2 million tourists every year. With its restaurants and lively nightlife, Maui is the only island that competes with Oahu in terms of entertainment; its charm lies in the fact that although entertainment is available, Maui's towns still feel like island villages compared to the heaving modern city of Honolulu.

Hawaii (The Big Island). The Big Island has the second-largest population of the Islands (almost 190,000) but feels sparsely settled due to its size. It's 4,038 square miles and growing—all the other Islands could fit onto the Big Island and there would still be room left over. The southernmost island in the chain (slightly southeast of Maui), the Big Island is home to Kilauea, the most active volcano on the planet. It percolates within Volcanoes National Park, which draws nearly 3 million visitors every year.

Kauai. The northernmost island in the chain (northwest of Oahu), Kauai is, at approximately 622 square miles, the fourth largest of all the Islands and the least populated of the larger Islands, with 68,000 residents. Known as the Garden Isle, this island is home to lush botanical gardens as well as the stunning Napali Coast and Waimea Canyon. The island is a favorite with honeymooners and others wanting to get away from it all—lush and peaceful, it's the perfect escape from the modern world.

Molokai. North of Lanai and Maui, and east of Oahu, Molokai is Hawaii's fifth-largest island, encompassing 260 square miles. On a clear night, the lights of Honolulu are visible from Molokai's western shore. Molokai is sparsely populated, with about 7,300 residents, the majority of whom are Native Hawaiians. Most of the island's 79,000 annual visitors travel from Maui or Oahu to spend the day exploring its beaches, cliffs, and former leper colony on Kalaupapa Peninsula.

Lanai. Lying just off Maui's western coast, Lanai looks nothing like its sister Islands, with pine trees and deserts in place of palm trees and beaches. Still, the tiny 140-square-mile island is home to about 3,200 residents and draws an average of 75,000 visitors each year to two resorts (one in the mountains and one at the shore), both operated by Four Seasons, and the small, 11-room Hotel Lanai.

Hawaii's Geology

The Hawaiian Islands comprise more than just the islands inhabited and visited by humans. A total of 19 islands and atolls constitute the State of Hawaii, with a total landmass of 6,423.4 square miles.

The Islands are actually exposed peaks of a submersed mountain range called

the Hawaiian Ridge-Emperor Seamounts chain. The range was formed as the Pacific plate moves very slowly (around 32 miles every million years—or about as much as your fingernails grow in one year) over a hot spot in the Earth's mantle. Because the plate moves northwestwardly, the Islands in the northwest portion of the archipelago (chain) are older, which is also why they're smaller—they have been eroding longer and have actually sunk back into the sea floor.

The Big Island is the youngest, and thus the largest, island in the chain. It is built from five different volcanoes, including Mauna Loa, which is the largest mountain on the planet (when measured from the bottom of the sea floor). Mauna Loa and Kilauea are the only Hawaiian volcanoes still erupting with any sort of frequency. Mauna Loa last erupted in 1984. Kilauea has been continuously erupting since 1983.

Mauna Kea (Big Island), Hualalai (Big Island), and Haleakala (Maui) are all in what's called the post-shield-building stage of volcanic development—eruptions decrease steadily for up to a million years before ceasing entirely. Kohala (Big Island), Lanai (Lanai), and Waianae (Oahu) are considered extinct volcanoes, in the erosional stage of development; Koolau (Oahu) and West Maui (Maui) volcanoes are extinct volcanoes in the rejuvenation stage—after lying dormant for hundreds of thousands of years, they began erupting again, but only once every several thousand years.

There is currently an active undersea volcano to the south and east of the Big Island called Kamaehu that has been erupting regularly. If it continues its current pattern, it should breach the ocean's surface in tens of thousands of years.

Hawaii's Flora and Fauna

More than 90% of native Hawaiian flora and fauna are endemic (they evolved into unique species here), like the koa tree and the yellow hibiscus. Long-dormant volcanic craters are perfect hiding places for rare native plants. The silversword, a rare cousin of the sunflower, grows on Hawaii's three tallest peaks: Haleakala, Mauna Kea, and Mauna Loa, and nowhere else on Earth. Ohia trees—thought to be the favorite of Pele, the volcano goddess—bury their roots in fields of once-molten lava, and one variety sprouts ruby pom-pom–like lehua blossoms. The deep yellow petals of ilima (once reserved for royalty) are tiny discs, which make elegant lei.

But most of the plants you see while walking around aren't Hawaiian at all and came from Tahitian, Samoan, or European visitors. Plumeria is ubiquitous; alien orchids run rampant on the Big Island; bright orange relatives of the ilima light up the mountains of Oahu. Though these flowers are not native, they give the Hawaiian lei their color and fragrance.

Hawaii's state bird, the nene goose, is making a comeback from its former endangered status. It roams freely in parts of Maui, Kauai, and the Big Island. Rare Hawaiian monk seals breed in the northwestern Islands. With only 1,500 left in the wild, you probably won't catch many lounging on the beaches, though they have been spotted on the shores of Kauai in recent years. Spinner dolphins and sea turtles can be found off the coast of all the Islands; and every year from November to April, the humpback whales migrate past Hawaii in droves.

WHEN TO GO

Long days of sunshine and fairly mild year-round temperatures make Hawaii an all-seasons destination. Most resort areas are at sea level, with average afternoon temperatures of 75°F–80°F during the coldest months of December and January; during the hottest months of August and September the temperature often reaches 90°F. Higher "upcountry" elevations typically have cooler and often misty conditions. Only at mountain summits do temperatures reach freezing.

Moist trade winds drop their precipitation on the north and east sides of the Islands, while the south and west sides remain warmer and drier. Rainfall can be higher in summer months, while winter brings higher surf and windier conditions.

Many travelers head to the Islands in winter, specifically from mid-November to mid-April. This high season means that fewer travel bargains are available; room rates average 10%–15% higher during this season than the rest of the year.

You can see humpback whales clearly off the western coast of Hawaii Island from November to May. The Ironman World Championship triathlon takes place every October in Kailua-Kona. Shortly after the Ironman, the first 10 days of November are devoted to the Kona Coffee Cultural Festival. Each day brings numerous caffeinated events including cooking, picking, and barista competitions, and, of course, the coveted cupping competition, which measures the taste and quality of coffee from participating estates. Connoisseurs from all over the world flock to Kona for the festival, nearly every local coffee farmer participates, and the whole west side of the island goes crazy for coffee.

Hawaii Holidays

If you happen to be in the Islands on March 26 or June 11, you'll notice light traffic and busy beaches full of families— these are state holidays not celebrated anywhere else. March 26 recognizes the birthday of Prince Jonah Kuhio Kalanianaole, a member of the royal line who served as a delegate to Congress and spearheaded the effort to set aside homelands for Hawaiian people. June 11 honors the first island-unifying monarch, Kamehameha I; locals drape his statues with lei and stage elaborate parades.

May 1 isn't an official holiday, but May Day marks an important time when school kids and civic groups celebrate Hawaiian culture and the quintessential island gift, the flower lei.

Statehood Day is celebrated on the third Friday in August (admission to the Union was August 21, 1959).

Most Japanese and Chinese holidays are widely observed. On Chinese New Year, homes and businesses display bright-red good-luck mottoes, lions dance in the streets, and everybody eats *gau* (steamed pudding) and *jai* (vegetarian stew).

THE HISTORY OF HAWAII

Hawaiian history is long and complex; a brief survey can put into context the ongoing renaissance of native arts and culture.

The Polynesians

Long before both Christopher Columbus and the Vikings, Polynesian seafarers set out to explore the vast stretches of the open ocean in double-hulled canoes. From western Polynesia, they traveled back and forth between Samoa, Fiji, Tahiti, the Marquesas, and the Society Isles, settling on the outer reaches of the Pacific, Hawaii, and Easter Island, as early as AD 300. The golden era of Polynesian voyaging peaked around AD 1200, after which the distant Hawaiian Islands were left to develop their own unique cultural practices and subsistence in relative isolation.

The Islands' symbiotic society was deeply intertwined with religion, mythology, science, and artistry. Ruled by an *alii*, or chief, each settlement was nestled in an *ahupuaa*, a pie-shaped land division from the uplands where the *alii* lived, through the valleys and down to the shores where the commoners resided. Everyone contributed, whether it was by building canoes, catching fish, making tools, or farming land.

A United Kingdom

When the British explorer Captain James Cook arrived in 1778, he was revered as a god. With guns and ammunition purchased from Cook, the Big Island chief, Kamehameha the Great, gained a significant advantage over the other *alii*. He united Hawaii into one kingdom in 1810, bringing an end to the frequent interisland battles that dominated Hawaiian life.

Tragically, the new kingdom was beset with troubles. Native religion was abandoned, and *kapu* (laws and regulations) were eventually abolished. The European explorers brought diseases with them, and within a few decades the Native Hawaiian population was decimated.

New laws regarding land ownership and religious practices eroded the underpinnings of pre-contact Hawaii. Each successor to the Hawaiian throne sacrificed more control over the Island kingdom. As Westerners permeated Hawaiian culture, so did social unrest.

Modern Hawaii

In 1893, the last Hawaiian monarch, Queen Liliuokalani, was overthrown by a group of Americans and European businessmen and government officials, aided by an armed militia. This led to the creation of the Republic of Hawaii, and it became a U.S. territory for the next 60 years. The loss of Hawaiian sovereignty and the conditions of annexation have haunted the Hawaiian people since the monarchy was deposed.

Pearl Harbor was attacked in 1941, which engaged the United States immediately into World War II. Tourism, from its beginnings in the early 1900s, flourished after the war and naturally inspired rapid real estate development in Waikiki. In 1959, Hawaii officially became the 50th state. Statehood paved the way for Hawaiians to participate in the American democratic process, which was not universally embraced by all Hawaiians. With the rise of the civil rights movement in the 1960s, Hawaiians began to reclaim their own identity, from language to hula.

HAWAIIAN PEOPLE AND THEIR CULTURE

By 2012, Hawaii's population was more than 1.3 million with the majority of residents living on Oahu. Ten percent are Hawaiian or other Pacific Islander, almost 40% are Asian American, 9% are Latino, and about 26% Caucasian. Nearly a fifth of the population list two or more races, making Hawaii the most diverse state in the United States.

Among individuals 18 and older, about 89% finished high school, half attained some college, and 29% completed a bachelor's degree or higher.

The Role of Tradition

The kingdom of Hawaii was ruled by a spiritual class system. Although the *alii*, or chief, was believed to be the direct descendent of a deity or god, high priests, known as *kahuna*, presided over every imaginable aspect of life and *kapu* (taboos) that strictly governed the commoners.

Each part of nature and ritual was connected to a deity—Kane was the highest of all deities, symbolizing sunlight and creation; Ku was the god of war; Lono represented fertility, rainfall, music, and peace; Kanaloa was the god of the underworld or darker spirits. Probably the most well known by outsiders is Pele, the goddess of fire.

The kapu not only provided social order, they also swayed the people to act with reverence for the environment. Any abuse was met with extreme punishment, often death, as it put the land and people's *mana*, or spiritual power, in peril.

Ancient deities play a huge role in Hawaiian life today—not just in daily rituals, but in the Hawaiians' reverence for their land. Gods and goddesses tend to be associated with particular parts of the land, and most of them are connected with many places, thanks to the body of stories built up around each.

One of the most important ways the ancient Hawaiians showed respect for their gods and goddesses was through the hula. Various forms of the hula were performed as prayers to the gods and as praise to the chiefs. Performances were taken very seriously, as a mistake was thought to invalidate the prayer, or even to offend the god or chief in question. Hula is still performed both as entertainment and as prayer; it is not uncommon for a hula performance to be included in an official government ceremony.

Who Are the Hawaiians Today?

To define the Hawaiians in a page, let alone a paragraph, is nearly impossible. Those considered to be indigenous Hawaiians are descendants of the ancient Polynesians who crossed the vast ocean and settled Hawaii. According to the government, there are Native Hawaiians or native Hawaiians (note the change in capitalization), depending on a person's background.

Federal and state agencies apply different methods to determine Hawaiian lineage, from measuring blood percentage to mapping genealogy. This has caused turmoil within the community because it excludes many who claim Hawaiian heritage. It almost guarantees that, as races intermingle, even those considered Native Hawaiian now will eventually disappear on paper, displacing generations to come.

Modern Hawaiian Culture

Perfect weather aside, Hawaii might be the warmest place anyone can visit. The Hawaii experience begins and ends with *aloha*, a word that envelops love, affection, and mercy, and has become a salutation for hello and good-bye. Broken

down, *alo* means "presence" and *ha* means "breath"—the presence of breath. It's to live with love and respect for self and others with every breath. Past the manicured resorts and tour buses, aloha is a moral compass that binds all of Hawaii's people.

Hawaii is blessed with some of the most unspoiled natural wonders, and aloha extends to the land, or *aina*. Hawaiians are raised outdoors and have strong ties to nature. They realize as children that the ocean and land are the delicate sources of all life. Even ancient gods were embodied by nature, and this reverence has been passed down to present generations who believe in *kuleana,* their privilege and responsibility.

Hawaii's diverse cultures unfold in a beautiful montage of customs and arts—from music, to dance, to food. Musical genres range from slack key to *Jawaiian* (Hawaiian reggae) to *hapa-haole* (Hawaiian music with English words). From George Kahumoku's Grammy-worthy laid-back strumming to the late Iz Kamakawiwoole's "Somewhere over the Rainbow" to Jack Johnson's more mainstream tunes, contemporary Hawaiian music has definitely carved its ever-evolving niche.

The Merrie Monarch Festival is celebrating more than 50 years of worldwide hula competition and education. The fine-dining culinary scene, especially in Honolulu, has a rich tapestry of ethnic influences and talent. But the real gems are the humble hole-in-the-wall eateries that serve authentic cuisines of many ethnic origins in one plate, a deliciously mixed plate indeed.

And perhaps, the most striking quality in today's Hawaiian culture is the sense of family, or *ohana*. Sooner or later, almost everyone you meet becomes an uncle or auntie, and it is not uncommon for near strangers to be welcomed into a home as a member of the family.

Until the last century, the practice of *hanai*, in which a family essentially adopts a child, usually a grandchild, without formalities, was still prevalent. While still practiced to a somewhat lesser degree, the *hanai*, which means to feed or nourish, still resonates within most families and communities.

How to Act Like a Local

Adopting local customs is a firsthand introduction to the Islands' unique culture. So live in T-shirts and shorts. Wear cheap rubber flip-flops, but call them slippers. Wave people into your lane on the highway, and, when someone lets you in, give them a wave of thanks in return. Never, ever blow your horn, even when the pickup truck in front of you is stopped for a long session of "talk story" right in the middle of the road.

Holoholo means to go out for the fun of it—an aimless stroll, ride, or drive. "Wheah you goin', braddah?" "Oh, holoholo." It's local speak for Sunday drive, no plan, it's not the destination but the journey. Try setting out without an itinerary. Learn to *shaka*: pinky and thumb extended, middle fingers curled in, waggle sideways. Eat white rice with everything. When someone says, "Aloha!" answer, "Aloha no!" ("And a real big aloha back to you"). And, as the locals say, "No make big body" ("Try not to act like you own the place").

KIDS AND FAMILIES

With dozens of adventures, discoveries, and fun-filled beach days, Hawaii is a blast with kids. Even better, the things to do here don't only appeal to small fry. The entire family, parents included, will enjoy surfing, discovering a waterfall in the rain forest, and snorkeling with sea turtles. And there are plenty of organized activities for kids that will give parents time for a few romantic beach strolls.

Choosing a Place to Stay

Resorts: Most of the big resorts make kids' programs a priority, and it shows. When you are booking your room, ask about "kids eat free" deals and the number of kids' pools at the resort. Also check out the size of the groups in the children's programs, and find out whether the cost of the programs includes lunch, equipment, and activities.

The Hilton Waikoloa Village is every kid's fantasy vacation come true, with multiple pool slides, one lagoon for snorkeling and one filled with dolphins, and even a choice between riding a monorail or taking a boat to your room. Not to be outdone, the Four Seasons Resort Hualalai has a great program that will keep your little ones happy and occupied all day.

Condos: Condo and vacation rentals are a fantastic value for families vacationing in Hawaii. You can cook your own food, which is cheaper than eating out and sometimes easier (especially if you have a finicky eater in your group), and you'll get twice the space of a hotel room for about a quarter of the price. If you decide to go the condo route, be sure to ask about the size of the complex's pool (some try to pawn off a tiny soaking tub as a pool) and whether barbecues are available. One of the best reasons to stay in your own place

is to hold a sunset family barbecue by the pool or overlooking the ocean.

Condos in Kailua-Kona (on or near Alii Drive) are the best value on the Big Island. We like Casa de Emdeko for its oceanfront pool and on-site convenience store. On the Kohala Coast, the Vista Waikoloa complex provides extra-large condos and is walking distance to beautiful Anaehoomalu Bay. Affordable food is available at restaurants in Kona, if you are looking for a family night out or, even better, a date night.

Ocean Activities

On the Beach: Most people like being in the water, but toddlers and school-age kids tend to be especially enamored of it. The swimming pool at your condo or hotel is always an option, but don't be afraid to hit the beach with a little one in tow. There are lots of family-friendly beaches on the Big Island, complete with protected bays and pleasant white sand. As always, use your judgment, and heed all posted signs and lifeguard warnings.

Calm beaches to try include Kamakahonu Beach and Kahaluu Beach Park in Kailua-Kona; Spencer Beach Park, Kaunaoa Bay (aka Mauna Kea Beach), and Hapuna Beach on the Kohala Coast; Ahalanui Beach Park in Puna; and Leleiwi Beach Park in Hilo.

On the Waves: Surf lessons are a great idea for older kids. Beginner lessons are always on safe and easy waves. Most surf schools also offer instruction in stand-up paddleboarding.

For school-age and older kids, book a four-hour surfing lesson with Ocean Eco Tours and either join the kids out on the break or say aloha to a little parents-only time.

The Underwater World: If your kids are ready to try snorkeling, Hawaii is a great place to introduce them to the underwater world. Even without the mask and snorkel, they'll be able to see colorful fish darting this way and that, and they may also spot turtles and dolphins at many of the island beaches.

The easily accessible Kahaluu Beach, in Kailua-Kona, is a great introductory snorkel spot because of its many facilities. Protected by a natural breakwater, these shallow reefs attract large numbers of sea creatures, including the Hawaiian green sea turtle. These turtles feed on seaweed near shore and sometimes can be spotted basking on the rocks.

On the southern tip of the island, Punaluu Black Sand Beach provides opportunities to see the sea turtles up close. Though the water can be rough, the sea turtles nest here and there are nearly always one or two napping on the beach. At nighttime, head to the Sheraton Kona Resort & Spa at Keauhou Bay, or Huggo's on the Rocks in Kailua-Kona, to view manta rays; each place shines a bright spotlight on the water to attract them. Anyone, but especially kids, could sit and watch them glide through the ocean in graceful circles for hours. No snorkel required!

Another great option is to book a snorkel cruise or opt to stay dry inside the Atlantis Submarine that operates out of Kailua-Kona. Kids love crawling down into a real-life submarine and viewing the ocean world through its little portholes.

Land Activities

In addition to beach experiences, Hawaii has easy waterfall hikes, botanical gardens, zoos, and hands-on museums that will keep your kids entertained and out of the sun for a day.

Hawaii Volcanoes National Park is a must for any family vacation. Even grumpy teenagers will acknowledge the coolness of lava tubes, steaming volcanic rocks, and a fiery nighttime lava show.

On the Hilo side, the Panaewa Rain Forest Zoo is small, but free, and lots of fun for the little ones, with a small petting zoo on Saturday. Your kids might even get to hold a Hawaiian hawk. Just a few miles north, on the Hamakua Coast, the Hawaii Tropical Botanical Garden makes a beautiful and fun stop for kids, filled with huge lily pads and noisy frogs.

School-age and older kids will get a kick out of the ATV tours on the rim above Waipio Valley, and horseback rides past the waterfalls of Waipio Valley via Naalapa Stables.

After Dark

At night, younger kids get a kick out of luau, and many of the shows incorporate young audience members, adding to the fun. Teens and adults alike are sure to enjoy the music and overall theatrical quality of the Sheraton Kona Resort & Spa's "Haleo," the story of the Keauhou *ahupuaa* (land division).

Stargazing from Mauna Kea is another treat. The visitor center has telescopes set up for all visitors to use. If you'd rather leave the planning to someone else, book a tour with Hawaii Forest & Trail. Its unbelievably knowledgeable guides are great at sharing that knowledge in a narrative form that kids—and adults, for that matter—enjoy.

TOP 10 HAWAIIAN FOODS TO TRY

Food in Hawaii is a reflection of the state's diverse cultural makeup and tropical location. Fresh seafood, organic fruits and vegetables, free-range beef, and locally grown products are the hallmarks of Hawaii regional cuisine. Its preparations are drawn from across the Pacific Rim, including Japan, the Philippines, Korea, and Thailand—and "local food" is a cuisine in its own right. Don't miss Hawaiian-grown coffee, either, whether it's smooth Kona from the Big Island or coffee grown on other islands.

Saimin

The ultimate hangover cure and the perfect comfort food during Hawaii's mild winters, *saimin* ranks at the top of the list of local favorites. In fact, it's one of the few dishes deemed truly local, having been highlighted in cookbooks since the 1930s. Saimin is an Asian-style noodle soup so ubiquitous it's even on McDonald's menus statewide. In mom-and-pop shops, a large melamine bowl is filled with homemade *dashi*, or broth, and wheat-flour noodles and then topped off with strips of omelet, green onions, bright pink fish cake, and *char siu* (Chinese roast pork) or canned luncheon meat, such as SPAM. Add *shoyu* (the "local" name for soy sauce) and chili pepper water, lift your chopsticks, and slurp away.

SPAM

Speaking of SPAM, Hawaii's most prevalent grab-and-go snack is SPAM *musubi*. Often displayed next to cash registers at groceries and convenience stores, the glorified rice ball is rectangular, topped with a slice of fried SPAM and wrapped in *nori* (seaweed). Musubi is a bite-size meal in itself. But just like sushi, the rice part hardens when refrigerated. So it's best to gobble it up right after purchase.

Hormel Company's SPAM actually deserves its own recognition—way beyond as a mere musubi topping. About 5 million cans are sold per year in Hawaii, and the Aloha State even hosts a festival in its honor. It's inexpensive protein and goes a long way when mixed with rice, scrambled eggs, noodles or, well, anything. The spiced luncheon meat gained popularity in World War II days, when fish was rationed. Gourmets and those with aversions to salt, high cholesterol, or high blood pressure may cringe at the thought of eating it, but SPAM in Hawaii is here to stay.

Manapua

Another savory snack is *manapua*, fist-size dough balls fashioned after Chinese *bao* (a traditional Chinese bun) and stuffed with fillings such as *char siu* (Chinese roast pork) and then steamed. Many mom-and-pop stores sell them in commercial steamer display cases along with pork hash and other dim sum. Modern-day fillings include curry chicken.

Fresh Ahi or Tako Poke

There's nothing like fresh ahi or *tako* (octopus) *poke* to break the ice at a back-yard party, except, of course, the cold beer handed to you from the cooler. The perfect *pupu*, poke (pronounced poh-kay) is basically raw seafood cut into bite-size chunks and mixed with everything from green onions to roasted and ground *kukui* nuts. Other variations include mixing the fish with chopped round onion, sesame oil, seaweed, and chili pepper water. Shoyu is the constant. These days, grocery stores sell a rainbow of varieties such as kimchi crab and anything goes, from adding mayonnaise to tobiko caviar. Fish lovers who want to take it to the next level order sashimi, the best cuts of ahi

sliced and dipped in a mixture of shoyu and wasabi.

Tropical Fruits
Tropical fruits such as apple banana and strawberry papaya are plucked from trees in Island neighborhoods and eaten for breakfast—plain or with a squeeze of fresh lime. Give them a try; the banana tastes like an apple and the papaya's rosy flesh explains its name. Locals also love to add their own creative touches to exotic fruits. Green mangoes are pickled with Chinese five spice, and Maui Gold pineapples are topped with *li hing mui* powder (heck, even margarita glasses are rimmed with it). Green papaya is tossed in a Vietnamese salad with fish paste and fresh prawns.

Plate Lunch
It would be remiss not to mention the plate lunch as one of the most beloved dishes in Hawaii. It generally includes two scoops of sticky white rice, a scoop of macaroni or macaroni-potato salad, heavy on the mayo, and perhaps kimchi or *koko* (salted cabbage). There are countless choices of main protein such as chicken *katsu* (fried cutlet), fried mahimahi, and beef tomato. The king of all plate lunches is the Hawaiian plate. The main item is laulau or kalua pig and cabbage along with poi, *lomilomi* salmon, chicken long rice, and sticky white rice.

Bento Box
The bento box gained popularity back in the plantation days, when workers toiled in the sugarcane fields. No one brought sandwiches to work then. Instead it was a lunch box with the ever-present steamed white rice, pickled *ume* (plum) to preserve the rice, and main meats such as fried chicken or fish. Today, many stores sell prepackaged bentos or you may go to an

okazuya (Japanese deli) with a hot buffet counter and create your own.

Malasadas
The Portuguese have contributed much to Hawaii cuisine in the form of sausage, soup, and sweetbread. But their most revered food is *malasadas*, hot, deep-fried doughnuts rolled in sugar. Malasadas are crowd-pleasers. Buy them by the dozen, hot from the fryer, placed in brown paper bags to absorb the grease. Or bite into gourmet malasadas at restaurants, filled with vanilla or chocolate cream.

Shave Ice
Much more than just a snow cone, shave ice is what locals crave after a blazing day at the beach or a hot-as-Hades game of soccer. If you're lucky, you'll find a neighborhood store that hand-shaves its ice, but it's rare. Either way, the counter person will ask you first if you'd like ice cream and/or adzuki beans scooped into the bottom of the cone or cup. Then they shape the ice into a giant mound and add colorful fruit syrups. First-timers should order the Rainbow, of course.

Crack Seed
There are dozens of varieties of crack seed in dwindling specialty shops and at the drugstores. Chinese call the preserved fruits and nuts *see mui* but somehow the Pidgin English version is what Hawaiians prefer. Those who like hard candy and salty foods will love *li hing* mangoes and rock salt plums, and those with an itchy throat will feel relief from the lemon strips. Peruse large glass jars of crack seed sold in bulk or smaller hanging bags—the latter make good gifts to give to friends back home.

BIG ISLAND'S BEST FARMERS' MARKETS

The Big Island has a wealth of farmers' markets, each offering a different range of goods, but all providing at the very least a good place to pick up fresh produce, jarred goods such as jams and salsa, as well as homemade local Hawaiian treats. Not surprisingly, locally grown mango, papaya, pineapple, passion fruit, coconut, and guava are available in abundance at great prices, but you can also find delicious avocados, organic peppers, fantastic goat cheese, and, of course, coffee. Local handmade gifts abound, too.

Hawaii's farmers are experimenting with dozens of varieties of exotic fruits such as dragon fruit, poha berries, bilimbi, and mamey sapoy. Due to state government restrictions, these fruits generally can't leave the island, so this is your only chance to sample them.

Markets listed from north to south. For additional markets, see the Shops and Spas chapter.

On the West Side

Under the Banyans Farmers' Market. Fresh produce, seasonal fruit, plants, and craft items are sold at this market way up north in the village of Hawi. It's open Saturday from 7:30 am until 1 pm.

Hawaiian Homesteaders Association Farmers' Market. Check out the crafts sold here in the Kuhio Hale Building before heading to Waimea's more expensive stores. Produce, flowers, plants, and baked goods are also available. It's open 7 am to noon every Saturday.

Keauhou Farmers' Market. Live music and plenty of local color permeate this down-home farmers' market held every Saturday from 8 to noon in the parking lot of the Keauhou Shopping Center.

South Kona Farmers Market. This popular market features coffee, baked goods, and local honey and jams. It's located at Amy B.H. Greenwell Ethnobotanical Garden in Captain Cook. It runs on Sunday morning from 9 am until 2 pm.

Kau Farmers' Market. On a trip to South Point, stock up on local produce and freshly baked pastries at this market held at the Naalehu Theater. It's open every Saturday, 8 am to 2 pm.

On the East Side

Downtown Honokaa Farmers Market. This good old-fashioned farmers' market in the midst of a charming old plantation town is a good stop during a drive up the Hamakua Coast. It begins at 7:30 am on Saturday.

Hilo Farmers Market. The biggest and best of the farmers' markets on the island runs Wednesday and Saturday 6 am to 4 pm.

Keaau Village Farmers Market. Fresh, local farm produce featuring sweet corn and flowers is on offer daily from 7 am to 5 pm. On Friday, vendors also sell handmade Hawaiian arts and crafts.

Makuu Farmers Market. Not only is there food and produce here, but also Hawaiian crafts, plants, jewelry, shells, books, and secondhand clothing. It's along the Keaau/Pahoa Highway, and is open Sunday 6 am to noon.

Pahoa Village Farmers Market. This great market, held in a large, covered, outdoor space, offers local produce, prepared foods, coffee, clothing, and live music 9 am to 3 pm every Sunday.

Volcano Village Farmers Market. This market sells local produce, fresh flowers, prepared foods, and baked goods, and hosts an occasional clothing swap. It's held in the Cooper Center 6 to 10 am Sunday.

HAWAII AND THE ENVIRONMENT

Sustainability—it's a word rolling off everyone's tongues these days. In a place known as the most remote island chain in the world (check your globe), Hawaii relies heavily on the outside world for food and material goods—estimates put the percentage of food arriving on container ships as high as 90. Like many places, though, efforts are afoot to change that. And you can help.

Shop Local Farms and Markets

From Kauai to the Big Island, farmers' markets are cropping up, providing a place for growers to sell fresh fruits and vegetables. There is no reason to buy imported mangoes, papayas, avocadoes, and bananas at grocery stores, when the ones you'll find at farmers' markets are not only fresher but tastier, too. Some markets allow the sale of fresh-packaged foods—salsa, say, or smoothies—and the on-site preparation of food—like pork *laulau* (pork, beef, and fish or chicken with taro, or luau, leaves wrapped and steamed in *ti* leaves) or roasted corn on the cob—so you can make your run to the market a dining experience.

Not only is the locavore movement vibrantly alive at farmers' markets, but Hawaii's top chefs are sourcing more of their produce—and fish, beef, chicken, and cheese—from local providers as well. You'll notice this movement on restaurant menus, featuring Kilauea greens or Hamakua tomatoes or locally caught mahimahi.

And while most people are familiar with Kona coffee farm tours on Big Island, if you're interested in the growing slow-food movement in Hawaii, you'll be heartened to know many farmers are opening up their operations for tours—as well as sumptuous meals.

Support Hawaii's Merchants

Food isn't the only sustainable effort in Hawaii. Buying local goods like art and jewelry, Hawaiian heritage products, crafts, music, and apparel is another way to "green up" the local economy. The County of Kauai helps make it easy with a program called **Kauai Made** (⊕ *www.kauaimade.net*), which showcases products made on Kauai, by Kauai people, using Kauai materials. The Maui Chamber of Commerce does something similar with **Made in Maui** (⊕ *www.madeinmaui.com*). Think of both as the Good Housekeeping Seal of Approval for locally made goods.

Then there are the crafty entrepreneurs who are diverting items from the trash heap by repurposing garbage. Take Oahu's **Muumuu Heaven** (⊕ *www.muumuuheaven.com*). They got their start by reincarnating vintage aloha apparel into hip new fashions.

Choose Green Tour Operators

Conscious decisions when it comes to Island activities go a long way to protecting Hawaii's natural world. The **Hawaii Ecotourism Association** (⊕ *www.hawaiiecotourism.org*) recognizes tour operators for, among other things, their environmental stewardship. The **Hawaii Tourism Authority** (⊕ *www.hawaiitourismauthority.org*) recognizes outfitters for their cultural sensitivity. Winners of these awards are good choices when it comes to guided tours and activities.

ONLY IN HAWAII

Traveling to Hawaii is as close as an American can get to visiting another country while staying within the United States. There's much to learn and understand about the state's indigenous culture, the hundred years of immigration that resulted in today's blended society, and the tradition of aloha that has welcomed millions of visitors over the years.

Aloha Shirt

To go to Hawaii without taking an aloha shirt home is almost sacrilege. The first aloha shirts from the 1920s and 1930s—called "silkies"—were classic canvases of art and tailored for the tourists. Popular culture caught on in the 1950s, and they became a fashion craze. With the 1960s' more subdued designs, Aloha Friday was born, and the shirt became appropriate clothing for work, play, and formal occasions. Because of its soaring popularity, cheaper and mass-produced versions became available.

Hawaiian Quilt

Although ancient Hawaiians were already known to produce fine *kapa* (bark) cloth, the actual art of quilting originated from the missionaries. Hawaiians have created designs to reflect their own aesthetic, and bold patterns evolved over time. They can be pricey because the quilts are intricately made by hand and can take years to finish. These masterpieces are considered precious heirlooms that reflect the history and beauty of Hawaii.

Popular Souvenirs

Souvenir shopping can be intimidating. There's a sea of Islands-inspired and often kitschy merchandise, so we'd like to give you a breakdown of popular and fun gifts that you might encounter and consider bringing home. If authenticity is important to you, be sure to check labels and ask shopkeepers. Museum shops are good places for authentic, Hawaiian-made souvenirs.

Fabrics. Purchased by the yard or already made into everything from napkins to bedspreads, modern Hawaiian fabrics make wonderful keepsakes.

Home accessories. Deck out your kitchen or dining room in festive luau style with bottle openers, pineapple mugs, tiki glasses, shot glasses, slipper and surfboard magnets, and salt-and-pepper shakers.

Lei and shell necklaces. From silk or polyester flower lei to kukui or puka shell necklaces, lei have been traditionally used as a welcome offering to guests (although the artificial ones are more for fun, real flowers are always preferable).

Lauhala products. *Lauhala* weaving is a traditional Hawaiian art. The leaves come from the *hala*, or *pandanus*, tree and are handwoven to create lovely gift boxes, baskets, bags, and picture frames.

Spa products. Relive your spa treatment at home with Hawaiian bath and body products, many of them manufactured with ingredients found only on the Islands.

Vintage Hawaii. You can find vintage photos, reproductions of vintage postcards or paintings, heirloom jewelry, and vintage aloha wear in many specialty stores.

Traditional Canoe

Hawaii's ancestors voyaged across 2,500 miles from Polynesia on board a double-hulled canoe with the help of the stars, the ocean swells, and the flight patterns of birds. The creation of a canoe spanned months and involved many religious ceremonies by the *kahuna kalai waa*, or high priest canoe builder. In 1973, the Polynesian Voyaging Society was founded to rediscover and preserve this ancestral

tradition. Since 1975, the group has built and launched the majestic *Hokulea* and *Hawaiiloa*, which regularly travel throughout the South Pacific. In 2014, Hokulea began an historic, three-year, around-the-world voyage.

Luau

The luau's origin, which was a celebratory feast, can be traced back to the earliest Hawaiian civilizations. In the traditional luau, the taboo or *kapu* laws were very strict, requiring men and women to eat separately. However, in 1819 King Kamehameha II broke the great taboo and shared a feast with women and commoners, ushering in the modern-era luau. Today, traditional luau usually commemorate a child's first birthday, graduation, wedding, or other family occasion. They also are a Hawaiian experience that most visitors enjoy, and resorts and other companies have incorporated the fire-knife dance and other Polynesian dances into their elaborate presentations.

Nose Flutes

The nose flute is an instrument used in ancient times to serenade a lover. For the Hawaiians, the nose is romantic, sacred, and pure. The Hawaiian word for kiss is *honi*. Similar to an Eskimo's kiss, the noses touch on each side, sharing one's spiritual energy or breath. The Hawaiian term, *ohe hano ihu*, simply translated to "bamboo," with which the instrument is made; "breathe," because one has to gently breathe through it to make soothing music; and "nose," as it is made for the nose and not the mouth.

Slack-Key Guitar and the Paniolo

Kihoalu, or slack-key music, evolved in the early 1800s when King Kamehameha III brought in Mexican and Spanish vaqueros to manage the overpopulated cattle that had run wild on the Islands. The vaqueros brought their guitars and would play music around the campfire after work. When they left, supposedly leaving their guitars to their new friends, the Hawaiian *paniolo,* or cowboys, began to infuse what they learned from the vaqueros with their native music and chants, and so the art of slack-key music was born.

Today, the paniolo culture thrives where ranchers have settled.

Ukulele

The word *ukulele* literally translates to the "the jumping flea" and came to Hawaii in the 1880s by way of the Portuguese and Spanish. Once a fading art form, today it brings international kudos as a solo instrument, thanks to tireless musicians and teachers who have worked hard to keep it by our fingertips.

One such teacher is Roy Sakuma. Founder of four ukulele schools and a legend in his own right, Sakuma and his wife Kathy produced Oahu's first Ukulele Festival in 1971. Since then, they've brought the tradition to the Big Island, Kauai, and Maui. The free event annually draws thousands of artists and fans from all over the globe.

Hula

"Hula is the language of the heart, therefore the heartbeat of the Hawaiian people." —Kalakaua, the Merrie Monarch.

Thousands—from tots to seniors—devote hours each week to hula classes. All these dancers need some place to show off their stuff. The result is a network of hula competitions (generally free or very inexpensive) and free performances in malls and other public spaces. Many resorts offer hula instruction.

TOP 5 BIG ISLAND OUTDOOR ADVENTURES

Getting out for active adventure is one of the top reasons people come to the Big Island.

There are endless options here for spending time outside, enjoying the land, the ocean, or the highest points of mountains and volcanoes. Here are a few of our favorites.

Bike Kulani Trails

Stands of 80-foot eucalyptus. Giant hapuu tree ferns. The sweet song of honeycreepers overhead. Add single-track of rock and root—no dirt here—and we're talking technical. Did we mention this is a rain forest? That explains the perennial slick coat of slime on every possible surface. Advanced cyclists only.

Snorkel at Kealakekua Bay

Yes, the snorkeling here is tops for the Big Island. Visibility reaches depths of 80 feet, and you'll spot colorful creatures swimming among jagged pinnacles and pristine coral habitats. But, to be real, the draw here is the Hawaiian spinner dolphins that come to rest in the bay during the daytime.

While it's enticing to swim with wild dolphins, getting too close can disrupt their sleep cycles. Observe from a distance and respect their space while still enjoying a fantastic experience communing with nature.

Search for Lava at Hawaii Volcanoes National Park

It's not too often that you can witness the creation of molten earth in action. That's just what happens at Hawaii Volcanoes National Park. The most dramatic examples occur where lava flows enter the sea. While Madame Pele rarely gives away her itinerary in advance, if you're lucky a hike or boat ride may pay off with spectacular sights. Just before dawn and nighttime make for the best viewing opportunities.

Go Horseback Riding in Waipio Valley

The Valley of the Kings owes its relative isolation and off-the-grid status to the 2,000-foot-high cliffs bookending the valley. Really, the only way to explore this sacred place is on two legs—or four.

We're partial to the horseback rides that wend deep into the rain forest to a series of waterfalls and pools—the setting for a perfect romantic getaway.

Wade Through Waterfalls on the Hilo Side

The east side of the Big Island—also called the Hilo side (as opposed to the western Kona side)—is essentially a rain forest, with an average rainfall of 130 inches a year. It's no wonder Hilo is called the City of Rainbows—and all that rain means tons of waterfalls. Some of our favorites include Peepee Falls (Boiling Pots) and Rainbow Falls, both easy to access from main roads.

BIG ISLAND'S TOP BEACHES

With over 265 miles of coastline, the Big Island—the largest and youngest island—offers the widest variety of beaches in Hawaii. Take your pick from black sand, soft white sand, crystalline green sand, award-winning beaches, and beaches off the beaten track.

Best Classic Beach

Mauna Kea (Kaunaoa) and nearby Hapuna Beach, Kohala Coast. Long, white stretches of pure soft sand and glistening, azure water are perfect for swimming, snorkeling, and sunbathing. These two beaches are consistently rated among the best in the world. Simply perfect.

Kekaha Kai State Park, Kona Coast. This beautiful beach in a postcard-like setting has outstandingly soft sand and great spots for swimming.

Best for Families

Spencer Park, Kohala Coast. This protected sandy beach has consistently gentle surf so it's safe for swimming.

Anaehoomalu Bay, Kohala Coast. In the heart of resort country, this white-sand beach is a spectacular spot for swimming, snorkeling, stand-up paddling, and spotting turtles. The glass-bottom boat ride is cool, too.

Onekahakaha Beach Park, Hilo. Parents can relax on the white-sand beach while kids explore the shallow, enclosed tide pools for exotic sea life.

Best for Interesting Sand

Punaluu Black Sand Beach Park, Kau. It's busy for a reason. Between the turtles and the black sand, it's tough not to camp out all day at this easily accessed beach.

Pololu Valley Beach, Kohala Coast. Jaw-droppingly scenic, this perfect crescent of black sand is backed by sheer green cliffs. The hike down to the beach is definitely worth the trip, but the surf can be treacherous.

Papakolea Beach, Kau. Sure it's a 2-mile hike, but where else are you going to see a beach with green sand? The dry, barren landscape is surreal, and the beach sparkles with olivine crystals formed during volcanic eruptions.

Best Snorkeling

Kahaluu Beach Park, Kailua-Kona. Protective reefs keep the waters calm, and the abundant fish are not shy, as they're used to swimming amid snorkelers.

Punaluu Black Sand Beach Park, Kau. You're almost guaranteed to see sea turtles who nest in the black sand and swim in the waters just offshore.

Best Surfing

Kahaluu Beach Park, Kailua-Kona. When the surf's up, this beach is irresistible for anyone who wants to take a beginner surf lesson.

Kua Bay (Kekaha Kai State Park), Kona Coast. Local surfers and body boarders love the challenge of the rough waves in winter.

Honolii Beach Park, Hilo. Even if you don't surf, Hilo's main drag for surfers is a great place to hang out and watch.

Best Sunsets

We're going to say it one last time: westward-facing **Hapuna Beach is** not to be missed.

WEDDINGS AND HONEYMOONS

There's no question that Hawaii is one of the country's foremost honeymoon destinations. Romance is in the air here, and the white-sand beaches, turquoise water, swaying palm trees, balmy tropical breezes, and perpetual sunshine put people in the mood for love. It's easy to understand why Hawaii is fast becoming a popular wedding destination as well, especially as the cost of airfare is often discounted, new resorts and hotels entice visitors, and same-sex marriage is now legal in the state. A destination wedding is no longer exclusive to celebrities and the superrich. You can plan a traditional ceremony in a place of worship followed by a reception at an elegant resort, or you can go barefoot on the beach and celebrate at a luau. There are almost as many wedding planners in the Islands as real estate agents, which makes it oh-so-easy to wed in paradise, and then, once the knot is tied, stay and honeymoon as well.

The Big Day

Choosing the Perfect Place. When choosing a location, remember that you really have two choices to make: the ceremony location and where to have the reception, if you're having one. For the former, there are beaches, bluffs overlooking beaches, gardens, private residences, resort lawns, and, of course, places of worship. As for the reception, there are these same choices, as well as restaurants and even luau. If you decide to go outdoors, remember the seasons—yes, Hawaii has seasons. If you're planning a winter wedding outdoors, be sure you have a backup plan (such as a tent), in case it rains. Also, if you're planning an outdoor wedding at sunset—which is very popular—be sure you match the time of your ceremony to the time the sun sets at that time of year. If you choose an indoor spot, be sure to ask

for pictures of the location when you're planning. You don't want to plan a pink wedding, say, and wind up in a room that's predominantly red. Or maybe you do. The point is, it should be your choice.

Finding a Wedding Planner. If you're planning to invite more than an officiant and your loved one to your wedding ceremony, seriously consider an on-island wedding planner who can help select a location; help design the floral scheme and recommend a florist as well as a photographer; help plan the menu and choose a restaurant, caterer, or resort; and suggest Hawaiian traditions to incorporate into your ceremony. And more: Will you need tents, a cake, music? Maybe transportation and lodging? Many planners have relationships with vendors, providing packages—which mean savings.

If you're planning a resort wedding, most have on-site wedding coordinators; however, there are many independents around the Islands and even those who specialize in certain types of ceremonies—by locale, size, religious affiliation, and so on. A simple "Hawaii weddings" Google search will reveal dozens. What's important is that you feel comfortable with your coordinator. Ask for references and call them. Share your budget. Get a proposal—in writing. Ask how long they've been in business, how much they charge, how often you'll meet with them, and how they select vendors. Request a detailed list of the exact services they'll provide. If your idea of your wedding doesn't match their services, try someone else. If you can afford it, you might want to meet the planner in person.

Getting Your License. The good news about marrying in Hawaii is that there is no waiting period, no residency or citizenship

requirement, and no blood test or shots are required. You can apply and pay the fee online; however, both the bride and groom must appear together in person before a marriage-license agent to receive the marriage license (the permit to get married). You'll need proof of age—the legal age to marry is 18. (If you're 19 or older, a valid driver's license will suffice; if you're 18, a certified birth certificate is required.) Upon approval, a marriage license is immediately issued and costs $60 (credit cards accepted online and in person; cash only accepted in-person). After the ceremony, your officiant will mail the marriage certificate (proof of marriage) to the state. Approximately four months later, you will receive a copy in the mail. (For $10 extra, you can expedite this process. Ask your marriage-license agent when you apply.) For more detailed information, visit ⊕ *marriage. ehawaii.gov.*

Also—this is important—the person performing your wedding must be licensed by the Hawaii Department of Health, even if he or she is a licensed officiant. Be sure to ask.

Wedding Attire. In Hawaii, basically anything goes, from long, formal dresses with trains to white bikinis. Floral sundresses are fine, too. For men, tuxedos are not the norm; a pair of solid-colored slacks with a nice aloha shirt is. In fact, tradition in Hawaii for the groom is a beautiful white aloha shirt (they do exist) with slacks or long shorts and a colored sash around the waist. If you're planning a wedding on the beach, barefoot is the way to go.

If you decide to marry in a formal dress and tuxedo, you're better off making your selections on the mainland and hand-carrying them aboard the plane. Yes, it can

be a pain, but ask your wedding-gown retailer to provide a special carrying bag. After all, you don't want to chance losing your wedding dress in a wayward piece of luggage.

Local Customs. The most obvious traditional Hawaiian wedding custom is the lei exchange in which the bride and groom take turns placing a lei around the neck of the other—with a kiss. Bridal lei are usually floral, whereas the groom's is typically made of *maile*, a green leafy garland that drapes around the neck and is open at the ends. Brides often also wear a *lei poo*—a circular floral headpiece. Other Hawaiian customs include the blowing of the conch shell, hula, chanting, and Hawaiian music.

The Honeymoon

Do you want champagne and strawberries delivered to your room each morning? A breathtaking swimming pool in which to float? A five-star restaurant in which to dine? Then a resort is the way to go. If, however, you prefer the comforts of a home, try a bed-and-breakfast. A small inn is also good if you're on a tight budget or don't plan to spend much time in your room. On the other hand, maybe you want your own private home in which to romp naked—or just laze around recovering from the wedding planning. Maybe you want your own kitchen so you can whip up a gourmet meal for your loved one. In that case, a private vacation-rental home is the answer. Or maybe a condominium resort. That's another beautiful thing about Hawaii: the lodging accommodations are almost as plentiful as the beaches, and there's one that will perfectly match your tastes and your budget.

CRUISING THE HAWAIIAN ISLANDS

Cruising has become popular in Hawaii. Cruises are a comparatively inexpensive way to see all of Hawaii, and you'll save travel time by not having to check in at hotels and airports on each Island. The limited amount of time in each port can be an argument against cruising, but you can make reservations for tours, activities, rental cars, and more aboard the cruise ship. This will also give you more time for sightseeing and shopping at ports.

The larger cruise lines such as Carnival, Princess, and Holland America offer itineraries of 10–16 days departing from the West Coast of the United States, most with stops at all the major Hawaiian Islands. Some cruise lines, such as Crystal, Cunard, and Disney, include ports in Hawaii on around-the-world cruises. All have plenty on board to keep you busy during the four to five days that you are at sea between the U.S. mainland and Hawaii.

Cruise ships plying the Pacific from the continental United States to Hawaii are floating resorts complete with pools, spas, rock-climbing walls, restaurants, nightclubs, shops, casinos, children's programs, and much more. Most hold thousands of passengers with an average staff-to-passenger ratio of three to one.

Prices for cruises are based on accommodation type: interior (no window, in an inside corridor); outside (includes a window or porthole); balcony (allows you to go outside without using a public deck); and suite (larger cabin, more amenities and perks). Passages start at about $1,000 per person for the lowest class accommodation (interior) and include room, on-board entertainment, and food. Ocean-view, balcony, and suite accommodations can run up to $6,500 and beyond per person.

Cruising to Hawaii

Carnival Cruises is great for families, with plenty of kid-friendly activities. Departing from Los Angeles or Vancouver, Carnival's "fun ships" show your family a good time, both on board and on shore (☎ 888/227–6482 ⊕ www.carnival.com). The grand dame of cruise lines, Holland America has a reputation for service and elegance. Their 14-day Hawaii cruises leave from and return to San Diego, with a brief stop at Ensenada (☎ 877/932–4259 ⊕ www.hollandamerica.com). More affordable luxury is what Princess Cruises offers. While their prices seem a little higher, you get more bells and whistles on your trip (more affordable balcony rooms, more restaurants to chose from, personalized service) (☎ 800/774–6237 ⊕ www.princess.com).

Cruising within Hawaii

Norwegian Cruise Lines is the only major operator to begin and end cruises in Hawaii. *Pride of Hawaii* (vintage America theme, family focus with lots of connecting staterooms and suites) offers a seven-day itinerary that includes stops on Maui, Oahu, the Big Island, and Kauai. This is the only ship to cruise Hawaii that does not spend days at sea visiting a foreign port, allowing you more time to explore destinations (☎ 800/327–7030 ⊕ www.ncl.com). Ocean conditions in the channels between islands can be a consideration when booking an interisland cruise on a smaller vessel such as Un-Cruise Adventures—a stately yacht accommodating only 36 passengers. This yacht's small size allows it to dock at less frequented islands such as Molokai and Lanai. The cruise is billed as "all inclusive"—your passage includes shore excursions, water activities, and a massage (☎ 888/862–8881 ⊕ www.un-cruise.com).

EXPLORING

Updated
by Kristina
Anderson

Nicknamed "The Big Island," Hawaii Island is a microcosm of Hawaii the state. From long white-sand beaches and crystal-clear bays to rain forests, waterfalls, valleys, exotic flowers, and birds, all things quintessentially Hawaii are well represented here.

An assortment of happy surprises also distinguishes the Big Island from the rest of Hawaii—an active volcano (Kilauea) oozing red lava and creating new earth every day, the clearest place in the world to view stars in the night sky (Mauna Kea), and some seriously good coffee from the famous Kona district, and also from neighboring Kau.

GEOLOGY AND BIOLOGY

Home to eight of the world's 13 sub-climate zones, this is the land of fire (thanks to active Kilauea volcano) and ice (compliments of not-so-active Mauna Kea, topped with snow and expensive telescopes). At just under a million years old, Hawaii is the youngest of the main Hawaiian Islands. Three of its five volcanoes are considered active: Mauna Loa, Hualalai, and Kilauea. The southeast rift zone of Kilauea has been spewing lava regularly since January 3, 1983; another eruption began at Kilauea's summit caldera in March 2008, the first since 1982. Back in 1984, Mauna Loa's eruptions crept almost to Hilo, and it could fire up again any minute—or not for years. Hualalai last erupted in 1801, and geologists say it will definitely do so again within 100 years. Mauna Kea is currently considered dormant but may very well erupt again. Kohala, which last erupted some 120,000 years ago, is inactive, but on volatile Hawaii Island, you can never be sure.

Most of the more than 2,200 plant species found in the Hawaiian Islands are not native to Hawaii. The red-and-green lobster claw is originally from South America.

AGRICULTURE

In the 19th- and mid-20th centuries sugar was the main agricultural and economic staple of all the Islands, but especially the Big Island. The drive along the Hamakua Coast, from Hilo or Waimea, illustrates diverse agricultural developments on the island. Sugarcane stalks have been replaced by orchards of macadamia-nut trees, eucalyptus, and specialty crops from lettuce to strawberries. Macadamia-nut orchards on the Big Island supply 90% of the state's yield, while coffee continues to be big business, dominating the mountains above Kealakekua Bay. Orchids keep farmers from Honokaa to Pahoa afloat, and small

DID YOU KNOW?

Most of the over 2,200 plant species found in the Hawaiian Islands are not native to Hawaii. The red-and-green lobster claw is originally from South America.

organic farms produce meat, fruits, vegetables, and even goat cheese for high-end resort restaurants.

HISTORY

Hawaii's history is deeply rooted in its namesake island, which was home to the first Polynesian settlements and now boasts the state's best-preserved *heiau* (temples) and *puuhonua* (refuges). Kamehameha, the greatest king in Hawaiian history and the man credited with uniting the Islands, was born here, raised in Waipio Valley, and died peacefully in Kailua-Kona. The other man who most affected Hawaiian history, Captain James Cook, spent the bulk of his time in the Islands here, docked in Kealakekua Bay. (He landed first on Kauai, but had little contact with the natives there.) Thus it was here that Western influence was first felt, and from here that it spread to the rest of Hawaii.

KAILUA-KONA

Kailua-Kona is about 7 miles south of the Kona airport.

A fun and quaint seaside town, Kailua-Kona has the souvenir shops and open-air restaurants you'd expect in a small tourist hub, plus a surprising number of historic sites. Quite a few nice oceanfront restaurants here offer far more affordable fare than those at the resorts on the Kohala Coast and in Waimea.

Except for the rare deluge, the sun shines year-round. Mornings offer cooler weather, smaller crowds, and more birds singing in the banyan trees; you'll see tourists and locals out running on Alii Drive, the town's main drag, by about 5 am every day. Afternoons sometimes bring clouds and soft rain, but evenings often clear up for cool drinks, brilliant sunsets, gentle trade winds, and lazy hours spent gazing out over the ocean. Though there are better beaches north of town on the Kohala Coast, Kailua-Kona is home to a few gems, including a fantastic snorkeling beach (Kahaluu) and a tranquil bay perfect for kids (Kamakahonu Beach, in front of the Courtyard King Kamehameha hotel).

Scattered among the shops, restaurants, and condo complexes of Alii Drive are Ahuhena Heiau, a temple complex restored by King Kamehameha the Great and the spot where he spent his last days (he died here in 1819); the last royal palace in the United States (Hulihee Palace); and a battleground dotted with the graves of ancient Hawaiians who fought for their way of life and lost. It was also here in Kailua-Kona that Kamehameha's successor, King Liholiho, broke and officially abolished the ancient *kapu* (roughly translated as "forbidden," it was the name for the strict code of conduct that islanders were compelled to follow) system by publicly sitting and eating with women. The following year, on April 4, 1820, the first Christian missionaries came ashore here, changing life in the Islands forever.

GETTING HERE AND AROUND

The town closest to Kona International Airport (it's about 7 miles away), Kailua-Kona is a convenient home base from which to explore the island.

Half a day is plenty of time to explore Kailua-Kona, as most of the town's sights are located in or near the downtown area. Still, if you add in a beach trip (Kahaluu Beach has some of the best and easiest snorkeling on the island), it's tempting to while away the day here. Another option for making a day of it is to tack on a short trip up a small hill to the charming, artsy village of Holualoa or to the coffee farms in the mountains just above Kealakekua Bay.

The easiest place to park your car is at Courtyard King Kamehameha's Kona Beach Hotel ($15 per day). Some free parking is also available: When you enter Kailua via Palani Road (Highway 190), turn left onto Kuakini Highway, drive for a half block, and turn right into the small marked parking lot. Walk *makai* (toward the ocean) on Likana Lane a half block to Alii Drive, and you'll be in the heart of Kailua-Kona.

TOURS

Kona Historical Society. To learn more about the village's fascinating past, arrange for a 90-minute walking tour with an interpretive guide. The tour includes a 24-page booklet with a map and more than 40 historic photos. You can also download the guide from the historical society's website and take the tour on your own. ✉ *81-6551 Mamalahoa Hwy., Kealakekua* ☏ *808/323–3222* ⊕ *www.konahistorical.org.*

TOP ATTRACTIONS

FAMILY **Astronaut Ellison S. Onizuka Space Center.** This informative museum, located at the airport, was opened as a tribute to Hawaii's first astronaut, who was killed in the 1986 *Challenger* disaster. The space center has computer-interactive exhibits. You can launch a miniature rocket and rendezvous with an object in space, feel the effects of gyroscopic stabilization, participate in hands-on science activities, and view educational films. ✉ *Keahole–Kona International Airport, 1 Keahole Airport Rd.* ☏ *808/329–3441* ⊕ *www.hawaiimuseums.org* 🎟 *$3* ⏲ *Daily 8:30–4:30.*

Fodor'sChoice **Hulihee Palace.** A lovely two-story oceanfront home surrounded by
★ jewel green grass and elegant coco palms and fronted by an elaborate wrought-iron gate, Hulihee Palace is one of only three royal palaces in America (the other two are in Honolulu). The royal residence was built by Governor John Adams Kuakini in 1838, a year after he completed Mokuaikaua Church. During the 1880s, it served as King David Kalakaua's summer palace. Built of lava rock, it features vintage koa furniture, weaving, portraits, tapa cloth, feather work, and Hawaiian quilts. The palace is on the National Register of Historic Places and is operated by the Daughters of Hawaii, a nonprofit organization dedicated to preserving the culture and royal heritage of the Islands. ✉ *75-5718 Alii Dr.* ☏ *808/329–1877* ⊕ *daughtersofhawaii.org* 🎟 *$8–$10* ⏲ *Tues.–Sat. 9–4.*

Kailua Pier. Though most fishing boats use Honokohau Harbor, this pier dating from 1918 is still a hub of ocean activity. Outrigger canoe teams practice and race, shuttles transport cruise ship passengers to and from town, and tour boats depart from these docks daily. Along the seawall, children and old-timers cast their lines. For youngsters, a bamboo pole and hook are easy to come by, and plenty of locals are

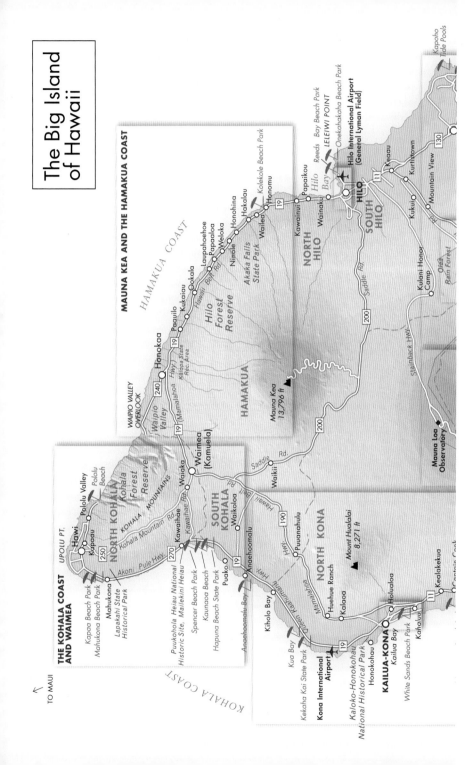

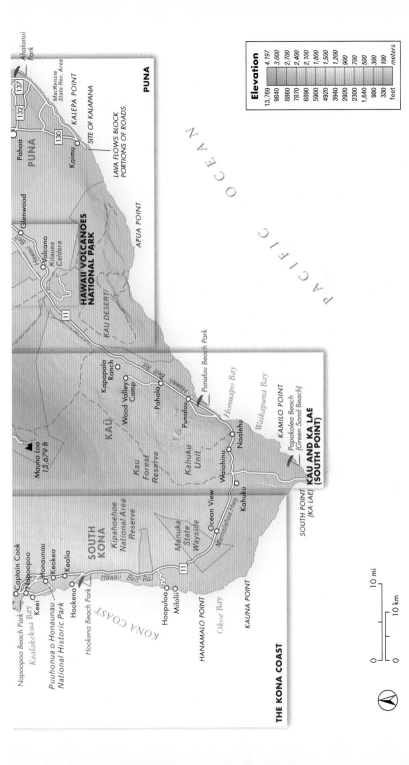

THE KONA COAST

PUNA

Aholanui Park

137

132

MacKenzie
State Rec. Area

KALEPA POINT

130

Pahoa

PUNA

Kaimu

SITE OF KALAPANA

Glenwood

LAVA FLOWS BLOCK
PORTIONS OF ROADS.

Hawaii Belt Rd.

Volcano
Kilauea
Caldera

APUA POINT

HAWAII VOLCANOES
NATIONAL PARK

11

KAU DESERT

PACIFIC OCEAN

Kapapala
Ranch

Wood Valley
Camp

Punaluu Beach Park

Pahala

Hawaii Belt Rd.

KAU

Punaluu

Mauna Loa
13,679 ft

Kau Forest
Reserve

Homuapo Bay

Kahuku
Unit

Waiohinu

Naalehu

Waikapuna Bay

South Kona

Captain Cook
Napoopoo
Keei
Honaunau
Keokea
Kealia

Puuhonua o Honaunau
National Historic Park

Kealakekua Bay
Napoopoo Beach Park

Kipahoehoe
National Area
Reserve

Hookena

Hookena Beach Park

Hawaii Belt Rd.

KONA COAST

Hoopuloa
Miloli'i

Okoe Bay

HANAMALO POINT

KAUNA POINT

Manuka
State
Wayside

11

Ocean View

Mamalahoa Hwy.

Kahuku

KAMILO POINT

Papakolea Beach
(Green Sand Beach)

KAU AND KA LAE
(SOUTH POINT)

SOUTH POINT
(KA LAE)

0   10 mi

0   10 km

Elevation

	feet	meters
	13,769	4,197
	9840	3,000
	8860	2,700
	7870	2,400
	6890	2,100
	5900	1,800
	4920	1,500
	3940	1,200
	2920	900
	2300	700
	1,640	500
	980	300
	330	100

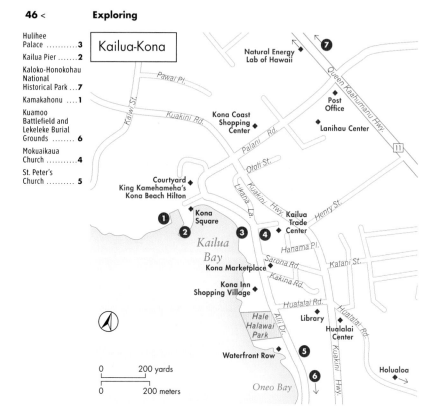

willing to give pointers. September brings the world's largest long-distance canoe race, while in October, 1,700 elite athletes leave from the pier to swim 2.4 miles as part of the famous Ironman World Championship triathlon. ✉ *Alii Dr., across from King Kamehameha's Kona Beach Hotel.*

QUICK BITES

Kope Lani. Grab a tasty croissant sandwich and locally made ice cream in tropical flavors, and knock back some of Kona's best coffee at Kope Lani, directly across from Hulihee Palace. ✉ *75-5719 Alii Dr.* ☎ *808/329-6152* ⊕ *www.kopelani.com.*

Kona Inn Restaurant. If it's sunset, it's time to unwind at this longstanding, oceanfront favorite. For tropical cocktails and *pupus* (appetizers), it doesn't get better than this. ✉ *75-5744 Alii Dr., #135* ☎ *808/329-4455* ⊕ *www.windandsearestaurants.com/konainn.*

Kamakahonu and Ahuena Heiau. In the early 1800s, King Kamehameha the Great built a royal compound at Kamakahonu, the bay fronting what is now the Courtyard King Kamehameha's Kona Beach Hotel. It was a four-acre homestead, complete with several houses and religious sites. In 1813, he rebuilt Ahuena Heiau, a stunning temple dedicated to Lono, the Hawaiian god of peace and prosperity, which was also used as a seat of government. Today it's on the National Register of Historic Places and a National Historic Landmark. One of the most revered and historically significant in all of Hawaii, the site sustained damage in the 2011 tsunami and is currently being repaired. ⊠ *75-5660 Palani Rd.* ⊕ *www.ahuena.net.*

Fodor's Choice **Mokuaikaua Church.** Site of the first Christian church in the Hawaiian
★ Islands, this strong lava-rock structure, built in 1836, is mortared with burned lime, coral, and kukui oil and topped by an impressive steeple. The ceiling and interior were crafted of timbers harvested from a forest on Hualalai and held together with wooden pegs, not nails. Incredibly, the church sustained no damage from recent earthquakes. Inside, behind a panel of gleaming koa wood, rests a model of the brig *Thaddeus* as well as a koa wood table crafted by Henry Boshard, pastor for 43 years. The gift shop is open most mornings, and a talk is given by the church historian Sunday at noon. The church still holds services and hosts community events. ⊠ *75-5713 Alii Dr.* ☎ *808/329–0655* ⊕ *www. mokuaikaua.org* ☞ *Free.*

WORTH NOTING

Kaloko–Honokohau National Historical Park. The trails at this sheltered 1,160-acre coastal park near Honokohau Harbor, just north of Kailua-Kona, are popular with walkers and hikers. The park is a good place to observe Hawaiian archaeological history and intact ruins, including a heiau, house platforms, ancient fishponds, and numerous petroglyphs, along the newly installed boardwalk. The park's wetlands provide refuge to a number of waterbirds, including the endemic Hawaiian stilt and coot. Two beaches here are good for swimming, sunbathing, and sea turtle spotting: **Aiopio**, a few yards north of the harbor, is a small beach with calm, protected swimming areas (good for kids) near the archaeological site of Puu Oina heiau, while **Honokohau Beach** is a ¾-mile stretch with ruins of ancient fishponds, also north of the harbor. Of the park's three entrances, the middle one leads to a visitor center with helpful rangers and lots of information. To go directly to the beaches, take the harbor road past the Kona Sailing Club, park in the gravel lot, and walk the sandy path to the water. ⊠ *74-425 Kealakehe Pkwy., off Hwy. 19 near airport* ☎ *808/329–6881* ⊕ *www.nps.gov/kaho* ☞ *Free* ⊗ *Kaloko Rd. gate daily 8–5.*

Kuamoo Battlefield and Lekeleke Burial Grounds. In 1819, an estimated 300 Hawaiians were killed on this vast lava field. Their spooky burial mounds are still visible at the south end of Alii Drive (called the "end of the world" by locals). After the death of his father, King Kamehameha, the newly crowned King Liholiho ate at a table with women, breaking the ancient *kapu* (taboo) system. Chief Kekuaokalani, his cousin and co-heir, held radically different views about religious traditions and unsuccessfully challenged Liholiho's forces in battle here. ⊠ *Alii Dr.*

St. Peter's Church. This tiny oceanfront chapel with crisp white-and-blue trim and an old-fashioned steeple sits next to the site of an ancient heiau, now marked by a dry-stack rock wall. This is not the church's original location, however. In 1912, it was dismantled and carried here piece by piece from a site across from Magic Sands Beach. Due to vandalism, the church is locked at all times other than mass on Saturday morning at 7:30. ⊠ *78-6684 Alii Dr., just north of mile marker 5, by Kahaluu.*

THE KONA COAST

South of Kailua-Kona, Highway 11 hugs splendid coastlines and rural towns, leaving busy streets behind. The winding, upcountry road takes you straight to the heart of coffee country, where fertile plantations and jaw-dropping views offer a taste of what Hawaii was like before the resorts took over. Tour one of the coffee farms to find out what the big deal is about Kona coffee, and enjoy a free sample while you're at it.

A half-hour drive off the highway from Kailua-Kona leads to beautiful Kealakekua Bay, where Captain James Cook arrived in 1778, dying here not long after. Hawaiian spinner dolphins frolic in the bay, now a Marine Life Conservation District, nestled alongside immensely high green cliffs that jut dramatically out to sea. Snorkeling is superb here, so you may want to bring your gear and spend an hour or so exploring the coral reefs. This is also a nice kayaking spot; the bay is normally extremely calm. ■ TIP→ **One of our favorite ways to spend a morning is to kayak in the pristine waters of Kealakekua Bay, paddling over to see the spot where Cook died. Guided tours are your best bet, and you'll likely see plenty of dolphins along the way.**

North of Kona International Airport, along Highway 19, brightly colored bougainvillea stand out in relief against miles of jet-black lava fields stretching from the mountain to the sea. The dry, barren landscape may not be what you'd expect to find on a tropical island, but it's a good reminder of the island's evolving volcanic nature.

SOUTH KONA AND KEALAKEKUA BAY

Kealakekua Bay is 14 miles south of Kailua-Kona.

Between its coffee plantations, artsy havens, and Kealakekua Bay—one of the most beautiful spots on the Big Island—South Kona has plenty of activities to occupy a day. Bring a swimsuit and snorkel gear, and hit Kealakekua Bay first thing in the morning. You'll beat the crowds, have a better chance of a dolphin sighting, and see more fish. After a morning of swimming or kayaking, head to one of the great cafés in nearby Kainaliu to refuel.

The winding road leading to Kealakekua Bay is home to a historic painted church, as well as several reasonably priced bed-and-breakfasts with great views. The communities surrounding the bay (Kealakekua and Captain Cook) are brimming with local and transplanted artists. They're great places to shop for gifts or antiques or to take an afternoon stroll.

The Kona Coast

Kiholo Bay

190

Ke Kahakai
State Park

**Astronaut Ellison S. Onizuka
Space Center**
Kona International Airport

Queen Ka ahumanu Hwy.

Mamalahoa Hwy.

Huehue Ranch

Kalaoa

**Natural Energy
Lab of Hawaii**

**NORTH
KONA**

Mountain
Thunder

Mount Hualalai
8,271 ft

**Kaloko-Honokohau
National Historical Park**

Hula Daddy

Honokohau

Kailua-Kona

Holualoa

Kailua Bay

White Sands Beach Park

11

Holualoa-Kona Coffee Company

Honalo

Kainaliu

Kealakekua

**Amy B.H. Greenwell
Ethnobotanical Garden**

Greenwell Farms and Store

Captain Cook

Napoopoo Beach Park

Captain Cook Monument

Napoopoo

Hikiau Heiau

Kealakekua Bay

Keel

**Kona Coffee Living
History Farm**

Royal Kona Coffee
Museum & Coffee Mill

160

Honaunau

Puuhonua O Honaunau

**St. Benedicts
Painted Church**

Keokea

**Lion's Gate
Farms**

Kealia

Hookena Beach Park

Hookena

**SOUTH
KONA**

PACIFIC OCEAN

Hawaii Bell Rd

Kipahoehoe
Natural Area
Reserve

Hoopuloa

Milolii Bay Beach Park

Milolii

11

HANAMALO POINT

Okoe Bay

**Manuka State
Wayside**

Mamalahoa Hwy.

0   6 mi
0   6 km

KAUNA POINT

Pohue Bay

GETTING HERE AND AROUND

To get to Kealakekua Bay, follow the signs off Highway 11 and park at Napoopoo Beach. It's not much of a beach, but it provides easy access into the water.

COFFEE FARMS

Several coffee farms around the Kona coffee-belt area welcome visitors to watch all or part of the coffee-production process, from harvest to packaging. Some tours are self-guided and most are free, with the exception of the Kona Coffee Living History Farm.

FAMILY **Greenwell Farms.** The Greenwell family played a significant role in the cultivation of the first commercial coffee in the Kona area. Depending on the season, the 20-minute walking tour of this working farm takes in various stages of coffee production, but it always includes a sample of Greenwell Farms' Kona coffee at the end and the opportunity to buy some from the gift shop. ⊠ *81-6581 Mamalahoa Hwy., between mile markers 112 and 111, Kealakekua* ☎ *808/323–2295* ⊕ *www.greenwellfarms.com* ⊠ *Free* ⊗ *Daily 8:30–4.*

Hula Daddy. On a walking tour of this working coffee orchard, visitors can learn the history of the farm, pick and pulp their own coffee beans, see a roasting demonstration, and have a tasting. And of course there's a gift shop. ⊠ *74-4944 Mamalahoa Hwy., Holualoa* ☎ *808/327–9744, 888/553–2339* ⊕ *www.huladaddy.com* ⊠ *Free* ⊗ *Mon.–Sat. 10–4.*

Kona Coffee Living History Farm (D. Uchida Farm). On the National Register of Historic Places, this perfectly preserved farm was completely restored by the Kona Historical Society. It includes a 1913 farmhouse surrounded by coffee trees, a Japanese bathhouse, *kuriba* (coffee-processing mill), and *hoshidana* (traditional drying platform). Caretakers still grow, harvest, roast, and sell the coffee exactly as they did 100 years ago. ⊠ *82-6199 Mamalahoa Hwy., mile marker 110, Captain Cook* ☎ *808/323–2006* ⊕ *www.konahistorical.org* ⊠ *$15* ⊗ *Tours weekdays 10–2.*

Lions Gate Farms. For a century, three generations have grown coffee on this pretty farm with spectacular ocean views in the heart of Honaunau. The coffee is processed in a mill that dates to 1942. Tours show how coffee and macadamia nuts are cultivated and harvested. ⊠ *Hwy. 11, mile marker 105, Honaunau* ☎ *808/989–4883* ⊕ *www.coffeeofkona.com* ⊗ *Tours by appointment.*

Mountain Thunder. This is the largest coffee grower and the most extensive organic coffee producer in Hawaii. Hourly "bean to cup" tours include a tasting and access to the processing plant, which shows dry milling, sizing, coloring, sorting, and roasting. Private VIP tours (small fee) let you be roast master for a day. Hawaiian teas, handmade chocolate, and macadamia nuts grown on-site are also available. ⊠ *73-1944 Hao St., Kailua-Kona* ☎ *888/414–5662* ⊕ *www.mountainthunder.com* ⊠ *Free* ⊗ *Tours daily 10–4.*

Royal Kona Coffee Museum & Coffee Mill. Take an easy self-guided tour by following the descriptive plaques located around the coffee mill. Then stop off at the small museum to see coffee-making relics and watch an informational film. ⊠ *83-5427 Mamalahoa Hwy., next to tree house,*

Kealakekua Bay is one of the most beautiful spots on the Big Island.

Captain Cook ☎ *808/328–2511* ⊕ *www.royalkonacoffee.com* ▨ *Free* ☉ *Daily 7:30–5.*

KONA'S COFFEE FESTIVAL

Kona Coffee Cultural Festival. This annual community-wide festival runs for 10 days in November and includes recipe competitions, parades with Miss Kona Coffee, concerts, special tours, an art stroll and coffee tasting in Holualoa, and the Gevalia Kona Cupping Competition (a judged tasting). ⊕ *www.konacoffeefest.com.*

TOP ATTRACTIONS

Fodor'sChoice ★ **Captain Cook Monument.** No one knows for sure what happened on February 14, 1779, when English explorer Captain James Cook was killed on this spot. He had chosen Kealakekua Bay as a landing place in November 1778. Arriving during the celebration of Makahiki, the harvest season, Cook was welcomed at first. Some Hawaiians saw him as an incarnation of the god Lono. Cook's party sailed away in February 1779, but a freak storm forced his damaged ship back to Kealakekua Bay. Believing that no god could be thwarted by a mere rainstorm, the Hawaiians were not so welcoming this time, and various confrontations arose between them and Cook's sailors. The theft of a longboat brought Cook and an armed party ashore to reclaim it. One thing led to another: shots were fired, daggers and spears were thrown, and Captain Cook fell, mortally wounded. A 27-foot-high obelisk marks the spot where he died. You can see it from a vantage point across the bay at Kealakekua Bay State Park. ✉ *Captain Cook* ⊕ *www.hawaiistateparks.org/parks.*

CLOSE UP

Kona Coffee

The Kona Coffee belt, some 16 miles long and about a mile wide, has been producing smooth, aromatic coffee for more than a century. The slopes of massive Mauna Loa at this elevation provide the ideal conditions for growing coffee: sunny mornings; cloudy, rainy afternoons; and rich, rocky, volcanic soil. More than 600 farms, most just three to seven acres in size, grow the delicious—and luxurious, at generally more than $25 per pound—gourmet beans. Only coffee from the North and South Kona districts can be called Kona, and Hawaii is the only U.S. producer of commercially grown coffee.

In 1828 Reverend Samuel Ruggles, an American missionary, brought a cutting over from the Oahu farm of Chief Boki, Oahu's governor. That coffee plant was a strain of Ethiopian coffee called Arabica, which is still produced today, although a Guatemalan strain of Arabica introduced in the late 1800s is produced in far higher quantities.

In the early 1900s, the large Hawaiian coffee plantations subdivided their lots and began leasing parcels to local tenant farmers, a practice that continues. Many tenant farmers were Japanese families. In the 1930s, local schools switched summer vacation to "coffee vacation," August to November, so that children could help with the coffee harvest, a practice that held until 1969.

Coffee is harvested as "cherries"—beans encased in a sweet, red shell. Kona coffee trees are hand-picked several times each season to guarantee the ripest product. The cherries are shelled, their parchment layer sun-dried and removed, and the beans roasted to perfection. Today most farms—owned and operated by Japanese-American families, west coast mainland transplants, and descendants of Portuguese and Chinese immigrants—control production from cultivation to cup.

Fodor's Choice ★ **Kealakekua Bay State Park.** This underwater marine reserve is one of the most beautiful spots in the state. Dramatic cliffs surround super-deep, crystal clear, turquoise water chock-full of stunning coral pinnacles and tropical fish. The dolphins that frequent the sanctuary should not be disturbed, as they use the bay to escape predators and sleep. The brown sand at west-facing **Napoopoo Beach,** washed away during Hurricane Iniki in 1992, is slowly returning. This is a nice, easy place to enter the water and swim, as it's well protected from currents. ⚠ **No lifeguards; at times, you may feel tiny jellyfish stings.** ✉ *Beach Rd., off Government Rd. from Puuhonua Rd. (Hwy. 160), Captain Cook* ⊕ *www.hawaiistateparks.org.*

NEED A BREAK?

The Coffee Shack. This cool roadside stop once declared, "Best Views of a Coffee Farm" on its signs. It's no exaggeration. Breakfast or lunch on the covered but breezy lanai comes with fantastic views of the restaurant's own coffee farm and Kealakekua Bay. The bread is home-baked, the eggs Benedict is a local favorite, the fruit plates and sandwiches are generous, and the staff is friendly. ✉ *83-5799 Mamalahoa Hwy., between mile*

DID YOU KNOW?

Coffee beans are actually the seeds of these cherry-like fruit, appropriately named coffee cherries. Be sure to sample some Kona brew while you're in the area.

markers 108 and 109, Kealakekua ☎ 808/328–9555 ⊕ www.coffeeshack. com ⊙ Daily 7:30–3.

Holualoa Town. Hugging the hillside along the Kona Coast, the artsy village of Holualoa is 3 miles up winding Hualalai Road from Kailua-Kona. Galleries here feature all types of artists—from painters, wood-workers, and jewelers to gourd-makers and potters—working in their studios in back and selling their wares up front. Formerly the exclusive domain of coffee plantations, Holualoa still has quite a few coffee farms offering free tours and inviting cups of joe. ⊠ *Holualoa ⊕ www. holualoahawaii.com.*

Fodor's Choice **Puuhonua O Honaunau National Historical Park** (*City of Refuge or Place of* ★ *Refuge*). This 420-acre National Historical Park houses the best pre-served *puuhonua* (place of refuge) in the state. Providing a safe haven for noncombatants, *kapu* (taboo) breakers, defeated warriors, and others, the puuhonua offered protection and redemption for anyone who could reach its boundaries, by land or sea. The oceanfront, 960-foot stone wall still stands and is one of the park's most prominent features. A number of ceremonial temples, including the restored **Hale o Keawe Heiau** (circa 1700), have served as royal burial chambers. An aura of ancient sacredness and serenity still embues the place. ⊠ *Rte. 160, about 20 miles south of Kailua-Kona, Honaunau ☎ 808/328–2288 ⊕ www. nps.gov/puho ⊠ $5 per vehicle ⊙ Park daily 7 am–sunset; visitor center daily 8–4:30.*

WORTH NOTING

Amy B.H. Greenwell Ethnobotanical Garden. Exhibiting a wealth of Hawaiian ethnobotanical traditions and some rare plants found only in cultivation, this 12-acre garden contains 250 types of plants typical of an early Hawaiian *ahupuaa*, the usually pie-shaped land divisions that ran from the mountains to the sea. The visitor center, now on the south side of the garden, includes a gift shop. The garden is 12 miles south of Kailua-Kona, across from the Manago Hotel. Call for information on guided tours. ⊠ *82-6160 Mamalahoa Hwy., just past mile marker 110, Captain Cook ☎ 808/323–3318 ⊕ www.bishopmuseum.org/greenwell ⊠ $7 ⊙ Tues.–Sun. 9–4.*

H.N. Greenwell Store Museum. Established in 1850, the homestead of Henry N. Greenwell served as cattle ranch, sheep station, store, post office, and family home all in one. Now, all that remains is the 1875 stone structure, which is listed on the National Register of Historic Places. It houses a fascinating museum with exhibits on ranching and coffee farming. It's also headquarters for the **Kona Historical Society,** which archives and preserves the history of the Kona district. ⊠ *81-6551 Mamalahoa Hwy., mile marker 112, Kealakekua ☎ 808/323–3222 ⊕ www.konahistorical.org ⊠ $7 ⊙ Mon.–Thurs. 10–2.*

Hikiau Heiau. This stone platform was once an impressive temple dedicated to the god Lono. When Captain Cook arrived in 1778, ceremonies in his honor were held here. ■TIP➔ It's still considered a religious site, so please visit with respect. ⊠ *Bottom of Napoopoo Rd.*

Kainaliu Town. This is the first town you encounter to the south heading upcountry from Kailua town. In addition to a ribbon of funky old stores, coffee bars, and bistros, a handful of galleries and shops have sprung up in the last few years. Browse around Oshima's, established in 1926, and Kimura's, founded in 1927, to find fabrics and Japanese goods beyond tourist trinkets. Pop into a local café for everything from burgers to authentic Italian. Peek into the 1932-vintage Aloha Theatre, where a troupe of community-theater actors might be practicing a Broadway revue. ⊠ *Hwy. 11, mile markers 112–114, Kainaliu.*

St. Benedict's Painted Church. In the late 1800s, Belgian-born priest and self-taught artist Father John Velge painted the walls, columns, and ceiling of this Roman Catholic church with religious scenes in the style of Christian folk art found throughout the South Pacific. The tiny church itself is of the European Gothic cathedral tradition and is listed on the Hawaii State Register of Historic Places and the National Register of Historic Places. Mass is offered daily. ⊠ *84-5140 Painted Church Rd., off Hwy. 160, Captain Cook* ☎ *808/328–2227* ⊕ *www. thepaintedchurch.org* ✉ *Donations welcome.*

NORTH KONA

Most of the lava flows in North Kona originate from the last eruptions of Hualalai, in 1800 and 1801, although some flows by the resorts hail from Mauna Loa. You will no doubt notice the white graffiti dotting the vast lava fields. This has been going on for decades, and locals still get a kick out of it, as do visitors. The first thing everyone asks is "where do the white rocks come from?" The answer is that they're bits of coral from the ocean, and if you want to write a message, you've got to use the coral that's already out there. This means that messages don't last long, but that's all part of the fun. Some local couples write their names in the same spot on the lava fields every anniversary. Other people greet friends as they arrive or depart Kona.

GETTING HERE AND AROUND
Head north from Kona International Airport and follow Highway 19 along the coast. Take caution driving at night between the airport and where resorts begin on the Kohala Coast; it's extremely dark and there are few road signs or traffic lights on this two-lane road.

WORTH NOTING
Natural Energy Lab of Hawaii Authority. Just south of Kona International Airport, a large mysterious group of buildings with an equally large and mysterious photovoltaic (solar) panel installation looks like some sort of top-secret military station. It's really the site of the Natural Energy Lab of Hawaii Authority, NELHA for short. Here, scientists, researchers, and entrepreneurs make use of a cold, deep-sea pipeline to develop and market everything from desalinated, mineral-rich drinking water and super-nutritious algae products to energy-efficient air-conditioning systems and environmentally friendly aquaculture techniques. Three types of facility tours are offered most days. ⊠ *73-4460 Queen Kaahumanu Hwy., Kailua-Kona* ☎ *808/329–8073*

DID YOU KNOW?

Kealakekua Bay is generally considered the best snorkeling spot on the Big Island, with stunning coral reefs—especially around the Captain Cook Monument—calm waters, and spinner dolphins.

⊕ *www.energyfuturehawaii.org* ✉ *$8 suggested donation for tours* ⊙ *Tours weekdays at 10 am.*

THE KOHALA COAST

2

The Kohala Coast is about 32 miles north of Kailua-Kona.

If you had only a weekend to spend on the Big Island, this is probably where you'd want to be. The Kohala Coast is a mix of the island's best beaches and swankiest hotels not far from ancient valleys and temples, waterfalls, and funky artist enclaves.

The resorts on the Kohala Coast lay claim to some of the island's finest restaurants, golf courses, and destination spas. But the real attraction here is the island's glorious beaches. On a clear day, you can see Maui, and during the winter months, numerous glistening humpback whales cleave the waters just offshore.

Rounding the northern tip of the island, the arid coast shifts rather suddenly to green villages and hillsides, leading to lush Pololu Valley in North Kohala, as the hot sunshine along the coast gives way to cooler temperatures.

As you drive north, you'll find the quaint sugar-plantation-towns-turned-artsy-villages of Hawi and Kapaau. New galleries are interspersed with charming reminders of old Hawaii—wooden boardwalks, quaint local storefronts, delicious neighborhood restaurants, friendly locals, and a delightfully slow pace. There's great shopping for everything from designer beachwear to authentic Hawaiian crafts.

GETTING HERE AND AROUND

Two days is sufficient time for experiencing each unique side of Kohala—one day for the resort perks: the beach, the spa, the golf, the restaurants; one day for hiking and admiring the waterfalls and valleys of North Kohala, coupled with a wander around Hawi and Kapaau.

Diving and snorkeling are primo along the Kohala coast, so bring or rent equipment. If you're staying at one of the resorts, they will usually have any equipment you could possibly want. If you're feeling adventurous, get your hands on a four-wheel-drive vehicle and head to one of the unmarked beaches along the Kohala Coast—you may end up with a beach to yourself.

The best way to explore the valleys of North Kohala is with a hiking tour. Look for one that includes lunch and a dip in one of the area's waterfall pools. There are a number of casual lunch options in Hawi and Kapaau (sandwiches, sushi, seafood, local-style "plate lunch"), and a few good dinner spots.

VISITOR INFORMATION

North Kohala Community Resource Center. This renovated plantation building has maps and information on North Kohala attractions. Take a seat on the lanai and talk story, have some cool water, or use the restroom or ATM. ✉ *55-3393 Akoni Pule Hwy., just past the "Welcome to Kohala" sign, North Kohala* ☎ *808/889-5523* ⊕ *www.northkohala.org* ✉ *Free* ⊙ *Weekdays 8:30–4:30, weekend hours vary.*

TOP ATTRACTIONS

Hawi and Kapaau. Near the birthplace of King Kamehameha, these North Kohala towns thrived during the plantation days, once bustling with hotels, saloons, and theaters—even a railroad. They took a hit when "Big Sugar" left the island, but both towns are blossoming once again, thanks to strong local communities, tourism, and an influx of artists keen on honoring the towns' past. They are full of lovingly restored vintage buildings housing fun and funky shops, galleries, and eateries.

Ackerman Gift Gallery. In Kapaau, browse through this longtime gallery's collections of local art, including glass, woodworks, bowls, fine art photography, and paintings. There's also a gift shop a couple of doors away. ✉ *54-3897 Akoni Pule Hwy., Hwy. 270, North Kohala* ☎ *808/889–5971 gallery, 808/889–5138 gift shop* ⊕ *www.ackermangalleries.com*

QUICK BITES **Kohala Coffee Mill & Tropical Dreams.** If you're looking for something sweet—or savory—this café in downtown Hawi serves great local coffee, breakfast (bagels, espresso-machine steamed eggs), and lunch (hot dogs, vegan soup), open until 6. Sit outside and watch the world go by as you enjoy locally made ice cream that is *ono* (delicious). ✉ *55-3412 Akoni Pule Hwy., Hawi* ☎ *808/889–5577.*

Keokea Beach Park. A newly renovated pavilion (damaged in the 2006 quake) welcomes visitors to this seven-acre beach park fronting the rugged shore in North Kohala. Enjoy the scenery, but don't try to swim here—the water is very rough, and be careful on the hairpin curve going down. ✉ *Hwy. 270, on the way to Pololu Valley near mile marker 27, North Kohala.*

Kohala Mountain Road Lookout. The road between North Kohala and Waimea is one of the most scenic drives in Hawaii, passing Parker Ranch, open pastures, and tree-lined mountains. There are a few places to pull over and take in the view; the lookout at mile marker 8 provides a splendid vista of the Kohala Coast and Kawaihae Harbor far below. On clear days, you can see well beyond the resorts to Maui, while other times an eerie, thick mist drifts over the view. ✉ *Kohala Mountain Rd. (Hwy. 250), Kamuela.*

Lapakahi State Historical Park. A self-guided, 1-mile walking tour leads through the ruins of the once-prosperous fishing village Koaie, which dates as far back as the 15th century. Displays illustrate early Hawaiian fishing and farming techniques, salt gathering, games, and legends. Because the shoreline near the state park is an officially designated Marine Life Conservation District (and part of the site itself is considered sacred), swimming, swim gear, and sunscreen are not allowed in the water. Restrooms are available but not drinking water. ✉ *Hwy. 270, mile marker 14 between Kawaihae and Mahukona, North Kohala* ☎ *808/327–4958* ⊕ *www.hawaiistateparks.org* 🎟 *Free* ⊙ *Daily 8–4.*

Continued on page 62

BIRTH OF THE ISLANDS

How did the volcanoes of the Hawaiian Islands evolve here, in the middle of the Pacific Ocean? The ancient Hawaiians believed that the volcano goddess Pele's hot temper was the key to the mystery; modern scientists contend that it's all about plate tectonics and one very hot spot.

Plate Tectonics & the Hawaiian Question: The theory of plate tectonics says that the Earth's surface is comprised of plates that float around slowly over the planet's molten interior. The vast majority of earthquakes and volcanic eruptions occur near plate boundaries—the San Francisco earthquakes in 1906 and 1989, for example, were the result of activity along the nearby San Andreas Fault, where the Pacific and North American plates meet. Hawaii, more than 1,988 miles from the nearest plate boundary, is a giant exception. For years scientists struggled to explain the island chain's existence—if not a fault line, what caused the earthquakes and volcanic eruptions that formed these islands?

What's a hotspot? In 1963, J. Tuzo Wilson, a Canadian geophysicist, argued that the Hawaiian volcanoes must have been created by small concentrated areas of extreme heat beneath the plates. Wilson hypothesized that there is a hotspot beneath the present-day position of the Big Island. Its heat produced a persistent source of magma by partly melting the Pacific Plate above it. The magma, lighter than the surrounding solid rock, rose through the mantle and crust to erupt onto the sea floor, forming an active seamount. Each flow caused the seamount to grow until it finally emerged above sea level as an island volcano. Plausible so far, but why then, is there not one giant Hawaiian island?

Holo Mai Pele, often played out in hula, is the Hawaiian creation myth. Pele sends her sister Hiiaka on an epic quest to fetch her lover Lohiau. Overcoming many obstacles, Hiiaka reaches full goddess status and falls in love with Lohiau herself. When Pele finds out, she destroys everything dear to her sister, killing Lohiau and burning Hiiaka's ohia groves. Each time lava flows from a volcano, ohia trees sprout shortly after, in a constant cycle of destruction and renewal.

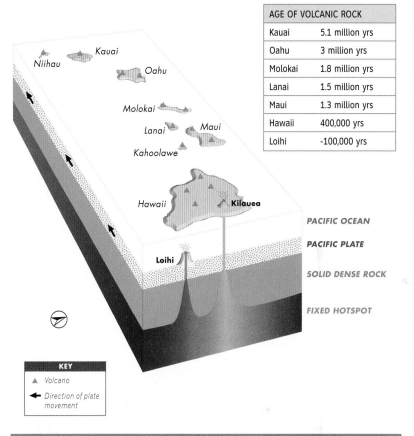

AGE OF VOLCANIC ROCK	
Kauai	5.1 million yrs
Oahu	3 million yrs
Molokai	1.8 million yrs
Lanai	1.5 million yrs
Maui	1.3 million yrs
Hawaii	400,000 yrs
Loihi	-100,000 yrs

PACIFIC OCEAN

PACIFIC PLATE

SOLID DENSE ROCK

FIXED HOTSPOT

KEY
▲ Volcano
◀ Direction of plate movement

Volcanoes on the Move: Wilson further suggested that the movement of the Pacific Plate itself eventually carries the island volcano beyond the hotspot. Cut off from its magma source, the island volcano becomes dormant. As the plate slowly moved, one island volcano would become extinct just as another would develop over the hotspot. After several million years, there is a long volcanic trail of islands and seamounts across the ocean floor. The oldest islands are those farthest from the hotspot. The exposed rocks of Kauai, for example, are about 5.1 million years old, but those on the Big Island are less than .5 million years old, with new volcanic rock still being formed.

An Island on the Way: Off the coast of the Big Island, the volcano known as Loihi is still submerged but erupting. Scientists long believed it to be a retired seamount volcano, but in the 1970s they discovered both old and new lava on its flanks, and in 1996 it erupted with a vengeance. It is believed that several thousand years from now, Loihi will be the newest addition to the Hawaiian Islands.

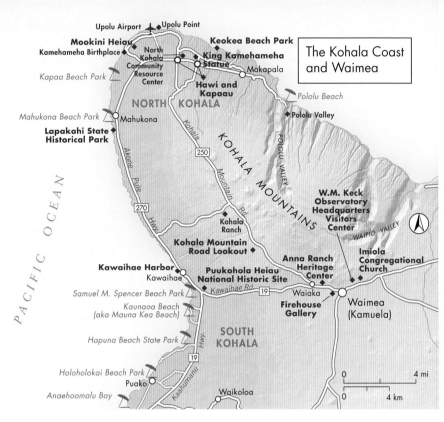

The Kohala Coast and Waimea

Upolu Airport
Upolu Point
Mookini Heiau
Kamehameha Birthplace
North Kohala Community Resource Center
Keokea Beach Park
King Kamehameha Statue
Makapala
Kapaa Beach Park
Hawi and Kapaau
NORTH KOHALA
Pololu Beach
Mahukona Beach Park
Mahukona
Pololu Valley
Lapakahi State Historical Park
KOHALA MOUNTAINS
POLOLU VALLEY
250
Kohala Mountain Rd.
Akone Pule Hwy.
270
Kohala Ranch
W.M. Keck Observatory Headquarters Visitors Center
WAIPIO VALLEY
Kohala Mountain Road Lookout
Imiola Congregational Church
Kawaihae Harbor
Kawaihae
Puukohola Heiau National Historic Site
Anna Ranch Heritage Center
Samuel M. Spencer Beach Park
Kawaihae Rd.
19
Waiaka
Waimea (Kamuela)
Kaunaoa Beach (aka Mauna Kea Beach)
Firehouse Gallery
Hapuna Beach State Park
SOUTH KOHALA
Kaahumanu Hwy.
19
Holoholokai Beach Park
Puako
Anaehoomalu Bay
Waikoloa
PACIFIC OCEAN
0   4 mi
0   4 km

Mookini Heiau. This isolated National Historic Landmark is so impressive in size and atmosphere that it may give you what locals call "chicken skin" (goose bumps). Its foundations date to about AD 480, but the high priest Paao from Tahiti expanded the heiau several centuries later and it continued to be used by Hawaiian religious leaders. You can still see the lava slab where hundreds of people were sacrificed, giving this place a truly haunted feel. Visit with utmost care and respect. Nearby is Kamehameha Akahi Aina Hanau, the birthplace of Kamehameha the Great. ⚠ Check conditions in the area before venturing. The access road is unpaved. When it's dry, it's not bad, but with pooled rainwater, it can be difficult, if not impossible, to traverse. Even with four-wheel drive, you could easily get stuck in the mud. ⊠ *Off Hwy. 270, turn at sign for Upolu Airport, near Hawi, and hike or drive 1½ miles south-west, North Kohala* ☎ *808/974–6200.*

Fodor'sChoice **Puukohola Heiau National Historic Site.** Quite simply, this is one of the
★ most historic sites in all of Hawaii. It was here in 1810, on top of Puukohala (Hill of the Whale), that Kamehameha the Great built the war heiau that would serve to unify the Hawaiian Islands. The ocean-front, fortress-like site is foreboding and impressive. A paved ½-mile, looped trail runs from the visitor center to the main temple sites. An even older temple, dedicated to the shark gods, lies submerged just

offshore, where sharks can be seen circling. A new museum displays ancient Hawaiian weapons, including clubs, spears, and a replica of a bronze cannon that warriors dragged into battle on an ancient Hawaiian sled. Stop on the lanai for a cool breeze and a spectacular view. A free audio tour can be heard on your cell phone. ⊠ *62-3601 Kawaihae Rd., Kawaihae* ☎ *808/882–7218* ⊕ *www.nps.gov/puhe/index.htm* 🎫 *Free* ⊗ *Daily 8–4:45.*

WORTH NOTING

Kawaihae Harbor. This no-frills industrial harbor, where in 1793 the first cattle landed in Hawaii, is a hub of commercial and community activity. It's especially busy on weekends, when paddlers and local fishing boats share the waters. Second in size only to Hilo Harbor on the east side, the port often shelters the *Makalii,* one of three traditional Hawaiian sailing canoes. King Kamehameha and his men launched their canoes from here when they set out to conquer the neighboring islands. ■ TIP➔ **Kawaihae has several restaurants with nice sunset views.** ⊠ *Kawaihae Harbor Rd., off Hwy. 270, Kawaihae.*

King Kamehameha Statue. A statue of Kamehameha the Great, the legendary king who united the Hawaiian Islands, stands watch over his descendants in North Kohala. The 8½-foot-tall figure bears the king's sacred feather *kihei, mahiole,* and *kaei* (cape, helmet, and sash). A replica of this statue fronts the Judiciary Building on King Street in Honolulu. Cast in Florence in 1880, it was lost at sea when the German ship transporting it sank near the Falkland Islands. A replica was then commissioned and shipped to Honolulu. Two years after its disappearance, the original statue was found in a junkyard in the Falkland Islands; it was missing an arm, which has since been replaced. This statue was transported to the remote northern tip of the Big Island, Kamehameha's birthplace: it's in front of the old Kohala Courthouse in Kapaau, next to the highway on the way toward Pololu Valley.

Every year on King Kamehameha Day (June 11), Kohala residents honor their most famous son with a celebration that involves a parade and draping the statue in dozens of handmade floral lei. ⊠ *54-3900 Kapaau Rd., Kapaau.*

WAIMEA

Waimea is 40 miles northeast of Kailua-Kona and 10 miles east of the Kohala Coast.

Thirty minutes over the mountain from Kohala, Waimea offers a completely different experience from the rest of the island. Rolling green hills, large open pastures, light rain, cool evening breezes and morning mists, abundant cattle, horses, and regular rodeos are just a few of the surprises you'll stumble upon here in *paniolo* (Hawaiian for "cowboy") country.

Waimea is also where some of the island's top Hawaii regional-cuisine chefs practice their art using local ingredients, which makes it an ideal place to find yourself at dinnertime. In keeping with the recent Big Island restaurant trend toward featuring locally farmed ingredients, a handful of Waimea farms and ranches supply most of the restaurants on the island, and many sell to the public as well. With its galleries, restaurants, beautiful countryside, and *paniolo* culture, Waimea is well worth a stop if you're heading to Hilo or Mauna Kea. ■**TIP**→ **And the short highway, or mountain road, that connects Waimea to North Kohala (Highway 250) affords some of our favorite Big Island views.**

GETTING HERE AND AROUND

You can see most of what Waimea has to offer in one day, but if you're heading up to Mauna Kea for stargazing (which you should), it could easily be stretched to two. If you stay in Waimea overnight (there are a few bed-and-breakfast options), spend the afternoon browsing through town or touring some of the area's ranches and historic sites. Then indulge in a gourmet dinner before heading up Saddle Road for world-renowned stargazing atop Mauna Kea.

A word to the wise—there are no services or gas stations on Saddle Road, the only way to reach the summit of Mauna Kea. Fill up on gas and bring water, snacks, and warm clothes with you (there are plenty of gas stations, cafés, and shops in Waimea).

TOP ATTRACTIONS

Fodor'sChoice
★
Anna Ranch Heritage Center. This stunning heritage property, on the National Register of Historic Places, belonged to the "first lady" of Hawaii ranching, Anna Lindsey Perry-Fiske. Here is a rare opportunity to see a fully restored cattle ranch compound and learn about the life of this fascinating woman, who butchered cattle by day and threw lavish parties by night. Wander the picturesque grounds and gardens on a self-guided walk, watch a master saddle maker and an ironsmith in action, and take a tour of the historic house, where Anna's furniture, gowns, and elaborate *pau* (parade riding) costumes are on display. The knowledgeable staff shares anecdotes about Anna's amazing life. ⊠ *65-1480 Kawaihae Rd.* ☎ *808/885–4426* ⊕ *www.annaranch.org* ⊠ *Guided tours $10* ☉ *Tues.–Fri. 10–3; guided tours by appointment.*

WORTH NOTING

Firehouse Gallery. Local Big Island artwork is featured at this historic gallery, an 80-year-old fire station at the intersection of Lindsey Road and old Mamalahoa Highway. Supporting the Waimea Arts Council, the gallery is home to annual juried shows as well as solo and group exhibitions by its many award-winning multimedia artists and artisans. ⊠ *67-1201 Mamalahoa Hwy., across from Waimea Chevron* ☎ *808/887–1052* ⊕ *www.waimeaartscouncil.org* ☉ *Wed.–Sat. 11–3.*

Imiola Congregational Church. Highlights of this church, which was established in 1832 and rebuilt in

---

WAIMEA OR KAMUELA?

Both, actually. Everyone knows it as Waimea, but the sign on the post office says Kamuela, which is Hawaiian for "Samuel," referring to Samuel Parker, the son of the founder of Parker Ranch. That designation is used to avoid confusion with communities named Waimea on the islands of Kauai and Oahu. But the official name of the town is Waimea.

DID YOU KNOW?

Accessed by a steep hiking
trail, the remote Pololu Valley
Beach, on the North Kohala
peninsula, is one of the Big
Island's most striking gray-
sand beaches.

Mauna Kea's snowcapped summit towers ahead on a drive south from Waimea.

1857, are a gleaming, restored koa interior and unusual wooden calabashes hanging from the ceiling. Be careful not to walk in while a service is in progress, as the front entry is behind the pulpit. ✉ *65-1084 Mamalahoa Hwy., on "Church Row"* ☎ *808/885–4987.*

W.M. Keck Observatory Headquarters Vistors Center. If you are keen on astronomy but don't have time to go all the way to the summit, visit Keck Observatory headquarters right in Waimea, with its educational exhibits and informed staff. You can see models and images taken from the twin 10-meter Keck telescopes on Mauna Kea and learn about the latest discoveries. ✉ *65-1120 Mamalahoa Hwy, across from hospital* ☎ *808/885–7887* ⊕ *www.keckobservatory.org* ☺ *Tues.–Fri. 10–2 (docent program).*

QUICK BITES

Waimea Coffee Company. This is a good stop for a steaming latté and a warm pastry, a cup of hot soup, or freshly made salad. The small lanai offers enjoyable views of Waimea's compact rolling hills dappled with rain, fog, and sunlight. ✉ *Parker Sq., 65-1279 Kawaihae Rd.* ☎ *808/885–8915* ⊕ *www.waimeacoffeecompany.com.*

MAUNA KEA

Fodor's Choice
★

Mauna Kea's summit is 18 miles southeast of Waimea and 34 miles northwest of Hilo.

Mauna Kea ("white mountain") offers the antithesis of the typical island experience. Freezing temperatures and arctic conditions are common at the summit, and snow can fall year-round. You can even snowboard or ski up here. Seriously. But just because you can doesn't mean you'll want to. You should be in very good shape and a close-to-expert boarder or skier to get down the slopes near the summit and then up again in the thin air with no lifts. During the winter months, lack of snow is usually not a problem.

But winter sports are the least of the reasons that most people visit this starkly beautiful mountain. From its base below the ocean's surface to its summit, Mauna Kea is the tallest island mountain on the planet. It's also home to little Lake Waiau, one of the highest natural lakes in the world, though lately, the word "pond" is closer to the truth.

Mauna Kea's summit—at 13,796 feet—is the best place in the world for viewing the night sky. For this reason, the summit is home to the largest and most productive astronomical observatories in the world—and $1 billion (with a "B") worth of equipment. Research teams from 11 different countries operate 13 telescopes on Mauna Kea, several of which are record holders: the world's largest optical–infrared telescopes (the dual Keck telescopes), the world's largest dedicated infrared telescope (UKIRT), and the largest submillimeter telescope (the JCMT). A still-larger 30-meter telescope has been cleared for construction and is slated to open its record-breaking eye to the heavens in 2018.

Mauna Kea is tall, but there are higher mountains in the world, so what makes this spot so superb for astronomy? It has more to do with atmosphere than with elevation. A tropical-inversion-cloud layer below the summit keeps moisture from the ocean and other atmospheric pollutants down at lower elevations. As a result, the air around the Mauna Kea summit is extremely dry, which helps in the measurement of infrared and submillimeter radiation from stars, planets, and the like. There are also rarely clouds up here; the annual number of clear nights here blows every other place out of the water. And, because the mountain is far away from any interfering artificial lights (not a total coincidence—in addition to the fact that the nearest town is nearly 30 miles away, there's an official ordinance limiting light on the island), skies are dark for the astronomers' research. To quote the staff at the observatory, astronomers here are able to "observe the faintest galaxies that lie at the very edge of the observable universe."

Teams from various universities around the world have used the telescopes on Mauna Kea to make major astronomical discoveries, including new satellites around Jupiter and Saturn, new Trojans (asteroids that orbit, similar to moons) around Neptune, new moons and rings around Uranus, and new moons around Pluto. Their studies of galaxies are changing the way scientists think about time and the evolution of the universe.

What does all this mean for you? A visit to Mauna Kea is a chance to see more stars than you've likely ever seen before, and an opportunity to learn more about mind-boggling scientific discoveries in the very spot where these discoveries are being made. For you space geeks, a trip to Mauna Kea may just be the highlight of your trip.

If you're in Hilo, be sure to visit the Imiola Astronomy Center. It has presentations and planetarium films about the mountain and the science being conducted there, as well as exhibits describing the deep knowledge of the heavens possessed by the ancient Hawaiians.

GETTING HERE AND AROUND

The summit of Mauna Kea isn't terribly far, but the drive takes about an hour and a half from Hilo and an hour from Waimea thanks to the steep road. Between the ride there, sunset on the summit, and stargazing, allot at least five hours for a Mauna Kea visit.

To reach the summit, you must take Saddle Road (Highway 200), which has been rerouted and repaved and is now a beautiful shortcut across the middle of the island. At mile marker 28, John A. Burns Way, the access road to the visitor center (9,200 feet), is fine, but the road from there to the summit is a lot more precarious because it's unpaved washboard and very steep. Only four-wheel-drive vehicles with low range should attempt this journey. Two-wheel-drive cars are unsafe, especially in winter conditions, and their lack of traction tears up the road. Rental car companies do not permit them to go to the summit; even if you rent a four-wheel-drive vehicle, make sure you are allowed to take it to the top. If you aren't and you go anyway, your contract will be void and you'll be responsible for any damages. This happens more often than you think. And if you're driving back down in the dark, slow and cautious is the name of the game.

Another factor to consider is altitude. ■TIP→ Take the change in altitude seriously—stop at the visitor center for at least an hour, and don't overexert yourself, especially at the top. The extreme altitude can cause disorientation, headaches, and light-headedness. Keeping hydrated is crucial. Scuba divers must wait at least 24 hours before traveling to the summit. Children under 16, pregnant women, and those with heart, respiratory, or weight problems should not go higher than the visitor center. And yes, you can park there and hike to the summit if you are in good shape, but the trip takes approximately six hours one way, and no camping is allowed. That means you must leave early and obtain a permit to hike, and remember that this is a wilderness area with no services.

The last potential obstacle: it's cold, as in freezing, usually with significant wind chill. Most summit tours provide parkas, but it's difficult to find cold-weather clothing in Hawaii, so if you plan to visit Mauna Kea, bring your favorite warm things from home.

ONIZUKA VISITOR CENTER

Fodor's Choice ★ **Onizuka Center for International Astronomy Visitor Information Station.** At 9,200 feet, this excellent amateur observation site has a handful of telescopes and a knowledgeable staff. You can enjoy the nightly stargazing sessions from 6 to 10, or just stop here to acclimate to the altitude if you're heading for the summit. Fortunately, it's a pleasure to do so. Sip hot chocolate and peruse exhibits on ancient Hawaiian celestial navigation, about the mountain's significance as a quarry for the best

CLOSE UP

Mauna Kea's Telescopes

There's a meeting of the minds on the mountaintop, with 13 telescopes operated by astronomers from around the world. Although the telescopes are owned and operated by various countries and organizations, any research team can book time on the equipment, paying several thousand dollars per day to do so, with up to a year's waiting list.

A U.S.–Japan team comprising astronomers from the University of Hawaii, University of Tokyo, Tohoku University, and Japan's Institute of Space and Astronautical Science made an important discovery of distant galaxies obscured by cosmic dust, using the JCMT telescope, which is jointly owned and operated by the United Kingdom, Canada, and the Netherlands. Similarly, a team of astronomers from the University of Hawaii used the Keck telescopes (owned and operated by Caltech and the University of California) to discover a distant galaxy that gives astronomers a glimpse of the Dark Ages, when galaxies and stars were first forming in the universe.

basalt in the Hawaiian Islands and as a revered spiritual destination, on modern astronomy, and about ongoing projects at the summit.

On weekends, the center offers free escorted caravan-style summit tours. Participants must arrive by 1 pm with their *own* low-range four-wheel-drive vehicle. Keep in mind that most summit telescope facilities are not open to the public, so your best bet for actual stargazing is at the visitor center. Nights are clear 90% of the year. ⊠ *Mauna Kea* ☎ *808/961–2180* ⊕ *www.ifa.hawaii.edu/info/vis* ⊠ *Donations welcome* ⊗ *Daily 9 am–10 pm.*

THE SUMMIT

Head to the summit before dusk so you can witness the stunning sunset and emerging star show. Only the astronomers are allowed to use the telescopes and other equipment, but the scenery is available to all. After the sun sinks, head down to the visitor center to warm up and stargaze, or do your stargazing first and then head up here. If you were blown away by the number of stars crowding the sky over the visitor center, this vantage point will make you speechless.

If you haven't rented a four-wheel-drive vehicle, don't want to deal with driving to the summit, or don't want to wait in line to use the handful of telescopes at the visitor center, consider booking a tour. Operators provide transportation to and from the summit along with expert guides; some also provide parkas, gloves, telescopes, dinner, hot beverages, and snacks. Excursion fees range from $90 to $212.

GUIDED TOURS OF THE SUMMIT

Arnott's Lodge & Hiking Adventures. This Mauna Kea summit tour focuses more on the experience of the mountain than on astronomy. Guides use laser lights to provide an informative lesson on major celestial objects and Polynesian navigational stars. The excursion departs from

Hilo and costs $180 per person, including parkas and hot beverages. The outfitter also offers lava and waterfall tours. ✉ *98 Apapane Rd., Hilo* ☎ *808/969–7097, 808/339–0921* ⊕ *www.arnottslodge.com.*

Fodor's Choice ★ **Hawaii Forest & Trail.** This comfortable, highly educational tour packs a lot of fun into a few hours. Guides are knowledgeable about astronomy and Hawaii's geologic and cultural history, and the small group size (max of 14) encourages camaraderie. Included in the tour are dinner at an old ranching station, catered by a favorite local restaurant; sunset on the summit; and a fantastic private star show mid-mountain. The company's powerful 11-inch Celestron Schmidt-Cassegrain telescope reveals lots of interesting celestial objects, including seasonal stars, galaxies, and nebula. The moon alone, if present, will knock your socks off. Everything from water bottles, parkas, and gloves to hot chocolate and brownies is included for $199. ✉ *74-5035 Queen Kaahumanu Hwy., 3 miles south of Kona airport, Kailua-Kona* ☎ *808/331–8505, 800/464–1993* ⊕ *www.hawaii-forest.com.*

Mauna Kea Summit Adventures. As the first company to specialize in tours to the mountain, Mauna Kea Summit Adventures focuses on stars. Cushy vans with panoramic windows go first to the visitor center, where participants eat dinner and acclimate for an hour before donning hooded arctic-style parkas and ski gloves for the sunset trip to the 14,000-foot summit. Stargazing through a powerful Celestron telescope happens mid-mountain with the help of knowledgeable guides. Tour, dinner, and west-side pickup cost $212 and run 364 days a year, weather permitting. ■**TIP**➜ You can save 15% by booking online. ✉ *Kailua-Kona* ☎ *808/322–2366, 888/322–2366* ⊕ *www.maunakea.com.*

THE HAMAKUA COAST

The Hamakua Coast is about 25 miles east of Waimea.

The spectacular waterfalls, mysterious jungles, emerald fields, and stunning ocean vistas along Highway 19 northwest of Hilo are collectively referred to as the Hilo–Hamakua Heritage Coast. Brown signs featuring a sugarcane tassel reflect the area's history: thousands of former acres of sugarcane are now idle, with little industry to support the area since "King Sugar" left the island in the early 1990s.

This is a great place to wander off the main road and see "real" Hawaii—untouched valleys, overgrown banyan trees, tiny coastal villages, and little plantation towns, Papaikou, Laupahoehoe, and Paauilo among them. Some small communities are still hanging on quite nicely, well after the demise of the big sugar plantations that first engendered them. They have homey cafés, gift shops, galleries, and a way of life from a time gone by.

The dramatic Akaka Falls is only one of hundreds of waterfalls here, many of which tumble into refreshing swimming holes, so bring your swimsuit when you explore this area. The pristine Waipio Valley was once a favorite getaway spot for Hawaiian royalty. The isolated valley floor has maintained the ways of old Hawaii, with taro patches, wild horses, and a handful of houses. The view from the lookout is breathtaking.

GETTING HERE AND AROUND

Though Highway 19 is the fastest route through the area, any turnoff along this coast could lead to an incredible view, so take your time and go exploring up and down the side roads. If you're driving from Kailua-Kona, rather than around the northern tip of the island, cut across on the Mamalahoa Highway (Highway 190) to Waimea, and then catch Highway 19 to the coast. It takes a little longer but is worth it.

■ TIP➔ **The "Heritage Drive," a 4-mile loop just off the main highway, is well worth the detour.** Signs mark various sites of historical interest, as well as scenic views along the 40-mile stretch of coastline. Keep an eye out for them and try to stop at the sights mentioned—you won't be disappointed.

Once back on Highway 19, you'll pass the road to Honokaa, which leads to the end of the road bordering Waipio Valley.

If you've stopped to explore the quiet little villages with wooden boardwalks and dogs dozing in backyards, or if you've spent several hours in Waipio Valley, night will undoubtedly be falling. Don't worry: the trip to Hilo via Highway 19 only takes about an hour, or you can go in the other direction to stop for dinner in Waimea before heading to the Kohala Coast (another 25 to 45 minutes). Although you shouldn't have any trouble exploring the Hamakua Coast in a day, a handful of romantic bed-and-breakfasts are available if you want to spend more time.

GUIDED TOURS

A guided tour is the best way to see Waipio Valley. You can walk down and up the steep narrow road yourself, but you won't see as much. Costs range from about $50 to $150, depending on the company and the transport mode.

Hawaiian Walkways. Knowledgeable guides lead personalized hiking tours for those who are serious about experiencing Hawaii intimately—from Waipio waterfall hikes to volcano discovery walks to a Saddle Road excursion. Tours range from 4½ to 8 hours and from $119 for the Waipio rim hike to $185 for the Saddle Road excursion. Hikes include lunch and hiking gear. It's best to email or call for reservations. ⊠ *Honokaa* ☎ *808/775–0372, 800/457–7759* ⊕ *www.hawaiianwalkways.com.*

Naalapa Stables. Friendly horses and friendly guides take guests on tours of the valley floor. The 2½-hour tours run Monday through Saturday (the valley rests on Sunday) with check-in times of 9 am and 12:30 pm. Cost is $88.50 per person. ⊠ *48-5416 Kukuihale Rd., Waipio Valley Artworks building, Honokaa* ☎ *808/775–0419* ⊕ *www.naalapastables.com.*

Waipio on Horseback and ATV Ranch Ride. This outfit offers guided horseback-riding trips on the valley floor for $88.54 and two- to three-hour ATV ranch tours up top (ages 16 and older), with awesome views of the valley and surrounding areas, for $104. Trips run every day but Sunday, and reservations are highly recommended. ⊠ *Hwy. 240, mile*

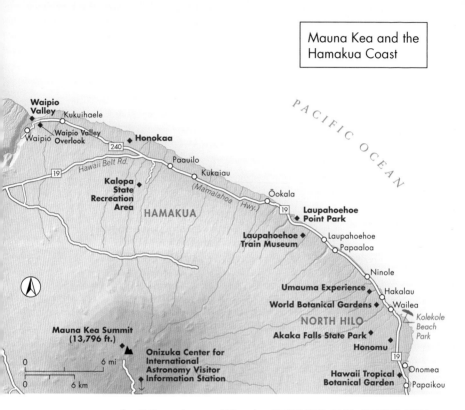

marker 7.5, northwest of Honokaa ☎ *808/775–7291, 877/775–7291*
⊕ *www.waipioonhorseback.com.*

Waipio Valley Shuttle. These informative, 1½–2-hour four-wheel-drive
tours explore the valley with lots of stops and run Monday through
Saturday. The windows on the van are removed, allowing guests to
snap unobstructed photos. The cost is $57.29. ✉ *48-5416 Kukuihaele
Rd., Honokaa* ☎ *808/775–7121* ⊕ *www.waipiovalleyshuttle.com.*

Waipio Valley Wagon Tours. Mule-drawn wagon tours take visitors
through the valley Monday through Saturday at 10:30, 12:30, and 2:30.
The excursion lasts 1½ hours and costs $62.50. Narration by friendly
guides offers history and cultural background. Reservations are highly
recommended. The pickup spot is at the Last Chance Store, 8 miles outside Honokaa. ✉ *48-5300 Kukuihaele Rd., Honokaa* ☎ *808/775–9518*
⊕ *www.waipiovalleywagontours.com.*

TOP ATTRACTIONS

Fodor's Choice **Akaka Falls State Park.** An easy, meandering 10-minute loop trail (a little
★ less than a half-mile) takes you to the best spots to see the spectacular
cascades of Akaka. The majestic upper Akaka Falls drops more than
442 feet, tumbling far below into a pool drained by Kolekole Stream
amid a profusion of fragrant white, yellow, and red torch ginger and
other tropical foliage. Another 400-foot falls is on the lower end of the

DID YOU KNOW?

The dramatic Akaka Falls is only one of hundreds of waterfalls on the Hamakua Coast. Many falls tumble into pristine swimming holes, so bring your swimsuit when you explore this area.

DID YOU KNOW?

At the mouth of the Waipio Valley, the Waipio River meets the ocean. The pristine valley used to be a favorite getaway spot for Hawaiian royalty.

trail. ⊠ *off Hwy. 19, 4 miles inland, near Honomu* ☎ *808/974–6200*
🚗 *$5 per vehicle (non-residents); $1 for walk-ins* ☉ *Daily 7–7.*

Hawaii Tropical Botanical Garden. Eight miles north of Hilo, stunning
coastline views appear around each curve of the 4-mile scenic jungle
drive that accesses this privately owned nature preserve beside Onomea
Bay. Paved pathways in the 17-acre botanical garden lead past ponds,
waterfalls, and more than 2,000 species of plants and flowers, including palms, bromeliads, ginger, heliconia, orchids, and ornamentals.
⊠ *27-717 Old Mamalahoa Hwy., Papaikou* ☎ *808/964–5233* ⊕ *www.
hawaiigarden.com* 🚗 *$15* ☉ *Daily 9–4.*

FAMILY   **Kalopa State Recreation Area.** Past the old plantation town of Paauilo,
at a cool elevation of 2,000 feet, lies this sweet 100-acre state park.
There's a lush forested area with picnic tables and restrooms, and an
easy ¾-mile loop trail with additional paths in the adjacent forest
reserve. Small signs identify some of the plants. Three campground
areas and four cabins can be reserved online. ⊠ *12 miles north of Laupahoehoe and 3 miles inland off Hwy. 19* ☎ *808/775–8852* 🚗 *Free*
☉ *Daily 7am–8 pm.*

Fodor'sChoice   **Waipio Valley.** Bounded by 2,000-foot cliffs, the "Valley of the Kings"
★   was once a favorite retreat of Hawaiian royalty. Waterfalls drop 1,200
feet from the Kohala Mountains to the valley floor, and the sheer cliff
faces make access difficult. Though completely off the grid today,
Waipio was once a center of Hawaiian life; somewhere between 4,000
and 20,000 people made it their home between the 13th and 17th
centuries.

To preserve this pristine part of the island, commercial-transportation
permits are limited—only four outfitters offer organized valley trips and
they're not allowed to take visitors to the beach: environmental laws
protect the swath of black sand. On Sunday the valley rests.

A road leads down from the **Waipio Valley Overlook,** but only four-
wheel-drive vehicles may attempt the *very* steep, treacherous road.
(Check your rental contract to see if it is allowed.) An information
booth at the lookout is staffed by volunteers who can answer questions.
There are no roads on the valley floor, and the going is often muddy.
The walk down into the valley is less than a mile from the lookout
point—just keep in mind the climb back gains 1,000 feet in elevation
and is strenuous. If you do visit here, please respect this area, as it is
considered highly sacred to Hawaiians. ⊠ *Hwy. 240, 8 miles northwest
of Honokaa.*

WORTH NOTING

Honokaa Town. This quaint, cliff-top village fronting the ocean was
built in the 1920s and 1930s by Japanese and Chinese workers who
quit the nearby plantations to start businesses that supported the sugar
economy. The intact historic character of the buildings, bucolic setting, and friendliness of the residents provide a nice reason to stop
and stroll. Cool antiques shops, a few interesting galleries, and good
cafés abound. Most restaurants close by 8 pm. ⊠ *Hwy. 240, Honokaa*
⊕ *www.honokaa.org.*

QUICK
BITES

Tex Drive-In. This place is famous for its *malasada*, a puffy, doughy, deep-fried Portuguese doughnut without a hole, best eaten hot. They also come in cream-filled versions, including vanilla, chocolate, and coconut. For more than a snack, go for the Hawaiian burger with a fat juicy slice of sweet pineapple on top or some good pizza. ⊠ *45-690 Pakalana St., at Hwy. 19, Honokaa* ☎ *808/775-0598* ⊕ *www.texdriveinhawaii.com.*

Back to the 50's Highway Fountain. Midway along the coast, there's a great lunch spot that serves good old-fashioned burgers, fries, onion rings, milk shakes, homemade pies plus lots of other entrées ranging from fish meatloaf to local specialties. The nicely restored vintage building is packed to the rafters with intriguing rock-and-roll and car culture memorabilia. Call for take-out or to check on hours, which vary. ⊠ *35-2074 Old Mamalahoa Hwy., Laupahoehoe* ☎ *808/962-0808* ⊗ *Closed Mon. and Tues.*

Honomu. Honomu did not die when sugar did. Its sugar-plantation past is reflected in the wooden boardwalks and metal-roofed buildings of this tiny town, which borders Akaka Falls State Park. It's fun to poke through old dusty shops filled with little treasures, check out homemade baked goods, or browse the local art at one of the fine galleries. ⊠ *1 mile inland from Hwy. 19 en route to Akaka Falls State Park.*

Laupahoehoe Point Park. Here the surf pounds the jagged black rocks at the base of a stunning point. This is not a safe place for swimming, however. Still vivid in the minds of longtime area residents is the 1946 tragedy in which 21 schoolchildren and three teachers were swept to sea by a tsunami. ⊠ *Hwy. 19, makai side, north of Laupahoehoe* ☎ *808/961-8311* 🎫 *Free* ⊗ *Daily 7 am–10 pm.*

Laupahoehoe Train Museum. Behind a stone loading platform of the once-famous Hawaii Consolidated Railway, constructed about 1900, the former manager's house is a poignant reminder of the era when sugar was the local cash crop. Today this museum displays artifacts from the sugar plantation era, the 1946 tsunami, local railway history, and the rich culture of the Hamakua Coast. The museum's Wye railyard has a vintage switch engine, large standard-gauge caboose, and narrow-gauge explosives box car. The trains even run a few yards along the restored tracks on special occasions. ⊠ *36-2377 Mamalahoa Hwy., Laupahoehoe* ☎ *808/962-6300* ⊕ *www.thetrainmuseum.com* 🎫 *$6* ⊗ *Thurs.– Sun. 10–5 and by appointment.*

FAMILY **Umauma Falls & Zipline Experience.** The only place to see the triple-tier Umauma Falls, this kid-friendly 200-acre park has 14 waterfalls and a classy visitor center. Like the World Botanical Gardens, next door, there's a river walk, zip line, and botanical gardens. Options include a zip and dip (a refreshing swim in a private waterfall pool after a nine-line zip), various à la carte adventures, a walk through the tropical grounds, a flume trail hike, kayaking, and a giant swing. ⊠ *Hwy. 19, mile marker 16, Honomu* ☎ *808/930-9477* ⊕ *www.ziplinehawaii.com* 🎫 *$12* ⊗ *Daily 7:45–5.*

FAMILY **World Botanical Gardens.** Just off the highway, this garden park is on more than 300 acres of former sugar cane land. With wide views of the countryside and the ocean, this is the place to see the beautiful Kamaee waterfalls. You can also follow a walking trail with old-growth tropical gardens including orchids, palm trees, ginger, hibiscus, and heliconia; visit the 10-acre arboretum, which includes a maze made of orange shrubs; explore the river walk; ride the zip line; and take the only off-road Segway adventure on the island. Admission into the gardens (not including zip line and Segway) is good for seven days; if you skip the zip line, you can see it all in a few hours. ⊠ *31-240 Old Mamalahoa Hwy., just past mile marker 16 from Hilo, on mountain side, Hakalau* ☎ *808/963–5427* ⊕ *www.wbgi.com* ✉ *$13* ☻ *Daily 9–5:30.*

HILO

Hilo is 55 miles southeast of Waimea, 95 miles northeast of Kailua-Kona, and just north of the Hilo Airport.

In comparison to Kailua-Kona, Hilo is often described as "the old Hawaii." With significantly fewer visitors than residents, more historic buildings, and a much stronger identity as a long-established community, this quaint, traditional town does seem more authentic. It stretches from the banks of the Wailuku River to Hilo Bay, where a few hotels line stately Banyan Drive. The characteristic old buildings that make up Hilo's downtown have been spruced up as part of a revitalization effort.

Nearby, the 30-acre Liliuokalani Gardens, a formal Japanese garden with arched bridges and waterways, was created in the early 1900s to honor the area's Japanese sugar-plantation laborers. It also became a safety zone after a devastating tsunami swept away businesses and homes on May 22, 1960, killing 60 people.

With a population of almost 50,000 in the entire district, Hilo is the fourth-largest city in the state and home to the University of Hawaii at Hilo. Although it is the center of government and commerce for the island, Hilo is clearly a residential town. Mansions with yards of lush tropical foliage share streets with older, single-walled plantation-era houses with rusty corrugated roofs. It's a friendly community, populated primarily by descendants of the contract laborers—Japanese, Chinese, Filipino, Puerto Rican, and Portuguese—brought in to work the sugarcane fields during the 1800s.

One of the main reasons visitors have tended to steer clear of the east side of the island is its weather. With an average rainfall of 130 inches per year, it's easy to see why Hilo's yards are so green and its buildings so weatherworn. Outside of town, the Hilo District has rain forests and waterfalls, a terrain unlike the hot and dry white-sand beaches of the Kohala Coast. But when the sun does shine—usually part of nearly every day—the town sparkles, and, during winter, the snow glistens on Mauna Kea, 25 miles in the distance. Best of all is when the mists fall and the sun shines at the same time, leaving behind the colorful arches that earn Hilo its nickname: the City of Rainbows.

The Merrie Monarch Hula Festival takes place in Hilo every year during the second week of April, and dancers and admirers flock to the city from all over the world. If you're planning a stay in Hilo during this time, be sure to book your room well in advance.

GETTING HERE AND AROUND

Hilo is a great base for exploring the eastern and southern parts of the island—just be sure to bring an umbrella for sporadic showers. If you're just passing through town or making a day trip, make the first right turn into the town off Highway 19 (it comes up fast) and grab a parking spot in the lot on your left or on any of the surrounding streets. Downtown Hilo is best experienced on foot.

There are plenty of gas stations and restaurants in the area. Hilo is a good spot to load up on food and supplies—just south of downtown there are several large budget chains. If you're here on Wednesday or Sunday, be sure to stop by the expansive Hilo Farmers' Market.

TOURS

Hilo Downtown Improvement Association. An excellent and free self-guided walking tour to downtown Hilo includes historical information, a map, and directions to 18 historic sites. You can obtain one from the association's website or downtown Hilo office. ⊠ *329 Kamehameha Ave.* ☎ *808/935–8850* ⊕ *www.downtownhilo.com* ☉ *Weekdays 8–4:30.*

TOP ATTRACTIONS

Fodor's Choice ★   **Imiloa Astronomy Center.** Part Hawaiian cultural center, part astronomy museum, this center provides an educational and cultural complement to the research being conducted atop Mauna Kea. Although visitors are welcome at Mauna Kea, its primary function is as a research center—not observatory, museum, or education center. Those roles have been taken on by Imiloa in a big way. With its interactive exhibits, full-dome planetarium shows, and regularly scheduled talks and events, the center is a must-see for anyone interested in the stars, the planets, or Hawaiian culture and history. Five minutes from downtown Hilo, the center also provides an important link between the scientific research being conducted at Mauna Kea and its history as a sacred mountain for the Hawaiian people. Admission includes one planetarium show and an all-day pass to the exhibit hall, which features more than 100 interactive displays. The lunch buffet at the adjoining Sky Garden Cafe is popular and affordable. ⊠ *600 Imiloa Pl., at the UH Hilo Science & Technology Park, off Nowelo and Komohana* ☎ *808/969–9700* ⊕ *www.imiloahawaii.org* ☑ *$17.50* ☉ *Tues.–Sun. 9–5.*

Liliuokalani Gardens. Designed to honor Hawaii's first Japanese immigrants, Liliuokalani Gardens' 30 acres of fish-filled ponds, stone lanterns, half-moon bridges, elegant pagodas, and a ceremonial teahouse make it a favorite Sunday destination. The surrounding area, once a busy residential neighborhood, was destroyed by a 1960 tsunami that caused widespread devastation and killed 61 people. ⊠ *Banyan Dr. at Lihiwai St.*

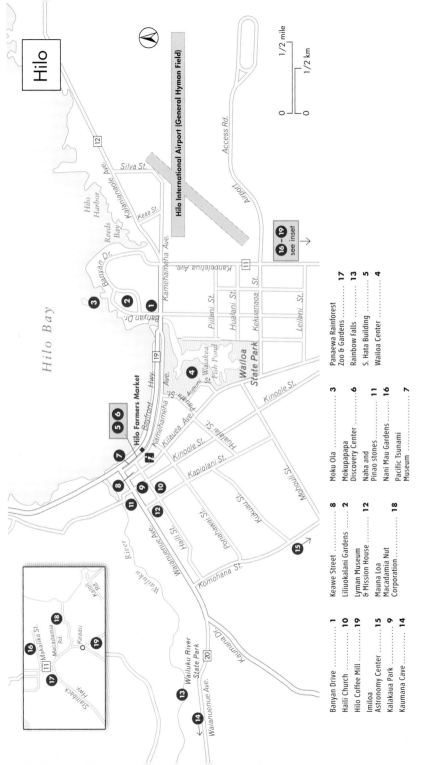

Hilo

Hilo International Airport (General Hyman Field)

0   1/2 mile
0   1/2 km

Banyan Drive 1
Haili Church 10
Hilo Coffee Mill 19
Imiloa
Astronomy Center 15
Kalakaua Park 9
Kaumana Cave 14

Keawe Street 8
Liliuokalani Gardens ... 2
Lyman Museum
& Mission House 12
Mauna Loa
Macadamia Nut
Corporation 18

Moku Ola 3
Mokupapapa
Discovery Center 6
Naha and
Pinao stones 11
Nani Mau Gardens 16
Pacific Tsunami
Museum 7

Panaewa Rainforest
Zoo & Gardens 17
Rainbow Falls 13
S. Hata Building 5
Wailoa Center 4

The world's largest optical and infrared telescopes are located at the Keck Observatory on Mauna Kea's summit.

FAMILY
Fodor's Choice
★

Panaewa Rainforest Zoo & Gardens. Billed as "the only natural tropical rainforest zoo in the United States," this sweet zoo is the home of white Bengal tiger Namaste, whose daily 3:30 feeding is quite a sight. Among the other animals here are such native Hawaiian species as the state bird, the *nene* goose, and the *io* (hawk), as well as lots of other rare birds, monkeys, and lemurs. To get here, turn left on Mamaki off Highway 11; it's just past the "Kulani 19, Stainback Hwy." sign. ⊠ *800 Stainback Hwy* ☎ *808/959-7224* ⊕ *www.hilozoo.com* ✉ *Donations encouraged* ⊙ *Daily 9–4.*

Wailuku River State Park (Boiling Pots). Four separate streams fall into a series of circular pools here, forming the Peepee Falls. The resulting turbulent action—best seen after a good rain—has earned this stretch of the Wailuku River the nickname Boiling Pots. ⚠ **There's no swimming allowed at Peepee Falls or anywhere in the Wailuku river, due to dangerous currents and undertows.** The falls are 3 miles northwest of Hilo off Waianuenue Avenue; keep to the right when the road splits and look for the sign. Open daylight hours. ⊠ *Peepee Falls Dr.* ⊕ *www.hawaiistateparks.org* ⊙ *Daily dawn–dusk.*

Wailuku River State Park (Rainbow Falls). After a hard rain, these falls thunder into the Wailuku River gorge, often creating magical rainbows in the mist. Sometimes known as the "Hilo Town Falls," they are located just above downtown Hilo. Take Waianuenue Avenue west for a mile; when the road forks, stay right and look for the Hawaiian warrior sign. Open daylight hours. ⊠ *Rainbow Dr.* ⊕ *www.hawaiistateparks. org* ⊙ *Daily dawn–dusk.*

A Walking Tour of Hilo

Put on some comfortable shoes, because all of the downtown destinations are within easy walking distance of each other. Start your excursion in front of the public library, on Waianuenue Avenue, four blocks from Kamehameha Avenue. Here, you'll find the massive Naha and Pinao stones, which legend says King Kamehameha I was able to move as a teenager, thus foretelling that someday he would be a powerful king. Cross the road to walk southeast along Kapiolani Street, and turn right on Haili Street to visit the historic Lyman Museum & Mission House. Back on Haili Street, follow this busy road toward the ocean; on your right you'll pass Haili Church.

Soon you'll reach Keawe Street with its plantation-style shop fronts. Stop at the Big Island Visitors Bureau on the right-hand corner for maps and brochures before taking a left. You'll bump into Kalakaua Street; for a quick respite turn left and rest on the benches in Kalakaua Park.

Continue *makai* (toward the ocean) on Kalakaua Street to visit the Pacific Tsunami Museum on the corner of Kalakaua and Kamehameha avenues. After heading three blocks east along the picturesque bay front, you'll come across the S. Hata Building, which has interesting shops and restaurants, and the free Mokupapapa Discovery Center, at the end of the block. Just next door, on either side of Mamo Street, is the Hilo Farmers' Market.

WORTH NOTING

Banyan Drive. More than 50 enormous banyan trees with aerial roots dangling from their limbs were planted some 60 to 70 years ago by visiting celebrities. Names such as Amelia Earhart and Franklin Delano Roosevelt can be seen on plaques affixed to the trees. A scenic loop beginning at the Hawaii Naniloa Resort makes a nice walk. ⊠ *93 Banyan Dr.* ⊕ *downtownhilo.com.*

Big Island Visitors Bureau. Marked by a red-and-white Hawaiian warrior sign, the bureau is worth a visit for brochures, maps, and up-to-date, friendly insider advice. ⊠ *250 Keawe St., at Haili St.* ☎ *808/961–5797, 800/648–2441* ⊕ *www.bigisland.org* ⊗ *Weekdays 8–4:30.*

Moku Ola (*Coconut Island*). This small island, just offshore from Liliuokalani Gardens, is accessible via a footbridge. It was considered a place of healing in ancient times. Today children play in the tide pools while fisherfolk try their luck. ⊠ *Banyan Dr.*

Haili Church. Constructed in 1859 by New England missionaries, this church is known for its choir, which sings hymns in Hawaiian during services. In 1902, Hawaiian musical legends Harry K. Naope Sr. and Albert Nahalea Sr. began the choral traditions still practiced by their descendants. ⊠ *211 Haili St.* ☎ *808/935–4847* ⊕ *www.hailichurch. org.*

Hilo Coffee Mill. With all the buzz about Kona coffee, it's easy to forget that coffee is produced throughout the rest of the island. The Hilo Coffee Mill is a pleasant reminder of that. In addition to farming its own coffee on-site, the mill has partnered with several small coffee farmers in East Hawaii in an effort to put the region on the world's coffee map. You can sample their efforts, tour the mill, and watch the roasters in action. ⌧ *17-995 Volcano Rd. (Hwy. 11), between mile markers 12 and 13, Mountain View* ☎ *808/968–1333* ⊕ *www.hilocoffeemill.com* ⌦ *Free* ☉ *Mon.–Sat. 7–4.*

Kalakaua Park. King Kalakaua, who revived the hula, was the inspiration for Hilo's Merrie Monarch Festival. A bronze statue, erected in 1988, depicts the king with a taro leaf in his left hand to signify the Hawaiian peoples' bond with the land. The park also has a huge spreading banyan tree and small fishponds, but no picnic or recreation facilities. In a local tradition, families of military personnel often leave leftover floral displays and funeral wreaths along the fishpond walkway as a way of honoring and celebrating their loved ones. ⌧ *Kalakaua and Kinoole Sts.* ☉ *Daily dawn–dusk.*

Kaumana Caves Park. Thanks to Hilo's abundant rainfall, this lava tube is lush with plant life. Concrete stairs lead down to the 2½-mile-long tube. Bring a flashlight and explore as far as you dare to go. There are restrooms and a covered picnic table at the cave, and parking across the street. Please heed all warning signs when entering. ⌧ *Waianuenue Ave., on right just past mile marker 4 (veer left going towards Saddle Rd.)* ⌦ *Free* ☉ *Daily dawn–dusk.*

Keawe Street. Buildings here have been restored to their original 1920s and '30s plantation styles. Although most shopping is along Kamehameha Avenue, the ambience on Keawe Street offers a nostalgic sampling of Hilo as it might have been 80 years ago. Downtown Hilo won a major paint retailer's contest, so you might see painting of these historic properties in progress. ⌧ *Keawe St.*

Lyman Museum & Mission House. Built in 1839, the beautifully restored Lyman Mission House is the oldest frame building on the island. (Tours are offered.) An adjacent museum has wonderful exhibits on volcanoes, island formation, island habitats and wildlife, marine shells, and minerals and gemstones. It also showcases native Hawaiian culture and immigrant ethnic groups, including a life-size replica of a traditional Korean home. The gift shop has great Hawaiian items. ⌧ *276 Haili St.* ☎ *808/935–5021* ⊕ *www.lymanmuseum.org* ⌦ *$10* ☉ *Mon.–Sat. 10–4:30.*

Mauna Loa Macadamia Nut Corporation. Acres of macadamia-nut trees lead to a giant roasting facility and processing plant with viewing windows and self-guided tours. A video depicts the harvesting and preparation of the nuts, and there are free samples and plenty of gift boxes with mac nuts in every conceivable form of presentation for sale in the visitor center. There is no factory processing on weekends or holidays. Children can burn off extra energy on a nature trail. ⌧ *16-701 Macadamia Rd., off Hwy. 11, 5 miles south of Hilo* ☎ *808/966–8618, 888/628–6256* ⊕ *www.maunaloa.com* ☉ *Daily 8:30–5.*

FAMILY **Mokupapapa Discovery Center.** This informative center teaches about the Papahanaumokuakea Marine National Monument, which encompasses about 140,000 square miles in the waters northwest of the main

CLOSE UP

Banyan Drive's Trees

The history of the giant trees lining Hilo's Banyan Drive is one of the Big Island's most interesting and least known stories. Altogether, some 50 or so banyans were planted by VIP visitors to Hilo between 1933 and 1972.

The majority are Chinese banyans, and each one is marked with a sign naming the VIP who planted it and the date on which it was planted. The first trees were planted on October 20, 1933, by a Hollywood group led by director Cecil B. DeMille, who was in Hilo making the film Four Frightened People. Soon after, on October 29, 1933, another banyan was planted by the one and only George Herman "Babe" Ruth, who was in town playing exhibition games.

President Franklin D. Roosevelt planted a tree on his visit to Hilo on July 25, 1934. And in 1935, famed aviator Amelia Earhart put a banyan in the ground just days before she became the first person to fly solo across the Pacific Ocean.

Trees continued to be planted along Banyan Drive until World War II. The tradition was then revived in 1952, when a young and aspiring U.S. senator, Richard Nixon of California, planted a banyan tree. Nixon's tree was later toppled by a storm and was replanted by his wife, Pat, during a Hilo visit in 1972. On a bright, sunny day, strolling down Banyan Drive is like walking through a green, shady tunnel. The banyans form a regal protective canopy over Hilo's own "Walk of Fame."

Hawaiian Islands and is a UNESCO World Heritage site. Giant graphics, murals, and 3-D maps depict the monument's extensive coral reefs and the more than 7,000 marine species that live there, one in four of which are found only in the Hawaiian archipelago. Knowledgeable staff or volunteers are on hand to answer questions. Interactive programs, a new aquarium, and short films give insight into marine life and environmental impact. It's worth a stop just to get an up-close look at the center's huge stuffed albatross, with wings outstretched. ⊠ *Old Koehnen's Building, 76 Kamehameha Ave.* ☎ *808/933–8195* ⊕ *www.papahanaumokuakea.gov/education/center.html* 🎫 *Free* 🕐 *Tues.–Sat. 9–4.*

Naha and Pinao stones. These two huge, oblong stones are legendary. The Pinao stone is purportedly an entrance pillar of an ancient temple built near the Wailuku River. King Kamehameha is said to have moved the 5,000-pound Naha stone when he was still in his teens. Legend decreed that he who did so would become king of all the islands. They're in front of the Hilo Public Library. ⊠ *300 Waianuenue Ave.*

Nani Mau Gardens. The name means "forever beautiful" in Hawaiian, and that's a good description of this 20-acre botanical garden filled with several varieties of fruit trees and hundreds of varieties of ginger, orchids, anthuriums, and other exotic plants. The restaurant has a lunch buffet. ⊠ *421 Makalika St., off Hwy. 11* ☎ *808/959–3500* ⊕ *www. nanimaugardens.com* 🎫 *$5* 🕐 *Daily 10–3.*

FAMILY **Pacific Tsunami Museum.** In downtown Hilo, businesses tend to be far from the bayfront. There's a reason for this. Tsunamis have killed more people in Hawaii than any other natural event, especially in Hilo. A small but informative museum in a 1931 building provides tsunami education and scientific information, and chronicles the poignant history of these devastating disasters, with accounts taken from tsunami survivors from Hawaii and worldwide. Exhibits include a wave machine and tsunami warning center simulation as well as detailing recent tsunamis in Japan, Alaska, and Indonesia. ✉ *130 Kamehameha Ave.* ☎ *808/935–0926* ⊕ *www.tsunami.org* 🖂 *$8* ⊗ *Mon.–Sat. 9–4.*

S. Hata Building. Built as a general store in 1912 by Sadanosuke Hata and his family, this historic structure now houses galleries, a restaurant, and other small shops. During World War II, Hata family members were interned and the building was confiscated by the U.S. government. When the war was over, a daughter repurchased it for $100,000. A beautiful example of Renaissance-Revival architecture, it won an award from the state for the authenticity of its restoration. ✉ *308 Kamehameha Ave., at Mamo St.*

Wailoa Center. In Wailoa State Recreation Area, this circular exhibition center mounts monthly shows featuring local artists. Work ranges from photography, contemporary painting, and woodworking to musical instruments and artwork depicting Hawaii's native species. ✉ *200 Piopio St., off Kamehameha Ave.* ☎ *808/933–0416* ⊗ *Mon., Tues., Thurs., and Fri. 8:30–4:30; Wed. noon–4:30.*

PUNA

Puna is about 6 miles south of Hilo.

The Puna District is wild in every sense of the word. The jagged black coastline is changing all the time; the trees are growing out of control, forming canopies over the few paved roads; the land is dirt cheap and there seem to be no building codes; and the people—well, there's something about living in an area that could be destroyed by lava at any moment (as Kalapana was in 1990) that makes the laws of modern society seem silly. So it is that Puna has its well-deserved reputation as an "outlaw" region of the Big Island.

That said, it's well worth a detour, especially if you're near this part of the island anyway. Volcanically heated springs and tide pools burst with interesting sea life, and some mighty fine people-watching opportunities exist in Pahoa, a funky little town that the "Punatics" call home.

This is also farm country (yes, that kind of farm, but also the legal sort). Local farmers grow everything from orchids and anthuriums to papayas, bananas, and macadamia nuts. Several of the island's larger, rural, residential subdivisions are between Keaau and Pahoa, including Hawaiian Paradise Park, Orchidland Estates, Hawaiian Acres, and Hawaiian Beaches.

When dusk falls here, the air fills with the high-pitched symphony of thousands of coqui frogs. Though they look cute on the signs and seem

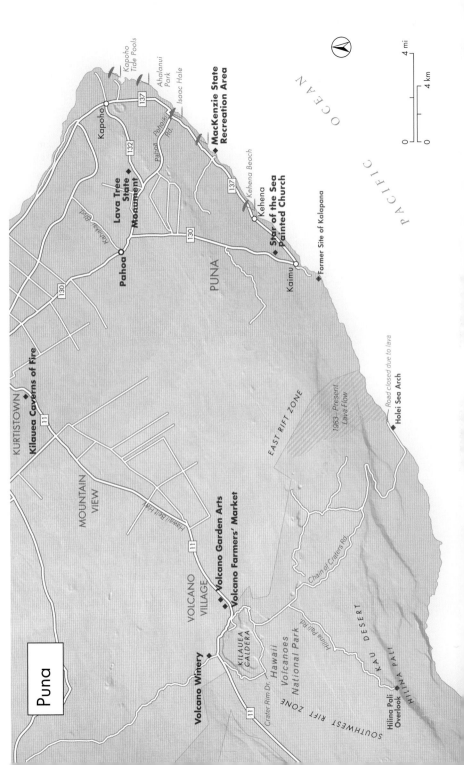

Puma

KURTISTOWN

Kilauea Caverns of Fire ◆

MOUNTAIN VIEW

Hawaii Belt Hwy.

VOLCANO VILLAGE

Volcano Garden Arts ◆
Volcano Farmers' Market ◆

Volcano Winery ◆

Crater Rim Dr.

KILAUEA CALDERA

Hawaii Volcanoes National Park

Chain of Craters Rd.

Hilina Pali Rd.

SOUTHWEST RIFT ZONE

EAST RIFT ZONE

KAU DESERT

HILINA PALI

Hilina Pali Overlook ◆

Holei Sea Arch ◆

Road closed due to lava

1983–Present Lava Flow

Kapoho
Tide Pools

Ahalanui Park

Isaac Hale

137

Kapoho

132

Kaohe Blvd.

Lava Tree State Monument ◆

Pahoa

130

Pahoa–Pohoiki Rd.

MacKenzie State Recreation Area ◆

Kehena Beach

137

Kehena ○

Star of the Sea Painted Church ◆

Kaimu ○

Former Site of Kalapana ◆

PUNA

PACIFIC OCEAN

0   4 km
0   4 mi

harmless, the invasive frogs are pests both to local crops and to locals tired of their shrieking, all-night calls.

GETTING HERE AND AROUND

The sprawling Puna District includes part of the Volcano area and stretches northeast down to the coast. If you're staying in Hilo for the night, driving around wild lower Puna is a great way to spend a morning.

The roads connecting Pahoa to Kapoho and the Kalapana coast form a loop that's about 25 miles long; driving times are from two to three hours, depending on the number of stops you make and the length of time at each stop. There are restaurants, stores, and gas stations in Pahoa, but services elsewhere in the region are spotty. Long stretches of the road may be completely isolated at any given point; this can be a little scary at night but beautiful and tranquil during the day.

Compared to big-city living, it's pretty tame, but there is a bit of a "locals-only" vibe in parts of Puna, and some areas suffer crime and drug problems. Don't wander around alone at night or get lost on backcountry roads.

WORTH NOTING

Lava Tree State Monument. Tree molds that rise like blackened smoke-stacks formed here in 1790, when a lava flow swept through the *ohia* forest. Some reach as high as 12 feet. A meandering trail provides close-up looks at some of Hawaii's tropical plants and trees. There are restrooms and a couple of picnic pavilions and tables. ■TIP➜ Mosquitoes live here in abundance, so come prepared. ⊠ *Hwy. 132, Pahoa* ☎ *808/974–6200* ☞ *Free* ☉ *Daily 8–4:30.*

MacKenzie State Recreation Area. This coastal park, on rocky shoreline cliffs in a breezy, cool ironwood grove, has a pavilion, picnic tables, restrooms, and a tent-camping area, but no drinking water. The park is significant for the restored section of the old King's Highway trail system, which circled the coast in the era before Hawaii was discovered by the Western world. In those days, regional chiefs used the trails to get between coastal villages, collect taxes, and maintain control over people. Views take in the rugged coast, rocky beach, and coastal dry forest. ⊠ *Hwy. 137, Pahoa.*

Pahoa Town. This eclectic little town is reminiscent of the Wild West, with its wooden boardwalks and vintage buildings—not to mention a reputation as a pot growers' haven. A throwback to the '60s and '70s, it attracts plenty of hippies, gurus, wwoofers (workers on organic farms), yoga students, and other colorful characters pursuing alternative lifestyles. Secondhand stores, tie-dye/hemp clothing boutiques, smoke shops, and art galleries add to the "trippy" experience. Pahoa's main street boasts a handful of local-style eateries. To get here, turn southeast onto Highway 130 at Keaau, and drive 11 miles to a marked right turn. ⊠ *Pahoa.*

Star of the Sea Painted Church. This historic church, now a community center, was moved to its present location in 1990 just ahead of the advancing lava flow that destroyed the Kalapana area. Dating from the 1930s, the church was built by a Belgian Catholic missionary priest, Father Evarest Gielen, who also painted the detailed scenes on the church's interior. Though similar in style, the Star of the Sea and St. Benedict's were painted by two different Belgian priests. Star of the Sea also boasts several lovely stained-glass windows and is on the National Register of Historic Places. ⊠ *Hwy. 130, 1 mile north of Kalapana, Kalapana* ⌦ *Donations welcome.*

HAWAII VOLCANOES NATIONAL PARK AND VICINITY

Fodor's Choice
★
Hawaii Volcanoes National Park is about 22 miles southwest from the start of the Puna district, and about 27 miles southwest of Hilo.

Few visitors realize that in addition to "the volcano" (Kilauea)—that mountain oozing new layers of lava onto its flanks—there's also Volcano, the village. Conveniently located next to Hawaii Volcanoes National Park, Volcano Village is a charming little hamlet in the woods that offers a dozen or so excellent inns and bed-and-breakfasts, a decent (although strangely expensive) Thai restaurant, and a handful of things to see and do that don't include the village's namesake.

For years, writers, artists, and meditative types have been coming to the volcano to seek inspiration, and many of them have settled in and around the village. Artist studios (open to the public by appointment) are scattered in the forest, laden with ferns and mists.

If you plan to visit the Halemaumau summit crater at night (which you absolutely should if it's glowing), or drive down to the coast to try to see lava steaming into the sea, spending a night in Volcano Village is the ideal way to go about it.

GETTING HERE AND AROUND

There is a handful of dining options, a couple of stores, and gas stations available in Volcano, so most of your needs should be covered. Kilauea Military Camp, inside the park, also runs a good general store and sells gas. If you can't find what you're looking for, Hilo is about a 35-minute drive away, and the Keeau grocery store and fast-food joints are 25 minutes away.

Many people choose to stay the night in Volcano to see the dramatic glow at the summit vent and to drive to the coast to see the lava flow into the sea. (If you do, bring a fleece or sweater, as temperatures drop at night and mornings are usually cool and misty.) ■TIP➜ **Chain of Craters Road is currently closed about 8 miles below the summit, however, so you will have to travel outside the boundaries of the park to see lava flows.**

For information on Hawaii Volcanoes National Park, see the highlighted feature in this chapter.

Continued on page 94

HAWAII VOLCANOES NATIONAL PARK

Exploring the surface of the world's most active volcano—from the moonscape craters at the summit to the red-hot lava flows on the coast to the kipuka, pockets of vegetation miraculously left untouched—is the ultimate ecotour and one of Hawaii's must-dos.

The park sprawls over 520 square miles and encompasses Kilauea and Mauna Loa, two of the five volcanoes that formed the Big Island nearly half a million years ago. Kilauea, youngest and most rambunctious of the Hawaiian volcanoes, erupted at its summit from the 19th century through 1982. Since then, the top of the volcano had been more or less quiet, frequently shrouded in mist; an eruption in the Halemaumau Crater in 2008 ended this period of relative inactivity.

Kilauea's eastern side sprang to life on January 3, 1983, shooting molten lava four stories high. This eruption has been ongoing, and lava flows are generally steady and slow, appearing and disappearing from view. Over 500 acres have been added to Hawaii's eastern coast since the activity began, and scientists say this eruptive phase is not likely to end anytime soon.

If you're lucky, you'll be able to catch creation at its most elemental—when molten lava meets the ocean, cools, and solidifies into brand-new stretches of coastline. Even if lava-viewing conditions aren't ideal, you can hike 150 miles of trails and camp amid wide expanses of *aa* (rough) and *pahoehoe* (smooth) lava. There's nothing quite like it.

P.O. Box 52, Hawaii Volcanoes National Park, HI 96718

808/985-6000

www.nps.gov/havo

$10 per vehicle; $5 for pedestrians and bicyclists. Ask about passes. Admission is good for seven consecutive days.

The park is open daily, 24 hours. Kilauea Visitor Center: 7:45 am–5 pm. Thomas A. Jaggar Museum: 8:30–5. Volcano Art Center Gallery: 9–5.

(top) Kilauea Iki Trail
(left) Fuming rim of Puu Oo, source of the current eruption

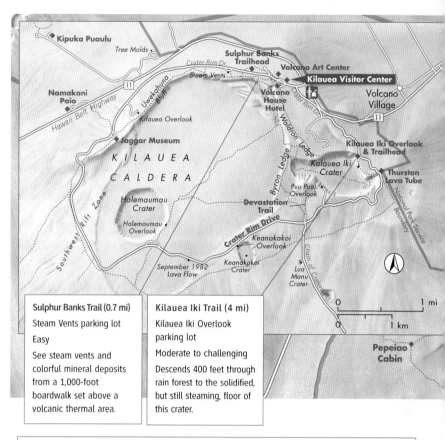

Sulphur Banks Trail (0.7 mi)	Kilauea Iki Trail (4 mi)
Steam Vents parking lot	Kilauea Iki Overlook parking lot
Easy	Moderate to challenging
See steam vents and colorful mineral deposits from a 1,000-foot boardwalk set above a volcanic thermal area.	Descends 400 feet through rain forest to the solidified, but still steaming, floor of this crater.

SEEING THE SUMMIT

The best way to explore the summit of Kilauea is to cruise along Crater Rim Drive to Kilauea Overlook. From Kilauea Overlook you can see all of Kilauea Caldera and Halemaumau Crater, an awesome depression in Kilauea Caldera measuring 3,000 feet across and nearly 300 feet deep. It's a huge and breathtaking view with pluming steam vents. At this writing, lava flows in the Southwest Rift Zone have closed parts of the 11-mile loop road indefinitely, including Halemaumau Overlook.

Near Kilauea Overlook is the Thomas A. Jaggar Museum, which offers similar views, plus geologic displays, video presentations of volcanic eruptions, and exhibits of seismographs once used by volcanologists at the adjacent Hawaiian Volcano Observatory (not open to the public).

Other Highlights along Crater Rim Drive include sulfur and steam vents, a walk-through lava tube, and deep fissures, fractures, and gullies along Kilauea's flanks. Kilauea Iki Crater, on the way down to Chain of Crater's Road, is smaller, but just as fascinating when seen from Puu Pai Overlook.

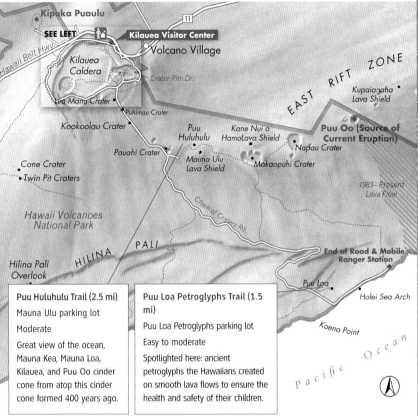

Kipuka Puaulu

SEE LEFT

Kilauea Visitor Center

Volcano Village

Hawaii Belt Hwy.

11

Kilauea Caldera

Crater Rim Dr.

Lua Manu Crater

Puhimau Crater

Kookoolau Crater

Pauahi Crater

Puu Huluhulu

Kane Nui o HamoLava Shield

EAST RIFT ZONE

Kupaianaha Lava Shield

Puu Oo (Source of Current Eruption)

Napau Crater

Cone Crater

Twin Pit Craters

Mauna Ulu Lava Shield

Makaopuhi Crater

Hawaii Volcanoes National Park

1983– Present Lava Flow

Chain of Craters Rd.

HILINA PALI

Hilina Pali Overlook

End of Road & Mobile Ranger Station

Puu Loa

Holei Sea Arch

Kaena Point

Pacific Ocean

Puu Huluhulu Trail (2.5 mi)

Mauna Ulu parking lot

Moderate

Great view of the ocean, Mauna Kea, Mauna Loa, Kilauea, and Puu Oo cinder cone from atop this cinder cone formed 400 years ago.

Puu Loa Petroglyphs Trail (1.5 mi)

Puu Loa Petroglyphs parking lot

Easy to moderate

Spotlighted here: ancient petroglyphs the Hawaiians created on smooth lava flows to ensure the health and safety of their children.

SEEING LAVA

Before you head out to find flowing lava, pinpoint the safe viewing spots at the Visitor Center. One of the best places usually is at the end of 18-mile Chain of Craters Road. Magnificent plumes of steam rise where the rivers of liquid fire meet the sea.

There are three guarantees about lava flows in HVNP. First: They constantly change. Second: Because of that, you can't predict when and where you'll be able to see them. Third: New land formed when lava meets the sea is highly unstable and can collapse at any time. Never go into areas that have been closed.

■ TIP➜ The view of brilliant red-orange lava flowing from Kilauea's east rift zone is most dramatic at night.

People watching lava flow at HVNP

PLANNING YOUR TRIP TO HVNP

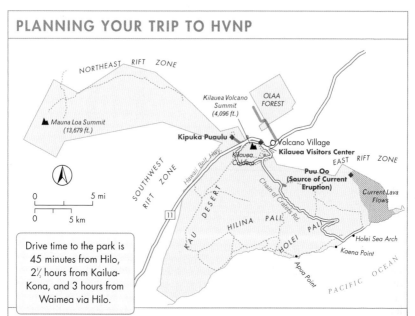

Drive time to the park is 45 minutes from Hilo, 2½ hours from Kailua-Kona, and 3 hours from Waimea via Hilo.

Lava entering the ocean

WHERE TO START

Begin your visit at the Visitor Center, where you'll find maps, books, and DVDs; information on trails, ranger-led walks, and special events; and current weather, road, and lava-viewing conditions. Free volcano-related film showings, lectures, and other presentations are regularly scheduled.

WEATHER

Weather conditions fluctuate daily, sometimes hourly. It can be rainy and chilly even during the summer; the temperature usually is 14° cooler at the 4,000-foot-high summit of Kilauea than at sea level.

Expect hot, dry, and windy coastal conditions at the end of Chain of Craters Road. Bring rain gear, and wear layered clothing, sturdy shoes, sunglasses, a hat, and sunscreen.

Photographer on lava table filming lava flow into ocean

FOOD
It's a good idea to bring your own favorite snacks and beverages; stock up on provisions in Volcano Village, 1½ miles away.

PARK PROGRAMS
Rangers lead daily walks at 10:30 and 1:30 into different areas; check with the Visitor Center for details as times and destinations depend on weather conditions and eruptions.

Over 60 companies hold permits to lead hikes at HVNP. Good choices are Hawaii Forest & Trail (www.hawaii-forest.com), Hawaiian Walkways (www.hawaiianwalkways.com), and Native Guide Hawaii (www.nativeguide hawaii.com).

CAUTION
"Vog" (volcanic smog) can cause headaches; breathing difficulties; lethargy; irritations of the skin, eyes, nose, and throat; and other health problems. Pregnant women, young children, and people with asthma and heart conditions are most susceptible, and should avoid areas such as Halemaumau Crater where fumes are thick.

Wear long pants and boots or closed-toe shoes with good tread for hikes on lava. Stay on marked trails and step carefully. Lava is composed of 50% silica (glass) and can cause serious injury if you fall.

Carry at least 2 quarts of water on hikes. Temperatures near lava flows can rise above 100°F, and dehydration, heat exhaustion, and sunstroke are common consequences of extended exposure to intense sunlight and high temperatures.

Remember that these are active volcanoes, and eruptions can cause parts of the park to close at any time. Check the park's website or call ahead for last-minute updates before your visit.

Volcanologists inspecting a vent in the East Rift Zone

You may see flowing lava from Kilauea, the Big Island's youngest and most active volcano.

WORTH NOTING

Kilauea Caverns of Fire. This way-out adventure explores the underbelly of the world's most active volcano via the Kazamura Lava Tube system. The largest lava tube system in the world—40 miles long, 80 feet wide, and 80 feet tall, it comprises four main tubes, each 500 to 700 years old and filled with bizarre lava formations and mind-blowing colors. Customized to groups' interest and skill level, tours through fascinating caves and lava tubes must be arranged in advance but are well worth the extra planning. Equipment is included. ⊠ *Hawaiian Acres, off Hwy. 11, between Kurtistown and Mountain View* ☎ *808/217–2363* ⊕ *www. kilaueacavernsoffire.com* 🖂 *$29 for walking tour, $89 for adventure tour* ☉ *By appointment only.*

Volcano Farmers' Market. Local produce, flowers, crafts, and food products, including fresh-baked breads, pastries, coffee, and homemade Thai specialties, are available every Sunday morning at one of the better farmers' markets on the island. It's best to get there early, before 7 am, as vendors tend to sell out of the best stuff quickly. There's also a great bookstore (paperbacks 50¢, hardbacks $1, and magazines 10¢) and a thrift store with clothes and knickknacks. ⊠ *Cooper Center, 19-4030 Wright Rd., Volcano* ☎ *808/936–9705* ⊕ *www.thecoopercenter.org* ☉ *Sun. 6–10 am.*

Volcano Garden Arts. This delightful gallery and garden lend credence to Volcano's reputation as an artists' haven. Located on beautifully landscaped grounds dotted with intriguing sculptures, this charming complex includes an eclectic gallery representing more than 100 artists, an excellent organic café housed in redwood buildings built in 1908, and a cute, one-bedroom artist's cottage, available for rent. If you're lucky, you'll get to meet the eccentric owner/"caretaker" of this enclave, the multitalented Ira Ono, known for his whimsical art, recycled trash creations, and friendly personality. ✉ *19-3834 Old Volcano Rd., Volcano* ☎ *808/985–8979* ⊕ *www.volcanogardenarts.com* 🖘 *Free* ☉ *Tues.–Sat. 10–4; gallery daily.*

Volcano Winery. Volcanic soil may not seem ideal for the cultivation of grapes, but that hasn't stopped this winery from producing some interesting vintages. The Macadamia Nut Honey wine is a nutty, very sweet after-dinner drink. The Infusion pairs estate-grown black tea with South Kona's fermented macadamia nut honey for a smooth concoction perfect for brunch through early evening. Though this isn't Napa Valley, the vintners take their wine seriously, and the staff is friendly and knowledgeable. Wine tasting is available, you can get wine and cheese to eat in the picnic area, and a gift store has a selection of local crafts. ✉ *35 Pi'i Mauna Dr., past entrance to Hawaii Volcanoes National Park, by golf course, Volcano* ☎ *808/967–7772* ⊕ *www. volcanowinery.com* ☉ *Daily 10–5:30; tours at 10 or by appointment.*

KAU AND KA LAE

Ka Lae (South Point) is 50 miles south of Kailua-Kona.

The most desolate region of the island, Kau, is nevertheless home to spectacular sights. Mark Twain wrote some of his finest prose here, where macadamia-nut farms, remote green-sand beaches, and tiny communities offer rugged, largely undiscovered beauty. The drive from Kailua-Kona to windswept Ka Lae (South Point) winds away from the ocean through a surreal moonscape of lava plains and patches of scrub forest. Coming from Volcano, as you near South Point, the barren lavascape gives way to lush vistas from the ocean to the hills.

At the end of the 12-mile two-lane road to Ka Lae, you can park and hike about an hour to Papakolea Beach (Green Sands Beach). Back on the highway, the coast passes verdant cattle pastures and sheer cliffs and the village of Naalehu on the way to the black-sand beach of Punaluu, a common nesting place of the Hawaiian green sea turtle.

GETTING HERE AND AROUND

Kau and Ka Lae are destinations usually combined with a quick trip to the volcano from Kona. This is probably cramming too much into one day, however. The volcano fills up at least a day (two is better), and the sights of this southern end of the island are worth more than a cursory glance.

Instead make Green Sands Beach or Punaluu a beach day, and see some of the other sights on the way there or back. Bring sturdy shoes, water, and a sun hat if Green Sands Beach is your choice (reaching the beach requires a hike). And be careful in the surf here. Don't go in unless you're used to ocean waves. There are no lifeguards at this remote beach. It's decidedly calmer and you can sometimes snorkel at Punaluu, but use caution at these and all Hawaii beaches.

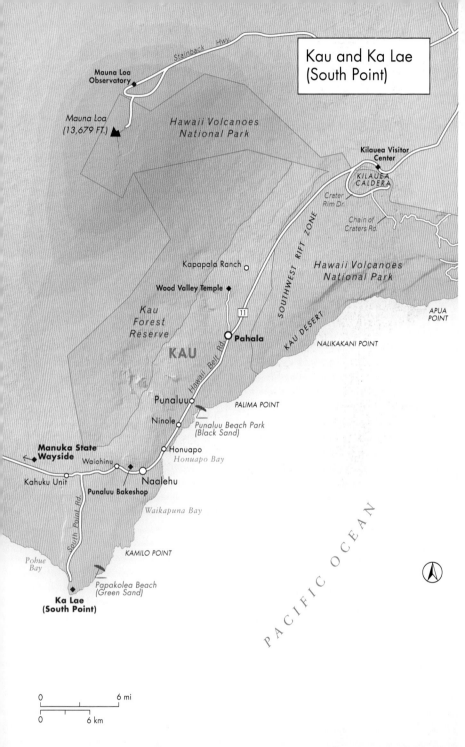

Kau and Ka Lae (South Point)

Stainback Hwy

Mauna Loa
Observatory

Mauna Loa
(13,679 FT.)

Hawaii Volcanoes
National Park

Kilauea Visitor
Center

KILAUEA
CALDERA

Crater
Rim Dr.

Chain of
Craters Rd.

Kapapala Ranch

Wood Valley Temple

Kau
Forest
Reserve

KAU

SOUTHWEST RIFT ZONE

Hawaii Volcanoes
National Park

APUA
POINT

11

Pahala

KAU DESERT

NALIKAKANI POINT

Hawaii Belt Rd.

Punaluu

PALIMA POINT

Ninole

Punaluu Beach Park
(Black Sand)

Manuka State
Wayside

Honuapo

Honuapo Bay

Waiohinu

Kahuku Unit

Naalehu

Punaluu Bakeshop

South Point Rd.

Waikapuna Bay

Pohue
Bay

KAMILO POINT

Papakolea Beach
(Green Sand)

Ka Lae
(South Point)

PACIFIC OCEAN

0   6 mi

0   6 km

The drive from Kailua-Kona to Ka Lae is a long one (roughly 2½ hours); from Volcano it's approximately 45 minutes. You can fill up on gas and groceries in Ocean View, or you can eat, fuel up, and get picnic fixings in Naalehu. Weather tends to be warm, dry, and windy.

TOP ATTRACTIONS

Fodor's Choice **Ka Lae (South Point).** It's thought that the first Polynesians came ashore
★ at this southernmost point of land in the United States, also a National Historic Landmark. Old canoe-mooring holes, visible today, were carved through the rocks, possibly by settlers from Tahiti as early as AD 750. To get here, drive 12 miles on the turnoff road, past rows of giant electricity-producing windmills powered by the nearly constant winds sweeping across this coastal plain. Bear left when the road forks, and park in the lot at the end. Walk past the boat hoists toward the little lighthouse. South Point is just past the lighthouse at the southernmost cliff. You may see brave locals jumping off the cliffs and then climbing up rusty old ladders, but swimming here is not recommended. ■TIP→ Don't leave anything of value in your car. ⊠ *South Point Rd., off Mamalahoa Hwy. at around mile marker 70, Kau* ☒ *Free.*

Manuka State Wayside. This upland forest spreads across several recent lava flows. A rugged trail follows a 2-mile loop past a pit crater, winding around interesting trees such as *hau* and *kukui*. It's a nice spot to get out of the car and stretch your legs—you can wander through the well-maintained arboretum, snap a few photos of the eerie forest, and let the kids scramble around trees so large they can't get their arms around them. The pathways can get muddy and rough, so bring appropriate shoes if you plan to hike. Restrooms, picnic areas, and camping sites (by permit) are available. ⊠ *Hwy. 11, north of mile marker 81* ☎ *808/974–6200* ⊕ *www.hawaiistateparks.org/parks/hawaii/index.cfm?park_id=53* ☒ *Free* ⊗ *Daily dawn–dusk.*

QUICK BITES

Punaluu Bakeshop. Billed as the southernmost bakery in the United States, it's a good spot to grab a snack, and the heavenly smell alone is worth the stop. Try the new house favorite, lilikoi-glazed *malasadas* (Portuguese doughnuts)—sweet with a touch of tart. (Be forewarned: One is never enough.) Local-style plate lunches and sandwiches on the bakeshop's famous sweetbread buns go well with Kau coffee. That's right, not Kona, but equally tasty. ⊠ *Hwy. 11, Naalehu* ☎ *808/929–7343, 866/366–3501* ⊕ *www.bakeshophawaii.com* ⊗ *Daily 9–5.*

OFF THE BEATEN PATH

Pahala. About 16 miles east of Naalehu, beyond Punaluu Beach Park, Highway 11 passes directly by this little town. You'll miss it if you blink. Pahala, once a booming sugar plantation company town, is sleepy today but still inhabited by retired cane workers and their descendants. Behind it, along a wide cane road, is Wood Valley, once a prosperous community, now just a peaceful road heavily scented by eucalyptus trees, coffee blossoms, and night-blooming jasmine and often laden in mist. ⊠ *Pahala.*

Wood Valley Temple (*Nechung Temple*). Behind Pahala, this serene and beautiful Tibetan Buddhist temple, established in 1973, has hosted more than 50 well-known lamas, including the Dalai Lama on two occasions. You can visit and meditate, leave an offering, walk the lush gardens shared by strutting peacocks, browse the gift shop, or stay in the temple's guesthouse, available for peaceful, nondenominational retreats. ⊠ *Pahala* ☎ *808/928–8539* ⊕ *www.nechung.org* ✉ *$5.*

3

BEACHES

Updated
by Kristina
Anderson

Don't believe anyone who tells you that the Big Island lacks beaches. It's just one of the myths about Hawaii's largest island that has no basis in fact. It's not so much that the Big Island has fewer beaches than the other islands, just that there's more island, so getting to the beaches can be slightly less convenient.

That said, there are plenty of those perfect white-sand stretches you think of when you hear "Hawaii," and the added bonus of black- and green-sand beaches, thanks to the relative young age of the island and its active volcanoes. New beaches appear and disappear regularly, created and destroyed by volcanic activity. In 1989, a black-sand beach, Kamoamoa, formed when molten lava shattered as it hit cold ocean waters; it was enjoyed for a few years before it was closed by new lava flows in 1992. It's part of the ongoing process of the volcano's creation-and-change dynamic.

Hawaii's largest coral reef systems lie off the Kohala Coast. Waves have battered them over millennia to create abundant white-sand beaches on the northwest side of the island. Black-sand and green-sand beaches lie in the southern regions, along the coast nearest the volcano. On the eastern side of the island, beaches tend to be of the rocky-coast–surging-surf variety, but there are still a few worth visiting, and this is where the Hawaiian shoreline is at its most picturesque.

KAILUA-KONA

There are a few good sandy beaches near town. However, the coastline is generally rugged black lava rock, so don't expect long stretches of white sand. The beaches in Kailua-Kona get lots of use by local residents, and visitors enjoy them, too. Excellent opportunities for snorkeling, scuba diving, swimming, kayaking, and other water sports are easy to find.

FAMILY **Kahaluu Beach Park.** This shallow and easily accessible salt-and-pepper beach is one of the Big Island's most popular swimming and snorkeling sites, thanks to the fringing reef that helps keep the waters calm, visibility high, and reef life—especially turtles and colorful fish—plentiful. Because it is so protected, it's great for first-time snorkelers, but outside the reef, very strong rip currents can run, so caution is advised. Never chase turtles or hand-feed the unusually tame reef fish here; it

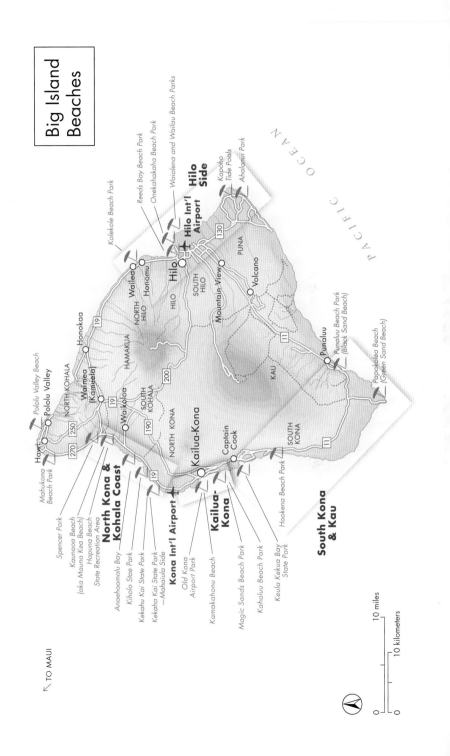

Big Island Beaches

↖ TO MAUI

PACIFIC OCEAN

Hilo Side

Kapoho Tide Pools
Ahalanui Park
Waiolena and Wailau Beach Parks
Onekahakaha Beach Park
Reeds Bay Beach Park
Kolekole Beach Park

Hilo Int'l Airport

Wailea
Honomu
Hilo

NORTH HILO
SOUTH HILO
HILO
HAMAKUA
PUNA
130
Mountain-View
Volcano
200
190
250
270
19
19
11
11

Honokaa
Waimea (Kamuela)
Waikoloa

NORTH KOHALA
SOUTH KOHALA
NORTH KONA
SOUTH KONA
KAU

Hawi
Pololu Valley
Kailua-Kona
Captain Cook
Punaluu

Punaluu Beach Park (Black Sand Beach)
Papakolea Beach (Green Sand Beach)

Pololu Valley Beach
Mahukona Beach Park
Spencer Park
Kaunaoa Beach (aka Mauna Kea Beach)
Hapuna Beach State Recreation Area

North Kona & Kohala Coast

Anaehoomalu Bay
Kiholo State Park
Kekahu Kai State Park
Kekaha Kai State Park —Mahaiula Side

Kona Int'l Airport

Old Kona Airport Park
Kamakahonu Beach

Kailua-Kona

Magic Sands Beach Park
Kahaluu Beach Park
Keula Kekua Bay State Park
Hookena Beach Park

South Kona & Kau

0   10 miles
0   10 kilometers

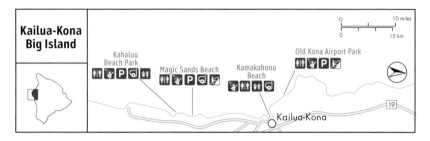

upsets the balance of the reef. ■TIP→ Experienced surfers find good waves beyond the reef, and scuba divers like the shore dives—shallow ones inside the breakwater, deeper ones outside. Snorkel equipment and boards are available for rent nearby, and surf schools operate here. Kahaluu was a favorite of the Hawaiian royal family, especially King Kalakaua. **Amenities:** food and drink; lifeguards; parking; showers; toilets. **Best for:** snorkeling; swimming. ⊠ *78-6720 Alii Dr., 5½ miles south of Kailua-Kona, across from the Beach Villas* ☎ *808/961–8311.*

FAMILY **Kamakahonu Beach.** This is where King Kamehameha spent his final days—the restored Ahuena Heiau sits on a platform across from the sand. Fronting the Courtyard King Kamehameha's Kona Beach Hotel and adjacent to Kailua Pier, this scenic crescent of white sand is one of few beaches in downtown Kailua-Kona. The water here is almost always calm and the beach clean, making this a perfect spot for kids. For adults, it's a great place for a swim, some stand-up paddleboarding, watching outrigger teams practice, or enjoying a lazy beach day. It can get crowded on weekends. Snorkeling can be good north of the beach, and snorkeling, SUP, and kayaking equipment can be rented nearby. ■TIP→ A little family of sea turtles likes to hang out next to the seawall, so keep an eye out. There's lots of grass and shade, and free parking in county lots is a short stroll away. **Amenities:** food and drink; showers; toilets; water sports. **Best for:** snorkeling; swimming. ⊠ *75-5660 Palani Rd., at Alii Dr.*

Magic Sands Beach Park (*White Sands Beach*). Towering coconut trees provide some shade and lend a touch of tropical beauty to this pretty little beach park (also called La'aloa), which may well be the Big Island's most intriguing stretch of sand. A migratory beach of sorts, it can disappear in winter, when waves wash away the small white-sand parcel (hence the name "Magic Sands"). In summer, the beach re-forms; you'll know you've found it when you see the body- and board surfers. Just south of Anthony's by the Sea Restaurant, this is a popular summer hangout for young locals. **Amenities:** lifeguards; parking (no fee); showers; toilets. **Best for:** surfing. ⊠ *77-6470 Alii Dr., 4½ miles south of Kailua-Kona* ☎ *808/961–8311.*

FAMILY **Old Kona Airport Park.** Hugging the long shoreline adjacent to the runway that served Kona's airport until 1970 (the old terminal is used for community events), this beach is flat, generally clean, and dotted with rocks and coral pieces. Calm waters make for good snorkeling, and a few accessible small coves of white sand offer safe water entry and tide

Calm Kailua Bay is an excellent spot for kayaking, snorkeling, and swimming.

pools for children. Shady areas are good for picnics or admiring the Kona skyline, complete with a whale (in season) and a cruise ship or two. A well-tended community jogging trail and dog park opposite the runway are worth checking out for the tropical landscape. Just north, an offshore surf break known as Old A's is popular with local surfers. It's usually not crowded, but this area can get busy on weekends. **Amenities:** parking (no fee); showers; toilets. **Best for:** sunset; walking. ⊠ *North end of Kuakini Hwy., where the road ends* ☎ *808/327–4958, 808/974–6200.*

THE KONA COAST

This ruggedly beautiful coastline harbors a couple of scenic beaches that take you off the beaten track. Napoopoo and Hookena offer great swimming, snorkeling, diving, and kayaking.

NORTH KONA

Kekaha Kai State Park—Kua Bay Side. This lovely beach is on the northernmost stretch of the park's coastline on an absolutely beautiful bay. The water is crystal clear, deep aquamarine, and peaceful in summer, but the park's paved entrance, amenities, and parking lot make it very accessible and, as a result, often crowded. Fine white sand sits amid black lava with little shade—bring umbrellas as it can get hot. Rocky shores on either side protect the beach from winds in the afternoon. Gates close daily at 7 pm. ⚠ In winter, surf can get very rough and often the sand washes away. **Amenities:** parking (no fee); showers; toilets. **Best for:**

surfing; swimming. ⊠ *Hwy. 19, north of mile marker 88, across from the Veterans Cemetery, Kailua-Kona.*

Fodor'sChoice **Kekaha Kai State Park—Mahaiula Side.** It's slow going, down a 1.8-mile,
★ bumpy, mostly unpaved road off Highway 19 to this beach park, but it's worth it. This state park encompasses three beaches (from south to north, Mahaiula, Makalawena, and Kua Bay, which has its own entrance). Mahaiula and Makalawena are beautiful, wide expanses of white-sand beach with dunes; there's a lot of space so you won't feel crowded. Makalawena has great swimming and boogie boarding. From there, a historic 4½-mile trail leads to Kua Bay. If you're game, work your way to the top of Puu Kuili, a 342-foot-high cinder cone whose summit offers a fantastic view of the coastline. However, be prepared for the heat and bring lots of water. Gates close promptly at 7 pm, so you need to leave the lot by 6:30. ⚠ Watch out for rough surf and strong currents. **Amenities:** toilets. **Best for:** sunset; swimming; walking. ⊠ *Hwy. 19, turnoff is about 2 miles north of Keahole–Kona International Airport, Kailua-Kona* ☎ *808/327–4958, 808/974–6200* ⊕ *www. hawaiistateparks.org.*

SOUTH KONA

FAMILY **Hookena Beach Park.** The 2½-mile road to this quiet, secluded little gem feels like you're venturing off the beaten path. The area is rich in cultural history, with remnants of an old steamship pier testifying to its former role as a thriving port. Frequented mostly by locals, the beach is usually only crowded on weekends. It has a clean, soft mix of dark brown and gray sand and is backed by steep embankments. The bay is usually calm, with small surf, good for swimming, snorkeling, kayaking, and diving. A community-county park partnership oversees the concessions and camping permits and rents camp gear. Trails along the shoreline make for good exploring. **Amenities:** food and drink; parking (no fee); showers; toilets; water sports. **Best for:** swimming. ⊠ *Hwy. 11, 23 miles south of Kailua-Kona between mile markers 101 and 102* ☎ *808/961–8311* ⊕ *www.hookena.org.*

Fodor'sChoice **Kealakekua Bay State Historical Park.** When Hurricane Iniki slammed into
★ Hawaii in 1992, this park lost all of its sand, which is slowly returning decades later. The shoreline is rocky but don't let that deter you. The area is surrounded by high green cliffs, creating calm conditions for superb swimming, snorkeling, and diving. Among the variety of marine life are dolphins, which come to rest and escape predators during the

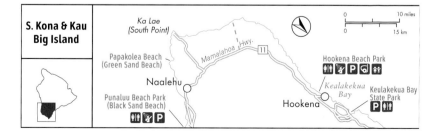

S. Kona & Kau Big Island

Ka Lae (South Point)

Papakolea Beach (Green Sand Beach)

Mamalahoa Hwy.

11

Naalehu

Punaluu Beach Park (Black Sand Beach)

Hookena Beach Park

Kealakekua Bay

Keulakekua Bay State Park

Hookena

0   10 miles
0   15 km

day. They are protected from harassment by federal law, so don't disturb them. This popular spot is also historically significant. Captain James Cook first landed in Hawaii here in 1778. When he returned a year later, he was killed in a skirmish with Hawaiians, now marked by a monument on the north end of the bay. Rocky but walkable trails lead to Hikiau Heiau, a sacred place for the Hawaiian people. Do not walk on or enter it. Parking is limited. ⚠ Be aware of the off-limits area (in case of rockfalls) marked by orange buoys. **Amenities:** parking (no fee); toilets. **Best for:** snorkeling; swimming. ⊠ *Napoopoo Rd., off Hwy. 11, just south of mile marker 111, Kealakekua* ☎ *808/961–9544.*

KOHALA COAST

Most of the Big Island's white sandy beaches are found on the Kohala Coast, which is also called the "Gold Coast" and is, understandably, home to the majority of the island's world-class resorts. Hawaii's beaches are public property and the resorts are required to provide public access, so don't be frightened off by a guard shack and a fancy sign. There is some limited public parking as well. Resort beaches aside, there are some real hidden gems, accessible only by boat, four-wheel drive, or a 15- to 20-minute hike. It's well worth the effort to get to at least one of these. ■TIP→ The west side of the island tends to be calmer, but the surf still gets rough in winter.

FAMILY
Fodor'sChoice
★

Anaehoomalu Bay (*A-Bay*). Also known as "A-bay," this expansive stretch of white sand fronts the Waikoloa Beach Marriott and is a perfect spot for swimming, windsurfing, snorkeling, and diving. Unlike some Kohala Coast beaches near hotel properties, this one is very accessible to the public and offers plenty of free parking. The bay is well protected, so even when surf is rough or trades are blasting, it's fairly calm here. (Mornings are calmest.) Snorkel gear, kayaks, and boogie boards are available for rent at the north end. Behind the beach are two ancient Hawaiian fishponds, **Kuualii** and **Kahapapa**, that once served ancient Hawaiian royalty. A walking trail follows the coastline to the Hilton Waikoloa Village next door, passing by tide pools, ponds, and a turtle sanctuary where sea turtles can often be spotted sunbathing on the sand. Footwear is recommended for the trail. **Amenities:** food and drink; parking (no fee); showers; toilets; water sports. **Best for:** snorkeling; swimming; walking. ⊠ *69-275 Waikoloa Beach Dr., just south of Waikoloa Beach Marriott; turn left at Kings' Shops, Kohala Coast.*

FAMILY
Fodor'sChoice
★

Hapuna Beach State Recreation Area. One of Hawaii's finest beaches, Hapuna is a ½-mile-long stretch of white perfection. The turquoise water is calm in summer with just enough rolling waves to make body-surfing and body boarding fun. Watch for the undertow; in winter it can be rough. There is excellent snorkeling around the jagged rocks that border the beach on either side, but high surf brings strong currents. Known for awesome sunsets, this is one of the best places on the island to see the "green flash" as the sun dips below a clear horizon. The north end of the beach fronts the Hapuna Beach Prince Hotel, which rents water-sports equipment and has a food concession with shaded picnic tables. There is ample parking, although the lot can fill

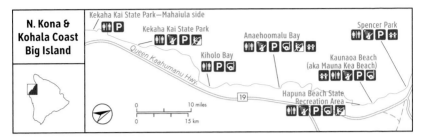

up by midday and the beach can get crowded on holidays. Lifeguards, on duty during peak hours, only cover the state park section, not areas north of the rocky cliff that juts out near the middle of the beach. **Amenities:** food and drink; lifeguards; parking (fee); showers; toilets; water sports. **Best for:** sunset; surfing; swimming; walking. ⊠ *Hwy. 19, near mile marker 69, just south of the Hapuna Beach Prince Hotel, Kohala Coast* ☎ *808/961–9544.*

FAMILY

Fodor's Choice

★

Kaunaoa Beach (*Mauna Kea Beach*). Hands-down one of the most beautiful beaches on the island, if not the whole state, Kaunaoa features a long crescent of pure white sand. The beach, which fronts the Mauna Kea Beach Hotel, slopes very gradually, and there's great snorkeling along the rocks. Classic Hawaii postcard views abound, especially in winter, when snow tops Mauna Kea. When conditions permit, waves are good for body- and board surfing also. Currents can be strong and powerful in winter, so be careful. ■TIP→ Public parking is limited to a few spaces, so arrive before 10 am or after 3 pm. If the lot is full, head to nearby Hapuna Beach, where there's a huge parking lot ($5 per vehicle). Try this spot again another day—it's worth it! **Amenities:** parking (no fee); showers; toilets; water sports. **Best for:** sunset; swimming; walking. ⊠ *62-100 Mauna Kea Beach Dr., entry through gate to Mauna Kea Beach Hotel, Kohala Coast.*

Kiholo State Park Reserve. One of the state park system's newest treasures, Kiholo Bay is still in the planning stage, so facilities are not yet complete. The brilliant turquoise waters of this stunning bay, set against stark black lava fields, are a cooling invitation on a warm Kohala day. The shore is rocky and the water's a bit cold and hazy due to freshwater springs, but there are tons of green sea turtles in residence year-round. The swimming and snorkeling are excellent when the tide is calm. Thanks to the eruptions of Mauna Loa, what was once the site of King Kamehameha's gigantic fishpond is now several freshwater ponds encircling the bay, with a picturesque lava-rock island in the middle. Along the shoreline southwest toward Kona, just past the big yellow house, is another public beach with naturally occurring freshwater pools inside a lava tube. This area, called Queen's Bath, is as cool as it sounds. Gates are locked promptly at 7 pm, and camping is allowed with fee and permit. **Amenities:** parking (no fee); toilets. **Best for:** snorkeling; walking. ⊠ *Hwy. 19, unmarked gravel road between mile markers 82 and 83, just south of the lookout, Kohala Coast* ☎ *808/974–6200* ⊕ *www. hawaiistateparks.org/parks/hawaii/index.cfm?park_id=58.*

DID YOU KNOW?

Most locals rate Hapuna
Beach, with its long expanse
of white sand, the best beach
on the island. Its turquoise
water is calm during summer
but rougher in winter.

Mahukona Beach Park. Snorkelers and divers make exciting discoveries in the clear waters of this park. Long ago, when sugar was the economic staple of Kohala, this harbor was busy with boats waiting for overseas shipments. Now it's a great swimming hole and an underwater museum of sorts. Remnants of shipping machinery, train wheels and parts, and what looks like an old boat are easily visible in the clear water. There's no actual beach here, but a ladder off the old dock makes getting in the water easy. It's best to venture out only on tranquil days, when the water is calm; conditions can get windy. A popular place for locals, Mahukona is busy on weekends. A camping area on the south side of the park has picnic tables and an old covered pavilion. A trail also leads to nearby Lapakahi State Park, about a ½-mile hike. **Amenities:** showers; toilets. **Best for:** snorkeling; swimming. ⊠ *Hwy. 270, about 7 miles south of Hawi, between mile markers 14 and 15, Kohala Coast* ☎ *808/961–8311.*

Pololu Valley Beach. On the North Kohala peninsula, this is one of the Big Island's most scenic black-sand beaches. After about 8 miles of lush, winding road past Hawi Town, Highway 270 ends at the overlook of Pololu Valley. Snap a few photos of the stunning view, then take the 15-minute hike down (twice as long back up) to the beach. The trail is steep and rocky; it can also be muddy and slippery, so watch your step. The beach itself is a wide expanse of fine black sand surrounded by sheer green cliffs and backed by high dunes and ironwood trees. A gurgling stream leads from the beach to the back of the valley. ⚠ **This is not a safe swimming beach even though locals do swim, body board, and surf here. Dangerous rip currents and usually rough surf pose a real hazard.** And because this is a remote, isolated area far from emergency help, extreme caution is advised. **Amenities:** none. **Best for:** hiking. ⊠ *Hwy. 270, end of the road, Kapaau.*

FAMILY **Spencer Park at Ohaiula Beach.** This white-sand beach is popular with local families because of its reef-protected waters. ■**TIP➜ It's probably the safest beach in West Hawaii for young children.** It's also safe for swimming year-round, which makes it a reliable spot for a lazy day at the beach. There is a little shade, plus a volleyball court and pavilion, and the soft sand is perfect for sand castles. It does tend to get crowded with families and campers on weekends, but the beach is generally clean. Although you won't see a lot of fish if you're snorkeling here, in winter you can usually catch sight of a breaching whale or two. The beach park lies just below Puukohola Heiau National Historic Park, site of the historic war temple built by King Kamehameha the Great in 1810 after uniting the Islands. **Amenities:** lifeguards (weekends and holidays only); parking (no fee); showers; toilets. **Best for:** sunset; swimming. ⊠ *Hwy. 270, toward Kawaihae Harbor, just after the road forks from Hwy. 19, Kawaihae* ☎ *808/961–8311.*

THE HAMAKUA COAST

Although there are no actual beaches along the jagged cliffs of the Hamakua Coast, a few surf spots and swimming holes tucked into the lush landscape deserve an afternoon stop.

Kua Bay is protected from wind by the rocky shores that surround it.

Honolii Beach Park. One of the most consistent places on the east side to catch a wave, Honolii is popular with the local surf crowd. The beach is a mix of black sand, coral, and sea glass, with plenty of rocks. A shady grassy area is great for picnics while you watch the surfers. ⚠ **The presence of surfers is not an indication that an area is safe for swimmers. Winter surf is very rough.** A pond just to the north is good for swimming, but it's deep and there is a drop-off. There's limited parking on the narrow roadside. Walk down the stairs and veer left over the rocks. **Amenities:** lifeguards; toilets. **Best for:** surfing. ⊠ *Hwy. 19, 1½ miles north of Hilo* ☎ *808/961–8311.*

Kolekole Beach Park. This lush park is tucked away under a high bridge that crosses a gulch along Highway 19, between Akaka and Umauma falls. The beach is composed of large, smooth, waterworn lava rocks, where the Kolekole stream meets the ocean. Although the shoreline is rocky and the ocean is rough, the stream is usually calm and great for swimming. There's even a rope swing tied to a banyan tree on the opposite side. The park is popular with locals, especially on weekends, when it can get rowdy. ■ **TIP➡ Where the stream meets the ocean, the surf is rough and the currents strong. Only very experienced swimmers should venture here. Amenities:** parking (no fee); showers; toilets. **Best for:** swimming. ⊠ *Hwy. 19, 13 miles north of Hilo, Honomu* ☎ *808/961–8311.*

BEACH SAFETY

Hawaii's world-renowned, beautiful beaches can be extremely dangerous at times due to large swells and strong currents—so much so that the state rates wave hazards using three signs: a yellow square (caution), a red stop sign (high hazard), and a black diamond (extreme hazard). Signs are posted and updated three times daily or as conditions change.

Visiting beaches with lifeguards is strongly recommended, and you should only swim when there's a normal caution rating. Never swim alone or dive into unknown water or shallow breaking waves. If you're unable to swim out of a rip current by swimming sideways, tread water and wave your arms in the air to signal for help.

Even in calm conditions, this is still the ocean and there are other dangerous things in the water to be aware of, including razor-sharp coral, jellyfish, eels, and sharks, to name a few.

Jellyfish cause the most ocean injuries, and signs are posted along beaches when they're present. Box jellyfish swarm Hawaii's leeward shores 9 to 10 days after a full moon. Portuguese man-of-wars are usually found when winds blow from the ocean onto land. Reactions to a sting range from usually mild (burning sensation, redness, welts) to severe (breathing difficulties). If you are stung by a jellyfish, pick off the tentacles, rinse the affected area with rubbing alcohol or urine (really) and apply ice. Seek first aid from a lifeguard if you experience a severe reaction.

According to state sources, the chances of a shark bite in Hawaiian waters are very low; sharks attack swimmers or surfers three or four times per year. Of the 40 species of shark found near Hawaii, tigers are considered the most dangerous because of their size and indiscriminate feeding behavior (they eat just about anything at the water's surface). Tiger sharks are easily recognized by their blunt snouts and vertical bars on their sides.

To reduce your shark-attack risk, avoid swimming at dawn, dusk, and night, when some shark species may move inshore to feed. Steer clear of murky waters, harbor entrances, areas near stream mouths (especially after heavy rains), channels, or steep drop-offs.

The website ⊕ *oceansafety.soest. hawaii.edu* provides beach hazard maps for Oahu, Maui, Kauai, and the Big Island, as well as weather and surf advisories, listings of closed beaches, and safety tips.

HILO

Hilo isn't exactly known for its beautiful white beaches, but there are a few in the area that provide good swimming and snorkeling opportunities, and most are surrounded by lush rain forest.

FAMILY **Onekahakaha Beach Park.** Shallow, rock-wall-enclosed tide pools and an adjacent grassy picnic area make this park a favorite among Hilo families with small children. The protected pools are great places to look for Hawaiian marine life like sea urchins and anemones. There isn't much white sand, but access to the water is easy. The water is

usually rough beyond the line of large boulders protecting the inner tide pools, so be careful if the surf is high. This beach gets crowded on weekends. **Amenities:** lifeguards (weekends, holidays, and summer only); parking (no fee); showers; toilets. **Best for:** swimming. ✉ *Onekahakaha Rd. and Kalanianaole Ave., via Kanoelehua St., 3 miles east of Hilo* ☎ *808/961–8311.*

Reeds Bay Beach Park. Safe swimming, proximity to downtown Hilo, and a freshwater-fed swimming hole, called the Ice Pond, that flows into the backwaters of Hilo Bay are the enticements of this cove. No, there really isn't ice in the swimming hole; it just feels that way on a hot sultry day. The large pond, between Hilo Seaside Hotel and Harrington's Restaurant, is a favorite of local kids, who enjoy jumping into and frolicking in the chilly fresh- and saltwater mix. The water is usually calm. **Amenities:** parking (no fee); showers. **Best for:** swimming. ✉ *Banyan Dr. and Kalaniana'ole Ave.* ☎ *808/961–8311.*

FAMILY **Waiolena and Wailua Beach Parks and Richardson Ocean Center.** Just east of Hilo, almost at the end of the road, three adjacent parks make up one beautiful spot with a series of bays, protected inlets, lagoons, and pretty parks. This is one of the best snorkeling sites on this side of the island, as rocky outcrops provide shelter for schools of reef fish, sea turtles, and dolphins. Local kids use the small black-sand pocket beach for body boarding. The shaded grassy areas are great for picnics. Be warned, this place is very crowded on weekends. **Amenities:** lifeguards (weekends, holidays, and summer only); parking (no fee); showers; toilets. **Best for:** snorkeling; walking. ✉ *2349 Kalaniana'ole Ave., 4 miles east of Hilo* ☎ *808/961–8311.*

PUNA

Puna's few beaches have some unusual attributes—swaths of new black sand, volcano-heated springs, and a coastline that is beyond dramatic (sheer walls of lava rock dropping into a dramatic blue ocean).

FAMILY **Ahalanui Park.** There's nothing like swimming in this natural, geothermally heated pool next to the ocean with palm trees swaying overhead. Popular with locals, this immaculate 3-acre beach park has a ½-acre pond of fresh spring water mixed with seawater that's heated by volcanic steam. There's no sand, but there is smooth, rocky access to the ocean as well as the pool. ⚠ Check with the lifeguard on duty, and heed all posted signs; this park sometimes closes temporarily due to possible

DID YOU KNOW?

You can see turtles at the Big Island's Punaluu Black Sand Beach Park, a popular resting and feeding spot for endangered Hawaiian green sea turtles. Absolutely no touching the animals—it's a hefty fine.

waterborne bacteria. The parking lot fills up quickly. **Amenities:** lifeguards; parking (no fee); showers; toilets. **Best for:** swimming. ⊠ *Hwy. 137, 2½ miles south of Hwy. 132, Puna* ☏ *808/961–8311.*

Fodor's Choice ★ **Kapoho Tide Pools.** Snorkelers find tons of coral and the fish who feed off it in this large network of tide pools at the end of Kapoho-Kai Road. This is a great place for getting close-up looks at Hawaii's interesting marine life. Some of the pools have been turned into private swimming pools in this residential area; those closest to the ocean are open to all. The pools are usually very calm, and some are volcanically heated and divine to soak in. It's best to come during the week, as the pools can get crowded on the weekend. Note: there is no real sandy beach here. Take the road to the end, turn left, and park. **Amenities:** none. **Best for:** snorkeling. ⊠ *Kapoho-Kai Rd., off Hwy. 13, about 9 miles southeast of Pahoa Town, Puna.*

KAU

You shouldn't expect to find sparkling white-sand beaches on the rugged and rocky coasts of Kau, and you won't. What you will find is something a bit rarer and well worth the visit: black- and green-sand beaches. And there's the chance to see the endangered Hawaiian green sea turtles close up.

Papakolea Beach (*Green Sands Beach*). Tired of the same old gold-, white-, or black-sand beach? Then how about a green-sand beach? You'll need good hiking shoes or sneakers to get to this olive-green crescent, one of the most unusual beaches on the island. It lies at the base of Puu O Mahana, at Mahana Bay, where a cinder cone formed during an early eruption of Mauna Loa. The greenish tint is caused by an accumulation of olivine crystals that form in volcanic eruptions. The dry, barren landscape is totally surreal but stunning, as aquamarine waters lap on green sand against reddish cliffs. The surf is often rough, and swimming is hazardous due to strong currents, so caution is advised. Drive down to Ka Lae (South Point); at the end of the 12-mile paved road, take the road to the left and park at the end. ⚠ Anyone trying to charge for parking is running a scam. To reach the beach, follow the 2¼-mile coastal trail, which ends in a steep and dangerous descent down the cliff side on an unimproved trail. The hike takes about two hours each way and it can get windy, so bring lots of drinking water. Four-wheel-drive vehicles are no longer permitted on the trail. **Amenities:** none. **Best for:** solitude. ⊠ *Hwy. 11, 2½ miles northeast of South Point, Naalehu.*

Fodor's Choice ★ **Punaluu Black Sand Beach Park.** A great stop on a south southeast–bound trip to the volcano, this easily accessible black-sand beach is backed by low dunes, brackish ponds, and tall coco palms. The shoreline is jagged, reefed, and rocky. Most days, large groups of sea turtles nap on the sand—a stunning sight. Resist the urge to get too close or disturb them; they're protected by federal and state law and fines for harassment can be hefty. Removing black sand is also prohibited. ⚠ Extremely strong rip currents prevail, so only experienced ocean swimmers should

SUN SAFETY

Hawaii's weather—seemingly never-ending warm, sunny days with gentle trade winds—can be enjoyed with good sun sense. Because of Hawaii's subtropical location, at 19 degrees north latitude, the sun here is particularly strong year-round, with a daily UV average of 14. Visitors should take precautions to avoid sunburns and long-term risks due to sun exposure.

Plan beach, golf, hiking, and other outdoor activities for the early morning or late afternoon, avoiding the sun between 10 am and 4 pm, when it's the strongest.

Apply a broad-spectrum sunscreen with a sun protection factor (SPF) of at least 30. Zinc products are best for the reefs, but some marine reserves don't allow sunscreen at all. Check posted instructions.

Cover areas that are most prone to burning like your nose, shoulders,

tops of feet, and ears. And don't forget to use lip balm with sunscreen. Apply sunscreen at least 30 minutes before you plan to be outdoors and reapply every two hours, even when it's cloudy. Clouds scatter sunlight so you can still burn on an overcast day.

Wear light, protective clothing, such as a long-sleeved shirt and pants, broad-brimmed hat, and sunglasses.

Stay in the shade whenever possible—especially on the beach—by using an umbrella. Remember that sand and water can reflect up to 85% of the sun's damaging rays.

Children need extra protection from the sun. Apply sunscreen frequently and liberally on children over six months of age, and minimize their time in the sun. Sunscreen is not recommended for children under six months.

consider getting in the water here. Popular with locals and tour buses alike, this beach park can get very busy, especially on weekends (the north parking lot is usually quieter). Shade from palm trees provides an escape from the sun, and at the northern end of the beach, near the boat ramp, lie the ruins of Kaneeleele Heiau, an old Hawaiian temple. The area was a sugar port until the 1946 tsunami destroyed the buildings. Developers tried to bring a resort experience here in the early 1990s, but that has mostly failed. (You'll drive by a few abandoned resort buildings on your way to the beach.) ■ TIP➔ Bring your camera and a picnic lunch. **Amenities:** parking (no fee); showers; toilets. **Best for:** walking. ⊠ *Hwy. 11, 27 miles south of Hawaii Volcanoes National Park between mile markers 55 and 56, Naalehu* ☏ *808/961–8311.*

4

WATER ACTIVITIES AND TOURS

Updated by Kristina Anderson

The ancient Hawaiians, who took much of their daily sustenance from the ocean, also enjoyed playing in the water. In fact, surfing was the sport of kings. Though it's easy to be lulled into whiling away the day baking in the sun on a white-, gold-, black-, or green-sand beach, getting into or onto the water is a highlight of most trips.

All of the Hawaiian Islands are surrounded by the Pacific Ocean, making them some of the world's greatest natural playgrounds. But certain experiences are even better on the Big Island: nighttime scuba diving trips to see manta rays; deep-sea fishing in Kona's fabled waters, where dozens of Pacific blue marlin of 1,000 pounds or more have been caught; and kayaking among the dolphins in Kealakekua Bay, to name a few.

From any point on the Big Island, the ocean is nearby. From body boarding and snorkeling to kayaking and surfing, there is a water sport for everyone. For most activities, you can rent gear and go it alone or with a group excursion with an experienced guide, who can offer security as well as special insights into Hawaiian marine life and culture. Want to try surfing? You can take lessons that promise to have you standing the first day out.

The Kona and Kohala coasts of West Hawaii boast the largest number of ocean sports outfitters and tour operators. They operate from the small-boat harbors and piers in Kailua-Kona, Keauhou, Kawaihae, and at the Kohala Coast resorts. There are also several outfitters in the East Hawaii and Hilo areas.

As a general rule, the waves are gentler here than on the other Islands, but there are a few things to be aware of. First, don't turn your back on the ocean. It's unlikely, but if conditions are right, a wave could come along and push you face-first into the sand or drag you out to sea. Second, when the Big Island does experience high surf, dangerous conditions prevail and can change rapidly. Watch the ocean for a few minutes before going out. Third, realize that ultimately you must keep yourself safe. We strongly encourage you to obey lifeguards and heed

DID YOU KNOW?

Kealakekua Bay, with its calm
waters and spinner dolphins,
is an excellent spot for kayaking as well as snorkeling.
Morning is the best time to
see dolphins.

the advice of outfitters from whom you rent equipment. It could save your trip, or even your life.

ADVENTURE CRUISES

Lava Ocean Adventures. The best lava boat operator on the island, Captain Shane Turpin takes the 24-passenger *Lava Kai* near lava flows spilling out of Kilauea's southeast vent. This is a once-in-a-lifetime chance to see molten earth hitting the sea in Mother Nature's most thrilling show. Tours are volcano dependent and leave from Pohoiki Boat Ramp at 5:30 am. ⊠ *Pohoiki* ☎ *808/966–4200* ⊕ *www.seelava.com* 🖃 *$150.*

BODY BOARDING AND BODYSURFING

According to the movies, in the Old West there was always friction between cattle ranchers and sheep ranchers. A somewhat similar situation exists between surfers and body boarders (and between surfers and stand-up paddleboarders). That's why they generally keep to their own separate areas. Often the body boarders, who lie on their stomachs on shorter boards, stay closer to shore and leave the outside breaks to the board surfers. Or the board surfers may stick to one side of the beach and the body boarders to the other. The truth is, body boarding (often called "boogie boarding," in homage to the first commercial manufacturer of this slick, little, flexible-foam board) is a blast. Most surfers also sometimes carve waves on a body board, no matter how much of a purist they claim to be. ■TIP➔ Novice body boarders should catch shore-break waves only. Ask lifeguards or locals for the best spots. You'll need a pair of short fins to get out to the bigger waves offshore (not recommended for newbies). As for bodysurfing, just catch a wave and make like Superman going faster than a speeding bullet.

BEST SPOTS

Fodor's Choice ★ **Hapuna Beach State Recreation Area.** Often considered one of the top 10 beaches in the world, Hapuna Beach State Recreation Area offers fine white sand, turquoise water, and easy rolling surf on most days, making it great for bodysurfing and body boarding at all levels. Ask the lifeguards—who only cover areas south of the rocky cliff that juts out near the middle of the beach—about conditions before heading into the water, especially in winter. Sometimes northwest swells create a dangerous undertow. Parking costs $5. ⊠ *Hwy. 19, near mile marker 69, just south of Mauna Kea Hotel, Kohala Coast* ⊕ *www.hawaiistateparks. org/parks/hawaii/hapuna.cfm.*

Honolii Cove. North of Hilo, this is the best body boarding spot on the east side of the island. ⊠ *Off Hwy. 19, near mile marker 4, Hilo.*

Magic Sands Beach Park (*White Sands Beach*). This white-sand, shore-break cove is great for beginning to intermediate bodysurfing and body boarding. Sometimes in winter, much of the sand here washes out to sea and forms a sandbar just offshore, creating fun wave conditions. Also known as White Sands, it's popular and can get crowded with locals,

Body boarding is popular on the Big Island.

especially when school is out. Watch for nasty rip currents at high tide. ■TIP→ If you're not using fins, wear reef shoes for protection against sharp rocks. ⊠ *Alii Dr., just north of mile marker 4, Kailua-Kona.*

EQUIPMENT

Equipment-rental shacks are located at many beaches and boat harbors, along the highway, and at most resorts. Body board rental rates are around $12–$15 per day and around $60 per week. Ask the vendor to throw in a pair of fins—some will for no extra charge.

Orchid Land Surf Shop. This shop has a wide variety of surf and other water sports equipment for sale or rent. It stocks professional custom surfboards, body boards, and surf apparel, and also does repairs. You can rent a body board for $12 a day, a surfboard for $20 a day. ⊠ *262 Kamehameha Ave., Hilo* ☎ *808/935–1533* ⊕ *www.orchidlandsurf.com.*

Pacific Vibrations. This family-owned surf shop—in business 35 years—holds the distinction of being the oldest, smallest surf shop in the world. Even at a compact 400 square feet, this place stocks tons of equipment, surf wear, surf gear, and GoPro cameras. You can rent a surfboard (under $20), stand-up paddleboard, or body board—$5 a day but you have to buy or bring your own fins. Right in the heart of downtown Kailua Town, it's worth a stop for the authentic Hawaii surf vibe. ⊠ *75-5702 Likana La. #B, at Alii Dr., Kailua-Kona* ☎ *808/329–4140.*

DEEP-SEA FISHING

The Kona Coast has some of the world's most exciting "blue-water" fishing. Although July, August, and September are peak months, with the best fishing and a number of tournaments, charter fishing goes on year-round. You don't have to compete to experience the thrill of landing a Pacific blue marlin or other big-game fish. Some 60 charter boats, averaging 26 to 58 feet, are available for hire, all of them out of **Honokohau Harbor,** north of Kailua-Kona.

Kona waters have the reputation of producing large marlin, mostly the Pacific blue variety. According to records, 63 marlin weighing 1,000 pounds or more have been caught off the Kona Coast, which has come to be known as "Grander Alley," a reference to the number of big fish that inhabit its waters. The largest "grander" ever, caught in 1984, weighed in at 1,649 pounds.

For an exclusive charter, prices generally range from $600 to $950 for a half-day trip (about four hours) and $800 to $1,600 for a full day at sea (about eight hours). For share charters, rates are about $100 to $140 per person for a half day and $200 for a full day. If fuel prices increase, expect charter costs to rise. Most boats are licensed to take up to six passengers, in addition to the crew. Tackle, bait, and ice are furnished, but you usually have to bring your own lunch. You won't be able to keep your catch, although if you ask, many captains will send you home with a few fillets.

Hawaiian International Billfish Tournament. Pacific blue marlin are sought after by deep-sea anglers the world over, who come to Kona's fabled waters, most notably during this five-day tournament in August. Since 1959, this granddaddy of big-game-fishing tourneys has attracted super-competitive teams in the finest boats imaginable. The powerful animals are caught or tagged and released. Occasionally, Kona waters produce a grander—over 1,000 pounds. ☎ *808/836–3422* ⊕ *www. hibtfishing.com.*

Honokohau Harbor's Fuel Dock. Show up around 11:30 am and watch the weigh-in of the day's catch from the morning charters, or around 3:30 pm for the afternoon charters. Weigh-ins are fun when the big ones come in, but it's not a sure thing. ■**TIP→** On Kona's Waterfront Row, look for the "Grander's Wall" of anglers with their 1,000-pound-plus prizes. ⊠ *Honokohau Harbor, Kealakehe Pkwy. at Hwy. 11, Kailua-Kona.*

BOATS AND CHARTERS

Before you sign up with anyone, think about the kind of trip you want. Looking for a romantic cruise? A rockin' good time with your buddies? Serious fishing in one of the "secret spots?" A family-friendly excursion? Be sure to describe your expectations so a booking agent can match you with a captain and a boat that suit your style.

Bwana Sportfishing. Full-, half-, quarter-, three-quarter-day, and over-night charters are available on the 46-foot *Bwana.* The boat features the latest electronics, top-of-the-line equipment, and air-conditioned cabins. Captain Teddy comes from a fishing family; father Peter is retired but still affiliated with the Kona Charter Skippers Association. ⊠ *Honokohau Harbor, Slip H-17, 74-381 Kealakehe Pkwy., just south of Kona airport, Kailua-Kona* ☎ *808/936–5168* ⊕ *www.teddyhoogs. com* ✉ *From $1,250.*

The Charter Desk at Honokohau Harbor. With about 60 boats on the books, this place can take care of almost anyone. You can make arrangements through hotel activity desks, but it's better to go directly to the desk at the harbor and look things over for yourself. ⊠ *Honokohau Harbor Fuel Dock, 74-381 Kealakehe Pkwy., Kailua-Kona* ☎ *808/329–5735, 888/566–2487* ⊕ *www.charterdesk.com.*

Charter Locker. This company offers half- and full-day charter fishing trips on 30- to 52-foot vessels. The luxurious *Blue Hawaii* has air-conditioned staterooms for overnight trips. Rates depend on the boat. ⊠ *Honokohau Harbor #16, 74-381 Kealakehe Pkwy., just south of Kona airport, Kailua-Kona* ☎ *808/326–2553* ⊕ *www.charterlocker.com.*

Humdinger Sportfishing. This game fisher guide has more than three decades of fishing experience in Kona waters, and the expert crew are marlin specialists. The 37-foot *Humdinger* has the latest in electronics and top-line rods and reels. ⊠ *Honokohau Harbor, Slip B-4, 74-381 Kealakehe Pkwy., Kailua-Kona* ☎ *808/936–3034, 800/926–2374* ⊕ *www.humdingersportfishing.com* ✉ *From $600.*

Illusions Sportfishing. Captain Tim Hicks is one of Kona's top fishing-tourney producers, with 20 years of experience. The 39-foot *Illusions* is fully equipped with galley, restrooms, an air-conditioned cabin, plus the latest in fishing equipment. ⊠ *Honokohau Harbor, 74-381 Kealakehe Pkwy., just south of Kona airport, Kailua-Kona* ☎ *808/960–7371* ⊕ *www.illusionssportfishing.com* ✉ *From $550.*

Kona Charter Skippers Association. In business since 1956, this company can help arrange half-day and full-day exclusive or share charters on several boats. Captain Pete is an old salt with plenty of Kona sea stories. ⊠ *Kailua-Kona* ☎ *808/936–5168.*

KAYAKING

The leeward west coast areas of the Big Island are protected for the most part from the northeast trade winds, making for ideal, near-shore kayaking conditions. There are miles and miles of uncrowded Kona and Kohala coastline to explore, presenting close-up views of stark, raw, lava-rock shores and cliffs; lava-tube sea caves; pristine, secluded coves; and deserted beaches.

Ocean kayakers can get close to shore—where the commercial snorkel and dive cruise boats can't reach. This opens up all sorts of possibilities for adventure, such as near-shore snorkeling among the expansive coral reefs and lava rock formations that teem with colorful tropical fish and Hawaiian green sea turtles. You can pull ashore at a quiet cove for a picnic and a plunge into turquoise waters. With a good coastal map and some advice from the kayak vendor, you might paddle by ancient battlegrounds, burial sites, bathing ponds for Hawaiian royalty, or old villages.

Kayaking can be enjoyed via a guided tour or on a self-guided paddling excursion. Either way, the kayak outfitter can brief you on recommended routes, safety, and how to help preserve and protect Hawaii's ocean resources and coral reef system.

■ Whether you're a beginning or experienced kayaker, choose appropriate location and conditions for your excursion.

■ Ask the outfitter about local conditions and hazards, such as tides, currents, and advisories.

■ Beginners should practice getting into and out of the kayak and capsizing (called a huli, the Hawaiian word for "flip") in shallow water.

■ Before departing, secure the kayak's hatches to prevent water intake.

■ Use a line to attach the paddle to the kayak to avoid losing it.

■ Always use a life vest or jacket, and wear a rash guard and plenty of sunblock.

■ Carry appropriate amounts of water and food.

■ Don't kayak alone. Create a float plan; tell someone where you're going and when you will return.

BEST SPOTS

Hilo Bay. This is a favorite kayak spot. The best place to put in is at **Reeds Bay Beach Park.** Parking is plentiful and free at the bayfront. Most afternoons you'll share the bay with local paddling clubs. Stay inside the breakwater unless the ocean is calm (or you're feeling unusually adventurous). Conditions range from extremely calm to quite choppy. ⊠ *Banyan Way and Banyan Dr., 1 mile from downtown Hilo.*

Kailua Bay and Kamakahonu Beach. The small, sandy beach that fronts the Courtyard King Kamehameha's Kona Beach Hotel is a nice place to rent or launch kayaks. You can unload in the cul-de-sac and park in nearby free lots. The water here is especially calm and the surroundings are historic and scenic. ⊠ *Alii Dr., next to Kailua Pier, Kailua-Kona.*

Kealakekua Bay State Historical Park. The excellent snorkeling and likelihood of seeing dolphins (morning is best) make Kealakekua Bay one of the most popular kayaking spots on the Big Island. An ocean conservation district, the bay is usually calm and tranquil. (Use caution and common sense during surf advisories.) Tall coral pinnacles and clear visibility surrounding the monument also make for stupendous snorkeling. Because of new regulations, only a few operators have permits to lead kayak tours in the park. ⊠ *Napoopoo Rd and Manini Bch. Rd., Captain Cook ⊕ www.hawaiistateparks.org/parks/hawaii.*

Oneo Bay. Right downtown, this is usually a placid place to kayak. It's fairly easy to get to. If you can't find parking along the road, there's a free lot across the street from the library and farmers' market. ⊠ *Alii Dr., Kailua-Kona.*

EQUIPMENT, LESSONS, AND TOURS

There are several rental outfitters on Highway 11 between Kainaliu and Captain Cook, but only a few are specially permitted to lead kayak trips in Kealakekua Bay.

Aloha Kayak Co. This outfitter is one of the few that is permitted to guide tours to the stunningly beautiful Kealakekua Bay, leaving from Napoopoo, including about 1½ hours at the Captain Cook Monument. The 3½-hour morning and afternoon tours ($99) include snacks and drinks. Local guides tell about the area's cultural, historical, and natural significance. You may see dolphins, but you must watch them from a distance only, as this is a protected marine reserve. Keauhou Bay tours are also offered: a four-hour morning tour for $89, a 2½-hour afternoon version for $69, and a two-hour evening manta ray tour, $89. Kayak rentals are $35 for a single, $60 for a double, and $85 for a triple. Stand-up paddleboard lessons at Keauhou Bay cost $75. ⊠ *79-7248 Mamalahoa Hwy., across from Teshima's Restaurant, Honalo* ☎ *808/322–2868, 877/322–1444* ⊕ *www.alohakayak.com.*

Aloha Living Services. Island-born Jonathon Ditto specializes in kayaking on the Kohala Coast, including Puako, and in teaching respectful, eco-friendly symbiosis with this pristine area. Private guided tours are available, and he also rents kayaks, boogie boards, stand-up paddleboards, snorkel gear, and road and mountain bikes. Free delivery. ⊠ *61-3636 Kawaihae Rd., Waimea* ☎ *808/430–0991* ⊕ *www.alohalivingservices. com* 🚣 *Rentals from $25.*

Fodor'sChoice
★
Kona Boys. On the highway above Kealakekua Bay, this full-service, environmentally conscious outfitter handles kayaks, body boards, surfboards, stand-up paddleboards, and snorkeling gear. Single-seat and double kayaks are offered. Surfing and stand-up paddling lessons are available for private or group instruction. Tours such as their Morning Magic and Midday Meander include two half-day guided kayaking and snorkeling trips with gear, lunch, snacks, and beverages. Kona Boys also run a beach shack fronting the King Kamehameha's Kona Beach Hotel and are happy to give advice on the changing regulations regarding South Kona bay usage. ■TIP→ The town location offers Hawaiian outrigger canoe rides, SUP lessons, and rentals of beach mats, chairs, and other gear. ⊠ *79-7539 Mamalahoa Hwy., Kealakekua* ☎ *808/328–1234, 808/329–2345* ⊕ *www.konaboys.com* 🚣 *Tours from $99; kayaks from $47; surf/paddle lessons from $75* 🚣 *75–5660 Palani Rd., Kailua-Kona.*

Ocean Safari's Kayak Adventures. On the guided 3½-hour morning sea-cave tour that begins in Keauhou Bay, you can visit lava-tube sea caves along the coast, then swim ashore for a snack. The kayaks will already be on the beach, so you won't have to hassle with transporting them. The cost is $68.50 per person. A two-hour, dolphin-spotting tour costs $35 per person. Kayak daily rental rates are $25 for singles and $40 for doubles. Stand-up boards are $25 for two hours. If you want a lesson, it's $60 including the board (two-person minimum). ⊠ *End of Kamehameha III Rd., next to Sheraton Kona Resort & Spa at Keauhou Bay, Kailua-Kona* ☎ *808/326–4699* ⊕ *www.oceansafariskayaks.com.*

4

Pineapple Park. Affiliated with a hostel with locations in Hilo, Kona, and Mountain View, Pineapple Park's Kealakekua location rents kayaks for $50 for a single and $65 for a double. The rental price includes paddles, life jackets, bags to keep all your gear dry, and harnesses to strap the kayak to your car. ⊠ *81-6363 Mamalahoa Hwy., Kealakekua* ☎ *808/323–2224, 877/800–3800* ⊕ *www.pineapple-park.com.*

SAILING

For old salts and novice sailors alike, there's nothing like a cruise on the Kona or Kohala Coast. Calm waters, serene shores, and the superb scenery of Mauna Kea, Mauna Loa, and Hualalai, the Big Island's primary volcanic peaks, make for a great sailing adventure. You can drop a line over the side and try your luck at catching dinner, or grab some snorkel gear and explore when the boat drops anchor in one of the quiet coves and bays. A cruise may well be the most relaxing and adventurous part of a Big Island visit.

BOATS AND CHARTERS

Maile Charters. Private sailing charters for 2 to 16 passengers are available on the *Maile*, a 50-foot Gulfstar sloop. You choose the itinerary, whether it's watching for dolphins and whales, snorkeling around coral reefs, or enjoying appetizers as the sun sinks below the horizon. Morning snorkels, sunset sails, and overnight trips are offered. Snorkeling equipment is provided, and food can be catered. ⊠ *Kawaihae Harbor, Hwy. 270, on the dock, Kawaihae* ☎ *808/960–9744* ⊕ *www. adventuresailing.com* 🕿 *From $997.*

SCUBA DIVING

The Big Island's underwater world is the setting for a dramatic diving experience. With generally warm and calm waters, vibrant coral reefs and rock formations, and plunging underwater drop-offs, the Kona and Kohala coasts offer some premier scuba diving. There are also some good dive locations in East Hawaii, not far from the Hilo area. Divers find much to occupy their time, including marine reserves teeming with tropical reef fish, Hawaiian green sea turtles, an occasional and critically endangered Hawaiian monk seal, and even some playful spinner dolphins. On special night dives to see manta rays, divers descend with bright underwater lights that attract plankton, which in turn attract these otherworldly creatures. The best spots to dive are all on the west coast.

BEST SPOTS

Garden Eel Cove. Only accessible by boat, this is a great place to see manta rays somersaulting overhead as they feast on a plankton supper. It's also home to hundreds of tiny garden eels darting out from their

Continued on page 130

SNORKELING IN HAWAII

The waters surrounding the Hawaiian Islands are filled with life—from giant manta rays cruising off the Big Island's Kona Coast to humpback whales giving birth in the warm waters surrounding Maui. Dip your head beneath the surface to experience a spectacularly colorful world: pairs of milletseed butterflyfish dart back and forth, redlipped parrotfish snack on coral algae, and spotted eagle rays flap past like silent spaceships. Sea turtles bask at the surface while tiny wrasses give them the equivalent of a shave and a haircut. The water quality is typically outstanding; many sites afford 30-foot-plus visibility. On snorkel cruises, you can often stare from the boat rail right down to the bottom.

Certainly few destinations are as accommodating to every level of snorkeler as Hawaii. Beginners can tromp in from sandy beaches while more advanced divers descend to shipwrecks, reefs, craters, and sea arches just offshore. Because of Hawaii's extreme isolation, the island chain has fewer fish species than Fiji or the Caribbean—but many of the fish that are here exist nowhere else. The Hawaiian waters are home to the highest percentage of endemic fish in the world.

The key to enjoying the underwater world is slowing down. Look carefully. Listen. You might hear the strange crackling sound of shrimp tunneling through coral, or you may hear whales singing to one another during winter. A shy octopus may drift along the ocean's floor beneath you. If you're hooked, pick up a waterproof fishkey from Long's Drugs. You can brag later that you've looked the Hawaiian turkeyfish in the eye.

Picasso Triggerfish	Milletseed Butterflyfish*	Yellow Tang
Moorish Idol	Hawaiian Whitespotted Toby*	Saddleback Wrasse*
Redlip Parrotfish	Hawaiian Turkeyfish*	Zebra Moray Eel
Stocky Hawkfish	Green Sea Turtle (Honu)	Spotted Eagle Ray

*endemic to Hawaii

POLYNESIA'S FIRST CELESTIAL NAVIGATORS: HONU

Honu is the Hawaiian name for two native sea turtles, the hawksbill and the green sea turtle. Little is known about these dinosaur-age marine reptiles, though snorkelers regularly see them foraging for *limu* (seaweed) and the occasional jellyfish in Hawaiian waters. Most female honu nest in the uninhabited Northwestern Hawaiian Islands, but a few sociable ladies nest on Maui and Big Island beaches. Scientists suspect that they navigate the seas via magnetism— sensing the earth's poles. Amazingly, they will journey up to 800 miles to nest—it's believed that they return to their own birth sites. After about 60 days of incubation, nestlings emerge from the sand at night and find their way back to the sea by the light of the stars.

SNORKELING

Many of Hawaii's reefs are accessible from shore.

The basics: Sure, you can take a deep breath, hold your nose, squint your eyes, and stick your face in the water in an attempt to view submerged habitats . . . but why not protect your eyes, retain your ability to breathe, and keep your hands free to paddle about when exploring underwater? That's what snorkeling is all about.

Equipment needed: A mask, snorkel (the tube attached to the mask), and fins. In deeper waters (any depth over your head), life jackets are advised.

Steps to success: If you've never snorkeled before, it's natural to feel a bit awkward at first, so don't sweat it. Breathing through a mask and tube, and wearing a pair of fins take getting used to. Like any activity, you build confidence and comfort through practice.

If you're new to snorkeling, begin by submerging your face in shallow water or a swimming pool and breathing calmly through the snorkel while gazing through the mask.

Next you need to learn how to clear water out of your mask and snorkel, an essential skill since splashes can send water into tube openings and masks can leak. Some snorkels have built-in drainage valves, but if a tube clogs, you can force water up and out by exhaling through your mouth. Clearing a mask is similar: lift your head from water while pulling forward on mask to drain. Some masks have built-in purge valves, but those without can be cleared underwater by pressing the top to the forehead and blowing out your nose (charming, isn't it?), allowing air to bubble into the mask, pushing water out the bottom. If it sounds hard, it really isn't. Just try it a few times and you'll soon feel like a pro.

Now your goal is to get friendly with fins—you want them to be snug but not too tight—and learn how to propel yourself with them. Fins won't help you float, but they will give you a leg up, so to speak, on smoothly moving through the water or treading water (even when upright) with less effort.

Flutter stroking is the most efficient underwater kick, and the farther your foot bends forward the more leg power you'll be able to transfer to the water and the farther you'll travel with each stroke. Flutter kicking movements involve alternately separating the legs and then drawing them back together. When your legs separate, the leg surface encounters drag from the water, slowing you down. When your legs are drawn back together, they produce a force pushing you forward. If your kick creates more forward force than it causes drag, you'll move ahead.

Submerge your fins to avoid fatigue rather than having them flailing above the water when you kick, and keep your arms at your side to reduce drag. You are in the water—stretched out, face down, and snorkeling happily away—but that doesn't mean you can't hold your breath and go deeper in the water for a closer look at some fish or whatever catches your attention. Just remember that when you do this, your snorkel will be submerged, too, so you won't be breathing (you'll be holding your breath). You can dive head-first, but going feet-first is easier and less scary for most folks, taking less momentum. Before full immersion, take several long, deep breaths to clear carbon dioxide from your lungs.

If your legs tire, flip onto your back and tread water with inverted fin motions while resting. If your mask fogs, wash condensation from lens and clear water from mask.

TIPS FOR SAFE SNORKELING

- Snorkel with a buddy and stay together.
- Plan your entry and exit points prior to getting in the water.
- Swim into the current on entering and then ride the current back to your exit point.
- Carry your flippers into the water and then put them on, as it's difficult to walk in them.
- Make sure your mask fits properly and is not too loose.
- Pop your head above the water periodically to ensure you aren't drifting too far out, or too close to rocks.
- Think of the water as someone else's home—don't take anything that doesn't belong to you, or leave any trash behind.
- Don't touch any sea creatures; they may sting.
- Wear a T-shirt over your swimsuit to help protect you from being fried by the sun.
- When in doubt, don't go without a snorkeling professional; try a guided tour.

Green sea turtle (Honu)

HAWAII'S MANTA RAYS

Manta rays, one of Hawaii's most fascinating marine-life species, can be seen on some nighttime diving excursions along the Kona and Kohala coasts. They are generally completely harmless to divers, though of course no wild animal is totally predictable. If you don't want to get wet, head to the beach fronting the Mauna Kea Beach Hotel, on the Kohala Coast, or to the Sheraton Kona Resort & Spa at Keauhou Bay, where each evening, visitors gather by the hotel's lights to watch manta rays feed in the shallows.

■ The manta ray (*Manta birostris*), called the devil fish by some, is known as *hahalua* by Hawaiians.

■ Its winglike fins, reaching up to 20 feet wide, allow the ray to skim through the water like a bird gliding through air.

■ The manta ray uses the two large flap-like lobes extending from its eyes to funnel food to its mouth. It eats microscopic plankton, small fish, and tiny crustaceans.

■ Closely related to the shark, the manta can weigh more than 3,000 pounds.

■ Its skeleton is made of cartilage, not bone.

■ A female ray gives birth to one or two young at a time; pups can be 45 inches long and weigh 20 pounds at birth.

sandy homes. There's a steep drop-off and lots of marine life. ⊠ *Rte. 19, near Kona airport, Kailua-Kona.*

Manta Village. Booking with a night-dive operator is required for the short boat ride to this area, one of Kona's best night-dive spots. If you're a diving or snorkeling fanatic, it's well worth it to experience manta rays drawn by the lights of the hotel. ■TIP→ If night swimming isn't your cup of tea, you can catch a glimpse of the majestic creatures from the Sheraton's deck. ⊠ *78-128 Ehukai St., off Sheraton Kona Resort & Spa at Keauhou Bay, Kailua-Kona.*

Pawai Bay Marine Preserve. Clear waters, abundant reef life, and interesting coral formations make Pawai Bay Marine Preserve ideal for diving. Explore sea caves, arches, and rock formations. Located one-half mile north of Old Airport, it can be busy with snorkel boats, but is an easy dive spot. ⊠ *Kuakini Hwy., north of Old Kona Airport Park, Kailua-Kona.*

Puako. Just south of Hapuna Beach State Recreation Area, beautiful Puako offers easy entry to some fine reef diving. Deep chasms, sea caves, and rock arches abound with varied marine life. ⊠ *Puako Rd., off Hwy. 19, Kohala Coast.*

EQUIPMENT, LESSONS, AND TOURS

There are quite a few good dive shops along the Kona Coast. Most are happy to take on all customers, but a few focus on specific types of trips. Trip prices vary, depending on whether you're already certified and whether you're diving from a boat or from shore. Instruction with PADI, SDI, or TDI certification in three to five days costs $600 to $850. Most instructors rent dive equipment and snorkel gear, as well as underwater cameras. Most organize otherworldly manta ray dives at night and whale-watching cruises in season.

Jack's Diving Locker. Good for novice and intermediate divers, Jack's has trained and certified tens of thousands of divers since 1981, with classrooms and a dive pool for instruction. Four boats that accommodate 10 to 24 divers (boats at capacity can feel cramped) visit more than 80 established dive sites along the Kona coast, yielding sightings of turtles, manta rays, garden eels, and schools of barracuda. Snorkelers can choose from morning trips and manta night trips, and dolphin-watch and reef snorkels. Combined sunset/night manta ray dives are offered as well. ■TIP→ Kona's best deal for scuba newbies is Jack's two-part introductory dive from Kailua Pier: pool instruction plus a one-tank beach dive, or a two-tank boat dive is offered as well. ⊠ 75-5813 Alii Dr., Kailua-Kona ☎ 808/329–7585, 800/345–4807 ⊕ www. jacksdivinglocker.com ⊠ Snorkel trips from $65.

Kohala Divers. The Kohala Coast's lava-tube caves, vibrant coral reefs, and interesting sealife make it a great diving destination. This full-service PADI dive shop has been certifying divers since 1984. A one-day intro dive course has you in the ocean the same day. A four-day, full certification course is offered, too. The company also rents equipment and takes divers to the best diving spots. ⊠ Kawaihae Harbor Shopping Center, Hwy. 270, Kawaihae ☎ 808/882–7774 ⊕ www.kohaladivers. com ⊠ One-day dive course, $175; four-day certification $650; two-tank dive $139 plus $35 for gear; snorkel rentals $35 per week.

Nautilus Dive Center. Across from Hilo Bay, Nautilus Dive Center is the oldest and most experienced dive shop on the island. It offers a broad range of services for both beginners and experienced divers. Owner Bill De Rooy has been diving around the Big Island for 30 years, and can provide you with underwater maps and show you the best dive spots in Hilo. He also provides PADI instruction and likes to repair gear. ⊠ 382 Kamehameha Ave., Hilo ☎ 808/935–6939 ⊕ www.nautilusdivehilo. com ⊠ Dive-equipment rentals from $35 per day.

Ocean Eco Tours and Harbor Dive Center. This eco-friendly outfitter is eager to share a wealth of ocean knowledge with beginners and advanced divers alike. Six to ten divers and snorkelers head out on one of two 30-foot crafts, and the day's destination—from among 80 sites, both north and south, that feature good reefs and other prime underwater spots—varies based on ocean conditions. Four-hour daytime dives or a nighttime dive to swim with manta rays are offered. PADI open-water certification can be completed in three or four days. Seasonal whale-watch tours are also offered. Ride-alongs are welcome on all charters. ⊠ Honokohau Harbor, 74-425 Kealakehe Pkwy., Kailua-Kona ☎ 808/324–7873, 808/331–2121 ⊕ www.oceanecotours.com ⊠ Excursions from $129; PADI open-water certification $650; whale-watch tours $95.

Shan's Scuba. For a personalized scuba-certification experience, certified PADI MSDT instructor Shannon Rhodes offers complete certification. Specializing in small groups, she's particularly good with those who feel intimidated about learning to dive. If you plan ahead, you can learn online with PADI before arrival, and Shannon will certify you in the water for a discounted price. ✉ *Captain Cook* ☎ *985/515–5990* 🖰 *Certification $400 ($300 with pre-online course).*

Torpedo Tours. Owner-operators Mike and Nikki Milligan, both dive instructors, love to take divers out on their 40-foot custom dive boat, the *Na Pali Kai II.* They specialize in small groups, which means you'll get personalized attention and spend more time diving and less time waiting to dive. Morning excursions feature two-tank dives. Both snorkelers and divers can try the torpedo scooters—devices that let you cover more area with less kicking. Manta ray night diving and snorkeling at Garden Eel Cove are offered. This is the only company that fishes between dives. Scout, the dive dog, loves to swim with the sea life. ✉ *Honokohau Harbor, 74-425 Kealakehe Pkwy., Kailua-Kona* ☎ *808/938–0405* ⊕ *www.torpedotours.com* 🖰 *Dives from $119; snorkeling from $85; torpedo scooters $30.*

SNORKELING

A favorite pastime on the Big Island, snorkeling is perhaps one of the easiest and most enjoyable water activities for visitors. By floating on the surface, peering through your mask, and breathing through your snorkel, you can see lava rock formations, sea arches, sea caves, and coral reefs teeming with colorful tropical fish. While the Kona and Kohala coasts boast more beaches, bays, and quiet coves to snorkel, the east side around Hilo and at Kapoho are also great places to get in the water.

If you don't bring your own equipment, you can easily rent all the gear needed from a beach activities vendor, who will happily provide directions to the best sites for snorkeling in the area. For access to deeper water and assistance from an experienced crew, you can opt for a snorkel cruise. Excursions generally range from two to five hours; be sure you know what equipment and food is included.

BEST SPOTS

Kahaluu Beach Park. Since ancient times, the waters around Kahaluu Beach have provided traditional throw net–fishing grounds. With super-easy access, the bay offers good swimming and outstanding snorkeling, revealing turtles, angelfish, parrot fish, needlefish, puffer fish, and many types of tang. ■ TIP➔ **Stay inside the breakwater and don't stray too far, as dangerous and unpredictable currents swirl outside the bay.** ✉ *Alii Dr., Kailua-Kona.*

Kapoho Tide Pools. Here you'll find the best snorkeling on the Hilo side. Fingers of lava from the 1960 flow that destroyed the town of Kapoho jut into the sea to form a network of tide pools. Conditions near the shore are excellent for beginners, while farther out is challenging enough for experienced snorkelers. ✉ *End of Kapoho-Kai Rd., off Hwy. 137, Hilo.*

Fodor's Choice ★ **Kealakekua Bay State Historical Park.** This protected Marine Life Conservation District is hands-down one of the best snorkeling spots on

The Kona Coast's relatively calm waters and colorful coral reefs offer excellent scuba diving.

the island, thanks to clear visibility, fabulous coral reefs, and generally calm waters. Pods of dolphins can be abundant, but they're protected under federal law and may not be disturbed or approached. Access to the area has been restricted in recent years, but a few companies are permitted to escort tours to the bay. ■TIP→ Overland access is difficult, so opt for one of the guided snorkel cruises permitted to moor here. ✉ Napoopoo, at end of Beach Rd. and Hwy. 160, Kailua-Kona ⊕ www.hawaiistateparks.org/parks/hawaii/index.cfm?park_id=46.

Magic Sands Beach Park. Also known as White Sands or Disappearing Sands Beach Park, this is a great place for beginning and intermediate snorkelers. In winter, it's also a prime spot to watch for whales. ✉ Alii Dr., Kailua-Kona.

Puuhonua O Honaunau. There is no swimming inside the national historical park here, but just to the north is a boat launch where the snorkeling is almost as good as at Kealakekua Bay. Parking is very limited. Be respectful of local fishermen who use the area. ✉ Hwy. 160, 20 miles south of Kailua-Kona.

EQUIPMENT, LESSONS, AND TOURS

FAMILY **Body Glove Cruises.** This operator is a good choice for families; kids love the waterslide and the high-dive platform, and parents appreciate the reasonable prices and good food. The 65-foot catamaran sets off for Red Hill from Kailua-Kona pier daily for a morning snorkel cruise that includes breakfast and a lunch buffet. A three-hour dinner cruise to Kealakekua Bay is a great way to relax, watch the sunset, and learn about Kona's history. It includes a buffet and live music. Seasonal whale-watch cruises are available, too. ⊠ *75-5629 Kuakini Hwy., Kailua-Kona* ☎ *808/326–7122, 800/551–8911* ⊕ *www.bodyglovehawaii. com* 🖃 *Snorkeling $128; dinner cruise $108; whale-watch cruises $88.*

Captain Zodiac Raft Expedition. A four-hour trip on a rigid-hull inflatable Zodiac raft takes you along the Kona Coast to explore gaping lava-tube caves, search for dolphins and turtles, and snorkel around Kealakekua Bay. Captains entertain you with Hawaiian folklore and Kona history. Trips depart at 8:15 am, 10 am, and 1 pm. A seasonal three-hour whale-watching cruise is offered. All equipment, such as Rx masks and flotation devices, are included. ⊠ *Honokohau Harbor, 74-425 Kealakehe Pkwy. #16, Kailua-Kona* ☎ *808/329–3199* ⊕ *www.captainzodiac.com* 🖃 *From $99 per person; whale-watching cruise $74.*

FAMILY **Fair Wind Cruises.** In business since 1971, Fair Wind offers morning and
Fodor'sChoice afternoon snorkel trips that are great for families with small kids. The
★ custom-built 60-foot catamaran has two 15-foot waterslides, freshwater showers, and a staircase descending directly into the water for easy access. Snorkel gear is included, with lots of pint-size flotation equipment and prescription masks available. The company is known for its delicious meals. Cruises last 4½ hours; 3½-hour snack cruises are offered, too. For ages seven and older, the company operates the *Hula Kai* snorkel cruise, a 55-foot luxury hydrofoil catamaran with theater-style seats for panoramic views. Their five-hour morning snorkel cruise includes a gourmet breakfast buffet and barbecue lunch. ⊠ *Keauhou Bay, 78-7130 Kaleiopapa St., Kailua-Kona* ☎ *808/322–2788, 800/677– 9461* ⊕ *www.fair-wind.com* 🖃 *Cruises from $75.*

SNUBA

Snuba—a cross between scuba and snorkeling—is a great choice for non-scuba divers who want to go a step beyond snorkeling. You and an instructor dive off a raft attached to a 25-foot hose and regulator, allowing a dive as deep as 20 feet or so. This is a good way to explore reefs a bit deeper than you can get to by snorkeling. If you need a break, the raft is ready to support you.

LESSONS

FAMILY **Snuba Big Island.** Meet your instructor at the beach rental area near the pool at the Courtyard King Kamehameha for a shallow-water dive experience without the hassle of scuba certification. Courses include a 30-minute class and a one-hour dive from the beach and three-hour boat dives that leave from Honakahou Harbor. Kids ages four to seven can come along on the Snuba Doo program, which keeps them doing snuba safely on the surface. The company also runs the 40-foot *Kaha Nuola* scuba boat, which accommodates all levels for a two-tank dive, not including gear. ⊠ *Courtyard King Kamehameha's Kona Beach Hotel, 75-5660 Palani Rd., Kailua-Kona* ☎ *808/324–1650* ⊕ *www. snubabigisland.com* 🖃 *Classes from $89; dives from $135.*

Passengers aboard the *Atlantis VII* submarine can visit the aquatic world without getting wet.

STAND-UP PADDLING

Stand-up paddling (or SUP for short), a sport with roots in the Hawaiian Islands, has grown popular worldwide in recent years. It's available for all skill levels and ages, and even novice stand-up paddleboarders can get up, stay up, and have a great time paddling around a protected bay or exploring the gorgeous coastline. All you need is a large body of water, a board, and a paddle. The workout tests your core strength as well as your balance, and offers an unusual vantage point from which to enjoy the beauty of island and ocean.

BEST SPOTS

Anaehoomalu Bay Beach (*A-Bay*). In this well-protected bay, even when surf is rough on the rest of the island, it's usually fairly calm here, though trades pick up in the afternoon. Boards are available for rent at the north end, and the safe area for stand-up paddling is marked by buoys. ⊠ *Off Waikoloa Beach Dr., south of Waikoloa Beach Marriott, Kohala Coast.*

Hilo Bay. At this favorite among locals, the best place to put in is at **Reeds Bay Beach Park.** Most afternoons you'll share the bay with local paddling clubs. Stay inside the breakwater unless the ocean is calm (or you're feeling unusually adventurous). Conditions range from extremely calm to quite choppy. ⊠ *Banyan Way and Banyan Dr., 1 mile from downtown Hilo.*

FAMILY **Kailua Bay and Kamakahonu Beach.** The small, sandy beach that fronts the Courtyard King Kamehameha's Kona Beach Hotel is great for kids; the water here is especially calm and gentle. If you're more daring, you can easily paddle out of the bay and along the coast for some great exploring. ⊠ *Alii Dr., next to Kailua Pier, Kailua-Kona.*

EQUIPMENT AND LESSONS

Ocean Sports. This outfitter rents equipment, offers lessons, and has the perfect location for easy access to the bay. Ocean Sports also operates rental shacks at the Hilton Waikoloa Village, Mauna Kea Beach Hotel, Whale Center Kawaihae, and Queens' MarketPlace. ⊠ *Waikoloa Beach Marriott, 69-275 Waikoloa Beach Dr., Waikoloa* ☎ *808/886–6666* ⊕ *www.hawaiioceansports.com* ⊠ *Stand-up paddleboard rentals $30 per hour.*

Sun and Sea Hawaii. This full-serve ocean sports shop rents 11-foot inflatable stand-up paddleboards for four hours and for a full day. Snorkel, scuba, surfing, and kayaking equipment is also available for sale or rent. ⊠ *Hilo Bay front, 244 Kamehameha Ave., Hilo* ☎ *808/934–0902* ⊠ *From $45.*

SUBMARINE TOURS

FAMILY **Atlantis Submarines.** Want to stay dry while exploring the undersea world? Climb aboard the 48-passenger *Atlantis X* submarine, anchored off Kailua Pier, across from Courtyard King Kamehameha's Kona Beach Hotel. A large glass dome in the bow and 13 viewing ports on each side allow clear views of the aquatic world more than 100 feet down. This is a great trip for kids and nonswimmers. ■ TIP➜ A $10 discount is available if you book online. ⊠ *75-5669 Alii Dr., Kailua-Kona* ☎ *808/326–7939, 800/381–0237* ⊕ *www.atlantisadventures.com* ⊠ *$109.*

SURFING

The Big Island does not have the variety of great surfing spots found on Oahu or Maui, but it does have decent waves and a thriving surf culture. Local kids and avid surfers frequent a number of places up and down the Kona and Kohala coasts of West Hawaii. Expect high surf in winter and much calmer activity during summer. The surf scene is much more active on the Kona side.

BEST SPOTS

Honolii Cove. North of Hilo, this is the best surfing spot on the eastern side of the island. It hosts many exciting surf contests. ⊠ *Off Hwy. 19, near mile marker 4, Hilo.*

Kahaluu Beach Park. Slightly north of this beach park and just past the calm lagoon filled with snorkelers, beginning and intermediate surfers can have a go at some nice waves. ⊠ *Alii Dr., Kailua-Kona.*

Old Kona Airport Park. This park is a good place for catching wave action. A couple of the island's outfitters conduct surf lessons here, as the break is far away from potentially dangerous rocks and reefs. ⊠ *Kuakini Rd., Kailua-Kona.*

Pine Trees. Also known as Kohanaiki, this community beach park is among the best places to catch waves. Keep in mind that it's a very popular local surf spot on an island where there aren't all that many surf spots, so be respectful. ⊠ *Off Hwy. 11, Kohanaiki entrance gate, about 2 miles south of Kona airport, Kailua-Kona.*

EQUIPMENT, LESSONS, AND TOURS

Hawaii Lifeguard Surf Instructors. This family-owned, lifeguard-certified school helps novices become wave riders and offers tours that take more experienced riders to Kona's top surf spots. A 1½-hour introductory lesson has one instructor per three students. Private instruction is available as well. If the waves are on the smaller side, they convert to stand-up paddleboard lessons for the same prices as surfing. ⊠ *75-5909 Alii Dr., Kailua-Kona* ☎ *808/324–0442, 808/936–7873* ⊕ *www. surflessonshawaii.com* ⊠ *$75 per person (group), $110 (private).*

Fodor'sChoice **Ocean Eco Tours Surf School.** Family owned and operated, Kona's oldest
★ surf school emphasizes the basics and specializes in beginners. It's one of a handful of operators permitted to conduct business in Kaloko-Honokohau National Historical Park, which gets waves even when other spots on the island are flat. All lessons are taught by certified instructors, and the school guarantees that you will surf. If you're hooked, sign up for a three-day package. There's an authentic soul surfer's vibe to these folks, and they are equally diehard about teaching you about the ocean and having you standing up riding waves on your first day. ⊠ *Honokohau Harbor, 74-425 Kealakehe Pkwy., Kailua-Kona* ☎ *808/324–7873* ⊕ *www.oceanecotours.com* ⊠ *From $95 per person; $270 for three-day package.*

Orchid Land Surf Shop. The shop has a wide variety of water sports and surf equipment for sale or rent. It stocks custom surfboards, body boards, and surf apparel. The staff also handles repairs. ⊠ *262 Kamehameha Ave., Hilo* ☎ *808/935–1533* ⊕ *www.orchidlandsurf.com.*

WHALE- AND DOLPHIN-WATCHING

Each winter, some two-thirds of the North Pacific humpback whale population (about 4,000–5,000 animals) migrate over 3,500 miles from the icy Alaska waters to the warm Hawaiian ocean to mate and, the following year, give birth to and nurse their calves. Recent reports indicate that the whale population is on the upswing—a few years ago one even ventured into the mouth of Hilo Harbor, which marine biologists say is quite rare. Humpbacks are spotted here from early December through the end of April, but other species, like sperm, pilot, and beaked whales as well as spinner, spotted, and bottlenose dolphins, can be seen year-round. ■TIP➜ If you take a morning cruise, you're more likely to see dolphins. *In addition to the outfitters listed below, see Snorkeling for more outfitters that offer whale- and dolphin-watching cruises.*

Humpback whales are visible off the coast of the Big Island between December and April.

TOURS

Blue Sea Cruises. The 46-foot *Makai* and the 70-foot *Spirit of Kona* cruise along the Kona Coast catching sight of dolphins, whales, and manta rays. Their "dry" cruise on a glass-bottom boat is good for kids. Both boats have snack bars and restrooms, and the double-decker *Spirit of Kona* also has a glass bottom. Their sunset dinner cruise has an open bar, gourmet meal, luau show, and dancing. ✉ *Kailua-Kona Pier, 75-5660 Palani Rd., Kailua-Kona* ☎ *808/331–8875* ⊕ *www. blueseacruisesinc.com* ✉ *From $84.*

Captain Dan McSweeney's Whale Watch Learning Adventures. This is probably the most experienced small operation on the island. Captain Dan McSweeney offers three-hour trips on his double-decker, 40-foot cruise boat. In addition to humpbacks (in winter), he'll try to show you dolphins and some of the six other whale species that live off the Kona Coast throughout the year. McSweeney guarantees you'll see whales or he'll take you out again for free. ✉ *Honokohau Harbor, 74-381 Kealakehe Pkwy., Kailua-Kona* ☎ *808/322–0028, 888/942–5376* ⊕ *www. ilovewhales.com* ✉ *$110.*

Dolphin Discoveries. The captains, certified marine mammal naturalists, lead dolphin- and whale-watching cruises on the Kona Coast in rigid-hull adventure crafts. Animals sighted include Hawaiian spinner, spotted, and bottlenose dolphins plus pilot and humpback whales (in season). Passengers can participate in a photo-ID research program. Cruises include fresh tropical fruits, snacks, and cold drinks. ✉ *Keauhou Bay, picnic table, Kailua-Kona* ☎ *808/322–8000* ⊕ *www. dolphindiscoveries.com* ✉ *From $99.*

5

GOLF, HIKING, AND OUTDOOR ACTIVITIES

Visit Fodors.com for advice, updates, and bookings

Updated by Kristina Anderson

With the Big Island's predictably mild year-round climate, it's no wonder you'll find an emphasis on outdoor activities. After all, this is the home of the annual Ironman World Championship triathlon. Whether you're an avid hiker or a beginning bicyclist, a casual golfer or a tennis buff, you'll find plenty of land-based activities to lure you away from the sun and surf.

You can explore by bike, helicopter, ATV, zip line, or horse, or you can put on your hiking boots and use your own horsepower. No matter how you get around, you'll be treated to breathtaking backdrops along the Big Island's 266-mile coastline and within its 4,028 square miles (and still growing!). Aerial tours take in the latest eruption activity and lava flows, as well as the island's gorgeous tropical valleys, gulches, and coastal areas. Trips into the backcountry wilderness explore the rain forest, private ranch lands, coffee farms, and old sugar-plantation villages that offer a glimpse of Hawaii's earlier days.

Golfers will find acclaimed championship golf courses at the Kohala coast resorts—Mauna Kea Beach Hotel, Hapuna Beach Prince Hotel, Mauna Lani Bay Hotel & Bungalows, Waikoloa Beach Resort, and Four Seasons Hualalai, among others. And during the winter, if snow conditions allow, you can go skiing on top of Mauna Kea (elevation: 13,796 feet). It's a skiing experience unlike any other.

AERIAL TOURS

There's nothing quite like the aerial view of a waterfall crashing down a couple of thousand feet into cascading pools, or watching lava flow to the ocean as exploding clouds of steam billow into the air. You can get this bird's-eye view from a helicopter or a small plane. All operators pay strict attention to safety. So how to get the best experience for your money? ■TIP→ Before you choose a company, be a savvy traveler

DID YOU KNOW?

A helicopter tour is one of the best ways to see the Big Island's most inaccessible areas. It's hard to beat an aerial view of a 2,600-foot waterfall plunging down a sheer cliff face into the valley below.

and ask the right questions. What kind of aircraft do they fly? What is their safety record?

Blue Hawaiian Helicopters. Hawaii's most comfortable ride is on the roomy, $3-million Eco-Star helicopter—so quiet you hardly realize you're taking off and with great views from every seat. Pilots are knowledgeable about the island but not overly chatty. In the Waimanu Valley, the craft hovers next to 2,500-foot cliffs and dramatic, cascading waterfalls. The two-hour Big Island Spectacular also takes in Kilauea Volcano lava flows. Prices range from $196 to $495 per person, depending on type of craft. Most flights leave from a private helipad in Waikoloa, but the 50-minute Circle of Fire tour departs Hilo for the volcano's wonders. ⊠ *Waikoloa Heliport, Hwy. 19, Waikoloa* ☎ *808/961–5600* ⊕ *www.bluehawaiian.com.*

Iolani Air. These two- to six-passenger Gippsland and Cessna aircraft depart from both the Hilo and Kona airports, following the coastline all the way around for an aerial tour of the entire Big Island. You'll get a good view of fascinating geographic and historical points of interest. Four air tours are available, from a 60-minute tour of volcanoes and waterfalls (Hilo only) at $175 per person to a 2½-hour full-circle tour starting at $299. Highlights include the volcano, Waipio Valley, and the Kona Coast. ☎ *808/329–0018, 800/538–7590* ⊕ *www.iolaniair.com.*

Fodor's Choice **Paradise Helicopters.** This friendly company offers great options no one
★   else does. On three landing tours, departing from Kona's airport, you can either touch down for a hike in a remote Kohala valley, experience a Hilo zip line, or spend a few hours exploring downtown Hilo. After flying over active lava flows, aircraft easily maneuver near the sheer valley walls of the east side. In a "doors off" adventure, four-passenger MD 500 helicopters (Hilo only) get so close, you can feel heat from the lava. Flights start at $200 for 50 minutes to $495 for three-hour landing tours. Pilots, many of whom have military backgrounds, are fun and knowledgeable. Free hotel shuttles run to and from the Kona and Hilo airports, where tours are based. ☎ *808/969–7392, 866/876–7422* ⊕ *www.paradisecopters.com.*

ATV TOURS

A fun way to experience the Big Island's rugged coastline and wild ranch lands is through an off-road adventure—a real backcountry experience. At higher elevations, the weather gets nippy and rainy, but views can be awesome. Protective gear is provided, and everyone gets a mini driving lesson. Generally, you must be 16 or older to ride your own ATV; some outfitters allow children seven and older as passengers.

ATV Outfitters Hawaii. These trips take in the scenic beauty of the rugged North Kohala Coast, traveling along coastal cliffs and into the forest in search of waterfalls. ATV Outfitters also offers double-seater ATVs for parents traveling with children or adults who don't feel comfortable operating their own vehicle. ⊠ *51-324 Lighthouse Rd., Kapaau* ☎ *808/889–6000, 888/288–7288* ⊕ *www.atvoutfittershawaii.com.*

Fodor'sChoice **Waipio Ride the Rim.** A fabulous way to experience the extraordinary
★ beauty atop lush Waipio Valley, the tour is led by fun and knowledgeable guides along private trails to the headwaters of the twin Hiilawe
Falls, Hawaii's highest single-fall waterfalls. You stop for a swim in a
ginger-laden grotto with a refreshing waterfall (disclaimer: it's cold!)
and travel to a series of lookouts—at times crossing the still-active
Kohala Ditch—where you can observe the valley and its black-sand
beach from all angles. Bring a bathing suit and be prepared to get wet
and muddy. Beginners are welcome. It's teen-tastically fun. (To drive
your own ATV, you must be over 16.) Prices start at $179, or take the
guided buggy tour if you're not up to driving. ⊠ *Waipio Valley Artworks Bldg., 48-5416 Kukuihaele Rd., Kukuihaele* ☎ *808/775–1450,
877/775–1450* ⊕ *www.ridetherim.com.*

BIKING

5

The Big Island's biking trails and road routes range from easy to moderate coastal rides to rugged backcountry wilderness treks that challenge
the most serious cyclists. You can soak up the island's storied scenic
vistas and varied geography—from tropical rain forest to rolling ranch
country, from high-country mountain meadows to dry lava deserts. It's
dry, windy, and hot on Kona's and Kohala's coastal trails and cool, wet,
and muddy in the upcountry Waimea and Volcano areas, as well as in
lower Puna. There are long distances between towns, few bike lanes,
narrow single-lane highways, and scanty services in the Kau, Puna,
South Kona, and Kohala Coast areas, so plan accordingly for weather,
water, food, and lodging before setting out.

Hawaii Cycling Club. This nonprofit club has tons of information on biking the Big Island. ⊕ *www.hawaiicyclingclub.com.*

BEST SPOTS

Fodor'sChoice **Kulani Trails.** This has been called the best ride in the state—if you really
★ want to get gnarly. The technically demanding ride, which passes majes-
tic eucalyptus trees, is for advanced cyclists. To reach the trailhead
from the intersection of Highway 11 and Highway 19, take Highway
19 south about 4 miles, turn right on Stainback Highway, continue 2½
miles, turn right at the Waiakea Arboretum, and park near the gate. A
permit is required, available from the Department of Land and Natural
Resources at Kawili Street and Kilauea Avenue in Hilo. ⊠ *Stainback
Hwy., Hilo.*

Old Puna Trail. A 10½-mile ride through the subtropical jungle in Puna,
this trail leads into one of the island's most isolated areas. It starts on
a cinder road, which becomes a four-wheel-drive trail. If it's rained
recently, you'll have to deal with puddles—the first few of which you'll
gingerly avoid until you give in and go barreling through the rest for the
sheer fun of it. This is a great ride for all abilities and takes about 90
minutes. To get to the trailhead from Highway 130, take Kaloli Road
to Beach Road. ⚠ Ride at your own risk; this is not a maintained trail.
⊠ *Kaloli Rd. at Hwy. 130, Puna.*

EQUIPMENT AND TOURS

There are several rental shops in Kailua-Kona and a couple in Waimea and Hilo. Many resorts rent bicycles that can be used around the properties. Most outfitters can provide a bicycle rack for your car, and all offer reduced rates for rentals longer than one day.

BikeVolcano.com. This outfitter leads three- or five-hour bike rides through Hawaii Volcanoes National Park, mostly downhill, that take in fantastic sights, from rain forests to craters. The three-hour tour costs $105; five hours, $129. There's also a spectacular seven-hour sunset tour that goes to the active lava flows (volcano depending). Equipment, support van, and food are included. ⊠ *Kilauea General Store, 19-3972 Old Volcano Rd., Volcano* ☎ *808/934–9199, 888/934–9199* ⊕ *www. bikevolcano.com.*

Bike Works. This outfitter caters to cyclists of all skill levels with tours for moderate to advanced riders and rentals of deluxe road bikes, full-suspension mountain bikes, and high-end triathlon bikes. Rentals start at $40 a day. ⊠ *Hale Hana Center, 74-5583 Luhia St., Kailua-Kona* ☎ *808/326–2453* ⊕ *www.bikeworkskona.com.*

Fodor's Choice **Cycle Station.** This shop, with exceptionally nice proprietors, has a variety of bikes for rent, from hybrids to racing models. Rentals run from ★ $20 to $75 per day and can be delivered to your hotel. Island-wide trips are also available. ⊠ *73-4976 Kamanu St., Kailua-Kona* ☎ *808/327–0087* ⊕ *www.konabikerentals.com.*

Mid Pacific Wheels. This downtown shop carries a full line of bikes and accessories and rents mountain bikes for exploring the Hilo area starting at $30 per day. The staff provides current trail information as well as expert advice on where to go and what to see and do on a self-guided tour. ⊠ *1133C Manono St., Hilo* ☎ *808/935–6211* ⊕ *www. midpacificwheelsllc.com.*

CAVING

The Kanohina Lava Tube system is about 1,000 years old and was used by the ancient Hawaiians for water collection and for shelter. More than 40 miles of these braided lava tubes have been mapped so far in the Kau District of the Big Island, near South Point. About 45 miles south of Kailua-Kona, these lava tubes are a great experience for cavers of all age levels and abilities.

Fodor's Choice **Kula Kai Caverns.** Expert cave guides lead groups into the fantastic under-★ world of these caverns near South Point. The braided lava-tube system attracts scientists from around the world, who come to study and map them (almost 40 miles so far). Tours start at $20 and range from The Crawl ($60) to the Two Hour, a deep-down-under spelunking adventure for $95. (Longer, customized tours are also available.) Programs are tailored to each group's interest and abilities, and all gear is provided. Tours start at an Indiana Jones-style expedition tent and divulge fascinating details about the caves' geologic and cultural history. Reservations are required. ⊠ *Kula Kai Estates, Lauhala Dr. at Kona Kai Blvd.* ☎ *808/929–9725* ⊕ *www.kulakaicaverns.com.*

TIPS FOR THE GREEN

Golf is golf, and Hawaii is part of the United States, but island golf nevertheless has its own quirks. Here are a few tips to make your golf experience in the Islands more pleasant.

■ Wear sunscreen, even in December. We recommend zinc-based, with a minimum SPF of 30, and that you reapply on the 10th tee.

■ Stay hydrated. Spending four-plus hours in the sun and heat means you'll perspire away considerable fluids and energy.

■ Private courses may allow you to play at their discretion.

■ All resort courses and many daily-fee courses provide rental clubs. In many cases, they're the latest lines from Titleist, Ping, Callaway, and the like. This is true for both men and women, as well as left-handers, which means you don't have to schlep clubs across the Pacific.

■ Pro shops at most courses are stocked with balls, tees, and other accoutrements, so even if you bring a bag, it needn't weigh a ton.

■ Come spikeless—very few Hawaii courses permit metal spikes.

■ Resort courses, in particular, offer more than the usual three sets of tees, sometimes four or five. So bite off as much or little challenge as you like. Tee it up from the tips and you'll end up playing a few 600-yard par-5s and see a few 250-yard forced carries.

■ In theory, you can play golf in Hawaii 365 days a year. But there's a reason the Hawaiian Islands are so green. Better to bring an umbrella and light jacket and not use them than to not bring them and get soaked.

■ Unless you play a muni or certain daily-fee courses, plan on taking a cart. Carts are mandatory at most courses and are included in the greens fee.

GOLF

For golfers, the Big Island is a big deal—starting with the Mauna Kea Golf Course, which opened in 1964 and remains one of the state's top courses. Black lava and deep blue sea are the predominant themes on the island. In the roughly 40 miles from the Kona Country Club to the Mauna Kea resort, nine courses are carved into sunny seaside lava plains, with four more in the hills above. Indeed, most of the Big Island's best courses are concentrated along the Kohala Coast, statistically the sunniest spot in Hawaii. Vertically speaking, although the majority of courses are seaside or at least near sea level, three are located above 2,000 feet, another one at 4,200 feet. This is significant because in Hawaii temperatures drop 3°F for every 1,000 feet of elevation gained.

Greens Fee: Greens fees listed here are the highest course rates per round on weekdays for U.S. residents. Courses with varying weekend rates are noted in the individual listings. (Some courses charge non–U.S. residents higher prices.) ■TIP→ Discounts are often available for resort guests and for those who book tee times on the web, as well as for those willing to play in the afternoon. Twilight fees are also usually offered.

Big Island Country Club. Set 2,000 feet above sea level on the slopes of Mauna Kea, this course is out of the way but well worth the drive. In 1997, Pete and Perry Dye created a gem that plays through upland woodlands—more than 2,500 trees line the fairways. On the par-5 15th, a giant tree in the middle of the fairway must be avoided with the second shot. Five lakes and a meandering natural mountain stream bring water into play on nine holes. The most dramatic is the par-3 17th, where Dye created a knockoff of his infamous 17th at the TPC at Sawgrass. ✉ *71-1420 Hawaii Belt Rd., Kailua-Kona* ☎ *808/325–5044* ⊕ *www.bigislandcountryclub.com* ⚐ *18 holes, 7075 yards, par 72* 🖃 *$89.*

Hamakua Country Club. While the typical, modern 18-hole golf course requires at least 250 acres, this 9-hole, par-33 public course fits into just 19. Compact is the word, and with several holes crisscrossing, this is BYO hard hat. Holes run up and down a fairly steep slope overlooking the ocean. Cheerfully billed as an Old World golf experience, the course has no clubhouse or other amenities, and the 9th green is square, but for 15 bucks, whaddaya expect? ✉ *Hwy. 19, at mile marker 41, 43 miles north of Hilo, Honokaa* ☎ *808/775–7244* ⚐ *9 holes, 2520 yards, par 33* 🖃 *$15.*

Hapuna Golf Course. Hapuna's challenging play and environmental sensitivity make it one of the island's most unusual courses. Designed by Arnold Palmer and Ed Seay, it is nestled into the natural contours of the land from the shoreline to about 700 feet above sea level. There are spectacular views of mountains and sea (Maui is often visible in the distance). Holes wind through kiawe scrub, beds of jagged lava, and tall fountain grasses. Hole 12 is favored for its beautiful views and challenging play. ✉ *62-100 Kanunaoa Dr., Kamuela* ☎ *808/880–3000* ⊕ *www.princeresortshawaii.com* ⚐ *18 holes, 6875 yards, par 72* 🖃 *$125.*

Hilo Municipal Golf Course. Hilo Muni is proof that you don't need sand bunkers to create a challenging course. Trees and several meandering creeks are the danger here. The course, which offers views of Hilo Bay from most holes, has produced many of the island's top players over the years. Taking a divot reminds you that you're playing on a volcano—the soil is dark black crushed lava. ✉ *340 Haihai St., Hilo* ☎ *808/959–7711* ⚐ *18 holes, 6325 yards, par 71* 🖃 *$35 weekdays, $40 weekends.*

Hualalai Resort. Named for the volcanic peak that is the target off the first tee, the Nicklaus Course at Hualalai is semiprivate, open only to guests of the adjacent Four Seasons Resort Hualalai. From the forward and resort tees, this is perhaps Jack Nicklaus's most friendly course in Hawaii, but the back tees play a full mile longer. The par-3 17th plays across convoluted lava to a seaside green, and the view from the tee is so lovely, you may be tempted to just relax on the koa bench and enjoy the scenery. ✉ *100 Kaupulehu Dr., Kohala Coast* ☎ *808/325–8480* ⊕ *www.*

Most of the Big Island's top golf courses are located on the sunny Kohala Coast.

fourseasons.com/hualalai ⅃ *18 holes, 7117 yards, par 72* ✉ *$250 for all-day access.*

Makalei Country Club. Set on the slopes of Hualalai, at an elevation of 2,900 feet, Makalei is one of the rare Hawaii courses with bent-grass putting greens, which means they're quick and without the grain associated with Bermuda greens. Former PGA Tour official Dick Nugent (1992) designed holes that play through thick forest and open to wide ocean views. Elevation change is a factor on many holes, especially the par-3 15th, whose tee is 80 feet above the green. In addition to fixed natural obstacles, wild peacocks and turkeys can make for an entertaining game. After noon, greens fees dip drastically. ✉ *72-3890 Hawaii Belt Rd., Kailua-Kona* ☎ *808/325–6625* ⊕ *www.makalei.com* ⅃ *18 holes, 7091 yards, par 72* ✉ *$85.*

Fodor's Choice ★
Mauna Kea Golf Course. Originally opened in 1964, this golf course is one of the most revered in the state. It underwent a tee-to-green renovation by Rees Jones, son of the original architect, Robert Trent Jones Sr. Hybrid grasses were planted, the number of bunkers increased, and the overall yardage was expanded. The par-3 3rd is one of the world's most famous holes—and one of the most photographed. You play from a cliff-side tee across a bay to a cliff-side green. Getting across the ocean is just half the battle because the green is surrounded by seven bunkers, each one large and undulated. The course is a shot-maker's paradise and follows Jones's "easy bogey, tough par" philosophy. ✉ *62-100 Kaunaoe Dr., Kamuela* ☎ *808/882–5400* ⊕ *www.maunakeagolf.com* ⅃ *18 holes, 7250 yards, par 72* ✉ *$250.*

Fodor's Choice   **Mauna Lani Resort.** Black lava flows, lush green turf, white sand, and
★   the Pacific's multihues of blue define the 36 holes at Mauna Lani. The
South Course includes the par-3 15th across a turquoise bay, one of
the most photographed holes in Hawaii. But it shares "signature hole"
honors with the 7th, a long par 3, which plays downhill over convoluted
patches of black lava, with the Pacific immediately to the left and a dune
to the right. The North Course plays a couple of shots tougher. Its most
distinctive hole is the 17th, a par 3 with the green set in a lava pit 50
feet deep. The shot from an elevated tee must carry a pillar of lava that
rises from the pit and partially blocks a view of the green. ✉ *68-1310
Mauna Lani Dr., Kohala Coast* ☎ *808/885–6655* ⊕ *www.maunalani.
com* ⛳ *North Course: 18 holes, 6057 yards, par 72; South Course: 18
holes, 6025 yards, par 72* 🖛 *$215.*

Volcano Golf & Country Club. Just outside Hawaii Volcanoes National
Park—and barely a stone's throw from Halemaumau Crater—this is
by far Hawaii's highest course. At 4,200-feet elevation, shots tend
to fly a bit farther than at sea level, even in the often cool, misty
air. Because of the elevation and climate, it's one of the few Hawaii
courses with bent-grass putting greens. The course is mostly flat, and
holes play through stands of Norfolk pines, flowering *lehua* trees,
and multitrunk *hau* trees. The uphill par-4 15th doglegs through a
tangle of hau. ✉ *Pii Mauna Dr., off Hwy. 11, Volcanoes National
Park* ☎ *808/967–7331* ⊕ *www.volcanogolfshop.com* ⛳ *18 holes,
6106 yards, par 72* 🖛 *$56.*

Fodor's Choice   **Waikoloa Beach Resort.** Robert Trent Jones Jr. built the Beach Course
★   at Waikoloa (1981) on an old flow of crinkly *aa* lava, which he used
to create holes that are as artful as they are challenging. The par-5
12th hole is one of Hawaii's most picturesque and plays through a
chute of black lava to a seaside green. At the Kings' Course (1990),
Tom Weiskopf and Jay Morrish built a links-esque track. It turns
out lava's natural humps and declivities replicate the contours of
seaside Scotland. But there are a few island twists—such as seven
lakes. This is "option golf," as Weiskopf and Morrish provide different risk-reward tactics on each hole. Beach and Kings' have separate
clubhouses. ✉ *600 Waikoloa Beach Dr., Waikoloa* ☎ *808/886–7888*
⊕ *www.waikoloabeachgolf.com* ⛳ *Beach Course: 18 holes, 6566
yards, par 70; Kings' Course: 18 holes, 7074 yards, par 72* 🖛 *$135
for guests, $165 for nonguests.*

Waikoloa Village Golf Course. Robert Trent Jones Jr., who created some
of the most expensive courses on the Kohala Coast, also designed this
little gem 20 minutes from the coast. At a 450-foot elevation, it offers
ideal playing conditions year-round. Holes run across rolling hills with
sweeping mountain and ocean views. ✉ *68-1792 Melia St., Waikoloa*
☎ *808/883–9621* ⊕ *www.waikoloavillagegolf.com* ⛳ *18 holes, 6230
yards, par 72* 🖛 *$83.50.*

Hawaii Volcanoes National Park's 150 miles of trails offer easy to moderately difficult hikes.

HIKING

Ecologically diverse, Hawaii Island has four of the five major climate zones and 8 of 13 sub-climate zones—a lot of variation for one island—and you can experience them all by foot. The ancient Hawaiians cut trails across the lava plains, through the rain forests, and up along the mountain heights. Many of these paths are still in use today. Part of the King's Trail at Anaehoomalu winds through a field of lava rocks covered with ancient carvings called petroglyphs. Many other trails, historic and modern, crisscross the huge Hawaii Volcanoes National Park and other parts of the island. Plus, the serenity of remote beaches, such as Papakolea Beach (Green Sands Beach), is accessible only to hikers.

Department of Land and Natural Resources, State Parks Division. The division provides information on all the Big Island's state parks. ⊠ *75 Aupuni St., Hilo* ☎ *808/961–9544* ⊕ *www.hawaiistateparks.org.*

BEST SPOTS

Fodor'sChoice
★ **Hawaii Volcanoes National Park.** Perhaps the Big Island's premier area for hikers, the park has 150 miles of trails providing close-up views of fern and rain-forest environments, cinder cones, steam vents, lava fields, rugged coastline, and current lava-flow activity. Day hikes range from easy to moderately difficult, and from one or two hours to a full day. For a bigger challenge, consider an overnight or multiday backcountry hike with a stay in a park cabin (available by a remote coast, in a lush forest, or atop frigid Mauna Loa). To do so, you must first obtain a

free permit at the backcountry permit office in the Visitor Emergency Operations Center. Daily guided hikes are led by knowledgeable, friendly park rangers. The bulletin board outside the visitor center has the day's schedule. ⊠ *Hwy. 11, 30 miles south of Hilo, Volcanoes National Park* ☎ *808/985–6000* ⊕ *www.nps.gov/havo/index.htm.*

Kekaha Kai State Park. A 1.8-mile unimproved road leads to Mahaiula Bay, a gorgeous little piece of paradise, while on the opposite end of the park is lovely Kua Bay. Connecting the two is the 4½-mile Ala Kahakai historic coastal trail. Mahaiula has picnic tables and *luas* (porta potties). Midway between the two white-sand beaches, you can hike to the summit of Puu Kuili,

> ## HIKING BIG ISLAND TRAILS
>
> ■ Trails on the eastern, or windward, side of the island are often wet and muddy, making them slippery and unstable, so wear good hiking shoes or boots.
>
> ■ Bring plenty of water, rain protection, a hat, sunblock, and a cell phone, but be aware that service can be spotty.
>
> ■ Don't eat any unknown fruits or plants.
>
> ■ Darkness comes suddenly here, so carry a flashlight if there's a chance you'll be out after sunset.

a 342-foot-high cinder cone with an excellent view of the coastline. It's dry and hot with no drinking water, so pack sunblock and water. Gates close at 7 pm sharp. ⊠ *Trailhead on Hwy. 19, about 2 miles north of Kona airport.*

Muliwai Trail. On the western side of mystical Waipio Valley, this trail leads to the back of the valley, then switchbacks up through a series of gulches, and finally emerges at Waimanu Valley. Only very experienced hikers should attempt the entire 18-mile trail, the hike of a lifetime. It can take two to three days of backpacking and camping, which requires camping permits from the Division of Forestry and Wildlife in Hilo. ⊠ *Trailhead at end of Hwy. 240* ☎ *808/974–4221* ⊕ *hawaiitrails. ehawaii.gov.*

Onomea Bay Trail. This short but beautiful trail is packed with stunning views of the cliffs, bays, and gulches of the Hamakua Coast, on the east side of the island. The trail is just under a mile and fairly easy, with access down to the shore if you want to dip your feet in, although we don't recommend swimming in the rough waters. Unless you pay the $15 entry fee to the nearby botanical garden, entering its gates (even by accident) will send one of the guards running after you to nicely but firmly point you back to the trail. ⊠ *Trailhead on Old Hawaiian Belt Rd., just before botanical garden* ⊕ *hawaiitrails.ehawaii.gov.*

TOURS

To get to some of the best trails and places, it's worth going with a skilled guide. Costs range from $95 to $165, and some hikes include picnic meals or refreshments, and gear, such as binoculars, ponchos,

Continued on page 154

HAWAII'S PLANTS 101

Hawaii is a bounty of rainbow-colored flowers and plants. The evening air is scented with their fragrance. Just look at the front yard of almost any home, travel any road, or visit any local park and you'll see a spectacular array of colored blossoms and leaves. What most visitors don't know is that many of the plants they are seeing are not native to Hawaii; rather, they were introduced during the last two centuries as ornamental plants, or for timber, shade, or fruit.

Hawaii boasts nearly every climate on the planet, excluding the two most extreme: arctic tundra and arid desert. The Islands have wine-growing regions, cactus-speckled ranchlands, icy mountaintops, and the rainiest forests on earth.

Plants introduced from around the world thrive here. The lush lowland valleys along the windward coasts are predominantly populated by non-native trees including yellow- and red-fruited **guava**, silvery-leafed **kukui**, and orange-flowered **tulip trees**.

The colorful **plumeria flower**, very fragrant and commonly used in lei making, and

the giant multicolored **hibiscus flower** are both used by many women as hair adornments, and are two of the most common plants found around homes and hotels. The umbrella-like **monkeypod tree** from Central America provides shade in many of Hawaii's parks including Kapiolani Park in Honolulu. Hawaii's largest tree, found in Lahaina, Maui, is a giant **banyan tree.** Its canopy and massive support roots cover about two-thirds of an acre. The native **ohia tree**, with its brilliant red brush-like flowers, and the **hapuu**, a giant tree fern, are common in Hawaii's forests and are also used ornamentally in gardens.

Bougainvillea

Guava

Monkeypod

Banyan

Ohia Lehua*

Tulip Tree

Plumeria

Pandanus

Hibiscus

Anthurium

Kukui

Hapuu

*endemic to Hawaii

DID YOU KNOW?

More than 2,200 plant species are found in the Hawaiian Islands, but only about 1,000 are native. Of these, 320 are so rare, they are endangered. Hawaii's endemic plants evolved from ancestral seeds arriving in the Islands over thousands of years as baggage with birds, floating on ocean currents, or drifting on winds from continents thousands of miles away. Once here, these plants evolved in isolation, creating many new species known nowhere else in the world.

and walking sticks. The outfitters mentioned here also offer customized adventure tours.

Hawaiian Walkways. With knowledgeable guides, this company conducts tours in unique spots—a botanical walk in a Kona cloud forest, a hike on Saddle Road between Mauna Kea and Mauna Loa, waterfall hikes, and jaunts through Hawaii Volcanoes National Park—as well as custom-designed trips. ⊠ *45-3625 Mamane St., Honokaa* ☎ *808/775–0372, 800/457–7759* ⊕ *www.hawaiianwalkways.com.*

Fodor'sChoice
★ **Hawaii Forest & Trail.** Since 1993, this locally owned and operated outfit has had a reputation for high-quality nature tours and eco-adventures. The company has access to thousands of acres of restricted or private lands and employs expert, certified guides. Its variety of programs includes a Hakalau Forest National Wildlife Refuge birdwatching tour, Kilauea Volcano excursion, Kohala waterfall trip, and the super-fun Kona Coffee & Craters adventure. The Twilight Volcano Adventure stays in the national park after dark to see the glowing red stuff. ⊠ *74-5035B Queen Kaahahumanu Hwy., Kailua-Kona* ☎ *808/331–8505, 800/464–1993* ⊕ *www.hawaii-forest.com.*

Kapoho Kine Adventures. This outfitter offers several hiking adventures in Hawaii Volcanoes National Park and surrounding areas, including a 12-hour tour that explores the region by day and sees the lava at night, a shorter day tour, and an evening tour complete with Hawaiian-style barbecue dinner. The Gold Coast/Cloud Forest Tour contrasts a hot day at a historic beach with misty hikes in a cool and endangered cloud forest teeming with birds. Tours depart from both Hilo and Kona. ⊠ *224 Kamehameha Ave. #106, next to Palace Theatre, on Haili St., Hilo* ☎ *808/964–1000, 866/965–9552* ⊕ *www.kapohokine.com* 🖃 *From $99.*

HORSEBACK RIDING

With its *paniolo* (cowboy) heritage and the ranches it spawned, the Big Island is a great place for equestrians. Riders can gallop through green pastures, or saunter through Waipio Valley for a taste of old Hawaii.

TOURS

Hamakua Adventures. One-and-a-half-hour morning and afternoon horseback rides ($79) travel through private ranchlands in the lush Onomea area near Hilo, stopping at the base of the 80-foot, twin Waikahalulu Falls. Refreshments are provided, with an optional ($20) barbecue lunch. ⊠ *27-2668 Hawaii Belt Rd., Pepeekeo* ☎ *808/871–5222* ⊕ *www.hamakuaadventures.com.*

King's Trail Rides. A four-hour excursion ($135) down an old Hawaiian trail leads to a scenic, uncrowded spot near Kealakekua Bay for snorkeling and lunch. A mask and snorkel are provided. ⊠ *Hwy. 11, mile marker 111, Kealakekua* ☎ *808/323–2388* ⊕ *www.konacowboy.com.*

Waipio Ridge Stables. Two different rides around the rim of Waipio Valley are offered—a 2½-hour trek for $85 and a 5-hour hidden-waterfall

DID YOU KNOW?

The Waipio Valley is a popular place to go horseback riding. Waipio means "curved water"; the valley is named for the Waipio River, which flows through it.

adventure (with swimming) for $165. Lunch is included. The meeting point is Waipio Valley Artworks. ✉ *48-5416 Kukuihaele Rd., off Hwy. 240, Honokaa* ☎ *808/775–1007, 877/757–1414* ⊕ *www.waipioridgestables.com.*

RUNNING

Ironman 70.3 Hawaii. The only Hawaii qualifier for the World Championship, the spring Ironman 70.3 Hawaii triathlon begins with swimming at Hapuna Beach, then moves to biking for 56 miles on Queen Kaahumanu Highway, and finishes with a 13-mile run through the Kohala resorts. ☎ *808/329–0063* ⊕ *www.ironman703hawaii.com.*

Ironman World Championship. Staged annually since 1978, the Ironman World Championship is the granddaddy of all triathlons. For about two weeks in early October, Kailua-Kona takes on the vibe of an Olympic Village as 2,000 top athletes from across the globe and their supporters roam the town, carbo-loading, training, and acclimating in advance of the world's premier swim-bike-run endurance event. The competition starts at Kailua Pier with a 2.4-mile open-water swim, followed by a 112-mile bicycle ride and a 26.2-mile marathon. ☎ *808/329–0063* ⊕ *www.ironmanworldchampionship.com.*

SKIING

Where else but Hawaii can you surf, snorkel, and snow ski on the same day? In winter, the 13,796-foot Mauna Kea (Hawaiian for "white mountain") usually has snow at higher elevations—and along with that, skiing. No lifts, no manicured slopes, no faux-alpine lodges, no après-ski nightlife, but the chance to ski some of the most remote (and let's face it, unlikely) runs on the planet. Some people have even been known to use body boards as sleds, but we don't recommend it. As long as you're up there, fill your cooler with the white stuff for a snowball fight on the beach later with local kids.

Ski Guides Hawaii. With the motto "Pray for pineapple powder," Christopher Langan of Mauna Kea Ski Corporation is the only licensed outfitter providing transportation, guide services, and ski equipment on Mauna Kea. Snow can fall from Thanksgiving to June, but the most likely months are February and March. The runs are fairly short, and hidden lava rocks and other dangers abound. Langan charges $450 per person for a daylong experience that includes lunch, equipment, guide service, transportation from Waimea, and a four-wheel-drive shuttle back up the mountain after each ski run. Ski or snowboard rentals are $50 per day. ☎ *808/885–4188* ⊕ *www.skihawaii.com.*

TENNIS

Many of the island's resorts allow nonguests to play for a fee. They also rent rackets, balls, and shoes. On the Kohala Coast, try the Fairmont Orchid Hawaii, the Hilton Waikoloa Village, and Waikoloa Beach

Marriott. In Kailua-Kona there's Island Slice at the site of the Keauhou Beach Hotel, now closed to everything but tennis; the Courtyard King Kamehameha's Kona Beach Hotel; and the Royal Kona Resort.

County of Hawaii Department of Parks and Recreation. The department has information on all public courts. ⊠ *25 Aupuni St., Hilo* ☎ *808/961–8311* ⊕ *www.hawaiicounty.gov/parks-and-recreation.*

Edith Kanakaole Multi-Purpose Tennis Stadium. Both indoor and outdoor courts are available for public use. ⊠ *Hoolulu County Park, Piilani and Kalanikoa Sts., Hilo* ☎ *808/961–8720.*

Higashihara Park. You can play for free at this park near Honalo. ⊠ *Off Hwy. 11, before Honalo, Kailua-Kona.*

Old Kona Airport Park. Tennis courts are available for play. ⊠ *North end of Kuakini Hwy., Kailua-Kona* ☎ *808/327–4958, 808/974–6200.*

ZIP LINE TOURS

One of the few ways to really see the untouched beauty of the Big Island is to fly over its lush forests, dense tree canopies, and glorious rushing waterfalls on a zip line. You strap into a harness, get clipped to a cable, step off a platform, and then zip, zip, zip your way through paradise. Most companies start you out easy on a slower, shorter line and graduate you to faster, longer zips. It's an exhilarating adventure for all ages and, between the zipping, rappelling, and suspension bridges, has been known to help some put aside their fear of heights (at least for a few minutes).

Big Island Eco Adventures II and Kona Zip. This company knows zip lines—it built the first one on the Big Island. For $169, the three-hour tour takes you on eight zip lines and a 200-foot suspension bridge. You experience exhilarating, crisscrossing thrills over the mountains and gulches of historic North Kohala, including the enormous Waianae Gulch. Along the way you get awesome views of the Pacific Ocean, and, on clear days, Maui. The eight-line Kona treetop zip is nestled in a pristine upcountry ohia forest, accompanied by the calls of rare native birds who live high in the canopy. ⊠ *53-496 Iole Rd., Kapau* ☎ *808/889–5111* ⊕ *www.thebigislandzipline.com.*

Kapoho Kine Adventures. In addition to offering volcano hikes, waterfall swims, and helicopter tours, this company does zipping exceptionally well, in combinations or à la carte adventures. It has one of the longest zip lines on the island, at 2,400 feet, as well as the only all-dual-track zip, which means you'll be able to traverse the eight stations more quickly and have a friend at your side the whole way. You'll soar over the lush rainforests of Hilo's Honolii River gorge, complete with thundering waterfalls, and get views of the smoking vent at Kilauea Volcano. Tours start at $169 and depart both Hilo and Kona. ⊠ *Historic Canario Complex, 224 Kamehameha Ave., Hilo* ☎ *800/964–100* ⊕ *www.kapohokine.com*

Kohala Zipline. This company features nine zips and five suspension bridges for a thrilling, above-the-canopy adventure in the forest. You'll bounce up to the site in a six-wheel-drive, military-style vehicle. Two certified guides accompany each small group. Designed for all ability levels, the Kohala Zipline focuses on fun and safety, offering a dual line for easy, confident braking. You'll soar hundreds of feet above the ground and feel like a pro by the last platform. Zip and Dip tours (combining zip line, nature walk, snacks, and swim) cost $169. ✉ *54-3676 Akoni Pule Hwy., Kapaau* ☎ *808/331–3620, 800/464–1993* ⊕ *www. kohalazipline.com.*

SHOPS AND SPAS

Updated by Karen Anderson

Residents like to complain that there isn't a lot of great shopping on the Big Island, but unless you're searching for winter coats, you can find plenty to deplete your pocketbook.

Dozens of shops in Kailua-Kona offer a range of souvenirs from far-flung corners of the globe and plenty of local coffee and foodstuffs to take home to everyone you left behind. Housewares and artworks made from local materials (lava rock, coconut, koa, and milo wood) fill the shelves of small boutiques and galleries throughout the island. Upscale shops in the resorts along the Kohala Coast carry high-end clothing and accessories, as do a few boutiques scattered around the island. Galleries and gift shops, many showcasing the work of local artists, fill historic buildings in Waimea, Kainaliu, Holualoa, and Hawi. Hotel shops generally offer the most attractive and original resort wear, but, as with everything else at resorts, the prices run higher than elsewhere on the island.

High prices are entirely too common at the island's resort spas, but a handful of unique experiences are worth every penny. Beyond the resorts, the Big Island is also home to independent massage therapists and day spas that offer similar treatments for lower prices, albeit usually in a slightly less luxurious atmosphere. In addition to the obvious relaxation benefits of any spa trip, the Big Island's spas have done a fantastic job incorporating local traditions and ingredients into their menus. Massage artists work with coconut or *kukui* (candlenut) oil, hot-stone massages are conducted with lava stones, and ancient healing techniques such as *lomilomi*—a massage technique with firm, constant movement—are a staple at every island spa.

SHOPS

In general, stores on the Big Island open at 9 or 10 am and close by 6 pm. Hilo's Prince Kuhio Plaza stays open until 8 pm on weekdays and 9 pm on Friday and Saturday. In Historic Kona Village, most shopping plazas geared to tourists remain open until 9 pm. Grocery stores such as KTA Superstore are open until 11 pm.

KAILUA-KONA

SHOPPING CENTERS

Coconut Grove Marketplace. This meandering oceanfront marketplace includes gift shops, cafés, restaurants (Outback Steakhouse, Humpy's Big Island Alehouse, Bongo Ben's, Lu Lu's), sports bars, sushi, boutiques, a frozen-yogurt shop, Jack's Diving Locker, and several art galleries. At night, locals gather to watch outdoor sand volleyball games held in the courtyard or grab a beer and enjoy live music. This place is always hopping, and it has the biggest free parking lot in downtown Kailua-Kona. ⊠ *75-5795–75-5825 Alii Dr.*

Crossroads Shopping Center. This in-town shopping center includes a Safeway with an excellent deli section for on-the-go snacks, as well as a Wal-Mart, where visitors can find affordable Hawaiian souvenirs including discounted Kona coffee and macadamia nuts. For a cheap meal, there's also a Denny's plus several fast-food joints. ⊠ *75-1000 Henry St.* ☎ *808/329–4822.*

Kaloko Light Industrial Park. This large retail complex near the airport includes the membership-store Costco, the best place to stock up on food if you're staying at a vacation rental. Cycle Station has bikes to rent, and Mrs. Barry's Kona Cookies sells beautifully packaged, delicious "souvenirs." ⊠ *Off Hwy. 19 and Hina Lani St., near Kona airport.*

Keauhou Shopping Center. About 5 miles south of Kailua Village, this neighborhood shopping center includes KTA Superstore, Longs Drugs, Kona Stories bookstore, and a multiplex movie theater. Kenichi Pacific, a great sushi restaurant, and Peaberry & Galette, a café that serves excellent crepes, are favorite eateries joined by Bianelli's Pizza and Sam Choy's Kai Lanai. You can also grab a quick bite at Los Habaneros, Subway, or L&L Hawaiian Barbecue. ⊠ *78-6831 Alii Dr.* ☎ *808/322–3000* ⊕ *www.keauhoushoppingcenter.com.*

King Kamehameha Mall. Around the corner from Courtyard King Kamehameha's Kona Beach Hotel, this tiny neighborhood center includes Bangkok House Thai Restaurant, Ocean Seafood Chinese Restaurant, Quilt Passions Quilt and Needlework Shop, and a clothier. ⊠ *75-5626 Kuakini Hwy.*

Kona Commons. This downtown center features big-box retailers, such as Sports Authority (for snorkel and swim gear), and Ross Dress for Less (for suitcases, shoes, swimsuits, and aloha wear). Food and drink options include fast-food standbys like Dairy Queen, Subway, Taco Del Mar, and Panda Express; Ultimate Burger, for local beef and delicious homemade fries; Genki Sushi, where the goods are delivered via conveyer belt; and Kona Wine Market, which has a great selection of wines and spirits along with gourmet gift items. ■ TIP➜ Target has fresh-flower leis for a fraction of the cost that local florists charge. ⊠ *75-5450 Makala Blvd.*

Kona Inn Shopping Village. Originally a hotel, the Kona Inn was built in 1928 to woo a new wave of wealthy travelers. As newer condos and resorts opened along the Kona and Kohala coasts, it was transformed into a low-rise, outdoor shopping village with dozens of clothing boutiques, art galleries, gift shops, and island-style eateries. Broad lawns with coconut trees on the ocean side provide a lovely setting for an afternoon picnic. The open-air Kona Inn Restaurant is a local favorite for evening mai tais. ⊠ *75-5744 Alii Dr.*

Kona Marketplace. On the *mauka* (mountain) side of Alii Drive, near Hulihee Palace, this small retail enclave in Historic Kailua Village includes galleries, T-shirt/souvenir shops, a tattoo parlor, and karaoke bar, Sam's Hideaway. Local favorite Hayashi's You Make the Roll offers shaded outdoor seating and affordable sushi to go. ⊠ *75-5744 Alii Dr.*

Makalapua Center. On the *mauka* (mountain) side of the highway above Kona's Old Industrial area, this shopping center attracts visitors with great souvenir bargains at Kmart as well as island-influenced clothing, jewelry, and housewares at the upscale Macy's, the best place in Kona to find aloha shirts. The center also has one of the island's largest movie theaters. ⊠ *Kamakaeha Ave. at Hwy. 19.*

ARTS AND CRAFTS

Eclectic Craftsman. This longtime favorite brimming with handmade Hawaiian collectibles focuses on local art and crafts. The 60 Big Island artists represented here include renowned local painters and woodworkers. Affordable gifts range from bookmarks to salad servers to wine-bottle toppers. You won't find these items anywhere else, and they're all made in Hawaii. ⊠ *Kona Inn Shopping Village, 75-5744 Alii Dr.* ☎ *808/334-0562.*

Fodor's Choice ★ **Hula Lamps of Hawaii.** Located in Kailua-Kona's Old Industrial complex, this one-of-a-kind shop features the bronze creations of Charles Moore. Inspired by the vintage hula-girl lamps of the 1930s, Moore creates art pieces sought by visitors and residents alike. Mix and match with an array of hand-painted lampshades. ⊠ *74-5599 Luhia St., Unit F-5* ☎ *808/326-9583* ⊕ *www.hulalamps.com.*

Just Ukes. As the name suggests, this place is all about ukuleles—from music books to T-shirts to accessories like cases and bags. The independently owned shop carries a variety of ukuleles ranging from low-priced starter instruments to high-end models made of koa and mango. There's another Just Ukes at the Shops at Mauna Lani. ⊠ *Kona Inn Shopping Village, 75-5744 Alii Dr.* ☎ *808/769-5101.*

BOOKSTORES

Kona Stories. With more than 10,000 titles, this bookstore also sells Hawaiiana, children's toys, and whimsical gifts. Special events, such as readings and book signings, are held weekly. ⊠ *Keauhou Shopping Center, 78-6831 Alii Dr.* ☎ *808/324-0350* ⊕ *www.konastories.com.*

CLOTHING AND SHOES

Hilo Hattie. The well-known Hawaii clothier offers his-and-her aloha wear and carries a huge selection of casual clothes, local art, books, music, jewelry, local gourmet items, coffee, and souvenirs. ∎**TIP**➔ **Call for free transportation from nearby hotels.** ⊠ *75-5597 Palani Rd.* ☎ *808/329-7200* ⊕ *www.hilohattie.com.*

Honolua Surf Company. Surfer chic, compliments of Roxy, Volcom, and the like, is for sale here for both men and women. This is a great place to shop for a bikini or board shorts, or to pick up a cool, retro-design T-shirt or Hawaii-style embroidered sweat jacket. Another location at the Waikoloa Beach Resort focuses on *wahine* (women's) apparel. ⊠ *Kona Inn Shopping Village, 75-5744 Alii Dr.* ☎ *808/329–1001* ⊕ *www.honoluasurf.com.*

Paradise Found. Carrying contemporary silk and rayon clothing for women, this reputable shop is in the upcountry town of Kainaliu, near Aloha Theatre, but there's also a branch at Keauhou Shopping Center. ⊠ *79-740 Mamalahoa Hwy., Kainaliu* ☎ *808/322–2111.*

FOOD AND WINE

Kailua Candy Company. This chocolate company has been satisfying sweet tooths for more than three decades with decadent desserts and sinful bites of chocolate heaven. Many truffles and candies incorporate local ingredients (passion-fruit truffles and chocolate-covered mango—yum). Cheesecakes and mousse cakes melt in your mouth. Of course, tasting is part of the fun. Through a glass wall you can watch the chocolate artists at work Monday through Saturday from 9 to 5. ⊠ *Kaloko Light Industrial Park, 73-5612 Kauhola St.* ☎ *808/329–2522* ⊕ *www. kailuacandy.com.*

Fodor'sChoice
★
Keauhou Store. This historic roadside store has been transformed into a combination convenience store, bakeshop, lunch stop, gift shop, and museum. When Kurt and Thea Brown purchased the property in 2010, they discovered a treasure trove of untouched inventory dating to the 1920s. These artifacts are on display, along with such gift items as koa bowls, cool retro T-shirts, and Kona coffee grown on-site. Stop by for fresh produce, beverages, spirits, ice cream, Thea's yummy fresh-baked cookies, or a burger or sandwich enjoyed on the outdoor lanai overlooking the coffee trees. ⊠ *78-7010 Mamalahoa Hwy., Holualoa* ☎ *808/322–5203* ⊕ *www.keauhoustore.com.*

Kona Coffee & Tea Company. Its location across from the Honokohau Harbor makes this family-owned coffee company's retail outlet a good bet for some easy gourmet gift shopping—or just a coffee or tea stop. Try different roasts or a selection of flavored coffees from the coffee bar, and shop for other Hawaiian-made treats, from honey and jams to chocolate-covered coffee beans. The shop is behind the Tesoro gas station. A branch, in downtown Kailua-Kona's Kona Coast Shopping Center, focuses on barista service. ⊠ *74-5035 Queen Kaahumanu Hwy., 4 miles south of Kona airport* ☎ *808/329–6577* ⊕ *www.konacoffeeandtea.com.*

Kona Wine Market. This wine shop carries both local and imported varietals (with more than 600 high-end wines), specialty liquors, 150 specialty beers, gourmet foods, and even cigars. As a bonus, the market delivers wine and gift baskets to hotels. ⊠ *Kona Commons, 74-5450 Makala Blvd.* ☎ *808/329–9400* ⊕ *www.konawinemarket.com.*

FAMILY **Mrs. Barry's Kona Cookies.** For 30 years, Mrs. Barry and her family have been serving yummy home-baked cookies, including mac nut, white chocolate–mac nut, oatmeal raisin, and coffee crunch. Packaged in beautiful gift boxes or bags, the cookies make excellent gifts for family back home. Stop by on your way to Costco or the airport and pick up a bag or two or three. Ah heck, just ask Mrs. Barry to ship your stash instead. ✉ *73-5563 Maiau St., below Costco* ☎ *808/329–6055* ⊕ *www. konacookies.com.*

Fodor's Choice
★
Westside Wines. Tucked away in a small downtown Kona retail center below Longs, this nifty gourmet wine and spirits shop offers restaurant-quality "wine list" wines at affordable prices. It's also the place to find large-format craft beers, French Champagne, single-malt scotches, organic vodka, small-batch bourbon, rye whiskey, fresh bread, and artisan cheese from around the world. George Clooney's Casamigos tequila is the store's house tequila. A certified wine specialist, proprietor Alex Thropp was one of the state's top wholesale wine reps for decades. Wine and tequila tastings take place Friday and Saturday afternoons from 3 to 6. ✉ *75-5660 Kopiko St. #4* ☎ *808/329–1777.*

GALLERIES

Kona Art Gallery. Gary and Elizabeth Theriault showcase a variety of local art here, including Gary's Big Island life photos and Elizabeth's hand-painted drums and rattles. The gallery owners also feature work from other artists, including Hawaiian *ipus* (gourds used as instruments in hula dancing), exotic wood items, paper sculptures, quilts, and jewelry. Be warned: it's only open Tuesday through Saturday 10 to 3. ✉ *Mamalahoa Hwy., Holualoa* ☎ *808/322–5125.*

MARKETS

Alii Gardens Marketplace. This mellow, parklike market, open Tuesday to Sunday 10 to 5, features outdoor stalls offering tropical flowers, produce, soaps, kettle corn, coffee, cookies, jewelry, koa wood, clothing, and kitschy crafts. A food kiosk serves shave ice, fish tacos, coconut water, fresh-fruit smoothies, and hamburgers, and you can also book surf lessons and kayak tours here. ✉ *75-6129 Alii Dr., 1½ mile south of Kona Inn Shopping Village.*

Keauhou Farmers Market. In the parking lot at Keauhou Shopping Center, this cheerful market is the place to go on Saturday morning, and for good reason: live music, local produce (much of it organic), goat cheese, honey, meat, flowers, macadamia nuts, fresh-baked pastries, Kona coffee, and plenty of local color. ✉ *Keauhou Shopping Center, 78-6831 Alii Dr.* ⊕ *www.keauhoufarmersmarket.com.*

Kona Inn Farmers' Market. An awesome florist creates custom arrangements while you wait at this touristy farmers' market. There are more than 40 vendors with lots of crafts for sale as well as the best prices on fresh produce and orchids in Kona. The market is held in a parking lot at the corner of Hualalai Road and Alii Drive, Wednesday to Sunday 7 to 4. ✉ *75-7544 Alii Dr.*

Kona International Market. This breezy, indoor-outdoor marketplace features coffee, Hawaii-made goods, and imported collectibles, novelty items, and clothing. There's also a shaded food court; try some authentic Filipino specialties at Trini's Mixed Plate Catering. The market is open daily 9 to 5, and a free shuttle from Kailua Pier runs on Wednesday. ✉ *74-5533 Luhia St.* ☎ *808/329–6262* ⊕ *www. konainternationalmarket.com.*

THE KONA COAST

ARTS AND CRAFTS

Antiques and Orchids Antique Mall. Housed in a historic building in Captain Cook, this boutique lives up to its name by offering a comprehensive collection of local antiques and Hawaiiana (check out the Duke Kahanamoku memorabilia) interspersed with orchids of assorted colors and varieties. Enjoy a cup of Kona coffee served in the store's quaint coffee shop. ⊠ *81-6224 Mamalahoa Hwy., Captain Cook* ☎ *808/323–9851.*

Kimura's Lauhala Shop. Originally a general store built in 1914, this historic shop features handmade products crafted by local lauhala weavers. Among the offerings are hats, baskets, containers, and mats, many of which are woven by the proprietors. Owner Alfreida Kimura-Fujita was born in the house behind the shop, and her daughter Renee is also an accomplished weaver. ⊠ *77-996 Mamalahoa Hwy., Holualoa* ☎ *808/324–0053.*

GALLERIES

Cliff Johns Gallery. Woodworker Cliff Johns has a knack for sourcing unique fine art handcrafted by Big Island artisans. The gallery features wood sculptures, paintings, carvings, and other crafts different from the standard fare. ⊠ *76-7460 Mamalahoa Hwy., Kealakekua* ☎ *808/322–6611.*

Holualoa Gallery. One of several excellent galleries along the narrow highway in this historic artists' village, this shop carries stunning contemporary *raku* pottery, original paintings by local artists, and other collectibles, including gallery owner Matt Lovein's famous Wish Keepers ceramic sculptures. ⊠ *76-5921 Mamalahoa Hwy., Holualoa* ☎ *808/322–8484* ⊕ *www.lovein.com.*

MARKET

South Kona Green Market. A favorite in Captain Cook, this Sunday farmers' market offers great hot breakfast and lunch items, produce from local farms, and artists selling their goods. ⊠ *Amy B.H. Greenwell Ethnobotanical Garden, 82-6160 Mamalahoa Hwy., Captain Cook* ⊕ *www.skgm.org.*

THE KOHALA COAST

SHOPPING CENTERS

Kawaihae Harbor Shopping Center. This almost-oceanfront shopping plaza houses the exquisite Harbor Gallery, which represents more than 200 Big Island artists. Stroll inside before or after your meal at the acclaimed Café Pesto, Kohala Burger and Taco, or Kawaihae Kitchen. Try the Big Island–made ice cream and shave ice (the best in North Hawaii) at local favorite Anuenue. Also here are Mountain Gold Jewelers and Kohala Divers. ⊠ *Hwy. 270, Kawaihae* ⊕ *www.kawaihaeshopping.com.*

Kings' Shops at Waikoloa Beach Resort. Stores here include Martin & MacArthur, featuring koa furniture and accessories, and Cariloha, which offers bamboo clothing items, as well as a small Macy's and high-end chains: Coach, Tiffany, L'Occitane, and Louis Vuitton. Gourmet offerings include Merriman's Mediterranean Café, Roy's Waikoloa Bar & Grill, and Three Fat Pigs. Stock your hotel fridge with fresh local produce from the Kings' Shops Farmers Market, held Wednesday 8:30 to 2. ⊠ *Waikoloa Beach Resort, 250 Waikoloa Beach Dr., Waikoloa* ☎ *808/886–8811* ⊕ *www.kingsshops.com.*

Queens' MarketPlace. The largest shopping complex on the Kohala Coast, Queens' MarketPlace houses fashionable clothing stores, jewelry boutiques, galleries, gift shops, and restaurants, including Sansei Seafood Restaurant & Sushi Bar and Romano's Macaroni Grill. Island Gourmet Markets and Starbucks are also here, as is an affordable food court. ⊠ *Waikoloa Beach Resort, 201 Waikoloa Beach Dr., Waikoloa* ☎ *808/886–8822* ⊕ *www.queensmarketplace.net.*

The Shops at Mauna Lani. The best part about this complex is its roster of restaurants, which includes Tommy Bahama Tropical Café, Ruth's Chris Steakhouse, Just Tacos Mexican Grill and Cantina, and Monstera, for noodles and sushi. You can find tropical apparel at Jams World, high-end housewares at Oasis Lifestyle, and original art at a number of galleries. Kids love the "adventure ride" theater, with the only "4-D" screens in Hawaii. ⊠ *68-1330 Mauna Lani Dr., Kohala Coast* ☎ *808/885–9501* ⊕ *www.shopsatmaunalani.com.*

ARTS AND CRAFTS

Elements Jewelry & Fine Crafts. The beautiful little shop carries lots of original, handmade jewelry made by local artists as well as carefully chosen gifts, including unusual ceramics, paintings, prints, glass items, baskets, fabrics, bags, and toys. ⊠ *55-3413 Akoni Pule Hwy., next to Bamboo Restaurant, Hawi* ☎ *808/889–0760* ⊕ *www. elementsjewelryandcrafts.com.*

Hawaiian Quilt Collection. The Hawaiian quilt is a work of art that is prized and passed down through generations. At this store, you'll find everything from hand-quilted purses and bags to wall hangings and blankets. You can even get a take-home kit and sew your very own Hawaiian quilt. ⊠ *Queens' MarketPlace, 201 Waikoloa Beach Dr., Waikoloa* ☎ *808/886–0494* ⊕ *www.hawaiian-quilts.com.*

Island Pearls by Maui Divers. Among the fine jewelry at this boutique is a wide selection of high-end pearl jewelry, including Tahitian black pearls, South Sea white and golden pearls, and chocolate Tahitian pearls. Also here are freshwater pearls in the shell, black coral (the Hawaii state gemstone), and diamonds. Prices are high but so is the quality. ⊠ *Queens' MarketPlace, 201 Waikoloa Beach Dr., Waikoloa* ☎ *808/886–4817* ⊕ *www.mauidivers.com.*

CLOTHING AND SHOES

As Hawi Turns. This North Kohala shop, housed in the historic 1932 Toyama Building, adds a sophisticated touch to resort wear with items made of hand-painted silk in tropical designs by local artists. There are plentiful vintage treasures, jewelry, gifts, hats, bags, and toys, plus handmade ukuleles by local luthier David Gomes. ⊠ *55-3412 Akoni Pule Hwy., Hawi* ☎ *808/889–5023.*

Blue Ginger. The Waikoloa branch of this fashion veteran offers really sweet matching aloha outfits for the entire family. There are also handbags, shoes, robes, jewelry, and lotions. ⊠ *Queens' MarketPlace, 201 Waikoloa Beach Dr., Waikoloa* ☎ *808/886–0022* ⊕ *www.blueginger. com.*

Cinnamon Girl. This store's feminine, flirty outfits—original print dresses, skirts, and tops designed and made in Hawaii—offer a contemporary twist on traditional aloha wear. The boutique also carries perfume, jewelry, hats, slippers, stuffed animals, and other trinkets and toys. ⊠ *Kings' Shops at Waikoloa Beach Resort, 250 Waikoloa Beach Dr., Waikoloa* ☎ *808/886–0241* ⊕ *www.cinnamongirl.com.*

Exclusive Designs. When it comes to Hawaiian-style apparel, everything from the traditional to the contemporary can be found here. The shop has casual, resort, and evening wear as well as swimwear, jewelry, and hats for women. Aloha styles are available for infants, children, men, and women. ⊠ *Queens' MarketPlace, 201 Waikoloa Beach Dr., Waikoloa* ☎ *808/886–0350.*

Persimmon. This darling little boutique is stocked with trendy women's clothing from lines such as Michael Stars, Free People, Blu Moon, and Hard Tail, plus local favorite Acacia swimwear. Gift items include stationery and cards, regional artwork, locally designed jewelry, and island-themed bath and body products. ⊠ *Queens' MarketPlace, 201 Waikoloa Beach Dr., Waikoloa* ☎ *808/886–0303* ⊕ *www. persimmonboutique.com.*

Reyn's. Reyn Spooner's dressy clothing has been a tradition in Hawaii since 1959 and remains popular among locals and visitors alike. The store offers aloha shirts for both men and boys, men's shorts, and some dresses for women and girls. The price may be high, but you're buying the best. ⊠ *Queens' MarketPlace, 303 Waikoloa Beach Dr., Waikoloa* ☎ *808/886–1162* ⊕ *www.reyns.com.*

GALLERIES

Ackerman Fine Art Gallery. This gallery is truly a family affair. Painter Gary Ackerman's daughter, Alyssa, and her husband, Ronnie, run the gallery that showcases Gary's art. Down the block is a second gallery, which features art by several of Gary's family members as well as gifts. The side-by-side gallery, café, and gift shop are near the King Kamehameha Statue. ⊠ *54-3897 Akoni Pule Hwy., Kapaau* ☎ *808/889–5971* ⊕ *www.ackermangalleries.com.*

Gallery at Bamboo. Inside Bamboo Restaurant, this gallery seduces with elegant koa-wood furniture and an array of gift items, such as boxes, jewelry, and even aloha shirts. ⊠ *Bamboo Restaurant, 55-3415 Akoni Pule Hwy., Hawi* ☎ *808/889–1441* ⊕ *www.bamboorestaurant.info.*

Harbor Gallery. Since 1990, this gallery has been enticing visitors with a vast collection of paintings and sculptures by more than 200 Big Island artists. There are also antique maps and prints, wooden bowls, paddles, koa furniture, jewelry, and glasswork. Chosen best art gallery by readers of *North Hawaii News* in 2013, the shop hosts two annual wood shows. ⊠ *Kawaihae Harbor Shopping Center, 61-3665 Akoni Pule Hwy., Kawaihae* ☎ *808/882–1510* ⊕ *www.harborgallery.biz.*

6

Rankin Gallery. Watercolorist and oil painter Patrick Louis Rankin show-cases his own work in his shop in a restored plantation store next to the bright-green Chinese community and social hall, on the way to Pololu Valley. The building sits right at a curve in the road, in the Palawa *ahu-puaa* (land division) past Kapaau. ⊠ *53-4380 Akoni Pule Hwy., Kapaau* ☎ *808/889–6849* ⊕ *www.patricklouisrankin.net.*

WAIMEA

SHOPPING CENTERS

Parker Ranch Center. With a snazzy ranch-style motif, this shopping hub includes a supermarket, some great local eateries (Village Burger and Lilikoi Café), a coffee shop, natural foods store, galleries, and clothing boutiques. The Parker Ranch Store and Parker Ranch Visitors Center and Museum are also here. ⊠ *67-1185 Mamalahoa Hwy.* ⊕ *www. parkerranchcenterads.com.*

Parker Square. Although the Gallery of Great Things is this center's star attraction, it's also worth looking in at the Waimea General Store; Sweet Wind, for books, chimes, and beads; and Kamuela Goldsmiths, which sells locally crafted gold jewelry. Waimea Coffee Company satisfies with salads, sandwiches, and Kona coffee. ⊠ *65-1279 Kawaihae Rd.*

FOOD AND WINE

Fodor'sChoice **Kamuela Liquor Store.** From the outside it doesn't look like much, but
★ this historic store sells the best selection of premium spirits, wines, and gourmet items on the island. Alvin, the owner, is a collector of fine wines, as evidenced by his multiple cellars. Wine-and-cheese tastings take place Friday afternoon—the store offers an extensive selection of artisanal cheeses from around the world. Favorites like duck mousse round out the inventory, and everything is priced within reason. ⊠ *64-1010 Mamalahoa Hwy.* ☎ *808/885–4674.*

Waimea General Store. Since 1970, this Waimea landmark has been a favorite of locals and visitors alike. Although specialty kitchenware takes center stage, the shop brims with local gourmet items, books, kimonos, and Hawaiian gifts and souvenirs. ⊠ *Parker Square, 65-1279 Kawaihae Rd., Suite 112* ☎ *808/987–1565* ⊕ *www.waimeageneralstore. com.*

GALLERIES

Fodor'sChoice **Gallery of Great Things.** You might lose yourself exploring the trove of fine
★ art and collectibles in every price range at this gallery, which represents hundreds of local artists and has a low-key, unhurried atmosphere. The "things" include hand-stitched quilts, ceramic sculptures, vintage kimo-nos, original paintings, koa-wood bowls and furniture, etched glass-ware, Niihau shell lei, and feather art by local artist Beth McCormick. ⊠ *Parker Square, 65-1279 Kawaihae Rd.* ☎ *808/885–7706* ⊕ *www. galleryofgreatthingshawaii.com.*

Wishard Gallery. A Big Island–born artist whose verdant landscapes and *paniolo* (cowboy)-themed paintings have become iconic throughout the Islands, Harry Wishard showcases his original oils at this gallery,

Continued on page 172

ALL ABOUT LEI

Lei brighten every occasion in Hawaii, from birthdays to bar mitzvahs to baptisms. Creative artisans weave nature's bounty—flowers, ferns, vines, and seeds—into gorgeous creations that convey an array of heartfelt messages: "Welcome," "Congratulations," "Good luck," "Farewell," "Thank you," "I love you." When it's difficult to find the right words, a lei expresses exactly the right sentiment.

WHERE TO BUY THE BEST LEI

In Honolulu's Chinatown, you'll encounter numerous lei "stands" that offer grand arrays of gorgeous garlands. Every florist shop in the Islands sells lei; you can also treat yourself to a lei while shopping for provisions at any supermarket or box store. And you'll always find lei sellers at crafts fairs and outdoor festivals.

LEI ETIQUETTE

■ To wear a closed lei, drape it over your shoulders, half in front and half in back. Open lei are worn around the neck, with the ends draped over the front in equal lengths.

■ Pikake, ginger, and other sweet, delicate blossoms are "feminine" lei. Men opt for cigar, crown flower, and ti leaf, which are sturdier and don't emit as much fragrance.

■ Lei are always presented with a kiss, a custom that supposedly dates back to World War II when a hula dancer fancied an officer at a U.S.O. show. Taking a dare from members of her troupe, she took off her lei, placed it around his neck, and kissed him on the cheek.

■ You shouldn't wear a lei before you give it to someone else. Hawaiians believe the lei absorbs your *mana* (spirit); if you give your lei away, you'll be giving away part of your essence.

ORCHID

Growing wild on every continent except Antarctica, orchids—which range in color from yellow to green to purple—comprise the largest family of plants in the world. There are more than 20,000 species of orchids, but only three are native to Hawaii—and they are very rare. The pretty lavender vanda you see hanging by the dozens at local lei stands has probably been imported from Thailand.

MAILE

Maile, an endemic twining vine with a heady aroma, is sacred to Laka, goddess of the hula. In ancient times, dancers wore maile and decorated hula altars with it to honor Laka. Today, "open" maile lei usually are given to men. Instead of ribbon, interwoven lengths of maile are used at dedications of new businesses. The maile is untied, never snipped, for doing so would symbolically "cut" the company's success.

ILIMA

Designated by Hawaii's Territorial Legislature in 1923 as the official flower of the island of Oahu, the golden ilima is so delicate it lasts for just a day. Five to seven hundred blossoms are needed to make one garland. Queen Emma, wife of King Kamehameha IV, preferred ilima over all other lei, which may have led to the incorrect belief that they were reserved only for royalty.

PLUMERIA

This ubiquitous flower is named after Charles Plumier, the noted French botanist who discovered it in Central America in the late 1600s. Plumeria ranks among the most popular lei in Hawaii because it's fragrant, hardy, plentiful, inexpensive, and requires very little care. Although yellow is the most common color, you'll also find plumeria lei in shades of pink, red, orange, and "rainbow" blends.

PIKAKE

Favored for its fragile beauty and sweet scent, pikake was introduced from India. In lieu of pearls, many brides in Hawaii adorn themselves with long, multiple strands of white pikake. Princess Kaiulani enjoyed showing guests her beloved pikake and peacocks at Ainahau, her Waikiki home. Interestingly, pikake is the Hawaiian word for both the bird and the blossom.

KUKUI

The kukui (candlenut) is Hawaii's state tree. Early Hawaiians strung kukui nuts (which are quite oily) together and burned them for light; mixed burned nuts with oil to make an indelible dye; and mashed roasted nuts to consume as a laxative. Kukui nut lei may not have been made until after Western contact, when the Hawaiians saw black beads from Europe and wanted to imitate them.

along with works by other renowned local artists like Kathy Long, Edward Kayton, and Lynn Capell. There's a second gallery location at Queens' MarketPlace. ⊠ *Parker Ranch Center, 67-1185 Mamalahoa Hwy.* ☎ *808/937–8772* ⊕ *www.wishardgallery.com.*

THE HAMAKUA COAST

ARTS AND CRAFTS

Glass from the Past. Near Akaka Falls, this is a fun place to shop for a quirky gift or just to poke around. The store is chock-full of old Hawaiian bottles, antiques, vintage clothing, Japanese collectibles, and interesting ephemera. There's often even a "free" table out front to add to the discovery. ⊠ *28-1672 Old Mamalahoa Hwy., Honomu* ☎ *808/963–6449.*

GALLERIES

Waipio Valley Artworks. In this quaint gallery in a vintage home, you can find finely crafted wooden bowls, koa furniture, paintings, and jewelry—all made by local artists. There's also a great little café where you can pick up a sandwich or ice cream before descending into Waipio Valley. ⊠ *Off Hwy. 240, Kukuihaele* ☎ *808/775–0958* ⊕ *www.waipiovalleyartworks.com.*

Woodshop Gallery. Run by local artists Peter and Jeanette McLaren, this Honomu gallery showcases their woodwork and photography collections along with beautiful ceramics, photography, glass, and paintings from other Big Island artists. The McLarens also serve up plate lunches, shave ice, homemade ice cream, and espresso to hungry tourists in the adjoining café. Their shop next door, called Same-Same, But Different, features made-in-Hawaii clothing and small gifts. The historic building still has a working soda fountain dating from 1935. ⊠ *28-1690 Old Government Rd., Honomu* ☎ *808/963–6363* ⊕ *www.woodshopgallery.com.*

HILO

SHOPPING CENTERS

Hilo Shopping Center. Among this shopping plaza's 40 shops are a day spa, a pharmacy, a trendy boutique, and popular Lanky's Pastries and Island Naturals Market and Deli, plus Sunlight Cafe and Restaurant Miwa. There's plenty of free parking. ⊠ *1261 Kilauea Ave.*

Prince Kuhio Plaza. The Big Island's most comprehensive mall has indoor shopping, entertainment (a multiplex), and dining, including KFC, Hot Dog on a Stick, Cinnabon, the island's only IHOP, and Maui Tacos. The kids might like the arcade (near the food court), while you enjoy the stores, anchored by Macy's, Sports Authority, and Sears. ⊠ *111 E. Puainako St., at Hwy. 11* ☎ *808/959–3555* ⊕ *www.princekuhioplaza.com.*

ARTS AND CRAFTS

Dan DeLuz's Woods. Master bowl-turner Dan DeLuz creates works of art from 50 types of exotic wood grown on the Big Island. The shop features a variety of items—from picture frames to jewelry boxes—made from koa, monkeypod, mango, kiawe, and other fine hardwoods. The store is closed Tuesday. ✉ *17-4003 Ahu Ahu Pl., past mile marker 12, Kurtistown* ☎ *808/968–6607.*

Most Irresistible Shop. This place lives up to its name by stocking unique gifts from around the Pacific, be it pure Hawaiian ohia lehua honey, kau coffee, aloha wear, or tinkling wind chimes. ✉ *256 Kamehameha Ave.* ☎ *808/935–9644.*

BOOKSTORES

FAMILY
Fodor's Choice
★

Basically Books. More than a bookstore, this bayfront shop stocks one of Hawaii's largest selections of maps, including topographical and relief maps, and Hilo's largest selection of Hawaiian music. Of course, it also has books about Hawaii, including great choices for children. ✉ *160 Kamehameha Ave.* ☎ *808/961–0144, 800/903–6277* ⊕ *www. basicallybooks.com.*

CLOTHING AND SHOES

Hilo Hattie. Set in an indoor mall, the east-side outlet of the well-known clothier is slightly smaller than its Kailua-Kona cousin, but offers plenty of the same his-and-her aloha wear, casual clothes, slippers, jewelry, and souvenirs. ✉ *Prince Kuhio Plaza, 111 E. Puainako St.* ☎ *808/961–3077* ⊕ *www.hilohattie.com.*

Sig Zane Designs. This acclaimed boutique sells distinctive island wearables with bold colors and motifs designed by the legendary Sig Zane, known for his artwork honoring native flora and fauna. All apparel is handcrafted in Hawaii, and is often worn by local celebrities and businesspeople. ✉ *122 Kamehameha Ave.* ☎ *808/935–7077* ⊕ *www. sigzane.com.*

FOOD

Big Island Candies. A local legend in the cookie- and chocolate-making business, Big Island Candies is a must-see if you have a sweet tooth. Enjoy a free cookie sample and a cup of Kona coffee as you watch sweets being made through a window. The store has a long list of interesting and tasty products, but it is best known for its chocolate-dipped shortbread cookies. ✉ *585 Hinano St., two blocks from Hilo airport* ☎ *808/935–8890* ⊕ *www.bigislandcandies.com.*

Hilo Coffee Mill. In addition to a fantastic coffee-farm tour, the Hilo Coffee Mill sells coffee from a variety of local producers, along with locally made baked goods, candies, artwork, and gifts. Free coffee samples are offered. The mill is closed Wednesday and Sunday and hosts a farmers' market Saturday 8 to 1. ✉ *17-995 Volcano Rd., between mile markers 12 and 13, Mountain View* ☎ *808/968–1333* ⊕ *www.hilocoffeemill.com.*

Two Ladies Kitchen. This hole-in-the-wall confections shop has made a name for itself thanks to its pillowy *mochi* (Japanese rice pounded into a sticky paste and molded into shapes). The proprietors are best known for their huge ripe strawberries wrapped in a white mochi covering, which won't last as long as a box of chocolates—most mochi items are only good for two or three days. To guarantee you get your fill, call and place your order ahead of time. It's closed Sunday and Monday. ⌧ *274 Kilauea Ave.* ☎ *808/961–4766.*

HOME DECOR

Dragon Mama. Step into this charming downtown Hilo spot to find authentic Japanese fabrics, futons, and gifts along with an elegant selection of clothing, sleepwear, slippers, and tea-service accoutrements. Handmade comforters, pillows, and futon pads are sewn of natural fibers on-site. ⌧ *266 Kamehameha Ave.* ☎ *808/934–9081* ⊕ *www. dragonmama.com.*

MARKET

Fodor's Choice ★ **Hilo Farmers Market.** The 200 vendors here—stretching a couple of blocks—sell a profusion of tropical flowers, locally grown produce, aromatic honey, tangy goat cheese, hot breakfast and lunch items, and fresh baked specialties at extraordinary prices. This colorful, open-air market—the most popular on the island—opens for business Wednesday and Saturday from 6 am to 4 pm. A smaller version on the other days features 20 to 30 vendors. ⌧ *Kamehameha Ave. and Mamo St.* ☎ *808/933–1000* ⊕ *www.hilofarmersmarket.com.*

HAWAII VOLCANOES NATIONAL PARK AND VICINITY

ARTS AND CRAFTS

Fodor's Choice ★ **Kilauea Kreations.** Beautiful hand-stitched Hawaiian quilts grace the walls here, quilting kits and books abound, and the vast inventory of tropical fabrics is amazing. The friendly proprietors also offer fine art, photography, cards, and cool souvenirs you won't find anywhere else. ⌧ *19-3972 Volcano Rd., Volcano* ☎ *808/967–8090* ⊕ *www. kilaueakreations.com.*

2400 Fahrenheit. At the end of Old Volcano Road near Volcano Village, this small gallery and studio has handblown glass inspired by the eruption of Kilauea and the colors of the tropics. You can see the artist in action Thursday through Monday from 10 to 4. ⌧ *Old Volcano Rd., off Hwy. 11 between mile markers 23 and 24, Volcano* ☎ *808/985–8667* ⊕ *www.2400f.com.*

SPAS

The Big Island's spa directors have produced menus full of "only in Hawaii" treatments well worth a splurge. Local specialties include *lomilomi* massages, hot-lava-stone massages, and scrubs and wraps that incorporate plenty of coconut, ginger, orchids, and macadamia nuts. Also expect to find Swedish and deep-tissue massages and, at some spas, Thai massage. And in romantic Hawaii, couples can be pampered side by side. ■ TIP➔ Lomilomi massage is a quintessential Hawaiian deep-tissue massage, and most practitioners are happy to adjust the pressure to your needs.

Most of the full-service spas on the Big Island are at the resorts. With the exception of the Four Seasons Spa at Hualalai, these spas are open to anyone. In fact, many of the hotels outsource spa management, and there is no price difference for guests and nonguests, although guests can receive in-room services.

KAILUA-KONA

A Ala Hawaii Massage and Spa. With oceanfront views of Kailua Bay, this spa offers a full menu of massage treatments as well as wraps, facials, and waxing. This is a convenient place to get pampered before hitting the village shops. ⊠ *Kona Inn Shopping Village, 75-5744 Alii Dr. #245, Kailua-Kona* ☏ *808/937–9707* ⊕ *www.oceanfrontmassage.com* ☞ *$79 60-min massage, $115 90-min massage. Services: Facials, massages, waxing, wraps. Classes and programs: Yoga.*

Hoola Spa at the Sheraton Kona Resort & Spa at Keauhou Bay. The hotel's oceanfront spa offers a menu of tropical delights with combination options that let you mix and match for a super heavenly—and affordable—treatment. The private outdoor lanai lets you melt into dreamland as you listen to waves lapping at the rocks inches away. In winter, you may hear a whale or two nearby. Massages, such as the combo *lomilomi,* shiatzu, pressure point, and Swedish full-body treatment, are given using only Ola organic oils made in Hawaii. Hot stones, steamed towels, and salt scrubs add to the luxury. Afterwards, you can rinse off with hot steam and cool water in the complimentary shower/steamroom. The spa recently debuted Hawaii's first Himalayan Salt Room, a natural therapy for spa-going guests. Couples' treatments take place outside on the secluded blacony and start with a private whirlpool bath followed by a side-by-side massage. ⊠ *Sheraton Kona Resort & Spa, 78-128 Ehukai St., Kailua-Kona* ☏ *808/930–4848* ⊕ *www.hoolaspa. com* ☞ *$120 50-min lomilomi massage, $165–$375 packages. Hair salon, sauna, steam room, whirlpool. Services: Aromatherapy, body scrubs and wraps, facials, massages, waxing.*

The Lotus Center. Tucked away on the first floor of the Royal Kona Resort, the Lotus Center provides a convenient option for massage treatments, facials, and waxing. There's also a chiropractor on the premises. Oceanside massage is available on a private patio outside the treatment rooms. Alternative offerings include Reiki and crystal-energy sessions, and biofeedback. ⊠ *Royal Kona Resort, 75-5852 Alii Dr., Kailua-Kona* ☏ *808/334–0445* ⊕ *www.konaspa.com* ☞ *$110–$150 lomilomi massage, $130–$165 hot-stone massage.*

Pau Hana Massage. This classy massage studio, owned and operated by resort-trained massage therapists and open weekdays, is conveniently located in downtown Kailua-Kona. In addition to traditional massage, you can get a five-star experience—warm coconut scalp massage, lemongrass-ginger hot stone foot soak, and other tropical specialties—at a fraction of resort prices. ⊠ *75-5741 Kuakini Hwy., Building A, Kailua-Kona* ☏ *808/327–5664* ⊕ *www.pauhanamassage.com* ☞ *$80 60-min massage, $115 90-min hot-stone massage, $120 hot-stone foot soak, foot scrub, and 60-min massage.*

Fodor's Choice ★ **The Spa at Hualalai.** For the exclusive use of Four Seasons Resort guests and members, this spa features 19 massage treatment areas. Tropical breezes waft through 10 outdoor massage *hales,* situated in beautiful garden settings. The therapists are top-notch, and a real effort is made to incorporate local traditions. Apothecary services allow you to customize your treatment with ingredients like kukui nuts, Hawaiian salts, and coconut. Massage options range from traditional *lomilomi* to Thai. ⊠ *Four Seasons Resort Hualalai, 72-100 Kaupulehu Dr., Kailua-Kona* ☎ *808/325–8000* ⊕ *www.fourseasons.com* ☞ *$175 50-min massage, $180 body scrub, $175 facials. Hair salon, outdoor hot tub, sauna, steam room. Gym with: Cardiovascular machines, free weights, weight-training equipment. Classes and programs: Personal training, Pilates, Spinning, yoga.*

THE KONA COAST

Kona Shiatsu Clinic. Tucked away in a vintage bungalow near Manago Hotel, this peaceful little clinic offers deep-tissue shiatsu massage, Japanese style. A master of shiatsu with more than 35 years experience, Tom Langenstein helps clients work out the kinks or recover from injuries. ⊠ *82-6161 Mamalahoa Hwy., Captain Cook* ☎ *808/323–3111* ⊕ *www. konashiatsu.com* ☞ *$65 60-min shiatsu massage.*

Mamalahoa Hot Tubs and Massage. Tucked into a residential neighborhood above Kealekekua, this is a welcome alternative to the large Kohala Coast resort spas. It feels like a secret hideaway aglow with tiki torches, and offers Hawaiian *lomilomi* and hot-stone massages at affordable prices. Soaking tubs, enclosed in their own thatched gazebo with roof portholes for stargazing, are great for a couple's soak. It's open Wednesday to Saturday. ⊠ *81-1016 St. John's Rd., Kealakekua* ☎ *808/323–2288* ⊕ *www.mamalahoa-hottubs.com* ☞ *$30 60-min soak; $95 30-min soak plus 60-min lomilomi, Swedish, or deep-tissue massage; $150 30-min soak plus 90-min hot-stone massage.*

THE KOHALA COAST

Hapuna Spa at the Hapuna Beach Prince Hotel. It's not unusual for locals to drive an hour each way to get their hair styled here. The salon is still the center of the operation, but it's joined by a full-service spa—nicely designed to let in lots of light—that has an extensive menu of massages, full facials, and body treatments. The most popular massage is the *lomilomi* (traditional Hawaiian massage). ⊠ *Hapuna Beach Prince Hotel, 62-100 Kaunaoa Dr., Kohala Coast* ☎ *808/880–3335* ⊕ *www. princeresortshawaii.com* ☞ *$145 50-min lomilomi massage, $439 half-day rejuvenation package. Hair salon. Services: body polish, facials, massages, waxing.*

Hawaii Island Retreat Maluhia Spa. This peaceful and elegant sanctuary in North Kohala offers three artfully appointed indoor treatment rooms and two outdoor massage platforms that overlook the valley. The spa is first-rate, with handcrafted wooden lockers, rain-style showerheads, and a signature line of lotions and scrubs that's made locally. The owners also create their own scrubs and wraps from ingredients grown on the property. The Papaya Delight lives up to its name, and features roasted ground papaya seeds mixed with goat yogurt and geranium.

The slate of massages includes *lomilomi,* Thai, and deep tissue. ✉ *250 Maluhia Rd., Kapaau* ☎ *808/889–6336* ⊕ *www.hawaiiislandretreat. com* ☞ *$130 60-minute lomilomi massage, $140 signature facial. Hot tub, infinity pool. Services: Facials, massages. Classes and programs: Aquacise, chi gung, yoga.*

Kohala Spa at the Hilton Waikoloa Village. Hawaii Island is known as the Orchid Isle. Kohala Spa pays it tribute with the Orchid Aromatherapy Massage, incorporating a specially blended, local *pikake* (jasmine) oil for calm and well-being. The island's volcanic character is expressed in lava rock soaking tubs and in treatments including the *Pohaku* hot-stone massage and reflexology with healing stones. Locker rooms are outfitted with a wealth of beauty and bath products, and the spa's retail facility offers signature Coco-Mango lotions, body washes, and shampoos. An open-air, seaside cabana provides a delightful spot for a massage overlooking the Pacific, while the fitness center has the latest machines and plentiful classes. ✉ *Hilton Waikoloa Village, 69-425 Waikoloa Beach Dr.* ☎ *808/886–2828, 800/445–8667* ⊕ *www.kohalaspa.com* ☞ *$145 50-min lomilomi massage, $554 half-day packages. Hair salon, hot tubs, sauna, steam room. Services: Aromatherapy, body scrubs and wraps, facials, massage. Gym with: Cardiovascular machines, free weights, weight-training equipment. Classes and programs: Aquaerobics, personal training, Pilates, Spinning, tai chi, yoga, Zumba.*

Mandara Spa at the Waikoloa Beach Marriott Resort. Overlooking the hotel's main pool with a distant view of the ocean, Mandara offers a complete, if not unique, spa menu, with *lomilomi,* scrubs, wraps, and more facial options than at the island's other spas. Mandara, which operates spas all over the world, uses Elemis products and incorporates local ingredients (lime and ginger in the scrubs, warm coconut milk in the wraps). The facility, which fuses contemporary and traditional Asian motifs, is beautiful. ✉ *Waikoloa Beach Marriott, 69-275 Waikoloa Beach Dr., Waikoloa* ☎ *808/886–8191* ⊕ *www.mandaraspa.com* ☞ *$188 50-min lomilomi massage. Steam room.*

Mauna Kea Spa by Mandara. Mandara blends European, Balinese, and indigenous treatments to create the ultimate spa experience. Though this facility is on the smaller side, the excellent treatments are up to the international company's exacting standards. Try the Elemis Tri-Enzyme Resurfacing Facial; the Mandara Four Hand Massage, where two therapists work out the kinks simultaneously; or an outdoor, ocean cabana massage. Traditional Hawaiian *lomilomi* is also available. The hotel operates a separate hair salon that offers manicures and pedicures. ✉ *Mauna Kea Beach Hotel, 69-100 Mauna Kea Beach Dr., Kohala Coast* ☎ *808/882–5630* ⊕ *www.mandaraspa.com* ☞ *$188 50-min lomilomi massage, $288 50-min outdoor massage. Services: Body treatments, facials, massages, waxing.*

Fodor'sChoice **Mauna Lani Spa.** This is a one-of-a-kind experience with a mix of tradi-
★ tional standbys (*lomilomi* massage, moisturizing facials) and innovative treatments influenced by ancient traditions and incorporating local products. Most treatments take place in outdoor thatched *hales* (huts) surrounded by lava rock. An exception is Watsu therapy, in which clients

are cradled in the arms of a certified therapist in warm salt water in a 1,000-square-foot grotto between two lava tubes. (It's great for people with disabilities who can't enjoy traditional massage.) Black volcanic clay applications are offered in a natural lava sauna. Aesthetic treatments incorporate high-end products from Epicuran and Emminence, so facials have lasting therapeutic effects. The spa also offers a full regimen of fitness and yoga classes. ⊠ *Mauna Lani Bay Hotel & Bungalows, 68-1365 Pauoa Rd., Kohala Coast* ☎ *808/881–7922* ⊕ *www. maunalani.com* ☞ *$175 60-min lomilomi massage, $185 50-min Lava Watsu Experience. Hair salon, hot tub, sauna, steam room. Services: Aquatic therapy, baths, body wraps, facials, massages, nail treatments, scrubs, tinting, waxing. Gym with: Cardiovascular machines, weight-training equipment. Classes and programs: Body sculpting, kickboxing, Pilates, spinning, weight training, yoga.*

FodorsChoice
★
Spa Without Walls at the Fairmont Orchid Hawaii. This ranks among the best massage facilities on the island, partially due to the superlative setting—private massage areas are situated amid the waterfalls, saltwater pools, and meandering gardens, as well as right on the beach. In fact, the Fairmont Orchid is one of the few resorts to offer beachside massage. Splurge on the 110-minute Alii Experience, offering hot coconut oil treatments, *lomilomi*, and hot-stone massage. Other great treatments include caviar facials, fragrant herbal wraps, and coffee-and-vanilla scrubs. Where else can you relax to the sounds of cascading waterfalls while watching tropical yellow tang swim beneath you through windows in the floor? ⊠ *Fairmont Orchid Hawaii, 1 N. Kaniku Dr., Kohala Coast* ☎ *808/887–7540, 808/885–2000* ⊕ *www.fairmont.com/ orchid* ☞ *$159–$179 50-min lomilomi massage. Sauna, steam room. Services: Baths, body wraps, facials, massages, scrubs. Classes and programs: Aquaerobics, guided walks, meditation, personal training, yoga.*

HAWAII VOLCANOES NATIONAL PARK AND VICINITY

Hale Hoola Spa in Volcano. Those staying in Volcano or Hilo have easy access to body treatments, massages, and facials at far more reasonable prices than on the other side of the island. Hale Hoola's menu features a bounty of local ingredients and traditional Hawaiian treatments, including *lomi hula*, which is *lomilomi* massage choreographed to hula music, and *laau hamo*, which blends *lomilomi* with traditional Hawaiian and Asian healing herbs and plant extracts. *Popokapai* is a divine blend of hot-stone massage and *laau hamo*, incorporating *lomilomi* with warm compresses filled with healing herbs. Facials and body scrubs use traditional ginger, coconut, and macadamia nuts, but also some surprises, including taro, vanilla, and volcanic clay. ⊠ *Mauna Loa Estates, 11-3913 7th St., Volcano* ☎ *808/756–2421* ⊕ *www.halehoola. net* ☞ *$75 60-min lomilomi massage, $190 rejuvenation package. Services: Aromatherapy, body scrubs and wraps, facials, hair removal, makeup, massages, waxing.*

ENTERTAINMENT AND NIGHTLIFE

Updated by Kristina Anderson

If you're the sort of person who doesn't come alive until after dark, you might be a little lonely on the Big Island. Blame it on the sleepy plantation heritage. People did their cane raising in the morning, thus very limited late-night fun.

Still, there are a few lively bars on the island, a handful of great local playhouses, half a dozen or so movie houses (including those that play foreign and independent films), and plenty of musical entertainment to keep you happy.

Also, many resorts have bars and late-night activities and events, and keep pools and gyms open late so there's something to do after dinner.

And let's not forget the luau. These fantastic dance and musical performances are combined with some of the best local food on the island and are plenty of fun for the whole family.

ENTERTAINMENT

DINNER CRUISES AND SHOWS

Luau on the Water Glass Bottom Dinner Cruise. Blue Sea Cruises offers a classier alternative to the booze cruise, with a buffet dinner, tropical cocktails, live entertainment, hula show, and conga dancing in a glass-bottom boat. The focus is on the sunset and the scenery, with the chance to see spinner dolphins and manta rays, as well as whales from November to May. ⊠ *Kailua Pier, Alii Dr., next to Courtyard King Kamehameha's Kona Beach Hotel, Kailua-Kona* ☎ *808/331–8875* ⊕ *www.blueseacruisesinc. com* ⛴ *$103* ☼ *Mon., Wed., Fri., and Sat., departure times vary.*

LUAU AND POLYNESIAN REVUES

KAILUA-KONA

Haleo Luau Dinner & Show at Sheraton Kona Resort. On the graceful grounds of the Sheraton Kona Resort, this luau takes you on a journey of song and dance, celebrating the historic Keauhou region, birthplace of King Kamehameha III. Before the show, you can participate in workshops on topics ranging from coconut-frond weaving to poi ball techniques. The excellent buffet is a feast of local favorites, including kalua pig, poi, ahi poke, chicken long rice, fish, and mango chutney. Generous mai tai refills are a plus, and it's all highlighted by a dramatic fire-knife finale. ⊠ *Sheraton Kona Resort & Spa at Keauhou Bay, 78-128 Ehukai St., Kailua-Kona* ☎ *808/930–4900* ⊕ *www.sheratonkona.com* ✉ *$85.78* ⊗ *Mon. at 5.*

Island Breeze Luau. With traditional dancing showcasing the interconnected Polynesian roots of Hawaii, Samoa, Tahiti, and New Zealand, the "We Are *Ohana* (family)" luau is not a hokey tourist-trap event. These performers take their art seriously. The historic oceanfront location at King Kamehameha's former royal compound near Ahuhena Heiau adds to the authenticity, and the bounty of food includes kalua pig cooked in an underground *imu* (oven). ⊠ *75-5660 Palani Rd., Kailua-Kona* ☎ *866/482–9775* ⊕ *www.islandbreezeluau.com* ✉ *$79.43* ⊗ *Tues., Thurs., and Sun. 5–8.*

Royal Kona Resort Lava Legends & Legacies. This resort lights its torches for a spectacular show and oceanfront buffet four times a week. Traditional luau fare is served along with succulent pork cooked in an authentic underground *imu* (oven), and an open bar offers mai tais and other tropical concoctions. An exciting fire-knife dancer caps off the show. ■ **TIP➔** Book online and save $15. ⊠ *Royal Kona Resort, 75-5852 Alii Dr., Kailua-Kona* ☎ *808/329–3111* ⊕ *www.royalkona. com* ✉ *$85* ⊗ *Mon.–Wed. and Fri. at 5.*

THE KOHALA COAST

Gathering of the Kings Polynesian Feast at Fairmont Orchid. Offering bang for your buck, this show is slickly produced and well choreographed, incorporating both traditional and modern dance and an array of beautiful costumes. The meal offers the most variety of any island luau, with four buffet tables representing New Zealand, Hawaii, Tahiti, and Samoa, and there's an open bar for mai tai refills. ⊠ *Fairmont Orchid Hawaii, 1 N. Kaniku Dr., Kohala Coast* ☎ *808/885–2000* ⊕ *www.fairmont.com/ orchid* ✉ *$109* ⊗ *Sat. at 5 pm.*

Hapuna Beach Prince Hotel's Let's Go Crabbing. While the Mauna Kea Beach Hotel's clambake gets all the acclaim, this meal is tastier and at a fraction of the price. Held on the hotel's ocean terrace, the all-you-can-eat buffet features everything from prime rib and roasted breast of turkey to Washington mussels, steamed Manila clams, excellent shrimp salads, and corn-and-crab bisque. Expect an array of crab offerings, including wok-fried Dungeness crab and chilled snow-crab claws. Homemade ice cream is the star attraction of the dessert bar, which features hot fudge and other toppings. ⊠ *Hapuna Beach Prince Hotel, 62-100 Kaunaoa Dr., Kohala Coast* ☎ *808/880–1111* ⊕ *www.princeresortshawaii.com* ✉ *$62* ⊗ *Fri. at 6.*

FAMILY **Legends of the Hawaii Luau at Hilton Waikoloa Village.** Presented outdoors at the Kamehameha Court, this new show is aptly subtitled, "Our Big Island Story." A delicious buffet offers Big Island–grown luau choices as well as more familiar fare and an open tropical bar. Pay a small fee and upgrade to Alii seating for a front-row vantage and your own buffet station. A children's station has kid favorites. Delicious desserts such as haupia cream puffs and Kona-coffee cheesecake top it all off. ⊠ *Hilton Waikoloa Village, 69-425 Waikoloa Beach Dr., Waikoloa* ☎ *808/886–1234* ⊕ *www.hiltonwaikoloavillage.com* 🗺 *$112* ⊙ *Tues., Fri., and Sun. at 6.*

Mauna Kea Beach Hotel Clambake. The weekly clambake here features an extensive menu with oysters on the half shell, Manila clams, Dungeness crab legs, sashimi, and Keahole lobster. There's even prime rib for meat lovers and a dessert station. Live Hawaiian music is often accompanied by a graceful hula dancer. ⊠ *Mauna Kea Beach Hotel, 62-100 Mauna Kea Beach Dr., Kohala Coast* ☎ *808/882–5810, 808/882–7222* ⊕ *www. maunakeabeachhotel.com* 🗺 *$92* ⊙ *Sat. at 6.*

Mauna Kea Beach Hotel Oceanfront Luau. On the oceanfront North Pointe Luau Grounds, you can sample the best of island cuisine—a traditional feast of imu-roasted kalua pig, island fish, lomi salmon, and sashimi—while enjoying the music and hula of the renowned Lim family. The luau includes an amazing fire-knife dance, spirited chanting, and traditional hula. *Keiki* (children) can learn the *hukilau* (a traditional song and dance), and you can relax under the stars. ⊠ *Mauna Kea Beach Hotel, 62-100 Mauna Kea Beach Dr., Kohala Coast* ☎ *808/882–5810, 808/882–7222* ⊕ *www.maunakeabeachhotel.com* 🗺 *$96* ⊙ *Tues. and Fri. at 5:45.*

Waikoloa Beach Marriott Sunset Luau. Overlooking beautiful Anaehoomalu Bay, the festivities at this luau include a spectacular Samoan fire dance performance as well as traditional song and dances from various Pacific Island cultures. Traditional dishes are served alongside more familiar Western fare, and there's also an open bar. ⊠ *Waikoloa Beach Marriott, 69-275 Waikoloa Beach Dr., Waikoloa* ☎ *808/886–6789* ⊕ *www. sunsetluau.com* 🗺 *$97* ⊙ *Wed. and Sat. 5–8:15.*

FESTIVALS

There is a festival dedicated to just about everything on the Big Island. Some of them are small community affairs, but a handful of film, food, and music festivals provide quality entertainment for visitors and locals alike. The following are our favorites:

Black and White Night. This lovely annual street party takes place in downtown Hilo. The stores stay open late, the sidewalks are dotted with live jazz bands, there are crafts and cultural info as well as a treasure hunt, and everyone dresses in black and white, some in shorts and tees and others in gowns and tuxes. ⊠ *329 Kamehameha Ave., Hilo* ☎ *808/935–8850* ⊕ *www.downtownhilo.com* ⊙ *First Friday in Nov.*

Chinese New Year. Every February, Hilo throws a big party complete with live music, food, and fireworks to commemorate this holiday. There's a smaller celebration along Alii Drive in Kona. ⊠ *329 Kamehameha Ave., Hilo* ☎ *808/935–8850* ⊕ *www.downtownhilo.com* ⊙ *Feb.*

King Kamehameha Day Celebration Parade. In this parade, at least 100 Hawaiian horseback riders represent the colorful flora of the Hawaiian Islands. A cultural festival usually follows. ⊠ *Kailua-Kona* ☎ *808/322–9944* ⊕ *www.konaparade.org* ⊙ *June.*

Kona Brewers Festival. At this lively annual celebration, 70 types of ales and lagers are showcased along with cuisine from 35 Hawaii chefs. There's

Hawaiian Music on the Big Island

It's easy to forget that Hawaii has its own music until you step off a plane onto the Islands—and then there's no escaping it. It's a unique blend of the strings and percussion favored by the early settlers and the chants and rituals of the ancient Hawaiians, reflecting the unique mixed heritage of this special place. Hawaiian music today includes Island-born tunings of acoustic guitar—slack key and steel guitar—along with the ukulele and vocals.

This is one of the few folk music traditions in the United States that is fully embraced by the younger generation, with no prodding from their parents or grandparents. A good many radio stations on the Big Island play Hawaiian/"Island"/reggae music, and concerts performed by Island favorites like Makana are filled with fans of all ages.

The best introduction is one of the annual festivals: the free **Annual Hawaii Slack Key Guitar Festival** (Labor Day weekend), with a handful of greats performing at the Sheraton Kona Resort; the **Annual Great Waikoloa Ukulele Festival** (March), which features prominent players and everything ukulele; and the **Annual Big Island Hawaiian Music Festival** (July), a weekend full of slack key, steel guitar, and ukulele madness at the UH Hilo Performing Arts Center.

Or you can catch live performances most nights at a handful of local bars and clubs, including **Huggo's on the Rocks, Island Lava Java**, and the **Kona Brewing Co.** in Kailua-Kona, and **Cronie's Bar and Grill** in Hilo.

also live music, fashion shows, a fun run, and a golf tournament. The multiday, sellout event is a community fundraiser and local favorite. ✉ *Courtyard King Kamehameha's Kona Beach Hotel, 75-5660 Palani Rd., Kailua-Kona* ☎ *808/331–3033* ⊕ *www.konabrewersfestival.com* ☉ *Early Mar.*

Kona Coffee Cultural Festival. Held over 10 days, the longest-running food festival in Hawaii includes coffee recipes, picking, and label-design contests; cupping competitions; a lecture series; and a colorful community parade featuring the newly crowned Miss Kona Coffee. During the Holualoa Village Coffee and Art Stroll, during you can meet artists and sample estate coffees. ☎ *808/323–2006* ⊕ *www.konacoffeefest.com* ☉ *Early Nov.*

Fodor'sChoice ★ **Merrie Monarch Festival.** The mother of all Hawaii festivals, the Merrie Monarch celebrates all things hula and completely overtakes Hilo for one fantastic week a year. The highly popular event honors the legacy of King David Kalakaua, the man responsible for reviving fading Hawaiian cultural traditions such as hula. The festival is staged at the spacious Edith Kanakaole Multi-Purpose Stadium during the first week following Easter Sunday. Hula *halau* (studios) worldwide come to compete in *kahiko* (ancient) and *auana* (modern) dance styles. ■ TIP→ You must reserve accommodations up to a year in advance. Ticket requests must be mailed after December 26 of the preceding year. ✉ *Edith Kanaka-*

ole Multi-Purpose Stadium, 350 Kalanikoa St., Hilo ☎ *808/935–9168* ⊕ *www.merriemonarchfestival.org* ⊗ *Apr.*

Moku O Keawe International Festival. This hula extravaganza, held on the big stage at Waikoloa Bowl, features *halau* (schools) from Hawaii and Japan competing under the stars. During the day, workshops and cultural fairs take place at the Waikoloa Beach Marriott Resort. ⊠ *Waikoloa Bowl, 69-150 Waikoloa Beach Dr., Hilo* ⊕ *www.mokif.com* ⊗ *Nov.*

Taste of the Hawaiian Range. Since 1995, this culinary event has given locals and visitors a taste of what the region's best chefs and ranches have to offer, from grass-fed beef, lamb, and mutton to succulent veal. ⊠ *Kailua-Kona* ☎ *808/981–5199* ⊕ *www.tasteofthehawaiianrange.com* ⊗ *Sept. or Oct.*

FILM

KAILUA-KONA

Regal Keauhou 7 Cinemas. This is a splendid theater complex with several pre- or post-movie food options in the shopping center. ⊠ *Keauhou Shopping Center, 78-6831 Alii Dr., Kailua-Kona* ☎ *808/324–0172* ⊕ *www.regmovies.com.*

Regal Makalapua Stadium Cinemas. This 10-screen theater has stadium seating and digital surround sound. ⊠ *Makalapua Ave., next to Kmart, Kailua-Kona* ☎ *808/327–0444* ⊕ *www.regmovies.com.*

HILO

Palace Theatre. After decades of neglect, this historic theater dating from the silent-movie era (1925) has been beautifully restored through community support. Today, it showcases everything from film festivals and old movies to musical productions and holiday concerts. ⊠ *38 Haili St., Hilo* ☎ *808/934–7010* ⊕ *www.hilopalace.com.*

Regal Kress Cinemas. Critically acclaimed films, kids' fare, and the occasional art-house flick are shown on four screens in this pretty art-deco building. Since the movies are not-so-recently released, the price is right at $1 to $1.75 per person. You can even get a hot dog for $1.75 and free refills on large popcorns and sodas. ⊠ *174 Kamehameha Ave., Hilo* ☎ *800/326–3264* ⊕ *www.regmovies.com/Theatres/Theatre-Folder/Regal-Kress-Cinemas-4-4548.*

Regal Prince Kuhio 9 Cinemas. First-run films are shown on nine screens here. ⊠ *Prince Kuhio Plaza, 111 E. Puainako St., Hilo* ☎ *800/326–3264.*

HONOKAA

Honokaa People's Theater. Screening art films during the week and more mainstream releases on weekends, this is the largest cinema on the Big Island, featuring a 50-foot screen as well as a huge stage and dance floor. Hula competitions, concerts, and other special events are also held here. ■ TIP→ Park properly, as cops regularly write tickets while moviegoers are watching the show. ⊠ *Mamane St., Honokaa* ☎ *808/775–0000* ⊕ *www.honokaapeople.com.*

THEATER

KAILUA-KONA

Aloha Theatre. Local groups stage musicals and plays at this charming 1930s-vintage theater in Kainaliu. ✉ *79-7384 Mamalahoa Hwy., Kainaliu* ☎ *808/322–9924* ⊕ *www.apachawaii.org.*

WAIMEA

Kahilu Theatre. This intimate theater regularly hosts internationally acclaimed performers. In recent seasons, Mikhail Barishnikov, the Szymanwski Quartet, Terence Blanchard, Ben Vereen, and the Martha Graham Company shared the calendar with regional modern-dance troupes and traditional Hawaiian musicians. Tremendous community support revived the theater after it closed in 2012. ✉ *Parker Ranch Center, 67-1185 Mamalahoa Hwy., Waimea* ☎ *808/885–6868* ⊕ *www.kahilutheatre.org.*

HILO

University of Hawaii at Hilo Performing Arts Center. This 600-seat venue hosts a full season of dance, drama, music, and other events. About 150 performances are held September to May. ✉ *200 W. Kawili St., Hilo* ☎ *808/932–7490* ⊕ *artscenter.uhh.hawaii.edu.*

VOLCANOES NATIONAL PARK

Volcano Art Center. Hawaiian music and dance, as well as theater performances, are hosted by this local art center. Locals drive here from all over the island for concerts. ✉ *19-4744 Old Volcano Rd., Volcano* ☎ *808/967–8222* ⊕ *www.volcanoartcenter.org.*

NIGHTLIFE

KAILUA-KONA

BARS

Humpy's Big Island Alehouse. Beer drinkers appreciate the fine craft brews on tap at this oceanfront restaurant. It's always busy with young, local revelers. Humpy's food can be hit or miss, but it's great for late-hour grill items. Happy-hour specials are available weekdays 3 to 6, and the bar stays open until 2 am. ✉ *75-5815 Alii Dr., Kailua-Kona* ☎ *808/324–2337* ⊕ *www.humpys.com/kona.*

Fodor'sChoice ★ **Kona Brewing Co. Pub & Brewery.** The only genuine brewpub in Kona, this spot is beloved by locals. Good pizzas and salads, great locally brewed beer (go for the sampler and try them all), and an outdoor patio with live music on Sunday night means this place can get crowded, especially on weekends. The main entrance is at the end of Pawai Street, in the Old Industrial area. ✉ *75-5629 Kuakini Hwy., Kailua-Kona* ☎ *808/334–2739* ⊕ *www.konabrewingco.com.*

Oceans Sports Bar & Grill. A popular gathering place, this sports bar in the back of the Coconut Grove Marketplace has a pool table and an outdoor patio, along with dozens of TVs screening the big game (whatever it happens to be that day). It really gets hopping on the weekends

Continued on page 190

7

HULA: MORE THAN A FOLK DANCE

Hula has been called "the heartbeat of the Hawaiian people" and also "the world's best-known, most misunderstood dance." Both are true. Hula isn't just dance. It is storytelling.

Chanter Edith McKinzie calls it "an extension of a piece of poetry." In its adornments, implements, and customs, hula integrates every important Hawaiian cultural practice: poetry, history, genealogy, craft, plant cultivation, martial arts, religion, protocol. So when 19th century Christian missionaries sought to eradicate a practice they considered depraved, they threatened more than just a folk dance.

With public performance outlawed and private hula practice discouraged, hula went underground for a generation. The fragile verbal link by which culture was transmitted from teacher to student hung by a thread. Even increasing literacy did not help because hula's practitioners were a secretive and protected circle.

As if that weren't bad enough, vaudeville, Broadway, and Hollywood got hold of the hula, giving it the glitz treatment in an unbroken line from "Oh, How She Could Wicky Wacky Woo" to "Rock-A-Hula Baby." Hula became shorthand for paradise: fragrant flowers, lazy hours. Ironically, this development assured that hundreds of Hawaiians could make a living performing and teaching hula. Many danced *auana* (modern form) in performance; but taught *kahiko* (traditional), quietly, at home or in hula schools.

Today, 30 years after the cultural revival known as the Hawaiian Renaissance, language immersion programs have assured a new generation of proficient—and even eloquent—chanters, songwriters, and translators. Visitors can see more, and more authentic, traditional hula than at any other time in the last 200 years.

Like the culture of which it is the beating heart, hula has survived.

Lei *poo*. Head lei. In kahiko, greenery only. In auana, flowers.

Face emotes appropriate expression.

Shoulders remain relaxed and still, never hunched, even with arms raised. No bouncing.

Eyes always follow leading hand.

Lei. Hula is rarely performed without neck lei.

Arms and hands remain loose, relaxed, below shoulder level—except as required by interpretive movements.

Traditional hula skirt is loose fabric, smocked and gathered at the waist.

Hip is canted over weight-bearing foot.

Knees are always slightly bent, accentuating hip sway.

Kupee. Ankle bracelet of flowers, shells, or foliage.

In kahiko, feet are flat. In auana, they may be more arched, but not tiptoes or bouncing.

BASIC MOTIONS

Speak or Sing

Moon or Sun

Grass Shack or House

Mountains or Heights

Love or Caress

At backyard parties, hula is performed in bare feet and street clothes, but in performance, adornments play a key role, as do rhythm-keeping implements.

In hula *kahiko* (traditional style), the usual dress is multiple layers of stiff fabric (often with a pellom lining, which most closely resembles *kapa*, the paperlike bark cloth of the Hawaiians). These wrap tightly around the bosom but flare below the waist to form a skirt. In pre-contact times, dancers wore only kapa skirts. Men traditionally wear loincloths.

Monarchy-period hula is performed in voluminous muumuu or high-necked muslin blouses and gathered skirts. Men wear white or gingham shirts and black pants.

In hula *auana* (modern), dress for women can range from grass skirts and strapless tops to contemporary tea-length dresses. Men generally wear aloha shirts, but sometimes grass skirts over pants or even everyday gear.

SURPRISING HULA FACTS

■ Grass skirts are not traditional; workers from Kiribati (the Gilbert Islands) brought this custom to Hawaii.

■ In olden-day Hawaii, *mele* (songs) for hula were composed for every occasion—name songs for babies, dirges for funerals, welcome songs for visitors, celebrations of favorite pursuits.

■ Hula *mai* is a traditional hula form in praise of a noble's genitals; the power of the *alii* (royalty) to procreate gave *mana* (spiritual power) to the entire culture.

■ Hula students in old Hawaii adhered to high standards: scrupulous cleanliness, no sex, daily cleansing rituals, certain food prohibitions, and no contact with the dead. They were fined if they broke the rules.

WHERE TO WATCH

If you're interested in "the real thing," there are annual hula festivals on each island. Check the individual island visitors' bureaus websites. The Merrie Monarch Hula Festival—held annually in Hilo (the Big Island) the week after Easter—is the best place to experience hula. Advance planning is required (⊕ www.merriemonarch.com).

If you can't make it to a festival, there are plenty of other hula shows—at most resorts, many lounges, and even at certain shopping centers. Ask your hotel concierge for performance information.

and for karaoke on Tuesday and Thursday. ✉ *Coconut Grove Marketplace, 75-5811 Alii Dr., Kailua-Kona* ☎ *808/327–9494.*

CLUBS

Huggo's on the Rocks. Jazz, island, and classic-rock bands perform here, and outside you may see people dancing in the sand. The food can be hit or miss, but the location, on the waterfront by the Royal Kona Resort, is worth it. ✉ *75-5828 Kahakai Rd., at Alii Dr., Kailua-Kona* ☎ *808/329–1493* ⊕ *www.huggos.com.*

Lulu's. On weekends, a young crowd gyrates to hot dance music under strobes. A DJ spins hip-hop, techno, and electronic beats, and the party lasts well into the wee hours. ✉ *Coconut Grove Marketplace, 75-5819 Alii Dr., Kailua-Kona* ☎ *808/331–2633* ⊕ *www.lulushawaii.com.*

> **BEST SUNSET MAI TAIS**
>
> **Huggo's on the Rocks** (Kailua-Kona). Table dining in the sand, plus live music Friday and Saturday.
>
> **Kona Inn** (Kailua-Kona). Wide, unobstructed view of the Kailua-Kona coastline.
>
> **Rays on the Bay at the Sheraton Kona Resort** (Kailua-Kona). Fantastic sunset views from plush lounge chairs, followed by spotlighted glimpses of nearby manta rays.
>
> **Waioli Lounge in the Hilo Hawaiian Hotel** (Hilo). A nice view of Coconut Island, live music Friday and Saturday nights.

THE KOHALA COAST

BARS

Fodor'sChoice ★ **Blue Dragon Restaurant & Spa.** Dancing under the stars in the open-air "Musiquarium," amid swaying coco palms and cooling trade winds, makes for some of the best nightlife in West Hawaii. Almost every night of the week, you can hear live music, including jazz, R&B, and Motown grooves, and sometimes there are special tango nights. Try Mediterranean appetizers and coffee if you need a break from dancing. ✉ *61-3616 Kawaihae Rd., across from harbor, Kawaihae* ☎ *808/882–7771.*

Luana Lounge. This wood-paneled lounge in the Fairmont Orchid has a large terrace and an impressive view. The bartenders are skilled, service is impeccable. The crowd is subdued, so it's a nice place for an early evening cocktail or after-dinner liqueur. ✉ *Fairmont Orchid, 1 N. Kaniku Dr., Kohala Coast* ☎ *808/885–2000* ⊕ *www.fairmont.com/orchid.*

Malolo Lounge. A favorite after-work spot for employees from the surrounding hotels, this lounge in the Hilton Waikoloa Village offers decent music, friendly bartenders, free Wi-Fi, and a pool table. ✉ *Hilton Waikoloa Village, 425 Waikoloa Beach Dr., Waikoloa* ☎ *808/886–1234* ⊕ *www.hiltonwaikoloavillage.com.*

The Mask-querade Bar. Hidden away in an unassuming strip mall, this is one of the Big Island's most venerable gay bars. Drag shows, hot DJs, live music, drink specials, fiestas, and Sunday barbecues are included in the roster of weekly events. All are welcome. ✉ *Kopiko Plaza, 75-5660 Kopiko St., behind Longs Drugs, Kailua-Kona* ☎ *808/329–8558* ⊕ *www.themask-queradebar.com.*

8

WHERE TO EAT

8

Updated by Karen Anderson

Between star chefs and myriad local farms, the Big Island restaurant scene has really heated up in the last 10 years. Food writers from national magazines are praising the chefs of the Big Island for their ability to turn the local bounty into inventive blends of the island's cultural heritage. The Big Island has become a destination for vacationing foodies, who are drawn by the innovative offerings and reputations of world-renowned chefs and premier restaurants.

Resorts along the Kohala Coast have long invested in culinary programs that offer memorable dining experiences that include inventive entrées, spot-on wine pairings, and customized chef's table options. But great food on the Big Island doesn't begin and end with the resorts. A handful of cutting-edge chefs have retired from the fast-paced hotel world and opened their own small bistros closer to the farms in upcountry Waimea, or other places off the beaten track. And, as some historic towns transform into vibrant arts communities, unique and wonderful restaurants have cropped up in Hawi, Kainaliu, and Holualoa, and on the east side of the island in Hilo.

Though the larger, gourmet restaurants (especially those at the resorts) tend to be very pricey, there are still *ono grindz* (Hawaiian slang for tasty local food) to be found at budget prices throughout the island, from greasy plate lunch specials to reasonably priced organic fare at a number of cafés and health food markets. Less populated areas like Kau, the Hamakua Coast, and Puna offer limited choices for dinner, but there are usually at least one or two spots that have a decent plate lunch or surprisingly good food.

In addition to restaurants, festivals devoted to island products draw hundreds of attendees to learn about everything from breadfruit and mango to avocado, chocolate, and coffee. Island tourism bureaus have also made an effort to promote agritourism, and it has turned into a fruitful venture for farmers. Farm tours afford the opportunity to meet with and learn from local producers and tour a variety of properties.

Some tours conclude with a meal of items sourced from the same farms. From goat farms churning creamy, savory goat cheese to Waimea farms planting row after row of bright tomatoes to high-tech aquaculture operations at NELHA (Natural Energy Lab of Hawaii Authority), visitors can see exactly where their next meal comes from and taste the difference that local, fresh, and/or organic production can make.

BIG ISLAND DINING PLANNER

WITH KIDS

Little ones are welcome almost everywhere on the kid-friendly Big Island; the exceptions are a small handful of fine-dining restaurants that cater to adults. The majority of restaurants feature a kids' menu, and many have toys and gimmicks to keep kids entertained.

SMOKING

Smoking is prohibited in all Hawaii restaurants and bars.

RESERVATIONS

Though it's rare to find a restaurant completely booked on the Big Island, a select few are sticklers about reservations. If you're bringing a large party or booking a special-occasion dinner, call ahead just in case, or check with your hotel concierge.

WHAT TO WEAR

There isn't a single place on the Big Island that requires formal attire. The general rule is anything goes, although there are a handful of restaurants (Ulu Ocean Grill and Sushi Lounge at the Four Seasons, the CanoeHouse at the Mauna Lani, and Merriman's) where you might feel out of place in your beach clothes. Resort wear, however, is acceptable at even the most upscale restaurants.

HOURS AND PRICES

Though it might seem at first glance like the Big Island's dining scene consists of either high-end restaurants or hole-in-the-wall dives, there is in fact a fairly large middle ground of good restaurants that cater to both local and visiting families, with new places cropping up all the time. Prices are generally higher than on the mainland due to the higher cost of living here.

Tipping is similar to elsewhere in the country: 15%–20% of the bill or $1 per drink at a bar. Bills for large parties generally include an 18% tip, as do bills at some resort restaurants, so be sure to check before leaving extra.

KAILUA-KONA

$ ✕ **Ba-Le.** Hidden away in a strip mall on Palani Road near KTA, Ba-Le
VIETNAMESE   serves a decent plate lunch. It also offers Vietnamese-influenced food such as *pho,* a soup laden with noodles, meat, and veggies. Sandwiches are served on French baguettes and stuffed with pickled daikon and carrots, cucumber, cilantro, homemade mayo, and your choice of Asian-style meats. ⑤ *Average main: $8* ✉ *Kona Coast Shopping Center,*

BEST BETS FOR BIG ISLAND DINING

Where can I find the best food the island has to offer? Fodor's writers and editors have selected their favorite restaurants by price, cuisine, and experience in the lists below. In the first column, the Fodor's Choice properties represent the "best of the best" across price categories. You can also search by area for excellent eats—just peruse our complete reviews on the following pages.

Fodor's Choice ★

Beach Tree at the Four Seasons Resort Hualalai, $$$, p. 203

Brown's Beach House at the Fairmont Orchid Hawaii, $$$$, p. 205

Café Pesto, $$, p. 205

CanoeHouse at the Mauna Lani Bay Hotel & Bungalows, $$$$, p. 205

Kona Brewing Co. Pub & Brewery, $, p. 198

Lava Lava Beach Club, $$, p. 208

Norio's Japanese Steakhouse and Sushi Bar, $$$, p. 209

Sushi Rock, $$, p. 210

Ulu Ocean Grill and Sushi Lounge at the Four Seasons Resort Hualalai, $$$$, p. 203

Village Burger, $, p. 212

By Price

$
Island Lava Java, p. 197

Kalama's, p. 202

Kona Brewing Co. Pub & Brewery, p. 198

Lemongrass Bistro, p. 199

Lilikoi Café, p. 211

Pau, p. 211

Sombat's Fresh Thai Cuisine, p. 219

Thai Rin Restaurant, p. 201

Village Burger, p. 212

$$
Café Pesto, p. 205

Jackie Rey's Ohana Grill, p. 197

Keei Café, p. 202

Kenichi Pacific, p. 198

Lava Lava Beach Club, p. 208

Mi's Italian Bistro, p. 202

Sushi Rock, p. 210

$$$
Beach Tree at the Four Seasons Resort Hualalai, p. 203

Kilauea Lodge, p. 220

Norio's Japanese Steakhouse and Sushi Bar, p. 209

$$$$
Brown's Beach House at the Fairmont Orchid Hawaii, p. 205

CanoeHouse at the Mauna Lani Bay Hotel & Bungalows, p. 205

Manta & Pavilion Wine Bar at the Mauna Kea Beach Hotel, p. 208

Merriman's, p. 208

Ulu Ocean Grill and Sushi Lounge at the Four Seasons Resort Hualalai, p. 203

By Cuisine

HAWAIIAN
Honu's on the Beach, $$$, p. 197

Kaaloa's Super Js Authentic Hawaiian Food, $, p. 201

Manago Hotel, $, p. 202

Roy's Waikoloa Bar and Grill, $$$, p. 209

Sam Choy's Kai Lanai, $$, p. 200

PLATE LUNCH
Big Island Grill, $, p. 195

Blane's Drive-In, $, p. 212

Café 100, $, p. 217

Kalama's, $, p. 202

By Experience

MOST ROMANTIC
Beach Tree at the Four Seasons Resort Hualalai, $$$, p. 203

CanoeHouse at the Mauna Lani Bay Hotel, $$$$, p. 205

Huggo's, $$$$, p. 197

Keei Café, $$, p. 202

Manta & Pavilion Wine Bar, $$$$, p. 208

Ulu Ocean Grill and Sushi Lounge, $$$$, p. 203

74-5588 Palani Rd., Kailua-Kona ☎ *808/327–1212* ⊕ *www.ba-le.com* ⊗ *No dinner Sun.*

$ ✕ **Bangkok House Thai Restaurant.** It may not look like much, with its
THAI small, dark interior, but this is the local go-to for good Thai food. One of few Thai restaurants on the island to add enough spice to their sauces, Bangkok serves up tasty curries, satays, and soups, along with a random assortment of Chinese entrées. The Rainbow salad, duck curry, and spring rolls are all standouts. Save room for homemade lychee ice cream. $ *Average main: $15* ✉ *King Kamehameha Mall, 75-5626 Kuakini Hwy., Kailua-Kona* ☎ *808/329–7764* ⊗ *No lunch weekends.*

$ ✕ **Big Island Grill.** This typical, local Hawaiian restaurant looks like an
HAWAIIAN old coffee shop or a Denny's—it's dark and nondescript inside, with
FAMILY booths along the walls and basic tables with bingo-hall chairs in the middle of the room. Local families love it for the huge portions of pork chops, loco moco, and an assortment of fish specialties at very reasonable prices. "Biggie's" also serves a decent breakfast—the prices and portions make this a good place to take large groups or families, if you want to feel like a real *kamaaina* (local), that is. $ *Average main: $12* ✉ *75-5702 Kuakini Hwy., Kailua-Kona* ☎ *808/326–1153* ⊗ *No lunch or dinner Sun.*

$ ✕ **Bite Me Fish Market Bar & Grill.** This cool sit-down bar and grill over-
SEAFOOD looks the boat ramp at Bite Me Fish Market in Honokohau Harbor, where you can pick up some fresh fish on the way out. Sit at the outdoor picnic tables and sip a beer while watching the day's catch get hoisted from the charter boats; chances are it will end up on your plate that day. Sandwiches are named after famous fishing lures in Kona (try the Kaya Bait Fish Reuben). Fish tacos can be ordered à la carte for a couple of bucks. Breakfast includes omelets, French toast, pancakes, and burritos. $ *Average main: $12* ✉ *Gentrys Kona Marina at Honokohau Harbor, 74-425 Kealakehe Pkwy., No. 17, Kailua-Kona* ☎ *808/327–3474* ⊕ *www.bitemefishmarket.com.*

$ ✕ **Bubba Gump Shrimp Company.** Okay, it's a chain, and a chain that
AMERICAN centers on an old Tom Hanks movie, no less. However, it has one of
FAMILY the nicest oceanfront patios in Historic Kailua Village, and the food's not bad, providing you know what to order. Anything with popcorn shrimp in it is a good bet, and the pear and berry salad (a combination of chicken, strawberries, pears, and glazed pecans) is the perfect size for lunch. Breakfast is now served seven days a week. $ *Average main: $10* ✉ *75-5776 Alii Dr., Kailua-Kona* ☎ *808/331–8442* ⊕ *www. bubbagump.com.*

$$ ✕ **Don the Beachcomber at the Royal Kona Resort.** The "original home of the
HAWAIIAN mai tai," Don the Beachcomber features a retro, tiki-bar setting with the absolute best view of Kailua Bay in town. There is a sizeable lunch and dinner menu at the bar, but dining in the main restaurant takes place only Thursday through Saturday. Try any of the nightly seafood specials or the Huli Huli chicken, but the Paniolo prime rib is the star attraction, slow roasted for flavor and tenderness. Save room for the Molten Lava Cake. $ *Average main: $20* ✉ *Royal Kona Resort, 75-5852 Alii Dr., Kailua-Kona* ☎ *808/329–3111* ⊕ *www.royalkona.com/Dining.cfm.*

8

196 < **Where to Eat**

CLOSE UP

The Plate Lunch Tradition

To experience island history firsthand, take a seat at one of Hawaii's popular "plate lunch" eateries, and order a segmented Styrofoam plate piled with rice, macaroni salad, and maybe some "pig and poi," or lomilomi salmon. On the sugar plantations, native Hawaiians and immigrant workers from many different countries ate together in the fields, sharing food from their *kau kau* kits, the utilitarian version of the Japanese *bento* lunchbox. From this melting pot came the vibrant language of pidgin and its equivalent in food: the plate lunch.

At beach parks and events, you might see a few tiny kitchens-on-wheels, another excellent venue for sampling plate lunch. These portable restaurants are descendants of lunch wagons that began selling food to plantation workers in the 1930s. Try the deep-fried chicken *katsu* (rolled in Japanese panko flour and spices). The marinated beef teriyaki is another good choice, as is miso butterfish. The noodle soup, *saimin*, with its Japanese fish stock and Chinese red-tinted barbecue pork, is a distinctly local medley. Koreans have contributed spicy barbecue *kalbi* ribs, often served with chili-laden kimchi (pickled cabbage). Portuguese bean soup and tangy Filipino adobo stew are also favorites. The most popular Hawaiian contribution to the plate lunch is the *laulau*, a mix of meat or fish and young taro leaves, wrapped in more taro leaves and ti, and steamed.

$$ ✕ **Fish Hopper.** With a bayside view in the heart of Historic Kailua Village, the open-air Hawaii location of the popular Monterey, California, restaurant has an expansive menu for breakfast, lunch, and dinner, with inventive fresh-fish specials alongside the fish-and-chips and clam chowder that the original is known for. The lunch menu is tantalizing, especially the seafood pasta entrées. There's also a comprehensive wine list, plus a happy hour menu 2–6 and 8–9:30. $ *Average main: $24* ✉ *75-5683 Alii Dr., Kailua-Kona* ☎ *808/326–2002* ⊕ *www.fishhopper. com/kona.*

SEAFOOD
FAMILY

$ ✕ **Harbor House.** This open-air restaurant on the docks at Kona's sleepy harbor is a fun place to grab a beer and a bite after a long day fishing, beaching, or diving. The venue is nothing fancy but Harbor House is a local favorite for fresh-fish sandwiches and a variety of fried fish-and-chip combos. The icy 18-ounce schooners of Kona Brewing Company ale don't hurt, either. $ *Average main: $10* ✉ *Honokohau Harbor, 74-425 Kealakehe Pkwy., Suite 4, Kailua-Kona* ☎ *808/326–4166* ⊕ *harborhouserestaurantkona.com.*

AMERICAN

$$ ✕ **Holuakoa Gardens and Cafe.** This respected slow-food restaurant in historic Holualoa Village features fine dining in a lush, open-air setting beneath the shade of an old monkeypod tree. The proprietors, top chefs from the Bay Area, strive to use all local and organic ingredients for such dishes as ahi succotash and chicken liver crostini toscani. In addition to serving only local meats plus vegetables harvested each morning, the restaurant makes its own organic pastas, baked goods, and des-

HAWAIIAN

serts. ⑤ *Average main: $20* ✉ *76-5900 Old Government Rd., Holualoa* ☎ *808/322–2233* ⊕ *www.holuakoacafe.com* ☾ *No dinner Sun.*

$$$ ✗ **Honu's on the Beach.** Featuring alfresco dining near the sand, this is
HAWAIIAN one of the only truly beachfront restaurants in Historic Kailua Village. Part of Courtyard King Kamehameha's Kona Beach Hotel, the venue offers prime views of Kailua Pier and Kamakahonu Bay. Steak and seafood dominate the menu, highlighted by Hawaii rancher's "natural" New York steak, fresh catch of the day, and sushi. A prime rib seafood buffet is available Friday and Saturday nights, and a breakfast buffet is served daily, with à la carte options available. ⑤ *Average main: $28* ✉ *Courtyard King Kamehameha's Kona Beach Hotel, 75-5660 Palani Rd., Kailua-Kona* ☎ *808/329–2911* ⊕ *www.konabeachhotel. com/dining.htm* ☾ *No lunch.*

$$$$ ✗ **Huggo's.** This is one of the only restaurants in town with prices and
HAWAIIAN atmosphere comparable to the splurge restaurants at the Kohala Coast resorts. Dinner offerings sometimes fall short, considering the prices, but the *pupus* (appetizers) and small plates are usually a good bet. The dining lanai overlooks the rocks at the ocean's edge, and at night you can almost touch the marine life swimming below. Relax with cocktails for two and feast on fresh local seafood; the certified Angus beef is a cut above USDA Choice. If you're on a budget, **Huggo's on the Rocks,** next door, is a popular outdoor bar in the sand, and the burgers are pretty darn good, too. It's also Kailua-Kona's hot spot for cocktails and live music on Friday night. ⑤ *Average main: $36* ✉ *75-5828 Kahakai Rd., off Alii Dr., Kailua-Kona* ☎ *808/329–1493* ⊕ *www.huggos.com* ☾ *No lunch.*

$ ✗ **Island Lava Java.** Open from 6:30 in the morning to 9:30 at night seven
AMERICAN days a week, this outdoor café is one of the most popular gathering spots in Kailua Village. Order at the counter and then sit outside at one of the umbrella-shaded tables, where you can sip 100% Kona coffee and take in the ocean view. The variety-filled menu includes island-style pancakes for breakfast, fresh-fish tacos for lunch, and braised lamb shanks or vegan cioppino for dinner, plus towering, fresh bistro salads. There are also pizzas, sandwiches, and plenty of choices for both vegetarians and meat eaters. Portions are large and most of the menu is fresh, local, and organic. For a quick snack, scones and pastries fill the display case. ⑤ *Average main: $14* ✉ *75-5799 Alii Dr., Kailua-Kona* ☎ *808/327–2161* ⊕ *www.islandlavajava.com.*

$$ ✗ **Jackie Rey's Ohana Grill.** This brightly decorated, open-air restaurant
AMERICAN is a favorite lunch and dinner destination of visitors and residents,
FAMILY thanks to generous portions and a nice variety of chef's specials, steaks, and seafood dishes. Meals pair well with selections from Jackie Rey's well-rounded wine list. The lunchtime menu offers great value on items like beer-battered fish-and-chips, a barbecued kalua-pork sandwich, and guava-glazed baby-back ribs. On the lighter side, inventive salads keep it healthy but flavorful. ⑤ *Average main: $23* ✉ *Pottery Terrace, 75-5995 Kuakini Hwy., Kailua-Kona* ☎ *808/327–0209* ⊕ *www. jackiereys.com* ☾ *No lunch weekends.*

$ ✗ **Kanaka Kava.** This is a popular local hangout, and not just because
HAWAIIAN the kava makes you mellow. (Used for relaxation, organic kava root is

8

harvested on the Hamakua Coast and transformed into a traditional, slightly bitter brew.) The Hawaiian proprietors also serve traditional Hawaiian food, including fresh poke; bowls of smoky, pulled kalua pork; and healthy organic greens, available in fairly large portions for less than you'll pay elsewhere. In addition, the restaurant offers fresh-fish plates, *opihi* (limpets), vegetarian options, and even traditional Hawaiian *laulau* (pork wrapped in taro leaves and steamed). Seating is at a premium, but don't be afraid to share a table and make friends. $ *Average main: $12* ⊠ *Coconut Grove Marketplace, 75-5803 Alii Dr., Space B6, Kailua-Kona* ☎ *808/327–1660* ⊕ *www.kanakakava.com.*

$$ ✕ **Kenichi Pacific.** With black-lacquer tables and lipstick-red banquettes,
JAPANESE   Kenichi offers a more sophisticated dining atmosphere than what's normally found in Kona. Its shopping center location feels like a secret, but it's worth seeking out. This is where residents go when they feel like splurging on top-notch sushi and steak. It's a little on the pricey side, but you'll leave feeling satisfied. The signature rolls are inventive, especially the always-popular Dynamite Shrimp. To save a buck or two, go early for happy hour (5 to 6:30 pm daily), when all sushi rolls are half price, or hang out in the cocktail lounge, where menu items average $6. $ *Average main: $25* ⊠ *Keauhou Shopping Center, 78-6831 Alii Dr., D-125, Kailua-Kona* ☎ *808/322–6400* ⊕ *www.kenichipacific.com* ☉ *No lunch. Closed Mon.*

$ ✕ **Kona Brewing Co. Pub & Brewery.** This ultra-popular destination with
AMERICAN   outdoor patio features an excellent and varied menu, including pulled-
Fodor'sChoice pork quesadillas, gourmet pizzas, and a killer spinach salad with Gor-
★   gonzola cheese, macadamia nuts, and strawberries. The best bet for lunch or dinner is the veggie slice and salad for under $8—the garden salad is generous and the pizza is the best in town. The beer-tasting menu offers a choice of four of the eight available microbrews in miniature glasses that add up to about two regular-size mugs for the price of one. The Hefeweizen is excellent. If you're staying in town, purchase beer to go in a half-gallon jug ("growler") filled on-site from the brewery's own taps. The Growler Shack also sells beer by the keg. $ *Average main: $12* ⊠ *75-5629 Kuakini Hwy., off Kaiwi St. at end of Pawai Pl., Kailua-Kona* ☎ *808/329–2739* ⊕ *www.konabrewingco.com.*

$$ ✕ **Kona Inn Restaurant.** This vintage open-air restaurant offers a beauti-
AMERICAN   ful, oceanfront setting on Kailua Bay. It's a great place to have a mai tai and some appetizers while watching the sunset, or to enjoy a calamari sandwich, clam chowder, or salad at lunch. Dinner is also available, but the entrées are less than stellar and for the prices there are better options once the sun disappears. $ *Average main: $20* ⊠ *75-5744 Alii Dr., Kailua-Kona* ☎ *808/329–4455* ⊕ *www.windandsearestaurants.com.*

$$$ ✕ **La Bourgogne.** A genial husband-and-wife team owns this quiet, coun-
FRENCH   try-style bistro with dark-wood walls and private booths (no windows; it's located in a nondescript office building). The traditional French cuisine might not impress visitors from France, but the average guest can enjoy classics such as escargots, beef with a cabernet sauvignon sauce, rack of lamb with roasted garlic and rosemary, and the less traditional venison with a pomegranate glaze. Call well in advance for reservations. $ *Average main: $30* ⊠ *77-6400 Nalani St., Kailua-Kona*

☎ *808/329–6711* ◁ *Reservations essential* ⊘ *Closed Sun. and Mon. No lunch.*

$ ✕ **Lemongrass Bistro.** This well-kept secret occupies a small but upscale
ASIAN venue near the Kona Inn Shopping Village. The Asian-fusion menu—
everything is made to order—includes Thai, Vietnamese, Japanese,
Laotian, and Filipino. Although dishes are presented with resort flair
(the proprietor is a former resort chef, and there's a second location at
Queens' MarketPlace at Waikoloa Beach Resort), entrées average an
afforable $14, with appetizers for $7. Best bets are the ono sashimi and
the grilled marinated chicken salad with crispy wonton. This is one of
the few restaurants in town open until 11 pm. Ⓢ *Average main: $14*
✉ *75-5742 Kuakini Hwy., Suite 103, across from library, Kailua-Kona*
☎ *808/331–2708* ⊕ *lemongrass-bistro.webs.com.*

$ ✕ **Los Habaneros.** Hidden in the corner of Keauhou Shopping Center
MEXICAN adjacent to the movie theater, Habaneros serves up fast, albeit average,
Mexican food for low prices. Favorites are usually combos, which can
be anything from enchilada plates to homemade sopes and chiles rel-
lenos. The burritos are a solid pick, stuffed with meat, beans, cheese,
and all the fixings. Wash it down with imported beer from Mexico.
Ⓢ *Average main: $7* ✉ *Keauhou Shopping Center, 78-631 Alii Dr.,
Kailua-Kona* ☎ *808/324–4688.*

$ ✕ **Pancho & Lefty's.** Across the street from the Kona Inn Shopping Village,
MEXICAN in Kailua Village, this upstairs Mexican restaurant is a good bet for
nachos and margaritas on a lazy afternoon, or to watch the passersby
below on Alii Drive. The food is marginal, but the hibiscus margarita
is a good bet. At 5 pm, the banyan tree across the street is filled with
hundreds of chirping birds, a veritable happy hour in bird land. Ⓢ *Average main: $15* ✉ *75-5719 Alii Dr., Kailua-Kona* ☎ *808/326–2171.*

$ ✕ **Peaberry & Galette.** The menu at this little crêperie includes Illy
CAFÉ espresso, teas, excellent sweet and savory crepes, sandwiches, soups,
salads, and rich desserts like lemon cheesecake and chocolate mousse,
made fresh daily. The small venue has a relaxed, urban-café vibe. It's
a nice place to hang for a bit if you're waiting for a movie at the theater next door or feel like taking a break from paradise to sip a decent
espresso and flip through the latest *W.* Ⓢ *Average main: $8* ✉ *Keauhou
Shopping Center, 78-6831 Alii Dr., Kailua-Kona* ☎ *808/322–6020*
⊕ *www.peaberryandgalette.com.*

$ ✕ **Pine Tree Café.** Next to Matsuyama's market along Highway 11 on
HAWAIIAN the way to the airport, the Pine Tree Café offers local classics such as
huli huli (Hawaiian-style rotisserie) chicken and loco moco, alongside
new inventions like crab curry bisque. The fresh-fish plate is decent, and
all meals are served with fries or rice and macaroni salad. The prices
are a bit higher than you might expect, but the portions are huge. It's
a good place to stop for a last-minute bite—breakfast, lunch, or dinner—before catching your flight back to the mainland. Ⓢ *Average main:
$12* ✉ *Kohanaiki Plaza, 73-4354 Mamalahoa Hwy. (Hwy. 11), Kailua-
Kona* ☎ *808/327–1234.*

$ ✕ **Quinn's Almost by the Sea.** With the bar in the front and the dining
AMERICAN patio in the back, Quinn's may seem like a bit of a dive at first glance,
but this venerable restaurant serves up the best darn cheeseburger and

8

fries in town. Appropriate for families, the restaurant stays busy for lunch and dinner, while the bar attracts a cast of colorful regulars. The menu has many tasty options, such as fish-and-chips, meat loaf, and beef tenderloin tips. If time gets away from you on a drive to the north beaches, Quinn's, which stays open until 11, awaits your return with a cheap beer and a basket of fried calamari. Drinks are strong—no watered-down cocktails here. Breakfast is sometimes served during football season. ■ TIP→ Park across the street at the Courtyard King Kamehameha's Kona Beach Hotel and get free one-hour parking with validation. ⑤ *Average main: $15* ⊠ *75-5655 Palani Rd., Kailua-Kona* ☎ *808/329–3822* ⊕ *quinnsalmostbythesea.com.*

$$
SOUTH PACIFIC
✕ **Rays on the Bay.** The Sheraton Kona's signature restaurant overlooks Keauhou Bay, offering nighttime views of the native manta rays that appear nightly beneath the balcony. The dinner menu includes surf and turf, fresh catch, and salads, plus seafood appetizers like sushi rolls and poke. Sit next to one of the many fire pits and soak up the starlit atmosphere. ⑤ *Average main: $25* ⊠ *Sheraton Kona Resort & Spa, 78-128 Ehukai St., Kailua-Kona* ☎ *808/930–4949* ⊕ *www.raysonthebay.com* ⌲ *Reservations not accepted* ⊗ *No lunch.*

$
JAPANESE
✕ **Restaurant Hayama.** Tucked into Kopiko Plaza, just below Long's, this local favorite for Japanese fare goes beyond sushi. Hayama serves traditional Japanese specialties like tempura, unagi, broiled fish, teriyaki, and *udon* noodles, all made from fresh local ingredients. Sushi is available as well, but only traditional *nigiri,* slices of raw fish layered with wasabi and rice, and sashimi. Dinner specials provide a three-course meal for two for $40. Despite its strip mall location, Hayama manages to pull off a Zen vibe that matches the quiet and attentive, albeit "island-time," service. ⑤ *Average main: $15* ⊠ *75-5660 Kopiko St., Kailua-Kona* ☎ *808/331–8888* ⊗ *Closed Sun. No lunch.*

$$
HAWAIIAN
✕ **Sam Choy's Kai Lanai.** Celebrity chef Sam Choy has transformed an old Wendy's perched on a bluff above a shopping center into a beautiful open-air restaurant with a bar that looks like a charter-fishing boat. Granite-topped tables offer ocean views from every seat. Open for lunch and dinner (and breakfast on weekends only), the venue presents reasonably priced entrées, highlighted by macadamia-nut-crusted chicken, Oriental lamb chops, and Sam's trio of fish served with shiitake-mushroom cream sauce. The ahi salad (served in a deep-fried flour tortilla bowl) is a great deal for $14. *Keiki* (children's) menus accommodate families, and yes, the restaurant can be noisy. Parking is at a premium, so you might have to park in the shopping center below, or opt for valet service. ■ TIP→ Arrive at 5 pm to nab the best patio seating. ⑤ *Average main: $22* ⊠ *Keauhou Shopping Center, 78-6831 Alii Dr., Suite 1000, Kailua-Kona* ☎ *808/333–3434* ⊕ *www.samchoy.com.*

$
MEXICAN
✕ **Tacos El Unico.** An array of authentic soft-taco choices (beef and chicken, among others), burritos, quesadillas, and excellent homemade tamales are served up at this local hideaway in Kailua Village, off Alii Drive. Breakfast entrées include traditional rancheros. Order at the counter, take a seat outside at one of a dozen yellow tables with blue umbrellas, and enjoy all the good flavors served up in those red plastic baskets. ⑤ *Average main: $9* ⊠ *Kona Marketplace, 75-5729 Alii Dr., Kailua-Kona* ☎ *808/326–4033.*

$ ✕ **Thai Rin Restaurant.** This dependable restaurant adjacent to Island Lava
THAI Java on Alii Drive offers an excellent selection of Thai food at decent
prices. Everything is cooked to order, and the menu is brimming with
choices, including five curries, a green-papaya salad, and a popular
platter that combines spring rolls, satay, beef salad, and *tom yum* (lem-
ongrass soup). For a real treat, try the deep-fried fish. Piña colada fans
appreciate the excellent cocktails here, and you can't beat the beautiful
view of Kailua Bay. Indoor and outdoor seating is available. ⑤ *Average
main: $11* ✉ *75-5799 Alii Dr., Kailua-Kona* ☎ *808/329–2929* ⊕ *www.
aliisunsetplaza.com.*

$ ✕ **Ultimate Burger.** Located in a Sports Authority shopping complex, this
DINER excellent burger joint may look like a chain, but it's an independent,
locally owned and operated eatery that serves 100% organic, grass-fed
Big Island beef on buns locally made. Be sure to order a side of seasoned
Big Daddy fries served with house-made aioli dipping sauce. ⑤ *Average
main: $8* ✉ *Kona Commons Shopping Center, 74-5450 Makala Blvd.,
Kailua-Kona* ☎ *808/329–2326.*

$$ ✕ **Wasabi's.** A tiny place hidden in the back of the Coconut Grove Mar-
JAPANESE ketplace on Alii Drive, Wasabi's features indoor and outdoor seating.
Prices may seem steep, but the fish is of the highest quality, highlighted
by a large selection of rolls and authentic Japanese offerings, along
with a few unique inventions. And for those who prefer their seafood
cooked, teriyaki, udon, and sukiyaki options abound. The restaurant
has recently unveiled a beer garden. ⑤ *Average main: $18* ✉ *Coconut
Grove Marketplace, 75-5803 Alii Dr., Kailua-Kona* ☎ *808/326–2352*
⊕ *www.wasabishawaii.com.*

THE KONA COAST

SOUTH KONA

$ ✕ **Annie's Island Fresh Burgers.** At the best upcountry burger restaurant
MODERN in Kona, the burgers are made of succulent, 100% island-raised beef.
AMERICAN Leather couches, hardwood floors, artwork, and live trees growing
through the floor and up through the roof create a casual yet well-
appointed feel. The homemade sauces are excellent, as are the onion
rings and basil french fries. ⑤ *Average main: $13* ✉ *Mango Court,
79-7460 Hawaii Belt Rd. #105, Kainaliu* ☎ *808/324–6000.*

$ ✕ **The Coffee Shack.** Visitors enjoy stopping here for breakfast or lunch
AMERICAN after a morning of snorkeling at Kealakekua Bay, and for good rea-
son: the views of the Honaunau coast from this roadside restaurant
are stunning. Breads are all homemade, and you get to choose your
favorite when ordering a generously sized sandwich brimming with
Black Forest ham and the like. If you're in the mood for a Hawaiian
smoothie, iced honey-mocha latte, scone, or homemade luau bread, it's
worth the detour, even though the parking lot can be tricky to maneu-
ver. ⑤ *Average main: $11* ✉ *83-5799 Mamalahoa Hwy., Captain Cook*
☎ *808/328–9555* ⊕ *www.coffeeshack.com* ☽ *No dinner.*

$ ✕ **Kaaloa's Super Js Authentic Hawaiian Food.** It figures that the best *lau-
HAWAIIAN lau* (meat wrapped in taro leaves and ti) in West Hawaii can be found

at a roadside hole-in-the-wall rather than at an expensive resort luau. In fact, this humble family-run eatery was featured on the *Food Network*'s "The Best Thing I Ever Ate." Plate lunches "to go" include tender chicken or pork laulau, steamed for up to 10 hours. The kalua pig and cabbage is delicious, and the *lomilomi* salmon features vine-ripened tomatoes. Owners John and Janice Kaaloa grind their own poi sourced from taro in Hilo and Waipio. $ *Average main: $7* ⊠ *83-5409 Mamalahoa Hwy., between mile markers 106 and 107, Honaunau* ☎ *808/328–9566* ▭ *No credit cards* ⊘ *Closed Sun.*

$ ✕ **Kalama's.** The little yellow café near Kealakekua Bay is a great place
HAWAIIAN to stop after a morning of kayaking or swimming with spinner dol-
FAMILY phins. The Kauai-born proprietors serve up excellent Hawaiian offer-
ings, such as the popular *laulau* burger made with cured pork, and complete entrées like grilled ahi or teriyaki short ribs. Eric's grilled mahimahi burger may be the best mahimahi you'll ever eat. For the kids, Kalama's offers shave ice, hot deli sandwiches, hot dogs, and burgers grilled on the barbecue and served on a soft potato bun. Everything is cooked to order, so grab a table, change your watch to island time, and enjoy. $ *Average main: $10* ⊠ *82-5674 Kahau Pl., at Napoopoo Rd., Captain Cook* ☎ *808/328–2828* ⊘ *No dinner.*

$$ ✕ **Keei Café at Hokukano.** This beautiful restaurant, perched above the
ECLECTIC highway just 15 minutes south of Kailua-Kona, serves delicious dinners with Brazilian, Asian, and European flavors highlighting fresh ingredients from local farmers. Favorites are the Brazilian seafood chowder or peanut-miso salad, followed by pasta primavera smothered with a basil-pesto sauce. There's an extensive wine list. Bob Miyashiro, the owner, is a Kona native, and his wife, Gina, is Brazilian. A husband-and-wife cooking team, also from Brazil, have been with the restaurant since its humble beginnings at its previous location in Honaunau. Toast your friendly hosts with a refreshing mojito before dinner. $ *Average main: $20* ⊠ *79-7511 Mamalahoa Hwy., ½ mile south of Kainaliu, Kealakekua* ☎ *808/322–9992* ⊕ *www.keeicafe.net* ⌱ *Reservations essential* ▭ *No credit cards* ⊘ *Closed Sun. and Mon. No lunch.*

$ ✕ **Manago Hotel.** About 20 minutes upcountry of Kailua-Kona, the his-
HAWAIIAN toric Manago Hotel is like a time warp. A vintage neon sign identifies the hotel, while Formica tables and old photos add to the authentically retro flavor. T-shirts brag that the restaurant has the best pork chops in town, and it's not false advertising. The fresh fish is excellent as well, especially the ono and ahi. Meals come with rice for the table and an assortment of changing side dishes, which usually include a macaroni, potato, and tuna salad, and a braised tofu and sautéed veggie dish. $ *Average main: $10* ⊠ *82-6155 Mamalahoa Hwy., Captain Cook* ☎ *808/323–2642* ⊕ *www.managohotel.com* ⊘ *Closed Mon.*

$$ ✕ **Mi's Italian Bistro.** This steady presence in the South Kona dining scene
ITALIAN is a friendly, white-tablecloth establishment in a hole-in-the-wall loca-
tion next to a liquor store on the mountain (*mauka*) side of Highway 11. The restaurant's husband-and-wife owners prepare homemade pastas and focaccia daily. Specials are always delicious and usually include lasagna, focaccia, and risotto. The homemade herb-cheese ravioli is rich and savory, and even the salad options are a notch above, with

ingredients such as candied macadamia nuts, roasted beets, and sautéed haricots verts. Homemade desserts are worth saving room for, particularly the banana-rum flambé. $ *Average main: $18* ⊠ *81-6372 Mamalahoa Hwy., Kealakekua* ☎ *808/323–3880* ⊕ *www.misitalianbistro.com* ◷ *No lunch.*

$ × **Teshima's.** Locals gather at this small, historic restaurant 15 minutes
JAPANESE south of Kailua-Kona whenever they're in the mood for fresh sashimi, puffy shrimp tempura, or *hekka* (beef and vegetables cooked in an iron pot) at a reasonable price. Teshima's doesn't look like much, inside or out, but it's been a *kamaaina* (local) favorite since 1929 for a reason. You might want to try *teishoku* (tray) No. 3, featuring sashimi, tempura, sukiyaki beef, rice, miso soup, and sunomono, or order the popular bento box lunch. Service is laid-back and friendly. Open for breakfast, lunch, and dinner, the restaurant has been family owned and operated by five generations of Teshimas. $ *Average main: $15* ⊠ *79-7251 Mamalahoa Hwy., Honalo* ☎ *808/322–9140.*

NORTH KONA

$$$ × **Beach Tree at the Four Seasons Resort Hualalai.** This beautifully designed
MODERN ITALIAN venue provides a relaxed and elegant setting for alfresco dining near the
FAMILY sand, with its boardwalk-style deck, outdoor seating under the trellis,
Fodor's Choice and enormous vaulted ceiling. Chef Nick Mastrascusa is a transplant
★ from the Four Seasons Hotel New York, bringing Italian and Spanish influences to his inventive menu. Outstanding entrées include the seafood paella for two and the grilled rib eye with shoestring fries. The tropical Peletini martini is a favorite, and at dinner, the premium wine list includes the Beach Tree's own signature reds and whites. There's also a great children's menu and chalkboard placemats for kids to play with. Live Hawaiian music is featured nightly. $ *Average main: $35* ⊠ *Four Seasons Resort Hualalai, 72-100 Kaupulehu Dr.* ☎ *808/325–8000* ⊕ *www.fourseasons.com/hualalai.*

$$$$ × **Ulu Ocean Grill and Sushi Lounge at the Four Seasons Resort Hualalai.**
MODERN Replacing the flagship Pahuia, this artfully renovated restaurant has the
HAWAIIAN same spectacular oceanfront setting with a more casual dining experi-
Fodor's Choice ence that highlights locally grown products. Breakfast can be à la carte
★ or buffet, but nighttime is when the magic happens, starting with an impressive wine program that includes boutique wines and world-class imports. Diverse menu choices—from roasted beet salad and corn-and-coconut soup to Big Island wild boar served with poha berry chutney, Kona lobster pad Thai, and local grass-fed tenderloin—make deciding what to order a challenge. There's also a full sushi menu. Reserve a table on the patio and you may spot whales while dining. $ *Average main: $35* ⊠ *Four Seasons Resort Hualalai, 72-100 Kaupulehu Dr., North Kona* ☎ *808/325–8000* ⊕ *www.fourseasons.com/hualalai* ◷ *No lunch.*

8

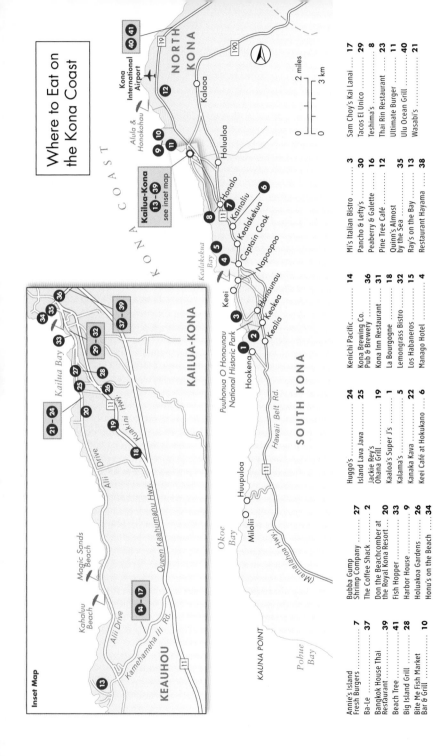

Where to Eat on the Kona Coast

NORTH KONA

Kona International Airport

Alula & Honokohau

Kailua-Kona
13–39
see inset map

KONA COAST

Kealakekua Bay

SOUTH KONA

Puuhonua O Honaunau National Historic Park

KAUNA POINT

Pohue Bay

Okoe Bay

Milolii

Huupuloa

Hookena

Keokea

Keokea

Kealia

Keei

Honaunau

Napoopoo

Captain Cook

Kealakekua

Kainaliu

Honalo

Holualoa

Kalaoa

Kalaoa

Kaahumanu Hwy

Hawaii Belt Rd.

(Mamalahoa Hwy)

0   2 miles
0   3 km

Inset Map

KEAUHOU

KAILUA-KONA

Kahaluu Beach

Magic Sands Beach

Kailua Bay

Alii Drive

Alii Drive

Kuakini Hwy

Queen Kaahumanu HWY

Kamehameha III Rd.

Annie's Island Fresh Burgers	**7**
Ba-le	**37**
Bangkok House Thai Restaurant	**39**
Beach Tree	**41**
Big Island Grill	**28**
Bite Me Fish Market Bar & Grill	**10**

Bubba Gump Shrimp Company	**27**
The Coffee Shack	**2**
Don the Beachcomber at the Royal Kona Resort	**20**
Fish Hopper	**33**
Harbor House	**9**
Holuakoa Gardens	**26**
Honu's on the Beach	**34**

Huggo's	**24**
Island Lava Java	**25**
Jackie Rey's Ohana Grill	**19**
Kaaloa's Super J's	**5**
Kalama's	**5**
Kanaka Kava	**22**
Keei Café at Hokukano	**6**

Kenichi Pacific	**14**
Kona Brewing Co. Pub & Brewery	**36**
Kona Inn Restaurant	**31**
La Bourgogne	**18**
Lemongrass Bistro	**32**
Los Habaneros	**15**
Manago Hotel	**4**

Mi's Italian Bistro	**3**
Pancho & Lefty's	**30**
Peaberry & Galette	**16**
Pine Tree Café	**12**
Quinn's Almost by the Sea	**35**
Ray's on the Bay	**13**
Restaurant Hayama	**38**

Sam Choy's Kai Lanai	**17**
Tacos El Unico	**29**
Teshima's	**8**
Thai Rin Restaurant	**23**
Ultimate Burger	**11**
Ulu Ocean Grill	**40**
Wasabi's	**21**

THE KOHALA COAST

$$ ✕ **Bamboo Restaurant.** This popular restaurant in the heart of Hawi pro-
ASIAN   vides a historic setting in which to enjoy a menu brimming with Hawai-
ian country flair. Creative entrées feature fresh island fish prepared
several ways. Try the seafood dish with sesame ginger, chili broth, garlic,
shiitake mushrooms, and Asian noodles; it's best accompanied with a
passion-fruit margarita or passion-fruit iced tea. Bamboo accents, bold
local artwork, and an old unfinished wooden floor make the restaurant
cozy. Sunday brunch includes omelets, pupus, salads, and sandwiches.
Local musicians entertain on Friday or Saturday, and drinks and pupus
are discounted during Tuesday to Thursday happy hours, from 4 to 6.
⑤ *Average main: $25* ✉ *55-3415 Akoni Pule Hwy. (Hwy. 270), Hawi*
☎ *808/889–5555* ⊕ *www.bamboorestaurant.info* ☾ *Closed Mon. No*
dinner Sun.

$$$$ ✕ **Brown's Beach House at the Fairmont Orchid Hawaii.** Nestled alongside the
MODERN   resort's sandy bay, Brown's Beach House offers beautiful sunset dining
HAWAIIAN   and innovative cuisine. Attention to detail is evident in the sophisti-
Fodor'sChoice   cated menu, like the Alae salt-roasted filet mignon served with kabo-
★   cha pumpkin mash and truffle foie gras demi. Seafood lovers might
like the crab-crusted Kona kampachi or the Sustainable Seafood Trio,
featuring fresh catch from the Kona Coast. The menu includes choices
that accommodate diet-specific preferences such as macrobiotic, raw,
vegan, gluten-free, and diabetic—amazingly, these offerings are as fla-
vorful and inventive as everything else on the main menu. ⑤ *Average*
main: $40 ✉ *Fairmont Orchid Hawaii, 1 N. Kaniku Dr., Kohala Coast*
☎ *808/885–2000* ⊕ *www.fairmont.com/orchid* ☾ *No lunch.*

$$ ✕ **Café Pesto.** In the sleepy harbor town of Kawaihae, the original Café
ITALIAN   Pesto ranks as a hidden find. Gourmet, wood-fired pizzas are topped
with eclectic goodies like pork and pineapple, chili-grilled shrimp, shii-
take mushrooms, and cilantro crème fraîche. The menu also includes
Asian-inspired pastas and risottos, fresh-fish entrées, and an excellent
array of salads, including the Volcano Mist, garnished with crisp, local
onion rings. Local brews and a full-service bar make this a good place
to end the evening, and the lounge-y bar area with sofas and comfy
chairs provides a nice place to grab a drink while waiting for a table.
⑤ *Average main: $25* ✉ *Kawaihae Harbor Shopping Center, 61-3665*
Akoni Pule Hwy. (Hwy. 270), Kawaihae ☎ *808/882–1071* ⊕ *www.*
cafepesto.com.

$$$$ ✕ **CanoeHouse at the Mauna Lani Bay Hotel & Bungalows.** This landmark
ECLECTIC   restaurant near the ocean showcases the inventive cuisine of Chef Allen
Fodor'sChoice   Hess, who previously worked at the famed Merriman's restaurant in
★   Waimea. The progressive menu—divided into the categories of Farmer,
Fisherman, and Rancher—draws its influences from locally grown and
raised products including grass-fed beef, lamb, fresh catch, shellfish,
and homemade sausage and bacon. For appetizers, try the goat tacos
served in a crispy bao bun. The Hawaii ranchers tenderloin is a good
bet for a main course, as is the furikaki-crusted ono served tataki style.
Each table has its own iPad that features a wine list to peruse by touch-
screen. Adjacent to the restaurant, The Lounge at the CanoeHouse
presents chef's bites, desserts, and signature cocktails from 5:30 to 9.

8

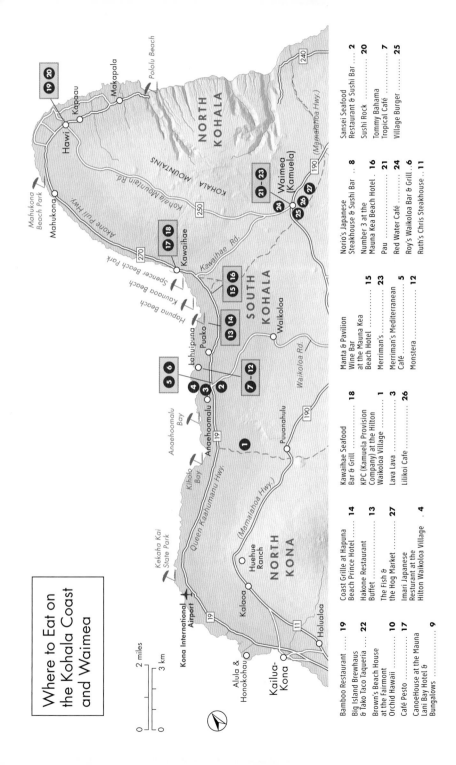

Where to Eat on the Kohala Coast and Waimea

0 ———— 2 miles

0 ———— 3 km

Bamboo Restaurant **19**
Big Island Brewhaus
& Tako Taco Taqueria **22**
Brown's Beach House
at the Fairmont
Orchid Hawaii **10**
Café Pesto **17**
CanoeHouse at the Mauna
Lani Bay Hotel &
Bungalows **9**

Coast Grille at Hapuna
Beach Prince Hotel **14**
Hakone Restaurant
Buffet **13**
The Fish &
the Hog Market **27**
Imari Japanese
Resturant at the
Hilton Waikoloa Village .. **4**

Kawaihae Seafood
Bar & Grill **18**
KPC (Kamuela Provision
Company) at the Hilton
Waikoloa Village **1**
Lava Lava **3**
Lilikoi Cafe **26**

Manta & Pavilion
Wine Bar
at the Mauna Kea
Beach Hotel **15**
Merriman's **23**
Merriman's Mediterranean
Café **5**
Monstera **12**

Norio's Japanese
Steakhouse & Sushi Bar .. **8**
Number 3 at the
Mauna Kea Beach Hotel .. **16**
Pau **21**
Red Water Café **24**
Roy's Waikoloa Bar & Grill .. **6**
Ruth's Chris Steakhouse .. **11**

Sansei Seafood
Restaurant & Sushi Bar ... **2**
Sushi Rock **20**
Tommy Bahama
Tropical Café **7**
Village Burger **25**

A customized dining program is offered at the Captain's Table. $ *Average main: $42* ⊠ *Mauna Lani Bay Hotel & Bungalows, 68-1400 Mauna Lani Dr., Kohala Coast* ☎ *808/885–6622* ⊕ *www.maunalani. com* ⊗ *No lunch.*

$$$
MODERN
HAWAIIAN

✕ **Coast Grille at Hapuna Beach Prince Hotel.** This open-air restaurant has high ceilings and a lanai that overlooks the pool and beach. American bistro-style dishes showcase the bounty of Big Island ingredients, including fresh Kona shrimp and lobster (raised at the Natural Energy Lab), seasonal fresh oysters, and other specially prepared seafood. A Friday alternative (the restaurant is closed on Friday and Saturday) is the Let's Go Crabbing night at the hotel's Ocean Terrace; a splendid buffet comes with everything from steamed Manilla clams and soft-shell crab tempura to crab-and-corn bisque and a full salad bar. $ *Average main: $30* ⊠ *Hapuna Beach Prince Hotel, 62-100 Kaunaoa Dr., Kohala Coast* ☎ *808/880–1111* ⊕ *www.princeresortshawaii.com* ⊗ *Closed Fri. and Sat. No lunch.*

$$$$
SEAFOOD

✕ **Hakone Restaurant Buffet.** Open on Saturday evening only, Hakone offers an excellent steak-and-seafood buffet featuring assorted sushi, daily catch, shrimp and veggie tempura, and grilled teriyaki steak. There's also a limited à la carte menu. The restaurant doesn't offer ocean views, but the upscale setting features Asian decor, fountains, shoji screens, and linen tablecloths. Be sure to try the signature martini—a hibiscus sake made with Sprite and a little cranberry juice. Yum. $ *Average main: $54* ⊠ *Hapuna Beach Prince Hotel, 62-100 Kaunaoa Dr., Kohala Coast* ☎ *808/880–1111* ⊕ *www.princeresortshawaii.com* ⊗ *Closed Sun.–Fri. No lunch.*

$$$$
JAPANESE

✕ **Imari Japanese Restaurant at the Hilton Waikoloa Village.** Decked out with an impressive display of Imari porcelain, waterfalls, and a teahouse, this elegant restaurant serves sukiyaki and tempura for mainland tastes and for a small fortune. (Menu items are a bit overpriced.) Other options include *teppanyaki* (beef or shrimp cooked table-side), *washoku* (an authentic Japanese dining experience with new-wave and classical cuisine), and a sushi–sashimi bar. Because the acoustics aren't the best, the restaurant can get loud when crowded. Private dining in the teahouse overlooks a koi pond. $ *Average main: $40* ⊠ *Hilton Waikoloa Village, 425 Waikoloa Beach Dr., Kohala Coast* ☎ *808/886–1234* ⊕ *www. hiltonwaikoloavillage.com* ⊗ *No lunch.*

$$
SEAFOOD

✕ **Kawaihae Seafood Bar & Grill.** Upstairs in a structure that dates from the 1850s, this seafood bar has been a hot spot since it opened in 2003, serving up a dynamite and well-priced bar menu with tasty *pupu* (appetizers), and an always expanding dinner menu that includes at least four fresh-fish specials daily. There's fare for landlubbers, too, including boneless braised short ribs, rib-eye steak, specialty pizza, and lots of salad options. Don't miss the escargot, oysters Rockefeller, and ginger steamed clams. At lunch, the menu ranges from sandwiches and burgers to sashimi and poke. Happy hour runs daily from 3 to 6 pm, and again from 10:30 pm until close (12 am). If you've got the late-night munchies, this is a great spot—food is served until 11. $ *Average main: $19* ⊠ *61-3642 Kawaihae Harbor, Hwy. 270, Kawaihae* ☎ *808/880–9393* ⊕ *www.seafoodbargrill.com.*

8

$$$$ ✕**KPC (Kamuela Provision Company) at the Hilton Waikoloa Village.** The
MODERN   breezy lanai has the most spectacular view of the leeward coast of any
HAWAIIAN   restaurant on the Big Island. Get here by 5:30 if you want to score a seat
for the sunset. It's the perfect accompaniment to the elegant yet down-
to-earth Hawaii regional cuisine. Specialty cocktails, like the mango
martini, are great, too. Entrées are on the pricey side, but the ginger-
steamed monchong (a deep-water Hawaiian fish) is a winner. Among
appetizers, the ahi carpaccio does not disappoint. The restaurant's num-
ber-one seller is the Kona Coffee Mud Slide, but the Baked Mauna Kea
(KPC's take on a baked Alaska) is equally decadent. ⑤ *Average main:
$36 ⊠ Hilton Waikoloa Village, 69-425 Waikoloa Beach Dr., Waiko-
loa ☎ 808/886–1234 ⊕ www.hiltonwaikoloavillage.com ⊗ No lunch.*

$$ ✕**Lava Lava Beach Club.** Dig your toes into the sand at Anaehoomalu
HAWAIIAN   Bay and enjoy one of the most happening, entertaining, and memorable
Fodor's Choice   bar/restaurants on the Kohala Coast. The atmosphere is super casual—
★   you can dine in your beach togs. There's always something going on:
the blowing of the conch shell at dusk, the lighting of the tiki torches,
tropical cocktails served in Hawaiiana ceramic ware, and live enter-
tainment featuring stellar Hawaiian recording artists. As for the food,
there's something for everybody, whether you want cocktails and *pupus*
(appetizers) for sunset or a fine-dining experience, with lobster-crusted
opakapaka with ginger and lemongrass, kiawe-smoked kalua pig, half
a chicken roasted in a smoker, or Chef Readman's signature gazpacho
topped with mac-nut pesto. ⑤ *Average main: $20 ⊠ 69-1081 Kuualii
Pl., Waikoloa ☎ 808/769–5282 ⊕ www.lavalavabeachclub.com.*

$$$$ ✕**Manta & Pavilion Wine Bar at the Mauna Kea Beach Hotel.** Perched on
MODERN   the edge of a bluff overlooking the sparkling waters of Kaunaoa Beach,
HAWAIIAN   the resort's flagship restaurant is a compelling spot for a romantic meal
at sunset, especially at one of the outside tables. The Enomatic wine
system lets guests sample 48 wines by the glass—from rare dessert
wines and ports to premier wines from France, Italy, and Argentina.
Executive Chef Peter Pahk's take on Hawaii regional cuisine includes
Kona kampachi prepared with black-sesame miso sauce, Japanese apri-
cot oil, and baby arugula salad. Waimea tomatoes, Puna goat cheese,
and rainbow chard from a nearby farm are some of the locally grown
ingredients. Among Sunday brunch's impressive spread are an omelet
station, prime rib, smoked salmon, tempura, lobster bisque, and a build-
your-own-sundae bar. ⑤ *Average main: $40 ⊠ Mauna Kea Beach Hotel,
62-100 Mauna Kea Beach Dr., Kohala Coast ☎ 808/882–5707 ⊕ www.
maunakeabeachhotel.com ⊗ No lunch. No dinner Sun. and Mon.*

$$ ✕**Merriman's Mediterranean Café.** From Peter Merriman, one of Hawaii's
MEDITERRANEAN   star chefs, comes a more affordable alternative to his upscale Waimea,
Kauai, and Maui restaurants. The Mediterranean-influenced menu
includes a variety of pasta dishes, tasty appetizers, and salads teeming with fresh ingredients from nearby Waimea farms. The outdoor
patio beckons locals and visitors alike. It's open daily for lunch, followed by happy hour from 3 to 5:30 and dinner until 9. ⑤ *Average
main: $25 ⊠ Kings' Shops at Waikoloa Beach Resort, 250 Waikoloa
Beach Dr., Waikoloa ☎ 808/886–1700 ⊕ www.merrimanshawaii.com/
mediterranean-cafe.*

$$ ✕ **Monstera.** It may not be beachfront with a view of the sunset, but this
JAPANESE   Shops at Mauna Lani eatery is worth a visit for its sophisticated Japa-
FAMILY   nese pub food with a touch of local inspiration. Chef Norio Yamamoto's
dinner menu includes his signature Original 69 Roll with Dungeness
crab. There are excellent sizzling plate items like short ribs and New
York steak, hot and cold noodle dishes, and, of course, outstanding
sushi. Most people make a meal out of sharing several small-plate items
to sample a bit of everything. For dessert, a tempura banana is drizzled
with chocolate and caramel. The *keiki* (children's) menu has chicken
nuggets and udon noodles. It's best to make a reservation; you can
also get some of the menu to go. ⑤ *Average main: $25* ⊠ *The Shops
at Mauna Lani, 68-1330 Mauna Lani Dr., Waikoloa* ☎ *808/887–2711*
⊕ *www.monterasushi.com* ⊘ *No lunch.*

$$$ ✕ **Norio's Japanese Steakhouse and Sushi Bar.** On the garden level of the
JAPANESE   Fairmont Orchid, this restaurant and Chef Darren Ogasawara's cuisine
Fodor'sChoice   appeal to both steak and seafood lovers, from Australian A6 Wagyu rib
★   eye (seasoned with five different kinds of Hawaiian sea salt) to hamachi-
and-avocado sashimi served with ponzu-garlic sauce. Dry-aged meats
from Kulana Farms are served on cedar planks, while free-range chicken
and sustainably caught Hawaiian seafood round out the offerings.
Everything is made from scratch, including the sauces, and the fish is
as fresh as it gets. Special dietary considerations are accommodated; the
gluten-free vegetable tempura and soy-free udon noodle are as flavorful
as the originals. ⑤ *Average main: $35* ⊠ *Fairmont Orchid Hawaii, 1
N. Kaniku Dr., Kohala Coast* ☎ *808/885–2000* ⊕ *www.fairmont.com/
orchid* ⊘ *Closed Tues. and Wed. No lunch.*

$$ ✕ **Number 3 at the Mauna Kea Beach Hotel.** Though it sits right on the edge
AMERICAN   of the hotel's golf course, this is not just a restaurant for golfers. A short
walk from the main entrance to the hotel, the spacious dining room has
seating both inside and out, and service is quick and correct. Number 3
serves up a great lunch menu with dishes such as ahi sashimi and beer-
battered fresh-fish tacos. ⑤ *Average main: $18* ⊠ *Mauna Kea Beach
Hotel, 62-100 Mauna Kea Beach Dr., Kohala Coast* ☎ *808/882–5707*
⊕ *www.maunakeabeachhotel.com* ⊘ *No dinner.*

$$$ ✕ **Roy's Waikoloa Bar & Grill.** Overlooking the lake at the Kings' Shops
MODERN   is, granted, not an oceanfront setting, but if you're staying nearby and
HAWAIIAN   are looking for decent food, this place fits the bill. In the mood for a
light meal? Choose from the enormous selection of great appetizers,
paired with something from the extensive wine-by-the-glass list. The
three-course meal is a good bet, as is the butterfish or Szechwan ribs,
a melt-in-your mouth encounter. The menu changes nightly and has a
lot of specials, like ancho-chili-pepper seared sea scallops and grilled
Hawaiian ono taco. ⑤ *Average main: $30* ⊠ *Kings' Shops at Waiko-
loa Village, 250 Waikoloa Beach Dr., Kohala Coast* ☎ *808/886–4321*
⊕ *www.roysrestaurant.com* ⊘ *No lunch.*

$$$$ ✕ **Ruth's Chris Steakhouse.** The Big Island location of the popular Loui-
STEAKHOUSE   siana steak house chain serves the sizzling steaks and heaping sides
the restaurant is known for. Early evening Prime Time specials consist
of a salad, entrée, side, and dessert for a fraction of the price. Otherwise, the tasty, classic sides, which include creamed spinach, sautéed

8

mushrooms, and potatoes au gratin, are à la carte. There *are* vegetarian options, but Ruth's Chris is a true steak house and is best suited to meat lovers. Nightly happy hour (5 to 7) provides substantial discounts on such items as escargot, barbecue shrimp, seared ahi, and prime-rib sliders. The beautiful bar area includes comfortable lounge seating in a sophisticated setting. $ *Average main: $40* ⊠ *The Shops at Mauna Lani, 68-1330 Mauna Lani Dr., Kohala Coast* ☎ *808/887–0800* ⊕ *www.ruthschris.com* ☯ *No lunch.*

$$
JAPANESE
✕ **Sansei Seafood Restaurant & Sushi Bar.** Heavenly interpretations of sushi and contemporary Asian cuisine are created by famed Hawaii chef D.K Kodama. More than a few dishes have won awards, including the shrimp dynamite in a creamy garlic masago aioli and unagi glaze, and the panko-crusted ahi sashimi sushi roll. Though it has tried-and-true mainstays, the menu is consistently updated to include new and exciting options, such as the Hawaiian *moi* sashimi rolls and the Japanese yellowtail nori aioli poke. You can certainly make a meal out of appetizers and sushi rolls, but Sansei's entrées, from both land and sea, are great. On Sunday and Monday from 5 to 6 pm, selected menu items are half off (limited seating; first come, first served). Or opt for a late-night meal on Friday and Saturday, when sushi and appetizers are half off from 9:30 until midnight, though you may have to put up with karaoke singers (21 and older). $ *Average main: $20* ⊠ *201 Waikoloa Beach Dr., 801 Queens' MarketPlace, Waikoloa* ☎ *808/886–6286* ⊕ *www. sanseihawaii.com* ☯ *No lunch.*

$$
JAPANESE
Fodor's Choice
★
✕ **Sushi Rock.** Located in historic Hawi Town, Sushi Rock isn't big on size—its narrow dining room is brightly painted and casually decorated with Hawaiian and Japanese knickknacks—but discerning locals and *akamai* (in-the-know) visitors come here for some of the island's best sushi. The restaurant prides itself on using local ingredients like grassfed beef tenderloin, goat cheese, macadamia nuts, and mango in the Island-inspired sushi rolls. It also serves up a variety of cooked seafood, chicken, noodle dishes, sandwiches, and salads for lunch and dinner. Everything is plated beautifully and served either at the sushi bar, at one of the handful of indoor tables, or on the covered front patio. Vegetarian, gluten-free, and vegan items are available, and a full bar even has house-infused vodka. $ *Average main: $23* ⊠ *55-3435 Akoni Pule Hwy., Hawi* ☎ *808/889–5900* ⊕ *sushirockrestaurant.net.*

$$$
MODERN
HAWAIIAN
✕ **Tommy Bahama Tropical Café.** This breezy, open-air restaurant, located upstairs at the Shops at Mauna Lani, offers an excellent roster of appetizers, including seared-scallop sliders and coconut-crusted crab cakes. The chef here has freedom to cook up his own daily specials, and the miso-marinated kampachi is a standout. Other entrées include rustic chicken pasta and crab-stuffed shrimp. Homemade breads and creamy butters set the stage for a nice meal, which most definitely should include one of Tommy's outstanding martinis, the tastiest and strongest anywhere on the island. Desserts are decadent and meant for sharing. There's live music every evening. $ *Average main: $34* ⊠ *The Shops at Mauna Lani, 68-1330 Mauna Lani Dr., No. 102, Kohala Coast* ☎ *808/881–8686* ⊕ *www.tommybahama.com.*

WAIMEA

$ $\quad$ ✕ **Big Island Brewhaus & Tako Taco Taqueria.** Tako Taco has always been
MEXICAN $\quad$ a favorite Waimea eatery, and owner Tom Kerns is a veteran brewer
who's now churning out some decent ales, lagers, and specialty beers
from his on-site brewery. With a focus on fresh ingredients, Tako Taco
whips up excellent tacos, burritos, Mexican salads, enchiladas, rellenos,
and quesadillas fresh to order. You'll want refills on the habanero salsa,
perhaps accompanied by a top-shelf margarita, either classic or *lilikoi*
(passion fruit). And nothing beats a cold local brew to wash down that
spicy enchilada. ⑤ *Average main: $11* ✉ *64-1066A Mamalahoa Hwy.,
Waimea* ☎ *808/887–1717* ⊕ *www.bigislandbrewhaus.com.*

$ $\quad$ ✕ **The Fish and the Hog Market Cafe.** Formerly Huli Sue's, this casual little
ECLECTIC $\quad$ restaurant along the highway serves up generous sandwiches, salads,
and melt-in-your-mouth barbecue items, including kiawe-smoked meat
like ribs, pork ribs, and brisket. Additional options range from pupu
platters, chowders, and crayfish boils to salads made with produce
grown in Waimea and a variety of seafood pasta dishes. Because the
owners are fisherpeople, the ceviche and poke use fish caught from
their boat. The on-site market sells fresh fish, homemade sausage, and
freshly made salad dressings and sauces. ⑤ *Average main: $15* ✉ *64-
957 Mamalahoa Hwy. (Hwy. 11), Waimea* ☎ *808/885–6268* ⊕ *www.
thefishandthehog.com.*

$ $\quad$ ✕ **Lilikoi Café.** This gem of a café is tucked away in the back of the Parker
EUROPEAN $\quad$ Ranch Center. Locals love that it's hard to find because they want to
keep its delicious breakfast crepes, freshly made soups, and croissants
Waimea's little secret. Owner and chef John Lorda creates an impressive selection of salad choices daily, including chicken curry, beet, fava
bean, chicken pesto, and Mediterranean pasta. The Israeli couscous
with tomato, red onion, cranberry, and basil is a hit, as is the half avocado stuffed with tuna salad. There's also a nice selection of sandwiches
and hot entrées. The food is fresh, many of the ingredients are organic,
and everything is homemade. ⑤ *Average main: $9* ✉ *Parker Ranch Cen-
ter, 67-1185 Mamalahoa Hwy. (Hwy. 11), Waimea* ☎ *808/887–1400*
⊗ *Closed Sun. No dinner.*

$$$$ $\quad$ ✕ **Merriman's.** Among the best restaurants in upcountry Waimea, this
MODERN $\quad$ is the signature restaurant of Peter Merriman, one of the pioneers of
HAWAIIAN $\quad$ Hawaii Regional Cuisine. Merriman's is the home of the original wok-
charred ahi: it's seared on the outside and sashimi on the inside. If
you prefer meat, try the Kahua Ranch braised lamb, raised locally to
the restaurant's specifications, or the prime bone-in New York steak,
grilled to order. The extensive wine list is impressive and includes many
selections poured by the glass. Although lunch prices are reasonable,
dinner is "resort pricey," so prepare to splurge. ⑤ *Average main: $45*
✉ *Opelo Plaza, 65-1227 Opelo Rd., Waimea* ☎ *808/885–6822* ⊕ *www.
merrimanshawaii.com* ⚑ *Reservations essential* ⊗ *No lunch weekends.*

$ $\quad$ ✕ **Pau.** Its name is Hawaiian for "done," perhaps an allusion to how
ITALIAN $\quad$ eagerly the sensational pizzas are gobbled up. On offer is a wide selection of appetizers, salads, sandwiches, pastas, and pizzas loaded with
lots of local, fresh ingredients. The Superfood salad, for example, has
quinoa, brown rice, edamame, grapes, and spiced nuts. All sauces and

8

salad dressings are made in-house. When it comes to the pizzas, any-thing goes; order one of Pau's 16-inch signature pies or create your own. Lunch is a deal if you order the Triple Slice: a quarter pizza cut into three slices plus a side salad for $9. A little tricky to find, the restaurant is near Merriman's. $ *Average main: $12* ⊠ *65-1227 Opelo Rd., Waimea* ☎ *808/885–6325* ⊕ *www.paupizza.com.*

$$$ ✕ **Red Water Cafe.** Chef David Abraham has transformed the former
ECLECTIC Fujimamas into a place for Hawaiian café food with a twist. The spe-
FAMILY cialty is "multicultural cuisine," like a Thai Caesar salad with crispy calamari croutons that is big enough to share. There's a full sushi bar as well. The Fuji roll has shrimp, ahi, crab, avocado, and cucumber, tempura-battered and deep-fried. Wash it all down with the signature saketini. Lunch is a great bet here, too, with a build-your-own *saimin* (broth with noodles), huge Cobb salad, and juicy 8-ounce burger with lots of fixings. This place is popular among locals and is a nice spot for the whole family—the kids' menu was developed by Abraham's eight-year-old daughter. $ *Average main: $30* ⊠ *65-1299 Kawaihae Rd., Waimea* ☎ *808/885–9299* ⊕ *www.redwater-cafe.com* ⊗ *Closed Sun.*

$ ✕ **Village Burger.** This little eatery brings a whole new meaning to gour-
AMERICAN met hamburgers. It serves up locally raised, grass-fed, hormone-free
Fodor's Choice beef that is ground fresh, hand-shaped daily on-site, and grilled to
★ perfection right before your eyes. Top your burger (be it ahi, veal, Kahua Ranch wagyu beef, Hamakua mushroom, or Waipio taro) with everything from local avocados, baby greens, and chipotle goat cheese to tomato marmalade. Even the ice cream for the milkshakes is made in Waimea, and the delicious brioche buns that house the juicy burgers are baked fresh in nearby Hawi. $ *Average main: $10* ⊠ *Parker Ranch Center, 67-1185 Mamalahoa Hwy., Waimea* ☎ *808/885–7319* ⊕ *www. villageburgerwaimea.com.*

HILO

$ ✕ **Bears' Coffee.** This favorite breakfast spot is much loved for its fresh-
DINER fruit waffles and tasty morning coffee. Service can be a little slow, but
FAMILY where are you running off to anyway? For lunch the little diner serves up huge deli sandwiches and decent entrée-size salads. In keeping with its name, it's full of stuffed bears, ceramic bears, even bear wallpaper. $ *Average main: $10* ⊠ *106 Keawe St., Hilo* ☎ *808/935–0708* ▬ *No credit cards* ⊗ *No dinner.*

$ ✕ **Big Island Pizza.** Gourmet pizza is the star here, topped with things
ITALIAN like shrimp and smoked salmon, but sandwiches, wraps, pastas, and salads are also served. There are only a handful of tables for eating in, but there's a brisk take-out business as well as delivery to the eastern side of the island. At another location above Costco in Kailua-Kona, the specialty is European-style pizzas with artisan crusts. $ *Average main: $15* ⊠ *760 Kilauea Ave., Hilo* ☎ *808/934–8000* ⊕ *www.bigislandpizza. com* ⊗ *No lunch Sun.*

$ ✕ **Blane's Drive-In.** With a vast menu second only to Ken's House of
HAWAIIAN Pancakes, Blane's serves up everything from standard hamburgers to

Continued on page 217

3

LUAU: A TASTE OF HAWAII

The best place to sample Hawaiian food is at a backyard luau. Aunts and uncles are cooking, the pig is from a cousin's farm, and the fish is from a brother's boat.

But even locals have to angle for invitations to those rare occasions. So your choice is most likely between a commercial luau and a Hawaiian restaurant.

Some commercial luau are less authentic; they offer little of the traditional diet and are more about umbrella drinks, spectacle, and fun.

For greater culinary authenticity, folksy experiences, and rock-bottom prices, visit a Hawaiian restaurant (most are in anonymous storefronts in residential neighborhoods). Expect rough edges and some effort negotiating the menu.

In either case, much of what is known today as Hawaiian food would be as foreign to a 16th-century Hawaiian as risotto or chow mein. The pre-contact diet was simple and healthy—mainly raw and steamed seafood and vegetables. Early Hawaiians used earth ovens and heated stones to cook seafood, taro, sweet potatoes, and breadfruit and seasoned their food with sea salt and ground kukui nuts. Seaweed, fern shoots, sweet potato vines, coconut, banana, sugarcane, and select greens and roots rounded out the diet.

Successive waves of immigrants added their favorites to the ti leaf–lined table. So it is that foods as disparate as salt salmon and chicken long rice are now Hawaiian—even though there is no salmon in Hawaiian waters and long rice (cellophane noodles) is Chinese.

AT THE LUAU: KALUA PORK

The heart of any luau is the *imu*, the earth oven in which a whole pig is roasted. The preparation of an imu is an arduous affair for most families, who tackle it only once a year or so, for a baby's first birthday or at Thanksgiving, when many Islanders prefer to imu their turkeys. Commercial luau operations have it down to a science, however.

THE ART OF THE STONE

The key to a proper imu is the *pohaku*, the stones. Imu cook by means of long, slow, moist heat released by special stones that can withstand a hot fire without exploding. Many Hawaiian families treasure their imu stones, keeping them in a pile in the backyard and passing them on through generations.

PIT COOKING

The imu makers first dig a pit about the size of a re-frigerator, then lay down *kiawe* (mesquite) wood and stones, and build a white-hot fire that is allowed to burn itself out. The ashes are raked away, and the hot stones covered with banana and ti leaves. Well-wrapped in ti or banana leaves and a net of chicken wire, the pig is lowered onto the leaf-covered stones. *Laulau* (leaf-wrapped bundles of meats, fish, and taro leaves) may also be placed inside. Leaves—ti, banana, even ginger—cover the pig followed by wet burlap sacks (to create steam). The whole is topped with a canvas tarp and left to steam for the better part of a day.

OPENING THE IMU

This is the moment everyone waits for: The imu is unwrapped like a giant present and the imu keep-ers gingerly wrestle out the steaming pig. When it's unwrapped, the meat falls moist and smoky-flavored from the bone, looking just like Southern-style pulled pork, but without the barbecue sauce.

WHICH LUAU?

Most resort hotels have luau on their grounds that include hula, music, and, of course, lots of food and drink. Each island also has at least one "authentic" luau. For lists of the best luau on each island, visit the Hawaii Visitors and Convention Bureau website: ⊕*www.gohawaii.com.*

MEA AI ONO
GOOD THINGS TO EAT

LAULAU
Steamed meats, fish, and taro leaf in ti-leaf bundles: fork-tender, a medley of flavors; the taro resembles spinach.

Laulau

LOMI LOMI SALMON
Salt salmon in a piquant salad or relish with onions, tomatoes.

POI
Poi, a paste made of pounded taro root, may be an acquired taste, but it's a must-try during your visit.

Consider: The Hawaiian Adam is descended from *kalo* (taro). Young taro plants are called "keiki"–children. Poi is the first food after mother's milk for many Islanders. Ai, the word for food, is synonymous with poi in many contexts.

Lomi Lomi Salmon

Not only that, we love it. "There is no meat that doesn't taste good with poi," the old Hawaiians said.

But you have to know how to eat it: with something rich or powerfully flavored. "It is salt that makes the poi go in," is another adage. When you're served poi, try it with a mouthful of smoky kalua pork or salty lomi lomi salmon. Its slightly sour blandness cleanses the palate. And if you don't like it, smile and say something polite. (And slide that bowl over to a local.)

Poi

8

E HELE MAI AI! COME AND EAT!

Hawaiian restaurants tend to be inconveniently located in well-worn storefronts with little or no parking, outfitted with battered tables and clattering Melmac dishes, but they personify aloha, invariably run by local families who welcome tourists who take the trouble to find them.

Many are cash-only operations and combination plates are a standard feature: one or two entrées, a side such as chicken long rice, choice of poi or steamed rice and—if the place is really old-style—a tiny portion of coarse Hawaiian salt and some raw onions for relish.

Most serve some foods that aren't, strictly speaking, Hawaiian, but are beloved of ka-maaina, such as salt meat with watercress (preserved meat in a tasty broth), or *akubone*

(skipjack tuna fried in a tangy vinegar sauce).

Our favorite: **Dani's Restaurant** (✉ 4201 Rice St., Lihue, ☎ 808/245–4991).

MENU GUIDE

Much of the Hawaiian language encountered during a stay in the Islands will appear on restaurant menus and lists of luau fare. Here's a quick primer.

ahi: *yellowfin tuna.*

aku: *skipjack, bonito tuna.*

amaama: *mullet; it's hard to get but tasty.*

bento: *a box lunch.*

chicken luau: *a stew made from chicken, taro leaves, and coconut milk.*

haupia: *a light, pudding-like sweet made from coconut.*

imu: *the underground oven in which pigs are roasted for luau.*

kalua: *to bake underground.*

kimchee: *Korean dish of fermented cabbage made with garlic, hot peppers, and other spices.*

Kona coffee: *coffee grown in the Kona district of the Big Island.*

laulau: *literally, a bundle. Laulau are morsels of pork, chicken, butterfish, or other ingredients wrapped with young taro leaves and then bundled in ti leaves for steaming.*

lilikoi: *passion fruit, a tart, seedy yellow fruit that makes delicious desserts, juice, and jellies.*

lomi lomi: *to rub or massage; also a massage. Lomi lomi salmon is fish that has been rubbed with onions and herbs; commonly served with minced onions and tomatoes.*

luau: *a Hawaiian feast; also the leaf of the taro plant used in preparing such a feast.*

luau leaves: *cooked taro tops with a taste similar to spinach.*

mahimahi: *mild-flavored dolphinfish, not the marine mammal.*

mai tai: *potent rum drink with orange liqueurs and pineapple juice, from the Tahitian word for "good."*

malasada: *a Portuguese deep-fried doughnut without a hole, dipped in sugar.*

manapua: *steamed chinese buns filled with pork, chicken, or other fillings.*

niu: *coconut.*

onaga: *pink or red snapper.*

ono: *a long, slender mackerel-like fish; also called wahoo.*

ono: *delicious; also hungry.*

opihi: *a tiny limpet, found on rocks.*

papio: *a young ulua or jack fish.*

poha: *Cape gooseberry. Tasting a bit like honey, the poha berry is often used in jams and desserts.*

poi: *a paste made from pounded taro root, a staple of the Hawaiian diet.*

poke: *cubed raw tuna or other fish, tossed with seaweed and seasonings.*

pupu: *appetizers or small plates.*

saimin: *long thin noodles and vegetables in broth, often garnished with small pieces of fish cake, scrambled egg, luncheon meat, and green onion.*

sashimi: *raw fish thinly sliced and usually eaten with soy sauce.*

ti leaves: *a member of the agave family. The leaves are used to wrap food while cooking and removed before eating.*

uku: *deep-sea snapper.*

ulua: *a member of the jack family that also includes pompano and amberjack. Also called crevalle, jack fish, and jack crevalle.*

CLOSE UP

Big Island Farm Tours

As local ingredients continue to play a prominent role on Big Island menus, chefs and farmers are working together to support a burgeoning agritourism industry in Hawaii. Several local farms make specialty items that cater to the island's gourmet restaurants. The **Hawaii Island Goat Dairy** (⊕ *www.hawaiiislandgoatdairy. com*) produces specialty cheese; **Volcano Island Honey Co.** (⊕ *www. volcanoislandhoney.com*) produces a rare and delicious white honey available not only in local restaurants but also on the shelves of high-end stores like Neiman Marcus; and the **Hamakua Heritage Farm** (⊕ *www. fungaljungle.com*) has turned harvested koa forests into a safe haven for gourmet mushrooms. A handful of farms—like **Mountain Thunder** (⊕ *www.mountainthunder.com*), which produces 100% organic Kona coffee, and **Hawaiian Vanilla Company** (⊕ *www.hawaiianvanilla.com*), which is cultivating vanilla from orchids on the Hamakua Coast—are open to the public and offer free tours.

popular chicken *katsu* to a gravy burger—comfort food for the local palate. A mean plate lunch with tons of fresh fish is only $7. At one point this was a real drive-in, with car service. Now, customers park, order at the window, and eat at one of the few picnic tables or take their food to go. There is a second location in Industrial Hilo (✉ *150 Wiwoole St.*), and two others in Honokaa and Orchidland. Ⓢ *Average main: $8 ✉ 217 Wainuenue Ave., Hilo ☎ 808/969–9494.*

$ ✕ **Café 100.** Established in 1948, this family-owned restaurant is famous
HAWAIIAN   for its tasty loco moco, prepared in more than three-dozen ways, and
FAMILY   its dirt-cheap breakfast and lunch specials. (You can stuff yourself for $3 if you order right.) The word "restaurant," or even "café," is used liberally here—you order at a window and eat on one of the outdoor benches provided—but you come here for the food, prices, and authentic, old Hilo experience. Ⓢ *Average main: $6 ✉ 969 Kilauea Ave., Hilo ☎ 808/935–8683 ⊕ www.cafe100.com ⊙ Closed Sun.*

$$ ✕ **Café Pesto.** Located in a beautiful and historic venue, Café Pesto offers
ITALIAN   exotic pizzas (with fresh Hamakua mushrooms, artichokes, and rose-
Fodor'sChoice   mary Gorgonzola sauce, for example), Asian-inspired pastas and risot-
★   tos, fresh seafood, delicious salads, and appetizers you can make a meal of. Products from local farmers feature heavily on the menu—Kulana free-range beef, Kawamata Farms tomatoes, and Kapoho Farms lehua-blossom honey are all made on the island. Local musicians provide entertainment at dinner Wednesday through Sunday. On the island's west side, another Café Pesto is located above Kawaihae Harbor. Ⓢ *Average main: $20 ✉ 308 Kamehameha Ave., Hilo ☎ 808/969–6640 ⊕ www.cafepesto.com.*

$ ✕ **Full Moon Cafe.** This cozy restaurant in a historic bayfront building
THAI   offers a small menu of American choices like burgers, fish, and steak, but where the eatery stands out is its fresh and tasty traditional Thai fare. The owners grow their own spices, herbs, and papayas organically on their Puna farm. The chefs sauté with olive oil to keep things heart-healthy. Good choices are the hot and sour Tom Yum soup, loaded with

8

fresh veggies; the pineapple curry; green papaya salad; and steamed salmon. There's outdoor seating on the lanai, and the adjacent Full Moon Coffee serves breakfast beginning at 6. ⑤ *Average main: $13* ✉ *51 Kalakaua St., Hilo* ☎ *808/961–0599.*

$
CHINESE
✕ **Happy Valley Seafood Restaurant.** Don't let the name fool you. Though Hilo's best Chinese restaurant does specialize in seafood (the salt-and-pepper prawns are fantastic), it also offers a wide range of other Cantonese treats, including a sizzling lamb platter, salt-and-pepper pork, Mongolian beef or chicken, and vegetarian specialties like garlic eggplant and crispy green beans. The food is decent, portions are large, and the price is right, but don't come here expecting any ambience—this is a funky and cheap Chinese restaurant, with a few random pieces of artwork tacked up here and there. ⑤ *Average main: $12* ✉ *1263 Kilauea Ave., Suite 320, Hilo* ☎ *808/933–1083* ⊙ *No lunch Sun.*

$$
AMERICAN
✕ **Hilo Bay Café.** This popular restaurant, previously located in a Walmart strip mall, now overlooks Hilo Bay from its towering perch on the waterfront. The sophisticated second-floor dining room looks like it's straight out of Manhattan. While some of the menu items have changed, old favorites are still available, including the traditional Blue Bay burger, shoestring fries, and eggplant Parmesan custard. A sushi bar now complements the excellent selection of fresh fish, gourmet sake, and premium wines. ⑤ *Average main: $20* ✉ *123 Lihiwai St., Hilo* ☎ *808/935–4939* ⊕ *www.hilobaycafe.com* ⊙ *No lunch Sun.*

$
DINER
✕ **Ken's House of Pancakes.** For years, this 24-hour diner on Banyan Drive between the airport and the hotels has been a gathering place for Hilo residents and visitors. Breakfast is the main attraction: Ken's serves 11 types of pancakes, plus all kinds of fruit waffles (banana, peach) and popular omelets, like Da Bradda, teeming with meats. The menu features 180 other tasty local specialties (loco moco, tripe stew, oxtail soup) and American-diner-inspired items from which to choose. Sunday is all-you-can-eat spaghetti night, Tuesday is all-you-can-eat tacos, and Wednesday is prime rib night. ⑤ *Average main: $10* ✉ *1730 Kamehameha Ave., Hilo* ☎ *808/935–8711* ⊕ *www.kenshouseofpancakes. com.*

$
HAWAIIAN
✕ **Kuhio Grille.** There's no atmosphere to speak of and water is served in unbreakable plastic, but if you're searching for local fare—that undefinable fusion of ethnic cuisines—this is the place. Sam Araki serves a 1-pound *laulau* (a steamed bundle of taro leaves and pork) that is worth the trip. Other *grindz* include loco moco, oxtail soup, plate lunches, pork chops, steaks, saimin, stir-fry, and daily specials. At the edge of Hilo's largest mall, above the parking lot near Longs, this local diner opens at 6 am. ⑤ *Average main: $9* ✉ *Prince Kuhio Plaza, 111 E. Puainako St., at Hwy. 11, Hilo* ☎ *808/959–2336* ⊕ *www.kuhiogrill. com.*

$
JAPANESE
✕ **Ocean Sushi.** What this restaurant lacks in ambience it certainly makes up for in quality and value. We're talking about light and crispy tempura; tender, moist teriyaki chicken; and about 25 specialty sushi rolls that, on average, cost a mere $5 per roll. Sushi lovers enjoy the "hospital roll," with shrimp tempura, cream cheese, cucumber, and spicy ahi, and the "volcano roll," akin to a California roll topped with flying-fish

eggs, dried fish shavings, green onions, and spicy mayo. Don't let the low price fool you—the service is quick and the food is fresh and filling. $ *Average main: $12* ⊠ *250 Keawe St., Hilo* ☎ *808/961–6625* ⊘ *Closed Sun.*

$ ✕ **Pescatore.** With dim lights, stately high-back chairs, and dark-ITALIAN wood paneling, Pescatore conjures up an Italian trattoria. The food
FAMILY is good, with plenty of Italian basics such as lasagna, chicken marsala, and chicken or veal parmigiana. Families love the simple pastas made to please choosy children. Lunch is served on Sunday only from 10 to 2. $ *Average main: $15* ⊠ *235 Keawe St., at Haili St., Hilo* ☎ *808/969–9090.*

$$ ✕ **Ponds Hilo.** Perched on the waterfront overlooking a scenic and serene
HAWAIIAN pond, this restaurant has the look and feel of an old-fashioned, harbor-
FAMILY side steak house and bar. The menu features a good range—burgers and salads, steak and seafood. Every Thursday is lobster night, with 8-ounce lobster tails served a variety of ways. Live music happens most evenings. $ *Average main: $20* ⊠ *135 Kalanianaole Ave., Hilo* ☎ *808/934–7663* ⊕ *www.pondshilohi.com.*

$ ✕ **Reuben's Mexican Restaurant.** It's not the best Mexican food you've
MEXICAN ever had, but if you're jonesing for some carne asada or chicken flautas, Reuben's has you pretty well covered. You can make a meal out of the warm chips and salsa alone. Known for pouring a stiff margarita in all sorts of interesting flavors, like *lilikoi* (passion fruit), guava, mango, coconut, and watermelon, the restaurant makes its own margarita mix. This is a lively place to spend an afternoon or evening. $ *Average main: $10* ⊠ *336 Kamehameha Ave., Hilo* ☎ *808/961–2552* ⊕ *www. reubensmexican.com.*

$$ ✕ **The Seaside Restaurant & Aqua Farm.** The Nakagawa family has been
SEAFOOD running this eatery since the early 1920s. The latest son to manage it
FAMILY has transformed both the menu and the decor, and that, paired with the setting (on a 30-acre natural, brackish fishpond) makes this one of the most interesting places to eat in Hilo. Islanders travel great distances for the fried *aholehole* (young Hawaiian flagtail), and mullet raised at the aqua farm. Other great dishes from the sea include furikake salmon, miso butterfish, and macadamia nut–crusted mahimahi, but the Pacific Rim menu includes plenty for landlubbers, too, like prime rib, chicken, and salads. Arrive before sunset and request a table by the window for a view of egrets roosting around the fishpond. $ *Average main: $23* ⊠ *1790 Kalanianaole Ave., Hilo* ☎ *808/935–8825* ⊕ *www. seasiderestaurant.com* ⊘ *Closed Mon. No lunch.*

$ ✕ **Sombat's Fresh Thai Cuisine.** There's a reason why locals flock to this
THAI hideaway for the best Thai cuisine in Hilo, and the name says it all. Fresh local ingredients highlight proprietor Sombat Saenguthai's menu (many of the herbs come from her own garden) to create authentic and tasty Thai treats like coconut curries, fresh basil rolls, eggplant stir-fry, and green papaya salad. Most dishes can be prepared with your choice of tofu, pork, beef, chicken, squid, or fish. The weekday lunch plate special is a steal ($7–$9). And if you can't leave the island without it, Sombat's famous pad thai sauce is available to take home in jars.

8

$⃣ *Average main: $13* ⊠ *Waiakea Kai Plaza, 88 Kanoelehue Ave., Hilo* ☎ *808/969–9336* ⊕ *www.sombats.com* ☾ *Closed Sun. No lunch Sat.*

$ ✕ **Verna's Drive-In.** Verna's is a favorite among locals, who come for the
HAWAIIAN   moist homemade burgers and filling plate lunches. The price is right
with a burger combo that includes fries and a drink for just $5.50. If
you're hungry for more, try the traditional Hawaiian plate with *laulau*,
beef stew, chicken long rice, *lomilomi* salmon; or the smoked meat plate
(a local specialty) smothered in onions and served with rice and macaroni salad. Whatever you choose, you won't leave hungry. Late-night
revelers take note: Verna's is one of the only joints in Hilo that's open
24 hours every day. $⃣ *Average main: $8* ⊠ *1765 Kamehameha Ave.,
Hilo* ☎ *808/935–2776.*

PUNA

$ ✕ **Luquin's Mexican Restaurant.** Long an island favorite for tasty, albeit
MEXICAN   greasy, Mexican grub, this landmark is still going strong in the funky
town of Pahoa. Breakfast includes huevos rancheros. Tacos are great
(go for crispy), especially when stuffed with grilled, seasoned local fish
on occasion. Chips are warm and salty, the salsa's got some kick, and
the beans are thick with lard and topped with melted cheese. Not something you'd eat before a long swim, but perfect after a long day of
exploring. $⃣ *Average main: $9* ⊠ *15-2942 Pahoa Village Rd., Pahoa*
☎ *808/965–9990* ⊕ *www.luquins.com.*

HAWAII VOLCANOES NATIONAL PARK AND VICINITY

Many park visitors stop in Volcano Village on their way in or out to
refuel at one of the handful of eateries here.

VOLCANO

$$$ ✕ **Kilauea Lodge.** Chef and owner Albert Jeyte combines contemporary
EUROPEAN   trends with traditional cooking styles from France and his native Ham-
burg, Germany. The menu changes daily and features such entrées as
venison, duck à l'orange with an apricot-mustard glaze, and lamb pro-
vençal garnished with papaya-apple-mint sauce. The coconut-crusted
Brie appetizer is melty and delicious, served with papaya salsa and
brandied apples. Savory soups and breads are made from scratch. Built
in 1937 as a YMCA camp, the restaurant still retains the original Fire-
place of Friendship, embedded with coins and plaques from around
the world. The roaring fire, koa-wood tables, and intimate lighting
are in keeping with this cozy lodge in the heart of Volcano Village.
$⃣ *Average main: $30* ⊠ *19-3948 Old Volcano Hwy., Volcano Village*
☎ *808/967–7366* ⊕ *www.kilauealodge.com.*

$ ✕ **Lava Rock Café.** This is an affordable place to grab a sandwich or
DINER   a coffee and check your email (Wi-Fi is free with purchase of meal)
FAMILY   before heading to Hawaii Volcanoes National Park. The homey, sit-
down diner caters to families, serving up heaping plates of pancakes and

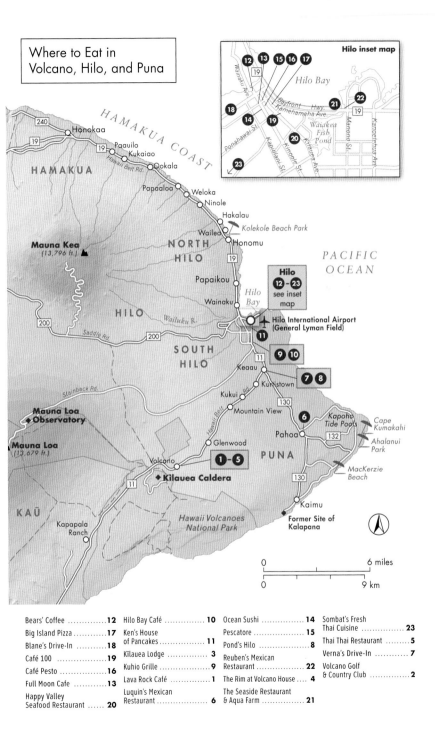

Where to Eat in Volcano, Hilo, and Puna

Hilo inset map

Hilo Bay

Bayfront Hwy.
Hamehameha Ave.

Waiakea
Fish
Pond

240

Honokaa

19

Paauilo

Kukaiao

Ookala

HAMAKUA

HAMAKUA COAST

Hawaii Belt Rd.

Papaaloa

Weloka

Ninole

Hakalau

Wailea

Kolekole Beach Park

Honomu

NORTH
HILO

19

Mauna Kea
(13,796 ft.)

Papaikou

Hilo
Bay

PACIFIC
OCEAN

Hilo
12 – 23
see inset
map

Wainaku

HILO

Wailuku R.

200

Saddle Rd.

200

Hilo International Airport
(General Lyman Field)

11

SOUTH
HILO

9 10

Keaau

11

7 8

Kurtistown

Kukui

Kukui Rd.

Mauna Loa
Observatory

130

Mountain View

6

Kapoho
Tide Pools

Cape
Kumakahi

Stainback Rd.

Hawaii Belt Rd.

Glenwood

Pahoa

132

Ahalanui
Park

Mauna Loa
(13,679 ft.)

Volcano

1 – 5

PUNA

130

MacKerzie
Beach

11

Kīlauea Caldera

KAŪ

Kapapala
Ranch

Hawaii Volcanoes
National Park

Kaimu

Former Site of
Kalapana

0   6 miles

0   9 km

Bears' Coffee **12**	Hilo Bay Café **10**	Ocean Sushi **14**	Sombat's Fresh Thai Cuisine **23**
Big Island Pizza **17**	Ken's House of Pancakes....................**11**	Pescatore **15**	Thai Thai Restaurant **5**
Blane's Drive-In **18**	Kīlauea Lodge **3**	Pond's Hilo **8**	Verna's Drive-In **7**
Café 100 ....**19**	Kuhio Grille **9**	Reuben's Mexican Restaurant **22**	Volcano Golf & Country Club **2**
Café Pesto **16**	Lava Rock Café **1**	The Rim at Volcano House **4**	
Full Moon Cafe **13**	Luquin's Mexican Restaurant **6**	The Seaside Restaurant & Aqua Farm **21**	
Happy Valley Seafood Restaurant **20**			

French toast for breakfast. For lunch, burgers range from bacon-cheese to turkey to Paniolo burgers made with Hawaii grass-fed beef. There are also generous sandwiches, loco moco, and soups; beef or chicken teriyaki; and haupia cake for dessert. A full bar serves draft beer. ⑤ *Average main: $10* ✉ *19-3972 Old Volcano Hwy., behind Kilauea General Store, Volcano* ☎ *808/967–8526* ⊙ *No dinner Sun. and Mon.*

$$ ✕ **The Rim at Volcano House.** The reopened Volcano House hotel houses
HAWAIIAN a fine-dining restaurant that overlooks the rim of Kilauea caldera and its fiery glow. Featuring two bars, a lounge, and live entertainment, it highlights island-inspired cuisine and incorporates locally sourced produce and other ingredients. Paired with Hilo coffee-rubbed rack of lamb, the creamy kabocha squash soup warms up a cool Volcano night. The Taste of Hawaii lunch menu comprises a choice of entrée (kalua pork, fresh catch, chicken, or stir-fry) and five local-style side dishes, such as poi, ahi poke wonton, and lilikoi cream puff, plus beverage; at $19, it's a great deal. ⑤ *Average main: $25* ✉ *Hawaii Volcanoes National Park, Crater Rim Dr., Volcano* ☎ *808/756–9625* ⊕ *www. hawaiivolcanohouse.com.*

$$ ✕ **Thai Thai Restaurant.** The food is authentic and the prices are reason-
THAI able at this little Volcano Village find. A steaming hot plate of curry is the perfect antidote to a chilly day at the volcano. The chicken satay is excellent—the peanut dipping sauce a good blend of sweet and spicy. And speaking of spicy, "medium" is more than spicy enough, even for hard-core chili addicts. The service is warm and friendly and the dining room pleasant, with white tablecloths, Thai art, and a couple of silk wall hangings. ⑤ *Average main: $20* ✉ *19-4084 Old Volcano Rd., Volcano* ☎ *808/967–7969* ⊙ *No lunch Wed.*

$ ✕ **Volcano Golf & Country Club.** This restaurant doesn't feel much like a
AMERICAN country club. It's simple and not at all fancy, with oak tables filled with old-timers talking story and chowing down on greasy local favorites. For lunch, the burgers and salads are best. Since there aren't many restaurants in Volcano Village, this is a great option. ⑤ *Average main: $9* ✉ *Pii Mauna Dr., off Hwy. 11, Volcano* ☎ *808/967–8228* ⊙ *No dinner.*

WHERE
TO STAY

Updated by Karen Anderson

Even among locals, there is an ongoing debate about which side of the Big Island is "better," so don't worry if you're having a tough time deciding where to stay. Our recommendation? Do both. Each side offers a different range of accommodations, restaurants, and activities.

Consider staying at one of the upscale resorts along the Kohala Coast or in a condo in Kailua-Kona for half of your trip. Then, shift gears and check into a romantic bed-and-breakfast on the Hamakua Coast, South Kona, Hilo, or near the volcano. If you've got children in tow, opt for a vacation home or a stay at one of the island's many family-friendly hotels. On the west side, explore the island's most pristine beaches or try some of the fine-dining restaurants; on the east side, hike through rain forests, witness majestic waterfalls, or go for a plate lunch.

Some locals like to say that the east is "more Hawaiian," but we argue that King Kamehameha himself made Kailua-Kona his final home during his sunset years. Another reason to try a bit of both: your budget. You can justify splurging on a stay at a Kohala Coast resort for a few nights because you'll spend the rest of your time paying one-third that rate at a cozy cottage in Volcano or a vacation rental on Alii Drive. And although food at the resorts is very expensive, you don't have to eat every meal there. Condos and vacation homes can be ideal for a family trip or for a group of friends looking to save money and live like *kamaainas* (local residents) for a week or two. Many of the homes also have private pools and hot tubs, lanai, ocean views, and more—you can go as budget or as high-end as you like.

If you choose a bed-and-breakfast, inn, or an out-of-the-way hotel, explain your expectations fully to the proprietor and ask plenty of questions before booking. Be clear about your travel and location needs. Some places require stays of two or three days. No matter where you stay, you'll want to rent a car. Some rental car companies do have restrictions about taking their vehicles to certain Big Island scenic spots, so make sure to ask about rules before you book.

BIG ISLAND LODGING PLANNER

HOTELS AND RESORTS

The resorts—most clustered on the Kohala Coast—are expensive, no two ways about it. That said, many offer free nights with longer stays (fifth or seventh night free) and sometimes team with airlines or consolidators to offer package deals that may include a rental car, spa treatments, golf, and other activities. Some hotels allow children under 17 to stay for free. Ask about specials when you book, and check websites as well—many resorts have Internet-only deals.

CONDOS AND VACATION RENTALS

Condos and vacation rental homes offer a range of options in every district of the island. With your own vacation pad, not only do you have more space to spread out, you can save a substantial amount of money by eating in.

See Condos and Vacation Rentals box for more information and rental agencies.

B&BS AND INNS

Bed-and-breakfasts and locally run inns offer a nice alternative to hotels or resorts in terms of privacy and location. Guests enjoy the perks of a hotel (breakfast and maid service), but without the extras that drive up rates.

Be sure to check industry association websites as well as property websites, and call to ask questions. There are still a few "B&Bs" that are really just dumpy rooms in someone's house, and you don't want to end up there. Members of the Big Island–based **Hawaii Island Bed & Breakfast Association** (⊕ *www.stayhawaii.com*) are listed with phone numbers and rates in a comprehensive online brochure. In order to join this network, bed-and-breakfasts must be evaluated and meet fairly stringent minimum requirements, including a yearly walk-through by association officers, to maintain their membership. Another bed-and-breakfast association includes **Hawaii's Best Bed & Breakfasts** (☎ *808/985–7488, 800/262–9912* ⊕ *www.bestbnb.com*).

RESERVATIONS

You'll almost always be able to find a room on the Big Island, but you might not get your first choice if you wait until the last minute. Make reservations six months to a year in advance if you're visiting during the peak seasons (summer, Christmas holiday, and spring break). During the week after Easter Sunday, for example, the Merrie Monarch Festival is in full swing, and most of Hilo's rooms are booked. Kailua-Kona is packed in mid-October during the Ironman World Championship triathlon. ■TIP➔ **September and February are great months to visit Hawaii; fares are lower, crowds are less, and accommodations prices are reduced.**

PRICES

Keep in mind that many of the resorts charge "resort fees" for things like parking, Internet, daily newspaper service, beach gear, and activities. Most condos and vacation rental owners charge an additional cleaning fee. Always ask about hidden fees as well as specials and discounts when you book. Look online for great package deals.

OUR REVIEWS

Prices in the hotel reviews are the lowest cost of a standard, double room in high season, which generally include taxes and service charges but not any optional meal plans. Prices for rentals are the lowest per-night cost for a one-bedroom unit in high season.

For expanded lodging reviews and current deals, visit Fodors.com.

KAILUA-KONA

Kailua-Kona, a bustling historic village full of restaurants, shops, and entertainment, boasts tons of lodging options. In addition to half a dozen hotels, oceanfront Alii Drive is brimming with condo complexes and vacation homes on both sides of the street. All the conveniences are here, and there are several grocery stores and big-box retailers nearby for those who choose to go the condo or vacation rental route and need to stock up on supplies. Kailua-Kona has a handful of beaches—Magic Sands, Kahaluu, and Kamakahonu (at the pier) among them. The downside to staying here is that you'll have to drive 30 to 45 minutes up the road to the Kohala Coast to visit Hawaii's signature, long, white-sand beaches. However, you'll also pay about half what you would at any of the major resorts, not to mention that Kailua-Kona offers a bit more local charm.

$$
RENTAL
Aston Kona by the Sea. Complete modern kitchens, tile lanai, and washer-dryer units are found in every suite of this comfortable oceanfront condo complex. **Pros:** oceanfront; swimming pool and Jacuzzi. **Cons:** no beach. $ *Rooms from: $210* ✉ *75-6106 Alii Dr., Kailua-Kona* ☎ *808/327–2300, 877/997–6667* ⊕ *www.astonhotels.com* ⤳ *72 units* ❍ *No meals.*

$
RENTAL
Casa de Emdeko. A large and pretty complex on the *makai* (oceanfront) side of Alii Drive, Casa de Emdeko offers a few more amenities than most condo complexes, including a florist, hair salon, and an on-site convenience store that makes sandwiches. **Pros:** oceanfront fresh- and saltwater pools; hidden from the street; very private. **Cons:** quality and prices depend on owner; not kid-friendly. $ *Rooms from: $110* ✉ *75-6082 Alii Dr., Kailua-Kona* ⊕ *www.casadeemdeko.org* ⤳ *106 units* ❍ *No meals.*

$$
HOTEL
Courtyard King Kamehameha's Kona Beach Hotel. This landmark hotel by Kailua Pier highlights Kona's rich history, whether on the grounds where King Kamehameha I spent his final years or in the jazzed-up lobby, which displays an impressive array of historical Hawaiian artifacts. **Pros:** central location; tastefully appointed rooms; historic ambience; aloha-friendly staff. **Cons:** most rooms have partial ocean views; some rooms face the parking lot. $ *Rooms from: $199* ✉ *75-5660 Palani Rd., Kailua-Kona* ☎ *808/329–2911* ⊕ *www.konabeachhotel.com* ⤳ *452 rooms* ❍ *No meals.*

$
B&B/INN
Hale Hualalai. Perfect for couples, Hale Hualalai offers two exceptionally large suites with exposed beams, whirlpool tubs, and private lanai, but perhaps most memorable is the food—owner Lonn Armour was

BEST BETS FOR BIG ISLAND LODGING

Fodor's writers and editors have selected their favorite hotels, resorts, condos, vacation rentals, and bed-and-breakfasts by price and experience. Fodor's Choice properties represent the "best of the best" across price categories. You can also search by area for excellent places to stay—check out our complete reviews on the following pages.

Fodor's Choice ★

Fairmont Orchid Hawaii, $$$$, p. 234

Four Seasons Resort Hualalai, $$$$, p. 233

Holualoa Inn, $$$$, p. 229

Mauna Lani Bay Hotel, $$$$, p. 238

Puakea Ranch, $$$, p. 238

Waianuhea, $$, p. 240

By Price

$

Coconut Cottage Bed & Breakfast, p. 242

Hale Ohia Cottages, p. 244

Kaawa Loa Plantation, p. 231

Kona Tiki Hotel, p. 230

Manago Hotel, p. 233

Royal Kona Resort, p. 230

Sheraton Kona Resort, p. 230

Waimea Gardens Cottage, p. 239

$$

Courtyard King Kamehameha's Kona Beach Hotel, p. 226

Hilton Waikoloa Village, p. 237

Kilauea Lodge, p. 244

Waianuhea, p. 240

$$$

Hapuna Beach Prince Hotel, p. 234

Puakea Ranch, p. 238

$$$$

Fairmont Orchid Hawaii, p. 234

Four Seasons Resort Hualalai, p. 233

Holualoa Inn, p. 229

Mauna Kea Beach Hotel, p. 237

Mauna Lani Bay Hotel & Bungalows, p. 238

Waikoloa Beach Marriott, p. 238

By Experience

BEST BEACH

Hapuna Beach Prince Hotel, $$$, p. 234

Mauna Kea Beach Hotel, $$$$, p. 237

Mauna Lani Bay Hotel & Bungalows, $$$$, p. 238

Waikoloa Beach Marriott, $$$$, p. 238

BEST HOTEL BAR

Four Seasons Resort Hualalai, $$$$, p. 233

Mauna Kea Beach Hotel, $$$$, p. 237

Mauna Lani Bay Hotel & Bungalows, $$$$, p. 238

Royal Kona Resort, $, p. 230

Sheraton Kona Resort & Spa at Keauhou Bay, $, p. 230

BEST B&BS AND INNS

Hawaii Island Retreat at Ahu Pohaku Hoomaluhia, $$$, p. 237

Holualoa Inn, $$$$, p. 229

Kane Plantation Guesthouse, $, p. 231

Kilauea Lodge, $$, p. 244

The Palms Cliff House Inn, $$, p. 240

Puakea Ranch, $$$, p. 238

Waianuhea, $$, p. 240

BEST SPA

Fairmont Orchid Hawaii, $$$$, p. 234

Hilton Waikoloa Village, $$, p. 237

Mauna Lani Bay Hotel & Bungalows, $$$$, p. 238

Sheraton Kona Resort & Spa at Keauhou Bay, $, p. 230

MOST KID-FRIENDLY

Courtyard King, $$, p. 226

Dolphin Bay Hotel, $, p. 240

Hapuna Beach Prince Hotel, $$$, p. 234

Hilton Waikoloa Village, $$, p. 237

Sheraton Kona Resort, $, p. 230

9

WHERE TO STAY ON THE BIG ISLAND

	Local Vibe	Pros	Cons
Kailua-Kona	Kailua-Kona is a bustling little village. Alii Drive is brimming with hotels and condo complexes.	Plenty to do, day and night; main drag of shops, historic landmarks, and seaside attractions within easy walking distance of most hotels; many grocery stores in the area.	More traffic than anywhere else on the island; limited number of beaches; traffic noise on Alii Drive.
South Kona and Kau	This area has some of the island's best snorkeling; there are plenty of bed-and-breakfasts and vacation rentals at or near Kealakekua Bay.	Kealakekua Bay is a popular destination for kayaking and snorkeling; several good dining options nearby; coffee-farm tours in Captain Cook and Kainaliu towns.	Vog (volcano fog) from Kilauea often settles here; fewer sand beaches in the area; farther south, the Kau district is quite remote.
The Kohala Coast	The Kohala Coast is home to most of the Big Island's major resorts. Blue, sunny skies prevail here, along with the island's best beaches.	Beautiful beaches; high-end shopping and dining; lots of activities for adults and children.	Pricey; long driving distances to Volcano, Hilo, and Kailua-Kona.
Waimea	Though it seems a world away, Waimea is only about a 15- to 20-minute drive from the Kohala Coast.	Beautiful scenery, paniolo (cowboy) culture; home to some exceptional local restaurants.	Can be cool and rainy year-round; nearest beaches are a 20-minute drive away.
The Hamakua Coast	A nice spot for those seeking peace, tranquility, and an alternative to the tropical-beach-vacation experience.	Close to Waipio Valley; foodie and farm tours in the area; good spot for honeymooners.	Beaches are an hour's drive away; convenience shopping is limited.
Hilo	Hilo is the wetter, more lush eastern side of the Big Island. It is also less touristy than the west side.	Proximity to waterfalls, rain-forest hikes, museums, and botanical gardens; good bed-and-breakfast options.	The best white-sand beaches are on the other side of the island; noise from coqui frogs can be distracting at night.
Puna	Puna doesn't attract nearly as many visitors as other regions on the island, so you'll find good deals on rentals and B&Bs here.	A few black-sand beaches; off the beaten path with lots of outdoor wilderness to explore; hot ponds; lava flows into the sea here.	Few dining and entertainment options; no resorts or resort amenities; noisy coqui frogs at night.
Hawaii Volcanoes National Park and Vicinity	If you are going to visit Hawaii Volcanoes National Park, stay the night at any number of enchanting bed-and-breakfast inns in the fern-shrouded Volcano Village.	Good location for watching lava at night bubbling inside Halemaumau Crater; great for hiking, nature tours, and bike riding; close to Hilo and Puna.	Not many dining options; not much nightlife; can be cold and wet.

a professional chef for 20 years. **Pros:** gourmet breakfasts; tastefully decorated house; whirlpool tubs; large living space. **Cons:** not kid-friendly; removed from local beaches and restaurants. ⑤ *Rooms from: $160 ⊠ 74-4968 Mamalahoa Hwy., Holualoa ☎ 808/326–2909 ⊕ www.hale-hualalai.com ⟿ 2 suites* ⍥ *Breakfast.*

$$$$
B&B/INN
Fodor's Choice
★

⌂ **Holualoa Inn.** Six spacious rooms and suites—plus a private, vintage, one-bedroom cottage that's perfect for honeymooners—are available at this beautiful cedar home on a 30-acre coffee-country estate, a few miles above Kailua Bay in the heart of the artists' village of Holualoa. **Pros:** within walking distance of art galleries and cafés; well-appointed, with wood floors, fine art, and lots of windows; panoramic views. **Cons:** not kid-friendly. ⑤ *Rooms from: $380 ⊠ 76-5932 Mamalahoa Hwy., Box 222, Holualoa ☎ 808/324–1121, 800/392–1812 ⊕ www.holualoainn.com ⟿ 6 rooms, 1 cottage* ⍥ *Breakfast.*

$
RESORT

⌂ **Holua Resort at Mauna Loa Village.** Tucked away by Keauhou Bay amid a plethora of coconut trees, this well-maintained enclave of blue-roofed villas offers lots of amenities, including an 11-court tennis center (with a center court, pro shop, and lights), swimming pools, hot tubs, fitness center, manicured gardens, waterfalls, covered parking, and a Tuesday-night hula show. **Pros:** tennis center; upscale feeling. **Cons:** no beach. ⑤ *Rooms from: $129 ⊠ 78-7190 Kaleiopapa St., Kailua-Kona ☎ 808/324–1550 ⊕ www.shellhospitality.com/Holua-Resort-at-Mauna-Loa-Village ⟿ 73 units* ⍥ *No meals.*

$
RENTAL

⌂ **Kona Bali Kai.** These slightly older condominium units, spread out among three low-rises on the ocean side of Alii Drive, are situated at Kona's most popular surfing spot, Banyans. **Pros:** close to town and beaches; convenience mart and beach-gear rental nearby. **Cons:** mountain-view rooms close to noisy street; oceanfront rooms don't have a/c. ⑤ *Rooms from: $175 ⊠ 76-6246 Alii Dr., Kailua-Kona ☎ 808/329–9381, 800/535–0085 ⊕ www.castleresorts.com ⟿ 67 units* ⍥ *No meals.*

$
RENTAL

⌂ **Kona Coast Resort.** Just below Keauhou Shopping Center, this resort offers furnished condos on 21 acres with pleasant ocean views and a host of on-site amenities including a swimming pool, beach volleyball, cocktail bar, hot tub, tennis courts, hula classes, equipment rental, and children's activities. **Pros:** nice location in Keauhou. **Cons:** dated decor; not on the beach. ⑤ *Rooms from: $140 ⊠ 78-6842 Alii Dr., Keauhou ☎ 808/324–1721 ⊕ www.shellhospitality.com ⟿ 268 units* ⍥ *No meals.*

KONA CONDO COMFORTS

The **Safeway** at Crossroads Shopping Center (⊠ *75-1000 Henry St., Kailua-Kona* ☎ *808/329–2207*) offers an excellent inventory of groceries and produce, although prices can be steep.

For pizza, **Kona Brewing Co. Pub & Brewery** (⊠ *75-5629 Kuakini Hwy., accessed through the Kona Old Industrial Park, Kailua-Kona* ☎ *808/329–2739*) is the best bet, if you can pick it up. Otherwise, for delivery, try **Domino's** (☎ *808/329–9500*).

9

$ RENTAL **Kona Magic Sands.** Cradled between a lovely grass park and Magic Sands Beach Park, this condo complex is great for swimmers, surfers, and sunbathers. **Pros:** next door to popular beach; affordable; oceanfront view from all units; restaurant and bar on-site. **Cons:** studios only; some units are dated. *Rooms from: $115 ✉ 77-6452 Alii Dr., Kailua-Kona ☎ 808/329–9393, 800/622–5348 ⊕ www.konahawaii.com/ms.htm 37 units No meals.*

$ HOTEL **Kona Tiki Hotel.** The best thing about this three-story walk-up budget hotel, about a mile south of downtown Kailua Village, is that all the units have lanai right next to the ocean. **Pros:** very low price; oceanfront lanai and pool; room fridges; friendly staff; free parking. **Cons:** older hotel in need of update; no TV in rooms; credit card payment only accepted via hotel website, not in person. *Rooms from: $85 ✉ 75-5968 Alii Dr., Kailua-Kona ☎ 808/329–1425 ⊕ www.konatikihotel.com 16 rooms No credit cards Breakfast.*

$ RENTAL **Nancy's Hideaway.** A few miles up the hill from downtown Kailua-Kona, this charming cottage and studio offer modern comforts; each has its own entrance, a lanai, ocean views, and a wet bar. **Pros:** plenty of privacy; ocean views. **Cons:** upcountry location in the clouds; not kid-friendly. *Rooms from: $130 ✉ 73-1530 Uanani Pl., off Kaloko Dr., Kailua-Kona ☎ 808/325–3132, 866/325–3132 ⊕ www.nancyshideaway.com 2 rooms. No Meals.*

$$$ RENTAL **Outrigger Kanaloa at Kona.** The 16-acre grounds provide a peaceful and verdant background for this low-rise condominium complex bordering the Keauhou-Kona Country Club and within a five-minute drive of the nearest beaches (Kahaluu and Magic Sands). **Pros:** within walking distance of Keauhou Bay; three pools with hot tubs; shopping center and restaurants nearby. **Cons:** no restaurant on property; mandatory cleaning fee at check-out. *Rooms from: $285 ✉ 78-261 Manukai St., Kailua-Kona ☎ 808/322–9625, 808/322–2272, 800/688–7444 ⊕ www.outrigger.com 63 units No meals.*

$ RESORT **Royal Kona Resort.** This is a great option if you're on a budget—the location is central; the bar, lounge, pool, and restaurant are right on the water; and the rooms feature contemporary Hawaiian decor with Polynesian accents. **Pros:** convenient location; waterfront pool; low prices. **Cons:** can be crowded; parking is tight. *Rooms from: $139 ✉ 75-5852 Alii Dr., Kailua-Kona ☎ 808/329–3111, 800/222–5642 ⊕ www.royalkona.com 436 rooms, 8 suites No meals.*

$ RESORT FAMILY **Sheraton Kona Resort & Spa at Keauhou Bay.** What this big concrete structure lacks in intimacy, it makes up for with its beautifully manicured grounds, historic sense of place, renovated interiors, and stunning location on Keauhou Bay. **Pros:** cool pool; manta rays on view nightly; restaurant; resort style at lower price. **Cons:** no beach; daily resort fee for Wi-Fi and parking. *Rooms from: $169 ✉ 78-128 Ehukai St., Kailua-Kona ☎ 808/930–4900 ⊕ www.sheratonkona.com 485 rooms, 24 suites No meals.*

$ RENTAL FAMILY **Silver Oaks Guest Ranch.** Three private cottages set on a 10-acre working ranch afford total privacy, with a few more amenities than a vacation house or condo. **Pros:** very private; deck with ocean views. **Cons:**

five-night minimum stay; not near the beach; dated decor. $Rooms from: $120 ✉ 73-4570 Mamalahoa Hwy., just north of Kaloko Dr., Kailua-Kona ☎ 877/325–2300, 808/325–2000 ⊕ www.silveroaksranch. com ⟲ 3 cottages.

THE KONA COAST

SOUTH KONA

There are no resorts in this area, but there are plenty of fantastic bed-and-breakfasts and vacation rental homes at Kealakekua Bay and in the hills above. The towns of Captain Cook and Kainaliu feature some excellent dining and shopping options, and there are several coffee farms open for tours as well. You can get to the volcano in about an hour and a half, and you're also close to several less well-known but wonderful beaches, including Hookena and Honomolino. Kailua-Kona is a 30-minute drive away from Captain Cook, while the great, sandy beaches of the Kohala Coast are an hour or more away.

$ **Aloha Guesthouse.** In the hills above Puuhonu O Honaunau, this
B&B/INN guesthouse offers quiet elegance, complete privacy, and ocean views from every room. **Pros:** eco-conscious; full breakfast; views of the South Kona coastline. **Cons:** remote location up a bumpy 1-mile dirt road. $Rooms from: $125 ✉ Old Tobacco Rd., off Hwy. 11 near mile marker 104, Honaunau ☎ 808/328–8955 ⊕ www.alohaguesthouse.com ⟲ 5 rooms ⊙ Breakfast.

$$$$ **Horizon Guest House.** Surrounded by McCandeless Ranch on 40 acres
B&B/INN in South Kona, this place may seem remote, but it's actually just a short drive from some of the best water attractions on the island, including Puuhonua O Honaunau, Kealakekua Bay, and Hookena Beach. **Pros:** private and quiet; heated pool with Jacuzzi; beautiful views. **Cons:** not on the beach; 40 minutes from Kailua-Kona. $Rooms from: $350 ✉ Mamalahoa Hwy., between mile markers 101 and 100, Captain Cook ☎ 808/328–2540 ⊕ www.horizonguesthouse.com ⟲ 4 suites ⊙ Breakfast.

$ **Kaawa Loa Plantation.** Proprietors Mike Martinage and Greg Nunn
B&B/INN operate a grand bed-and-breakfast inn on a 5-acre coffee farm above Kealakekua Bay. **Pros:** nice views; excellent breakfast; Hawaiian steam room. **Cons:** not within walking distance of bay; some rooms share a bath. $Rooms from: $129 ✉ 82-5990 Napoopoo Rd., Captain Cook ☎ 808/323–2686 ⊕ www.kaawaloaplantation.com ⟲ 2 rooms, 1 suite, 1 cottage ⊙ Breakfast.

$ **Kane Plantation Guesthouse.** The historic former home of the late leg-
B&B/INN endary artist Herb Kane, this luxury boutique guesthouse occupies a 16-acre avocado farm overlooking the South Kona coastline. **Pros:** privacy; upscale amenities. **Cons:** not on the beach. $Rooms from: $155 ✉ 84-1120 Telephone Exchange Rd., off Hwy. 11, ¼ mile past mile marker 105, south of Captain Cook, Honaunau ☎ 808/328–2416 ⊕ www.kaneplantationhawaii.com ⟲ 4 suites.

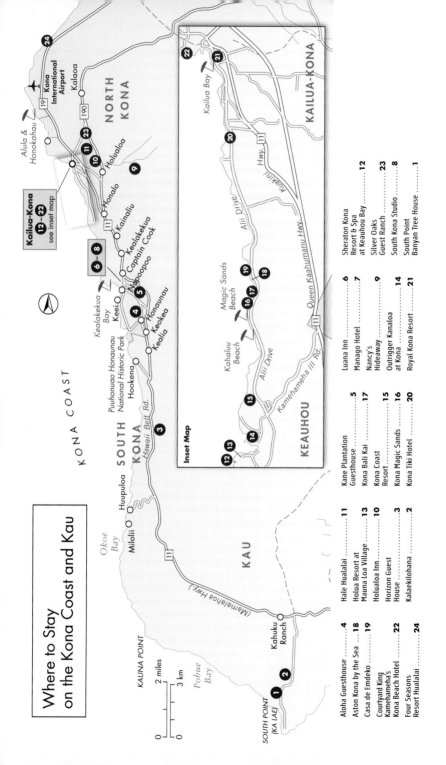

Where to Stay
on the Kona Coast and Kau

KONA COAST

SOUTH POINT (KA LAE)

KAUNA POINT

Pohue Bay

Okoe Bay

Miloli'i

Huupuloa

SOUTH KONA

Kahuku Ranch

KAU

(Mamalahoa Hwy.)

Hawaii Belt Rd.

Kealia

Keokea

Honaunau

Keei

Kealakekua Bay

Puʻuhonua o Honaunau National Historic Park

Hookena

Honaunau

Napoopoo

Captain Cook

Kealakekua

Kainaliu

Honalo

Holualoa

Kona International Airport

Kalaoa

Alula & Honokohau

Kaloa

NORTH KONA

KAILUA-KONA

Kailua-Kona 12–22 see inset map

Inset Map

Kailua Bay

Kahaluu Beach

Magic Sands Beach

Aliʻi Drive

Kuakini Hwy.

Queen Kaahumanu Hwy.

Kamehameha III Rd.

KEAUHOU

$ · B&B/INN · ⟨T⟩ **Luana Inn.** The best part of this bed-and-breakfast near Kealakekua Bay is the fabulous gourmet breakfast prepared by proprietors Ken and Erin. **Pros:** excellent food; sterling hospitality. **Cons:** not on the bay or beach; room decor is dated. ⟨$⟩ *Rooms from: $169* ⊠ *82-5856 Napoopoo Rd., Captain Cook* ☎ *808/328–2612* ⊕ *www.luanainn.com* ⇔ *5 rooms* ⟨Ö⟩ *Breakfast.*

$ · HOTEL · ⟨T⟩ **Manago Hotel.** This historic hotel is a good option if you want to escape the touristy thing but still be close to the water and attractions like Kealakekua Bay and Puuhonua O Honaunau National Historical Park. **Pros:** local color; rock-bottom prices; terrific on-site restaurant. **Cons:** not the best sound insulation between rooms. ⟨$⟩ *Rooms from: $36* ⊠ *81-6155 Mamalahoa Hwy., Box 145, Captain Cook* ☎ *808/323–2642* ⊕ *www. managohotel.com* ⇔ *64 rooms, 42 with bath* ⟨Ö⟩ *No meals.*

$ · RENTAL · ⟨T⟩ **South Kona Studio.** This little studio is a great find for travelers on a budget. **Pros:** budget friendly; snorkel gear included; ocean views; last-minute availability. **Cons:** remote location; two guests max. ⟨$⟩ *Rooms from: $79* ⊠ *Kaohe Rd. and Hwy. 11, Captain Cook* ☎ *808/938–1172* ⇔ *1 room* ⟨Ö⟩ *No Meals.*

KAU

Far from the West Hawaii resorts, Kau is a good place for those looking to get away from it all. You won't find a lot in terms of amenities, but there are several nice options including vacation rental cottages, B&B inns, and a condo resort complex with golf course. The main visitor attraction is the beautiful Punaluu Black Sand Beach, home of the endangered hawksbill turtle.

$$ · B&B/INN · ⟨T⟩ **Kalaekilohana.** You wouldn't really expect to find a top-notch bed-and-breakfast in Kau, but just up the road from South Point, this grand yellow residence offers large, comfortable private suites with beautiful, locally harvested hardwood floors, private lanai with ocean and mountain views, and big, comfy beds decked out with high-thread-count sheets and fluffy down comforters. **Pros:** luxurious beds; beautiful decor reminiscent of Old Hawaii; delicious breakfast; dinner Friday and Saturday. **Cons:** not for children under 10; no pool. ⟨$⟩ *Rooms from: $249* ⊠ *94-2152 South Point Rd., Naalehu* ☎ *808/939–8052* ⊕ *www. kau-hawaii.com* ⇔ *4 rooms* ⟨Ö⟩ *Multiple meal plans.*

$ · RENTAL · ⟨T⟩ **South Point Banyan Tree House.** Ideal for romance, this charming little tree cottage is built into a Chinese banyan tree. **Pros:** secluded and romantic; interesting architecture; lily pond; hot tub with a view. **Cons:** remote location not within walking distance of grocery store or restaurants; no pool or beach. ⟨$⟩ *Rooms from: $100* ⊠ *Hwy. 11 at Pinao St., near South Point, Waiohinu* ☎ *808/217–2504* ⊕ *www.southpointbth. com* ⇔ *1 cottage* ⟨Ö⟩ *No meals.*

9

NORTH KONA

$$$$ · RESORT · Fodor's Choice · ★ · ⟨T⟩ **Four Seasons Resort Hualalai.** Beautiful views everywhere, polished wood floors, custom furnishings and linens in warm earth and cool white tones, and Hawaiian fine artwork make this resort a peaceful retreat. **Pros:** beautiful location; excellent restaurants. **Cons:** not the

best beach among the resorts. ⑤ *Rooms from: $695* ✉ *72-100 Kaupu-lehu Dr., Box 1269, Kailua-Kona* ☎ *808/325–8000, 800/819–5053, 888/340–5662* ⊕ *www.fourseasons.com/hualalai* ↝ *243 rooms, 51 suites* ⑩ *No meals.*

THE KOHALA COAST

The Kohala Coast is home to most all of the Big Island's megaresorts. (As of this writing, Kona Village Resort remains closed indefinitely due to tsunami damage in March 2011. It's expected to reopen after extensive renovations are completed.) Dotting the coastline, manicured lawns and golf courses, luxurious hotels, and white-sand beaches break up the long expanse of black lava rock along Queen Kaahumanu Highway. Many visitors to the Big Island check in here and rarely leave, except to try the restaurants, spas, or golf courses at neighboring resorts. If you're looking to be pampered (for a price) and lounge on the beach or by the pool all day with an umbrella drink in hand, this is where you need to be. That's not to say that staying at a resort makes it difficult to see the rest of the island. On the contrary, most of the hiking and adventure-tour companies offer pickups at the Kohala Coast resorts, and many of the hotels have offers with various rental car agencies so you can be as active or lazy as you like.

$$
RENTAL
Aston Shores at Waikoloa. Villas with terra cotta–tile roofs are set amid landscaped lagoons and waterfalls at the edge of the championship Waikoloa Village Golf Course. **Pros:** good prices for the area; great location; fully self-sufficient condos with maid service. **Cons:** no restaurants. ⑤ *Rooms from: $239* ✉ *69-1035 Keana Pl., Waikoloa* ☎ *808/886–5001, 800/922–7866* ⊕ *www.astonhotels.com* ↝ *56 units* ⑩ *No meals.*

$$$$
RESORT
Fodor's Choice
★
Fairmont Orchid Hawaii. This first-rate resort overflows with tropical gardens, cascading waterfalls, sandy beach cove, beautiful wings with "open sesame" doors, a meandering pool, and renovated rooms with all the amenities. **Pros:** oceanfront location; great restaurants; excellent pool; aloha hospitality. **Cons:** top resort features come at a high price. ⑤ *Rooms from: $569* ✉ *1 N. Kaniku Dr., Kohala Coast* ☎ *808/885–2000, 800/845–9905* ⊕ *www.fairmont.com/orchid* ↝ *486 rooms, 54 suites* ⑩ *No meals.*

$
B&B/INN
FAMILY
Hale Hoonanea. A comfortable home with two detached guest suites, this 3-acre property in the Kohala Estates, above Kawaihae Harbor, lives up to the English translation of its name, "House of Relaxation." **Pros:** detached suites for maximum privacy; panoramic ocean views from private lanai; good price for the neighborhood. **Cons:** not within walking distance to restaurants; no pool. ⑤ *Rooms from: $110* ✉ *Kohala Estates, 59-513 Ala Kahua Dr., Kawaihae* ☎ *808/882–1653, 877/882–1653* ⊕ *www.houseofrelaxation.com* ↝ *2 suites* ⑩ *Breakfast.*

$$$
RESORT
FAMILY
Hapuna Beach Prince Hotel. More reasonably priced than its neighbor resorts, this hotel occupies the northern corner of the largest sand beach on the Big Island. **Pros:** extra-large rooms, all ocean-facing; direct access to one of island's best beaches. **Cons:** fitness center is a 10-minute walk from the golf course; daily fees for Wi-Fi and parking. ⑤ *Rooms from: $289* ✉ *62-100 Kaunaoa Dr., Kohala Coast* ☎ *808/880–1111, 866/774–6236*

CONDOS AND VACATION RENTALS

Renting a condo or vacation house gives you much more living space than the average hotel, plus the chance to meet more people (neighbors are usually friendly), lower nightly rates, and the option of cooking or barbecuing rather than eating out. When booking, remember that most properties are individually owned, with rates and amenities that differ substantially depending on the place. Some properties are handled by rental agents or agencies while many are handled directly through the owner. The following is a list of our favorite booking agencies for various lodging types throughout the island. Be sure to call and ask questions before booking.

Abbey Vacation Rentals (⊕ *www. waikoloarentals.com*) has luxury condos on the Kohala Coast.

Big Island Villas (⊕ *www. bigislandvillas.com*) lists a variety of condos attached to the Four Seasons Hualalai, Mauna Kea, and Mauna Lani resorts.

CJ Kimberly Realty (⊕ *www. cjkimberly.com*) offers fantastic deals on some oceanfront homes and condos.

Hawaiian Beach Rentals (⊕ *www. hawaiianbeachrentals.com*) and **Tropical Villa Vacations** (⊕ *www. tropicalvillavacations.com*) are excellent for high-end, ocean- or beach-front homes.

Hawaii Vacation Rentals (⊕ *www. vacationbigisland.com*) lists several properties on the beach in Puako, a sleepy beach settlement just up the road from the Kohala Coast resorts.

Keauhou Property Management (⊕ *www.konacondo.net*) has condos along the Kona Coast, just south of Kailua-Kona around Keauhou Bay.

Kolea Vacations (⊕ *www. koleavacations.com*) lists dozens of condos at the Kolea at Waikoloa complex as well as a stunning oceanfront home on Alii in Kailua-Kona.

Kona Coast Vacations (⊕ *www. konacoastvacations.com*) offers a large variety of condos on the west side of the island and wins high marks for good service.

Kona Hawaii Vacation Rentals (⊕ *www.konahawaii.com*) offers very affordable condos in Kailua-Kona.

Knutson and Associates (⊕ *www. konahawaiirentals.com*) handles rentals for a wide variety of Kailua-Kona condos and oceanfront vacation homes.

Property Network (☎ *808/329–7977* ⊕ *www.hawaii-kona.com*) lists and manages dozens of condo rentals in and around Kailua-Kona.

Rent Hawaii Home (⊕ *www. renthawaiihome.com*) offers several affordable cottage and beach-house rentals, ideal for those who are staying for a while and want some room and privacy but don't want to spend half a year's salary on a beachfront palace.

South Kohala Management (⊕ *www.southkohala.com*) lists a wide variety of luxury Kohala Coast condos.

Vacation Rental By Owner (⊕ *www.vrbo.com*) has homes and condos for rent all over the island.

9

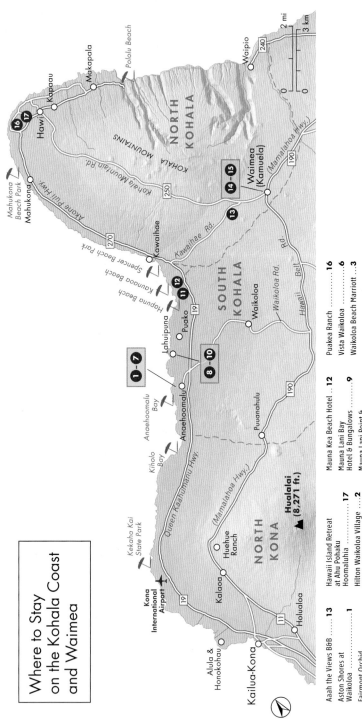

Where to Stay on the Kohala Coast and Waimea

2 mi

3 km

NORTH KOHALA

Pololu Beach

Waipio

240

Makapala

Kapaau

Hawi

KOHALA MOUNTAINS

Kohala Mountain Rd.

Akoni Pali Hwy.

Mahukona Beach Park

Mahukona

270

Spencer Beach Park

Kawaihae

250

Kawaihae Rd.

190

Waimea (Kamuela)

(Mamalahoa Hwy.)

Hapuna Beach

Kaunaoa Beach

Puako

Lahuipuna

SOUTH KOHALA

Waikoloa

Waikoloa Rd.

Hawaii Belt Rd.

19

Anaehoomalu Bay

Anaehoomalu

Kiholo Bay

Kekaha Kai State Park

Puuanahulu

190

Queen Kaahumanu Hwy.

(Mamalahoa Hwy.)

Huehue Ranch

NORTH KONA

Hualalai (8,271 ft.)

Kona International Airport

19

Kalaoa

Holualoa

111

Kailua-Kona

Alula & Honokohau

Aaah the Views B&B **13**	Hawaii Island Retreat at Ahu Pohaku Hoomaluhia **1**
Aston Shores at Waikoloa **1**	Hilton Waikoloa Village **2**
Fairmont Orchid Hawaii **8**	Kolea at Waikoloa Beach Resort **5**
Hapuna Beach Prince Hotel **11**	Lava Lava Beach Club **7**
Mauna Kea Beach Hotel .. **12**	Puakea Ranch **16**
Mauna Lani Bay Hotel & Bungalows **9**	Vista Waikoloa **6**
Mauna Lani Point & Islands of Mauna Lani **10**	Waikoloa Beach Marriott ... **3**
Outrigger Fairway Villas at Waikoloa **4**	Waimea Country Lodge .. **15**
	Waimea Gardens Cottage **14**

⊕ *www.princeresortshawaii.com*
⤴*351 rooms, 37 suites* ⏃No meals.*

$$$ ⛫ **Hawaii Island Retreat at Ahu Pohaku**
B&B/INN **Hoomaluhia.** Here, above the seacliffs in North Kohala's Hawi, sustainability meets luxury without sacrificing comfort. **Pros:** stunning location; ancient Hawaiian spiritual sites; eco-friendly. **Cons:** not within walking distance of restaurants; off the beaten path. ⑤*Rooms from: $275* ⊠*250 Maluhia Rd., off Hwy. 270 in Hawi, Kapaau* ☎808/889–6336 ⊕ *www.hawaiiislandretreat.com* ⤴*9 rooms, 7 yurts* ⏃*Breakfast.*

$$ ⛫ **Hilton Waikoloa Village.** Dolphins
RESORT swim in the lagoon; pint-size guests
FAMILY zoom down the 175-foot waterslide; a bride poses on the grand staircase; a fire-bearing runner lights the torches along the seaside path at sunset—these are some of the typical scenes at this 62-acre

KOHALA CONDO COMFORTS

If you require anything not provided by the management, both the **Kings' Shops** (⊠ *250 Waikoloa Beach Dr., Waikoloa* ☎ *808/886–8811*) and the **Queens' MarketPlace** (⊠ *201 Waikoloa Beach Dr., Waikoloa* ☎ *808/886–8822*) in the Waikoloa Beach Resort are good places to go. There are a small grocery store, a liquor store, and several nice restaurants at the Kings' Shops. The newer Queens' MarketPlace also has a food court, as well as a gourmet market where you can get pizza baked to order. It's not exactly cheap, but you're paying for the convenience of not having to drive into town.

megaresort. **Pros:** family-friendly; lots of restaurant and activity options. **Cons:** gigantic; crowded; lots of kids; restaurants are pricey. ⑤*Rooms from: $229* ⊠*69-425 Waikoloa Beach Dr., Waikoloa* ☎808/886–1234, 800/445–8667 ⊕ *www.hiltonwaikoloavillage.com* ⤴*1,241 rooms, 58 suites* ⏃*No meals.*

$$$ ⛫ **Kolea at Waikoloa Beach Resort.** These modern, impeccably furnished
RENTAL condos appeal to the high-end visitor typically associated with the Mauna
FAMILY Lani Bay Hotel & Bungalows. **Pros:** high design; close to beach and activities; resort amenities of nearby Hilton. **Cons:** pricey; no on-property restaurants. ⑤*Rooms from: $300* ⊠*Waikoloa Beach Resort, 69-1000 Kolea Kai Circle, Waikoloa* ☎808/987–4519 ⊕ *www.waikoloavacationrentals. com/kolea-rentals* ⤴*40 villas, 4 houses* ⏃*No meals.*

$$$$ ⛫ **Lava Lava Beach Club.** Spend the day swimming steps away from your
RENTAL private lanai and fall asleep to the sound of the ocean at these four artfully decorated one-room cottages, on the beach at Anaehoomalu Bay. **Pros:** on the beach; fully air-conditioned; free Wi-Fi. **Cons:** beach is public, so there will be people on it in front of cottage. ⑤*Rooms from: $475* ⊠*69-1081 Kuualii Pl., Waikoloa* ☎808/769–5282 ⊕ *www. lavalavabeachclub.com* ⤴*4 cottages* ⏃*No meals.*

$$$$ ⛫ **Mauna Kea Beach Hotel.** The grande dame of the Kohala Coast has long
RESORT been regarded as one of the state's premier vacation resort hotels, and it borders one of the island's finest white-sand beaches, Kaunaoa. **Pros:** beautiful beach; premier tennis center; extra-large contemporary rooms; on-site restaurants. **Cons:** small swimming pool; overpriced sundries shop. ⑤*Rooms from: $445* ⊠*62-100 Mauna Kea Beach Dr., Kohala*

9

Coast ☎ *808/882–7222, 866/977–4589* ⊕ *www.maunakeabeachhotel. com* ⤳ *254 rooms, 10 suites* ⊚️ *No meals.*

$$$$ 🛏 **Mauna Lani Bay Hotel & Bungalows.** Popular with honeymooners and
RESORT   anniversary couples for decades, this elegant Kohala Coast classic is
Fodor'sChoice   still one of the most beautiful resorts on the island, highlighted by a
★   breathtaking, open-air lobby with cathedral-like ceilings, Zen-like koi
ponds, and illuminated sheets of cascading water. **Pros:** beautiful design;
award-winning spa; no hidden fees; complimentary valet parking. **Cons:**
no luau. $ *Rooms from: $400* ✉ *68-1400 Mauna Lani Dr., Kohala
Coast* ☎ *808/885–6622, 800/367–2323* ⊕ *www.maunalani.com* ⤳ *318
rooms, 18 suites, 5 bungalows* ⊚️ *No meals.*

$$$ 🛏 **Mauna Lani Point and Islands of Mauna Lani.** Surrounded by the emer-
RENTAL   ald greens of a world-class ocean-side golf course, spacious two-story
suites at Islands of Mauna Lani offer a private, independent home, while
Mauna Lani Point villas are closer to the beach. **Pros:** privacy; soaking
tubs; extra-large units. **Cons:** pricey. $ *Rooms from: $275* ✉ *68-1050
Mauna Lani Point Dr., Kohala Coast* ☎ *808/885–5022, 800/642–6284*
⊕ *www.maunalanipoint.com* ⤳ *72 units* ⊚️ *No meals.*

$$ 🛏 **Outrigger Fairway Villas at Waikoloa.** These large and comfy town
RENTAL   houses and condominiums are located just off the fairway of the
Waikoloa golf course and are a short walk from Anaehoomalu Bay.
Pros: good location for beach, shopping, dining, and golf; infinity pool;
kid-friendly. **Cons:** no ocean views. $ *Rooms from: $185* ✉ *Waikoloa Beach Resort, 69-200 Pohakulana Pl., Waikoloa* ☎ *808/886–0036*
⊕ *www.outrigger.com* ⤳ *70 units* ⊚️ *No meals.*

$$$ 🛏 **Puakea Ranch.** Four beautifully restored ranch houses and bungalows
RENTAL   occupy this historic country estate in Hawi, where guests enjoy their
Fodor'sChoice   own private swimming pools, horseback riding, round-the-clock con-
★   cierge availability, and plenty of fresh fruit to pick from the orchards.
Pros: horseback lessons and trail riding; charmingly decorated; beautiful
bathrooms; private swimming pools. **Cons:** not on the beach. $ *Rooms
from: $289* ✉ *56-2864 Akoni Pule Hwy., Kohala Coast* ☎ *808/315–0805*
⊕ *www.puakearanch.com* ⤳ *4 bungalows, 2 cottages* ⊚️ *No meals.*

$$ 🛏 **Vista Waikoloa.** Older and more reasonably priced than most of the
RENTAL   condo complexes along the Kohala Coast, the well-appointed, two-
bedroom, two-bath Vista condos offer ocean views and two lanai per
unit. **Pros:** centrally located; reasonably priced; very large units; 75-foot
lap pool. **Cons:** hit or miss on decor because each unit is individually owned. $ *Rooms from: $180* ✉ *Waikoloa Beach Resort, 69-1010
Keana Pl., Waikoloa* ☎ *808/886–3594* ⤳ *122 units* ⊚️ *No meals.*

$$$$ 🛏 **Waikoloa Beach Marriott.** Covering 15 acres with ancient fishponds,
RESORT   historic trails, and petroglyph fields, the Marriott has rooms with sleek
FAMILY   modern beds, bright white linens, Hawaiian art, and private lanai.
Pros: more low-key than the Hilton Waikoloa; sunset luau Wednesday and Saturday; sand-bottom pool for kids. **Cons:** only one restaurant. $ *Rooms from: $410* ✉ *69-275 Waikoloa Beach Dr., Waikoloa*
☎ *808/886–6789, 800/228–9290* ⊕ *www.marriott.com* ⤳ *525 rooms,
22 suites* ⊚️ *No meals.*

WAIMEA

Though it seems a world away, Waimea is only about a 15- to 20-minute drive from the Kohala Coast resorts, which means it takes less time to get to the island's best beaches from Waimea than it does from Kailua-Kona. Yet few visitors think to book lodging in this pleasant upcountry ranching community, where you can enjoy cool mornings and evenings after a day spent basking in the sun. To the delight of residents and visitors, a few retired resort chefs have opened up their own little projects in Waimea. Sightseeing is easy from here, too: Mauna Kea is a short drive away, and Hilo and Kailua-Kona can be reached in about an hour. Because Waimea doesn't attract as many visitors as the coast, you won't find as many condos and hotels, but there are some surprising bed-and-breakfast and cottage options, some of which offer great deals, especially considering their vantage point. Many have spectacular views of Mauna Kea, the ocean, and the beautiful, green hills of Waimea.

$

B&B/INN

🖼 **Aaah the Views Bed and Breakfast.** The name aptly sums up the experience at this tranquil, stream-side inn built specifically to be a bed-and-breakfast—and it's the only lodging in Waimea that hosts a full, sit-down breakfast. **Pros:** away from it all; friendly hosts; beautiful countryside views; free beach gear. **Cons:** no pool. $ *Rooms from: $139* ✉ *66-1773 Alaneo St., off Akulani St., just past mile marker 60 on Hwy. 19, Waimea* ☎ *808/885–3455* ⊕ *www.aaahtheviews.com* ↙ *3 suites* ⦿ *Breakfast.*

$

HOTEL

🖼 **Waimea Country Lodge.** In the heart of cowboy country, this modest ranch house–style lodge offers views of the green, rolling slopes of Mauna Kea. **Pros:** affordable; large rooms equipped with kitchenettes. **Cons:** rooms could use some updating; no pool. $ *Rooms from: $135* ✉ *65-1210 Lindsey Rd., Waimea* ☎ *808/885–4100, 800/367–5004* ⊕ *www.castleresorts.com* ↙ *21 rooms* ⦿ *No meals.*

$

B&B/INN

🖼 **Waimea Gardens Cottage.** Surprisingly luxe, yet cozy and quaint, three charming country cottages at this historic Hawaiian homestead are surrounded by flowering private gardens and a backyard stream. **Pros:** no detail left out; beautiful self-contained cottages; gardens; complete privacy. **Cons:** requires payment in full six weeks prior to arrival. $ *Rooms from: $155* ✉ *Waimea* ☎ *808/885–8550* ⊕ *www.waimeagardens.com* ↙ *2 cottages, 1 studio* ⊟ *No credit cards* ⦿ *Breakfast.*

THE HAMAKUA COAST

A stretch of coastline between Waimea and Hilo, the Hamakua Coast is an ideal spot for those seeking peace, tranquility, and beautiful views, which is why it can be a favorite with honeymooners. Several über-romantic bed-and-breakfasts dot the coast, each with its own personality and views. As with Hilo, the beaches are an hour's drive away or more, so most visitors spend a few nights here and a few closer to the beaches on the west side. A handful of vacation homes provide an extra level of privacy for couples, groups, or families. Honokaa Town is a charming area with a couple of restaurants, banks, and convenience stores.

$$ 🏠 **The Palms Cliff House Inn.** This handsome Victorian-style mansion, 15
B&B/INN   minutes north of downtown Hilo and a few minutes from Akaka Falls,
is perched on the sea cliffs 100 feet above the crashing surf of the tropical coast. **Pros:** stunning views; terrific breakfast; comfortable rooms
with every amenity; all rooms have private entrances from the exterior. **Cons:** no pool; no lunch or dinner on-site; remote location means
you have to drive to Hilo for dinner. $ *Rooms from: $239* ✉ *28-3514
Mamalahoa Hwy., Honomu* ☎ *866/963–6076, 808/963–6076* ⊕ *www.
palmscliffhouse.com* ➷ *4 rooms, 4 suites* ⎮◎⎮ *Breakfast.*

$$ 🏠 **Waianuhea.** Defining Hawaiian upcountry elegance, this gorgeous
B&B/INN   country inn, which is fully self-contained and runs off solar power,
Fodor's Choice   sits in a forested area on the Hamakua Coast in Ahualoa. **Pros:** eco-
★   friendly hotel; hot and healthy breakfast; beautiful views of Mauna
Kea. **Cons:** very remote location; unreliable phone access. $ *Rooms
from: $225* ✉ *45-3503 Kahana Dr., Box 185, Honokaa* ☎ *888/775–
2577, 808/775–1118* ⊕ *www.waianuhea.com* ➷ *4 rooms, 1 suite*
⎮◎⎮ *Breakfast.*

$ 🏠 **Waipio Wayside.** Nestled amid the avocado, mango, coffee, and kukui
B&B/INN   trees of a historic plantation estate (circa 1932), this serene home provides a retreat close to the Waipio Valley. **Pros:** close to Waipio; gracious owner. **Cons:** remote location; close quarters; no lunch or dinner
on property. $ *Rooms from: $110* ✉ *42-4226 Waipio Rd. (Hwy. 240),
Honokaa* ☎ *808/775–0275, 800/833–8849* ⊕ *www.waipiowayside.
com* ➷ *5 rooms* ⎮◎⎮ *Breakfast.*

HILO

Hilo is the wetter, more lush eastern side of the Big Island, which means
if you stay here you'll be close to waterfalls and rain-forest hikes, but
not to the warm, dry, white-sand beaches of the Kohala Coast. Locals
have taken a greater interest in Hilo; signs of that interest are showing in new restaurants, restored buildings, and a handful of clean and
pleasant parks. Hilo has a few decent hotels, but none of the high-end
resorts that are the domain of the west side. So, get into the groove at
one of Hilo's fantastic bed-and-breakfasts. Some have taken over lovely
historic homes and serve breakfast comprising ingredients from backyard gardens. The volcano is only a 30-minute drive, as are the sights
of the Puna region. There are also a number of nice beaches and surf
spots, though not in the class of the resort beaches of South Kohala.

$ 🏠 **The Bay House.** Overlooking Hilo Bay and just steps away from the
B&B/INN   Singing Bridge near Hilo's historic downtown area, this small, quiet
bed-and-breakfast is vibrantly decorated, with Hawaiian-quilted beds
and private lanai in each of the three rooms. **Pros:** free Wi-Fi; ample
parking; cliffside hot tub; Hilo Bay views. **Cons:** only two people per
room. $ *Rooms from: $175* ✉ *42 Pukihae St., Hilo* ☎ *888/235–8195,
808/961–6311* ⊕ *www.bayhousehawaii.com* ➷ *3 rooms* ⎮◎⎮ *Breakfast.*

$ 🏠 **Dolphin Bay Hotel.** Units in this circa-1950s motor lodge are modest,
HOTEL   but charming, clean, and inexpensive. **Pros:** great value; full kitchens
FAMILY   in all units; extremely helpful and pleasant staff; weekly rates are a
good deal. **Cons:** no pool; no phones in the rooms. $ *Rooms from:*

$119 ⊠ 333 Iliahi St., Hilo ☎ 808/935–1466 ⊕ www.dolphinbayhotel. com ⟿ 18 rooms, 12 studios, 4 1-bedroom units, 1 2-bedroom unit ⊚ No meals.

$
B&B/INN
Hale Kai. On a bluff above Honolii surf beach, this modern 5,400-square-foot home is 2 miles from downtown Hilo and features four rooms—each with patio, deluxe bedding, and grand ocean views within earshot of the surf. **Pros:** delicious hot breakfast; pool; panoramic views of Hilo Bay; hot tub; free Wi-Fi; smoke-free property. **Cons:** no kids under 13. *⑤ Rooms from: $165 ⊠ 111 Honolii Pl., Hilo ☎ 808/935–6330 ⊕ www.halekaihawaii.com ⟿ 3 rooms, 1 suite ⊚ Breakfast.*

$$
HOTEL
Hilo Hawaiian Hotel. This recently renovated landmark hotel has large bay-front rooms offering spectacular views of Mauna Kea and Coconut Island on Hilo Bay. **Pros:** Hilo Bay views; private lanai in most rooms; large rooms. **Cons:** daily fee for in-room Internet. *⑤ Rooms from: $245 ⊠ 71 Banyan Dr., Hilo ☎ 808/935–9361, 800/367–5004 from mainland, 800/272–5275 interisland ⊕ www.castleresorts.com ⟿ 264 rooms, 21 suites ⊚ No meals.*

$
B&B/INN
Hilo Honu Inn. A charming old Craftsman home lovingly restored by a friendly and hospitable couple from North Carolina, the Hilo Honu offers quite a bit of variety. **Pros:** beautifully restored home; spectacular Hilo Bay views; a/c in two of the rooms; free Wi-Fi. **Cons:** no toddlers in the upstairs suite. *⑤ Rooms from: $140 ⊠ 465 Haili St., Hilo ☎ 808/935–4325 ⊕ www.hilohonu.com ⟿ 1 room, 2 suites ⊚ Breakfast.*

$
HOTEL
Hilo Seaside Hotel. A bit noisy due to its proximity to the airport, this local-flavor destination is a friendly, laid-back, and otherwise peaceful place, with tropical rooms that have private lanai. **Pros:** private lanai; friendly staff. **Cons:** noise from overhead planes can be disruptive. *⑤ Rooms from: $155 ⊠ 126 Banyan Way, Hilo ☎ 808/935–0821, 800/560–5557 ⊕ www.hiloseasidehotel.com ⟿ 135 rooms ⊚ No Meals.*

$
B&B/INN
The Inn at Kulaniapia Falls. Overlooking downtown Hilo and the ocean beyond, this inn sits next to a 120-foot waterfall that tumbles into a 300-foot-wide natural pond—ripe for swimming, conditions permitting. **Pros:** waterfalls on property; good value; complementary yoga. **Cons:** isolated; dark road challenging to navigate at night. *⑤ Rooms from: $179 ⊠ 100 Kulaniapia Dr., Hilo ☎ 808/935–6789 ⊕ www. waterfall.net ⟿ 10 rooms, 1 guesthouse ⊚ Breakfast.*

$$
B&B/INN
Shipman House Bed & Breakfast Inn. This historic bed-and-breakfast on 5½ verdant acres on Reed's Island is furnished with antique koa and period pieces, some dating from the days when Queen Liliuokalani came to tea. **Pros:** 10-minute walk to downtown Hilo; historic home; friendly and knowledgeable local hosts. **Cons:** not a great spot for kids; two-night minimum. *⑤ Rooms from: $219 ⊠ 131 Kaiulani St., Hilo ☎ 808/934–8002, 800/627–8447 ⊕ www.hilo-hawaii.com ⟿ 5 rooms ⊚ Breakfast.*

9

PUNA

Puna is a world apart—wild jungles, volcanically heated hot springs, and not a resort for miles around. There are, however, a handful of vacation homes and bed-and-breakfasts, most of which are a great deal. Puna doesn't attract nearly as many visitors as other regions on the island. This is not a typical vacation spot: there are a few black-sand beaches (some of them clothing-optional), few dining or entertainment options, and quite a few, er, interesting locals. That said, for those who want to have a unique experience, get away from everything, witness molten lava flowing into the ocean (depending on activity), and don't mind the sound of the chirping coqui frogs at night, this is the place to do it. The volcano and Hilo are both within driving distance.

$ **Coconut Cottage Bed & Breakfast.** This cottage has quickly become a
B&B/INN   favorite for its beautiful grounds, the hosts' attention to detail, and its proximity to different island adventures. **Pros:** great breakfast; convenient to the lava-flow area, black-sand beach, and Kapoho tide pools for snorkeling; free Wi-Fi; laundry facility. **Cons:** some may have a hard time sleeping with the coqui frogs chirping. $ *Rooms from: $140* ⊠ *13-1139 Leilani Ave., Pahoa* 📞 *808/965–0973, 866/204–7444* ⊕ *www.coconutcottagehawaii.com* ↪ *3 rooms, 1 bungalow* ⦿| *Breakfast.*

$ **Yoga Oasis.** With its exposed redwood beams, Balinese doorways,
B&B/INN   and imported art, Yoga Oasis draws those who seek relaxation and rejuvenation, and perhaps a free morning yoga lesson or two. **Pros:** daily yoga; focus on relaxation; breakfast and other meals may be available; very low prices. **Cons:** remote location; rooms in main building share bathrooms. $ *Rooms from: $65* ⊠ *Box 1935, 13-677 Pohoiki Rd., Pahoa* 📞 *808/936-7710, 800/274–4446* ⊕ *www.yogaoasis.org* ↪ *4 rooms with shared bath, 4 cabins, 2 houses* ⦿| *No meals.*

HAWAII VOLCANOES NATIONAL PARK AND VICINITY

If you are going to visit Hawaii Volcanoes National Park, and we highly recommend that you do, stay the night in Volcano Village. This allows you to see the glow of Halemaumau Crater at night—if there's activity, that is—without worrying about driving an hour or more back to your condo, hotel, or bed-and-breakfast. There are plenty of places to stay in the area, and many of them are both charming and reasonable. Volcano Village has just enough dining and shopping options to satisfy you for a day or two, and you're also close to Hilo, the Puna region, and Punaluu Black Sand Beach, should you decide to make Volcano your home base for longer.

$ **Chalet Kilauea Collection.** Comprising three inns and lodges and five
HOTEL   vacation houses in and around Volcano Village, the collection has rooms, suites, and homes ranging from a historic lodge with no-frills, basic bedrooms to a deluxe inn with themed rooms and its own six-person hot tub. **Pros:** free Wi-Fi at all facilities; free afternoon tea at main office; friendly front desk; large variety of lodging types to choose from;

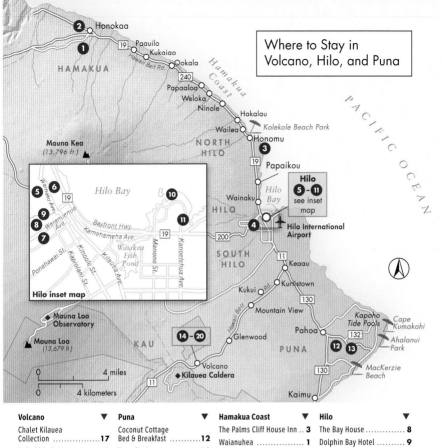

Where to Stay in
Volcano, Hilo, and Puna

Hilo inset map

hot tub; fireplace. **Cons:** office closes at 5 pm—late arrivals allowed with formal check-in the following morning. $ *Rooms from: $55* ✉ *19-4178 Wright Rd., Volcano* ☎ *808/967–7786, 800/937–7786* ⊕ *www.volcano-hawaii.com* ↝ *14 rooms, 3 suites, 5 houses* ❂ *No meals.*

$ ⌂ **Hale Ohia Cottages.** A stately and comfortable Queen Anne–style man-
RENTAL sion, Hale Ohia was built in the 1930s as a summer home for a wealthy Scotsman (the property is listed on the State Historic Register). **Pros:** unique architecture; central, quiet location; free Wi-Fi and parking; privacy. **Cons:** no TVs. $ *Rooms from: $115* ✉ *11-3968 Hale Ohia Rd., off Hwy. 11, Volcano* ☎ *808/967–7986, 800/455–3803* ⊕ *www. haleohia.com* ↝ *4 rooms, 3 cottages, 1 suite* ❂ *Breakfast.*

$$ ⌂ **Kilauea Lodge.** A mile from the entrance of Hawaii Volcanoes
HOTEL National Park, this lodge was initially built as a YMCA camp in the 1930s; now it is a pleasant inn, tastefully furnished with European antiques. **Pros:** great restaurant; close to volcano; fireplaces. **Cons:** no TV or phone in lodge rooms. $ *Rooms from: $180* ✉ *19-3948 Old Volcano Rd., 1 mile northeast of Volcano Store, Box 116, Volcano* ☎ *808/967–7366* ⊕ *www.kilauealodge.com* ↝ *12 rooms, 4 cottages (off property)* ❂ *Breakfast.*

$ ⌂ **My Island Bed & Breakfast Inn.** This three-story, family-operated
B&B/INN inn occupies a historic home built in 1886 by the Lyman missionary family and set on a 7-acre botanical estate. **Pros:** historic home; full breakfast. **Cons:** some shared bathrooms; not every room has a TV. $ *Rooms from: $94* ✉ *19-3896 Old Volcano Hwy., Volcano Village* ☎ *808/967–7216* ⊕ *www.myislandinnhawaii.com* ↝ *6 rooms, 1 guesthouse* ❂ *Breakfast.*

$$$ ⌂ **Volcano Mist Cottage.** Both rustic and Zen, this magical cottage in the
RENTAL rain forest features cathedral ceilings, spruce walls, cork flooring, and amenities not usually found at Volcano vacation rentals, like bathrobes, a Bose home theater system, and Trek mountain bikes. $ *Rooms from: $275* ✉ *11-3932 9th St., Volcano Village* ☎ *808/895–8359* ⊕ *www. volcanomistcottage.com* ↝ *1 cottage.*

$ ⌂ **Volcano Places.** A collection of lovely vacation rental cottages, these
RENTAL accommodations range from a simple cottage in the rain forest to the stunning cedar-paneled Nohea, with its own hot tub. **Pros:** unique architecture; accommodates families; competitively priced, with discounts for three or more nights. **Cons:** no nightlife nearby. $ *Rooms from: $135* ✉ *Volcano Village* ☎ *808/967–7990, 877/967–7990* ⊕ *www. volcanoplaces.com* ↝ *2 2-bedroom cottages, 1 1-bedroom unit, 1 studio* ❂ *No meals.*

$$ ⌂ **Volcano Teapot Cottage.** A near-perfect spot for couples seeking a
RENTAL romantic getaway in Volcano Village, this historic 1912 two-bedroom cottage evokes a vintage country feeling in keeping with the summer homes of the era. **Pros:** hot tub; fireplace; laundry facilities. **Cons:** not quite large enough to accommodate four people—three people max. $ *Rooms from: $195* ✉ *19-4041 Kilauea Rd., Volcano Village* ☎ *808/967–7112* ⊕ *www.volcanoteapot.com* ↝ *1 cottage* ❂ *Breakfast.*

UNDERSTANDING
THE BIG ISLAND

HAWAIIAN VOCABULARY

Although an understanding of Hawaiian is by no means required on a trip to the Aloha State, a *malihini*, or newcomer, will find plenty of opportunities to pick up a few of the local words and phrases. Traditional names and expressions are widely used in the Islands. You're likely to read or hear at least a few words each day of your stay.

With a basic understanding and some uninhibited practice, anyone can have enough command of the local tongue to ask for directions and to order from a restaurant menu. One visitor announced she would not leave until she could pronounce the name of the state fish, the *humuhumunukunukuāpua'a*.

Simplifying the learning process is the fact that the Hawaiian language contains only eight consonants—H, K, L, M, N, P, W, and the silent *'okina*, or glottal stop, written '—plus one or more of the five vowels. All syllables, and therefore all words, end in a vowel. Each vowel, with the exception of a few diphthongized double vowels such as *au* (pronounced "ow") or *ai* (pronounced "eye"), is pronounced separately. Thus *'Iolani* is four syllables (ee-oh-la-nee), not three (yo-la-nee). Although some Hawaiian words have only vowels, most also contain some consonants, but consonants are never doubled.

Pronunciation is simple. Pronounce *A* "ah" as in *father*; *E* "ay" as in *weigh*; *I* "ee" as in *marine*; *O* "oh" as in *no*; *U* "oo" as in *true*.

Consonants mirror their English equivalents, with the exception of *W*. When the letter begins any syllable other than the first one in a word, it is usually pronounced as a *V*. *'Awa*, the Polynesian drink, is pronounced "ava," *'ewa* is pronounced "eva."

Almost all long Hawaiian words are combinations of shorter words; they are not difficult to pronounce if you segment them. *Kalaniana'ole*, the highway running east from Honolulu, is easily understood as *Kalani ana 'ole*. Apply the standard pronunciation rules—the stress falls on the next-to-last syllable of most two- or three-syllable Hawaiian words—and Kalaniana'ole Highway is as easy to say as Main Street.

Now about that fish. Try *humu-humu nuku-nuku āpu a'a*.

The other unusual element in Hawaiian language is the *kahakō*, or macron, written as a short line (¯) placed over a vowel. Like the accent (´) in Spanish, the kahakō puts emphasis on a syllable that would normally not be stressed. The most familiar example is probably *Waikīkī*. With no macrons, the stress would fall on the middle syllable; with only one macron, on the last syllable, the stress would fall on the first and last syllables. Some words become plural with the addition of a macron, often on a syllable that would have been stressed anyway. No Hawaiian word becomes plural with the addition of an *S*, since that letter does not exist in the language.

The Hawaiian diacritical marks are not printed in this guide.

Pidgin

You may hear pidgin, the unofficial language of Hawai'i. It is a Creole language, with its own grammar, evolved from the mixture of English, Hawaiian, Japanese, Portuguese, and other languages spoken in 19th-century Hawai'i, and it is heard everywhere.

Glossary

What follows is a glossary of some of the most commonly used Hawaiian words. Hawaiian residents appreciate visitors who at least try to pick up the local language.

'a'ā: rough, crumbling lava, contrasting with *pāhoehoe*, which is smooth.

'ae: yes.

aikane: friend.

āina: land.

akamai: smart, clever, possessing savoir faire.

akua: god.

ala: a road, path, or trail.

ali'i: a Hawaiian chief, a member of the chiefly class.

aloha: love, affection, kindness; also a salutation meaning both greetings and farewell.

'ānuenue: rainbow.

'a'ole: no.

'apōpō: tomorrow.

'auwai: a ditch.

auwē: alas, woe is me!

'ehu: a red-haired Hawaiian.

'ewa: in the direction of 'Ewa plantation, west of Honolulu.

hala: the pandanus tree, whose leaves (*lau hala*) are used to make baskets and plaited mats.

hālau: school.

hale: a house.

hale pule: church, house of worship.

ha mea iki or **ha mea 'ole:** you're welcome.

hana: to work.

haole: ghost. Since the first foreigners were Caucasian, *haole* now means a Caucasian person.

hapa: a part, sometimes a half; often used as a short form of *hapa haole,* to mean a person who is part-Caucasian.

hau'oli: to rejoice. *Hau'oli Makahiki Hou* means Happy New Year. *Hau'oli lā hānau* means Happy Birthday.

heiau: an outdoor stone platform; an ancient Hawaiian place of worship.

holo: to run.

holoholo: to go for a walk, ride, or sail.

holokū: a long Hawaiian dress, somewhat fitted, with a yoke and a train. Influenced by European fashion, it was worn at court, and at least one local translates the word as "expensive mu'umu'u."

holomū: a post–World War II cross between a *holokū* and a mu'umu'u, less fitted than the former but less voluminous than the latter, and having no train.

honi: to kiss; a kiss. A phrase that some tourists may find useful, quoted from a popular hula, is *Honi Ka'ua Wikiwiki:* Kiss me quick!

honu: turtle.

ho'omalimali: flattery, a deceptive "line," bunk, baloney, hooey.

huhū: angry.

hui: a group, club, or assembly. A church may refer to its congregation as a *hui* and a social club may be called a *hui.*

hukilau: a seine; a communal fishing party in which everyone helps to drive the fish into a huge net, pull it in, and divide the catch.

hula: the dance of Hawai'i.

iki: little.

ipo: sweetheart.

ka: the. This is the definite article for most singular words; for plural nouns, the definite article is usually *nā.* Since there is no *S* in Hawaiian, the article may be your only clue that a noun is plural.

kahuna: a priest, doctor, or other trained person of old Hawai'i, endowed with special professional skills that often included prophecy or other supernatural powers; the plural form is kāhuna.

kai: the sea, saltwater.

kalo: the taro plant from whose root *poi* (paste) is made.

kamā'aina: literally, a child of the soil; it refers to people who were born in the Islands or have lived there for a long time.

kanaka: originally a man or humanity, it is now used to denote a male Hawaiian or part-Hawaiian, but is occasionally taken as a slur when used by non-Hawaiians. *Kanaka maoli,* originally a full-blooded Hawaiian person, is used by some Native Hawaiian rights activists to embrace part-Hawaiians as well.

kāne: a man, a husband. If you see this word on a door, it's the men's room. If you see *kane* on a door, it's probably a misspelling; that is the Hawaiian name for the skin fungus tinea.

kapa: also called by its Tahitian name, *tapa,* a cloth made of beaten bark and usually dyed and stamped with a repeat design.

kapakahi: crooked, cockeyed, uneven. You've got your hat on *kapakahi.*

kapu: keep out, prohibited. This is the Hawaiian version of the more widely known Tongan word *tabu* (taboo).

kapuna: grandparent; elder.

kēia lā: today.

keiki: a child; *keikikāne* is a boy, *keiki-wahine* a girl.

kona: the leeward side of the Islands, the direction (south) from which the *kona* wind and *kona* rain come.

kula: upland.

kuleana: a homestead or small plot of ground on which a family has been installed for some generations without necessarily owning it. By extension, *kuleana* is used to denote any area or department in which one has a special interest or prerogative. You'll hear it used this way: If you want to hire a surfboard, see Moki; that's his *kuleana.*

lā: sun.

lamalama: to fish with a torch.

lānai: a porch, a balcony, an outdoor living room. Almost every house in Hawai'i has one. Don't confuse this two-syllable word with the three-syllable name of the island, Lāna'i.

lani: heaven, the sky.

lau hala: the leaf of the *hala,* or pandanus tree, widely used in handicrafts.

lei: a garland of flowers.

limu: sun.

lolo: stupid.

luna: a plantation overseer or foreman.

mahalo: thank you.

makai: toward the ocean.

malihini: a newcomer to the Islands.

mana: the spiritual power that the Hawaiians believe inhabit all things and creatures.

manō: shark.

manuwahi: free, gratis.

mauka: toward the mountains.

mauna: mountain.

mele: a Hawaiian song or chant, often of epic proportions.

Mele Kalikimaka: Merry Christmas (a transliteration from the English phrase).

Menehune: a Hawaiian pixie. The *Menehune* were a legendary race of little people who accomplished prodigious work, such as building fishponds and temples in the course of a single night.

moana: the ocean.

mu'umu'u: the voluminous dress in which the missionaries enveloped Hawaiian women. Now made in bright printed cottons and silks, it is an indispensable garment. Culturally sensitive locals have embraced the Hawaiian spelling but often shorten the spoken word to "mu'u." Most English dictionaries include the spelling "muumuu."

nani: beautiful.

nui: big.

ohana: family.

'ono: delicious.

pāhoehoe: smooth, unbroken, satiny lava.

Pākē: Chinese. This *Pākē* carver makes beautiful things.

palapala: document, printed matter.

pali: a cliff, precipice.

pānini: prickly pear cactus.

paniolo: a Hawaiian cowboy, a rough transliteration of *español,* the language of the Islands' earliest cowboys.

pau: finished, done.

pilikia: trouble. The Hawaiian word is much more widely used here than its English equivalent.

puka: a hole.

pupule: crazy, like the celebrated Princess Pupule. This word has replaced its English equivalent in local usage.

pu'u: volcanic cinder cone.

waha: mouth.

wahine: a female, a woman, a wife, and a sign on the ladies' room door; the plural form is *wāhine.*

wai: freshwater, as opposed to saltwater, which is *kai.*

wailele: waterfall.

wikiwiki: to hurry, hurry up (since this is a reduplication of *wiki,* quick, neither W is pronounced as a V).

TRAVEL SMART
BIG ISLAND

GETTING HERE AND AROUND

Unless you have a travel agent in the family, you're probably among millions who book arrangements online. But it pays to know the options, especially for complicated destinations like Hawaii. Online Travel Agencies (OTAs) and discounters (like Priceline, Expedia, and Pleasant Holidays) have websites for booking airline, hotel, and car reservations without directly contacting the company itself. Aggregators (like Kayak and Hipmunk) compare travel offerings so you don't have to. These businesses offer good prices from their relationships with wholesalers, who make cheap, bulk reservations for resale. Yet another option is to consult a Hawaii-based inbound travel company. Because the travel industry has changed so much over the years, these companies can give you the best of both worlds—the personal service of an old-fashioned travel agent and connections to wholesalers as well as the local travel industry. Sometimes they offer deals that beat what you can find yourself.

Hawaii-Aloha Travel ⊠ *6800 Kalanianaole Hwy., Honolulu* ☎ *800/843–8771* ⊕ *www. hawaii-aloha.com.*

▌ AIR TRAVEL

Flying time to the Big Island is about 10 hours from New York, 8 hours from Chicago, 5 hours from Los Angeles, and 15 hours from London, not including layovers. Some of the major airline carriers serving Hawaii fly direct to the Big Island, allowing you to bypass connecting flights out of Honolulu and Maui. If you're a more spontaneous traveler, island-hopping flights depart daily every 20 to 30 minutes or so.

Although the Big Island's airports are smaller and more casual than Honolulu International, during peak times they can also get quite busy. Allow extra travel time getting to all airports during morning and afternoon rush-hour traffic periods. Plan to arrive at the airport 45 to 60 minutes before departure for interisland flights.

Plants and plant products are highly restricted by the Department of Agriculture, both upon entering and leaving Hawaii. When you leave the Islands, both checked and carry-on bags will be screened and tagged at the airport's agricultural inspection stations. Pineapples and coconuts with the packer's agricultural inspection stamp pass freely; papayas must be treated, inspected, and stamped. All other fruits are banned for export to the U.S. mainland. Flowers pass except for gardenia, rose leaves, jade vine, and mauna loa. Also banned are insects, snails, soil, cotton, cacti, sugarcane, and all berry plants.

You'll have to leave dogs and other pets at home. A 120-day quarantine is imposed to prevent the introduction of rabies, which is nonexistent in Hawaii. If specific pre- and post-arrival requirements are met, animals may qualify for a 30-day or 5-day-or-less quarantine.

Airlines and Airports Airline and Airport Links.com ⊕ *www.airlineandairportlinks.com.*

Airline Security Issues Transportation Security Administration. Transportation Security Administration can be consulted for up-to-the-minute changes to airport and traveling security. ⊕ *www.tsa.gov.*

Air Travel Resources in HawaiiState of Hawaii Airports Division Offices ☎ *808/836–6413* ⊕ *www.hawaii.gov/hnl.*

AIRPORTS

Honolulu International Airport (HNL) is the main gateway for most domestic and international flights into Hawaii. From Honolulu, interisland flights to the Big Island depart regularly from early morning through mid-evening. From Honolulu, the travel time is about 35 minutes. From Maui, it's about 20 minutes. Many carriers now offer nonstop service directly from the mainland to the Kona International Airport at Keahole (KOA) and Hilo International Airport (ITO). The two Big Island airports are "jetway free," meaning you can enjoy those balmy trade winds the moment you step off the plane, a welcome and rather quaint way to arrive in the Islands.

HONOLULU/OAHU AIRPORT

Hawaii's major airport is Honolulu International, on Oahu, 20 minutes (9 miles) west of Waikiki. To travel to the Big Island from Honolulu, you will depart from either the interisland terminal or the commuter-airline terminal (also called the "old interisland terminal" by locals), located in two separate structures adjacent to the main overseas terminal building. A free shuttle bus, the Wiki Wiki Shuttle, operates between terminals.

Information Honolulu International Airport (HNL) ⊠ *300 Rodgers Blvd., Honolulu* ☎ *808/836–6413* ⊕ *www.honoluluairport.com.*

BIG ISLAND AIRPORTS

Those flying to the Big Island regularly land at one of two fields. Kona International Airport at Keahole, on the west side, serves Kailua-Kona, Keauhou, the Kohala Coast, and points south. There are Visitor Information Program (VIP) booths located at all baggage-claim areas to assist travelers. Additionally, the airport is home to newsstands and lei stands, Maxwell's Landing restaurant, and a small gift shop.

Hilo International Airport is more appropriate for those planning visits based on the east side of the island. Here, you'll find VIP booths across from the Centerplate Coffee Shop near the departure lobby and in the arrival areas at each end of the terminal. In addition to the coffee shop, services include a Bank of Hawaii ATM, a gift shop, newsstands and lei stands. Waimea-Kohala Airport, called Kamuela Airport by residents, is used primarily for private flights between islands, but has recently welcomed one commercial carrier.

Information Hilo International Airport (ITO) ⊠ *2450 Kekuanaoa St., Suite 215, Hilo* ☎ *808/961–9300* ⊕ *www.hawaii.gov/ito.* **Kona International Airport at Keahole (KOA)** ⊠ *73-200 Kupipi St., Kailua-Kona* ☎ *808/329–3423* ⊕ *www.hawaii.gov/koa.* **Waimea-Kohala Airport (MUE)** ⊠ *Waimea-Kohala Airport Rd., Waimea* ☎ *808/887–8126* ⊕ *www.hawaii.gov/mue.*

GROUND TRANSPORTATION

Check with your hotel to see if it runs an airport shuttle. If you're not renting a car, you can choose from among 17 taxi companies serving the Hilo Airport. The approximate taxi rate is $3 for the initial fare, plus 30¢ every 1/8 mile, with surcharges for waiting time (30¢ per minute) and baggage ($1 per bag). Cab fares to locations around the island are estimated as follows: Banyan Drive hotels $11, Hilo Town $12, Hilo Pier $13, Volcano $75, Keaau $22, Pahoa $50, Honokaa $105, Kamuela/Waimea $148, Waikoloa $188, and Kailua Town $240.

At the Kona International Airport, taxis are available. SpeediShuttle also offers transportation between the airport and hotels, resorts, and condominium complexes from Waimea to Keauhou.

Contacts SpeediShuttle ⊠ *Kona International Airport, Kailua-Kona* ☎ *877/242–5777* ⊕ *www.speedishuttle.com.*

FLIGHTS

Serving Kona are Air Canada, Alaska Air, American, Delta, go!, Mokulele, Hawaiian, Island Air, United, US Airways, and Westjet. Go!, Hawaiian, Mokulele, and United fly into Hilo. Airlines schedule flights seasonally, meaning the number of daily flights varies according to demand.

Airline Contacts Air Canada ☎ *888/247–2262* ⊕ *www.aircanada.com.* **Alaska Airlines** ☎ *800/252–7522* ⊕ *www.alaskaair.com.* **American Airlines** ☎ *800/433–7300* ⊕ *www.aa.com.*

Delta Airlines ☎ *800/221–1212 for U.S. reservations* ⊕ *www.delta.com.* **United Airlines** ☎ *800/864–8331 for U.S. reservations,*

800/538–2929 for international reservations ⊕ www.united.com. **US Airways** ☎ 800/428–4322 ⊕ www.usairways.com. **Westjet** ☎ 888/937–8538 ⊕ www.westjet.com.

INTERISLAND FLIGHTS

Should you wish to visit neighboring islands, go!, Hawaiian, Island Air, and Mokulele offer regular service. Prices for interisland flights have increased quite a bit in recent years, while flight schedule availability has been reduced. Mokulele now serves Waimea. Planning ahead is your best bet.

Interisland Carriers Mokulele Airlines ☎ 888/435–9462 ⊕ www.mokuleleairlines.com. **Hawaiian Airlines** ☎ 800/367–5320 ⊕ www.hawaiianair.com. **Island Air** ☎ 800/388–1105 ⊕ www.islandair.com.**go! Airlines** ☎ 888/326–7070 ⊕ www.iflygo.com.

CHARTER FLIGHTS

Iolani Air Taxi, based on the Big Island, offers on-demand service between islands. If you're interested in getting off the beaten track, Iolani can fly you to remote airstrips.

Charter Companies Iolani Air Taxi ☎ 808/329–0018, 800/538–7590 ⊕ www.iolaniair.com.

▌ BUS TRAVEL

Travelers can take advantage of the affordable Hawaii County Mass Transit Agency's Hele-On Bus, which travels several routes throughout the island. Mostly serving local commuters, the Hele-On Bus costs $2 per person (students and senior citizens pay $1). Just wait at a scheduled stop and flag down the bus. A one-way journey between Hilo and Kona takes about four hours. There's regular service in and around downtown Hilo, Kailua-Kona, Waimea, North and South Kohala, Honokaa, and Pahoa.

Visitors staying in Hilo can take advantage of the Transit Agency's Shared Ride Taxi program, which provides door-to-door transportation in the area. A one-way fare is $2, and a book of 15 coupons

can be purchased for $30. Visitors to Kona can also take advantage of free shuttles operated by local shopping centers.

Information Hele-On Bus ☎ 808/961–8744 ⊕ www.heleonbus.org.

▌ CAR TRAVEL

Visitors who rent a car on the Big Island quickly learn it's a big, big island. Fortunately, when you circle the island by car, you are treated to miles and miles of wondrous vistas of every possible description. In addition to using compass directions, Hawaii residents often refer to places as being either *mauka* (toward the mountains) or *makai* (toward the ocean).

It's difficult to get lost along the main roads of the Big Island. Although their names may challenge the visitor's tongue, most roads are well marked; in rural areas look for mile marker numbers. Free publications containing basic road maps are available at most retailers, but if you are doing a lot of driving, invest about $4 in the standard Big Island map.

Turning right on a red light is legal, except where noted. Hawaii has a strict seat-belt law that applies to both drivers and passengers. The fine for not wearing a seat belt is $92. Many police officers drive their own cars while on duty, strapping the warning lights to the roof. Because of the color, locals call them "blue lights."

GASOLINE

You can count on having to pay more at the pump for gasoline on the Big Island than almost anywhere on the U.S. mainland. Prices tend to be higher in Kailua-Kona and cheaper in Hilo. Gas stations in rural areas can be few and far between, and it's not unusual for them to close early. If you notice that your tank is getting low, don't take any chances.

PARKING

Parking can be a challenge in historic Kailua Village. A few municipal lots near Alii Drive offer convenient parking on an honor system. (You'll be ticketed if you

Car Rental Resources

Automobile Associations		
American Automobile Association	☎ 315/797–5000	⊕ www.aaa.com
Local Agencies		
AA Aloha Cars-R-Us	☎ 800/655–7989	⊕ www.hawaiicarrental.com
Happy Campers Hawaii	☎ 888/550–3918	⊕ www.happycampershawaii.com
Harper Car and Truck Rental (Big Island)	☎ 800/852–9993	⊕ www.harpershawaii.com
Hawaiian Discount Car Rentals	☎ 800/882–9007	⊕ www.hawaiidrive-o.com
Kona Harley-Davidson	☎ 866/326–9887	⊕ www.hawaiiharleyrental.com
Major Agencies		
Alamo	☎ 800/479–0000	⊕ www.alamo.com
Avis	☎ 800/831–2847	⊕ www.avis.com
Budget	☎ 800/221–8822	⊕ www.budget.com
Dollar	☎ 877/492–9379	⊕ www.dollar.com
Enterprise	☎ 808/334–1810	⊕ www.enterprise.com
Hertz	☎ 800/654–3131	⊕ www.hertz.com
National Car Rental	☎ 800/227–7368	⊕ www.nationalcar.com
Thrifty	☎ 800/847–4389	⊕ www.thrifty.com

don't pay.) There is one free county lot downtown. In Hilo, you'll find plenty of free parking.

ROAD CONDITIONS

Roads on the Big Island are generally well maintained and can be easily negotiated. Most of the roads are two-lane highways with limited shoulders—and yes, even in paradise, there is traffic, especially during the morning and afternoon rush hours and before and after school. Jaywalking and hitchhiking are very common, so pay careful attention to the roads, especially while driving in rural areas. Also use caution during heavy downpours, especially if you see signs warning of flash floods and falling rocks.

RENTALS

Should you plan to sightsee around the Big Island, it is best to rent a car. With more than 260 miles of coastline—and attractions as varied as Hawaii Volcanoes National Park, Akaka Falls State Park, Puuhonua o Honaunau National Historic Park, and Puukohola Heiau National Historic Site—ideally you should split up your stay between the east and west coasts of the island. Even if all you want to do is relax at your resort, you may want to hop in the car to check out one of the island's popular restaurants.

While on the Big Island, you can rent anything from an econobox to a sports car to a motor home. Rates are usually better if you reserve though a rental agency's website. It's wise to make reservations far in advance and make sure that a confirmed reservation (usually free) guarantees you a car, especially if visiting during peak seasons or for major conventions or sporting events. It's not uncommon to find several car categories sold out during major events on the island, such as the Merrie Monarch Festival in Hilo in April or the Ironman World Championship triathlon in Kailua-Kona in October. ∎TIP➡ If **you're planning on driving to the 13,796-foot summit of Mauna Kea for stargazing, you'll need a four-wheel-drive vehicle.** Harper Car and Truck Rental, with offices in Hilo and Kona, is the only company that allows its vehicles to be driven to the summit.

For some, renting an RV or motor home might be an appealing way to see the island. Harper has motor homes available and Hilo-based Happy Campers Hawaii rents out classic Volkswagen Westfalia camping vans. And if exploring the island on two wheels is more your speed, Kona Harley-Davidson rents motorcycles.

Rates begin at about $25 to $35 a day for an economy car with air-conditioning, automatic transmission, and unlimited mileage. This does not include the airport concession fee, general excise tax, rental vehicle surcharge, or vehicle license fee. When you reserve a car, ask about cancellation penalties and drop-off charges should you plan to pick up the car in one location and return it to another. Many rental companies in Hawaii offer coupons for discounts at various attractions.

In Hawaii, you must be 21 years of age to rent a car, and you must have a valid driver's license and a major credit card. Those under 25 pay a daily surcharge of $15 to $25. Request car seats and extras such as GPS when you book. Hawaii's Child Restraint Law requires that all children three years and younger be in an approved child safety seat in the backseat of a vehicle. Children ages four to seven must be seated in a rear booster seat or child restraint such as a lap and shoulder belt. Car seats and boosters range from $5 to $8 per day.

In Hawaii, a valid mainland driver's license is valid for a rental for up to 90 days.

Because the road circling the Big Island can be two-lane, narrow, and windy in places, allow plenty of time to return your vehicle so that you can make your flight. Traffic can be heavy during morning and afternoon rush hours, especially in the Kona area. Roadwork is ongoing and often unscheduled. Give yourself about 3½ hours before departure time to return your vehicle.

CAR-RENTAL INSURANCE

Everyone who rents a car wonders whether the insurance that the rental companies offer is worth the expense. No one—including us—has a simple answer. It all depends on how much regular insurance you have, how comfortable you are with risk, and whether or not money is an issue.

If you own a car and carry comprehensive car insurance for both collision and liability, your personal auto insurance probably covers a rental, but call your auto insurance company to confirm. If you don't have auto insurance, then you will need to buy the collision- or loss-damage waiver (CDW or LDW) from the rental company. The CDW allows you to walk away from most incidents, so it might be worth the peace of mind. Some credit cards offer CDW coverage, but it's usually supplemental to your own insurance and rarely covers SUVs, minivans, and luxury models. If your coverage is secondary, you may still be liable for loss-of-use costs from the car-rental company (again, read the fine print). But no credit-card insurance is valid unless you use that card for *all* transactions, from reserving to paying the final bill.

∎TIP➡ **Diners Club offers primary CDW coverage on all rentals reserved and paid for with the card. This means that Diners Club's company—not your own car insurance—pays in case of an accident. It doesn't mean that your car insurance** company won't raise your rates once it discovers you had an accident.

You may also be offered supplemental liability coverage; the car-rental company is required to carry a minimal level of liability coverage insuring all renters, but it's rarely enough to cover claims in a really serious accident if you're at fault. Your own auto-insurance policy will protect you if you own a car; if you don't, you have to decide whether you are willing to take the risk.

U.S. rental companies sell CDWs and LDWs for about $15 to $25 a day; supplemental liability is usually more than $10 a day. The car-rental company may offer you all sorts of other policies, but they're rarely worth the cost. Personal accident insurance, which is basic hospitalization coverage, is an especially egregious rip-off if you already have health insurance.

■TIP→ You can decline the insurance from the rental company and purchase it through a third-party provider such as Travel Guard (⊕ www.travelguard. com)—$9 per day for $35,000 of coverage. That's sometimes just under half the price of the CDW offered by some car rental companies.

ESSENTIALS

▮ COMMUNICATIONS

INTERNET

If you've brought your laptop or tablet with you to the Big Island, you should have no problem checking email or connecting to the Internet. Most of the major hotels and resorts offer high-speed access in rooms or lobbies. You should check with your hotel in advance to confirm that access is wireless; if not, ask whether in-room cables are provided. In some cases, there will be an hourly or daily charge posted to your room. If you're staying at a small inn or bed-and-breakfast without Internet access, ask the proprietor for the nearest café or shopping center with wireless access.

Contacts Cybercafes. Cybercafes lists over 4,000 Internet cafés worldwide. ⊕ *www. cybercafes.com.*

▮ HEALTH

Hawaii is known as the Health State. The life expectancy here is 79 years, the longest in the nation. Balmy weather makes it easy to remain active year-round, and the low-stress aloha attitude certainly contributes to general well-being. When visiting the Islands, however, there are a few health issues to keep in mind.

The Hawaii State Department of Health recommends that you drink 16 ounces of water per hour to avoid dehydration when hiking or spending time in the sun. Use zinc-based sunblock, wear UV-reflective sunglasses, and protect your head with a visor or hat for shade. If you're not acclimated to warm, humid weather you should allow plenty of time for rest stops and refreshments. When visiting freshwater streams, be aware of the tropical disease leptospirosis, which is spread by animal urine and carried into streams and mud. Symptoms include fever, headache, nausea, and red eyes. If left untreated, it

WORD OF MOUTH

Did the resort look as good in real life as it did in the photos? Did you sleep like a baby, or were the walls paper-thin? Did you get your money's worth? Rate hotels and write your own reviews in Travel Ratings or start a discussion about your favorite places in the Forums on ⊕ *www. fodors.com.* Your comments might even appear in our books. Yes, you, too, can be a correspondent!

can cause liver and kidney failure, respiratory failure, internal bleeding, and even death. To avoid this, don't swim or wade in freshwater streams or ponds if you have open sores and don't drink from any freshwater streams or ponds.

On the Big Island, you may experience the effects of "vog," an airborne stew of gases released from volcanic vents at Kilauea. Depending on your location and the level of volcanic activity, you may notice a strong sulfur smell and hazy horizons. These gases can exacerbate respiratory and other health conditions, especially asthma or emphysema. If susceptible, avoid visiting the volcano, stay indoors, and get emergency assistance if needed.

The Islands have their share of bugs and insects that enjoy the tropical climate as much as visitors do. Most are harmless but annoying. When planning to spend time outdoors in hiking areas, wear long-sleeve clothing and pants and use mosquito repellent containing DEET. In very damp or rocky places, you may encounter the dreaded local centipede. Blue or brown in color, the centipedes can grow as long as eight inches but are not overly aggressive. If surprised, they might sting, which might feel like a bee or wasp sting. When camping, shake out your sleeping bag before climbing in, and check your shoes in the morning, as centipedes like warm, moist places. If planning on hiking or traveling in remote areas, always carry a first-aid kit and appropriate medications for sting reactions.

▌HOURS OF OPERATION

Even people in paradise have to work. Generally local business hours are weekdays 8–5. Banks are usually open Monday through Thursday 8:30–4 and until 6 on Friday. Some banks offer Saturday-morning hours.

Only a handful of service stations are open around the clock. Many operate from around 7 am until 10 pm. U.S. post offices are open weekdays 8:30 am–4:30 pm and Saturday 8:30–noon.

Most museums generally open their doors between 9 am and 10 am and stay open until 5 pm Tuesday through Saturday. Many museums operate with afternoon hours only on Sunday and close on Monday. Visitor-attraction hours vary throughout the state, but most sights are open daily with the exception of major holidays such as Christmas and New Year's Day.

Stores in resort areas sometimes open as early as 8 am, with shopping-center opening hours varying from 9:30 to 10 am on weekdays and Saturday, a bit later on Sunday. Bigger malls stay open until 9 pm weekdays and Saturday and close at 5 pm on Sunday. Boutiques in resort areas may stay open as late as 11 pm.

▌MONEY

Automatic teller machines for easy access to cash are everywhere on the Islands. ATMs can be found in shopping centers, small convenience and grocery stores, and hotels and resorts as well as outside most bank branches. For a directory of locations, call ☎ *800/424–7787* for the MasterCard/Cirrus/Maestro network or ☎ *800/843–7587* for the Visa/Plus network.

CREDIT CARDS

It's a good idea to inform your credit-card company before you travel, especially if you're going abroad and don't travel internationally very often. Otherwise, the credit-card company might put a hold on your card owing to unusual activity—not a good thing halfway through your trip. Record all your credit-card numbers—as well as the phone numbers to call if your cards are lost or stolen—in a safe place, so you're prepared should something go wrong. Both MasterCard and Visa have general numbers you can call (collect if you're abroad) if your card is lost, but you're better off calling the number of your issuing bank, since MasterCard and Visa usually just transfer you to your bank. Your bank's number is usually printed on your card.

Reporting Lost Cards American Express ☎ *800/528–4800 in the U.S., 336/393–1111 collect from abroad* ⊕ *www.americanexpress. com.* **Diners Club** ☎ *800/234–6377 in the U.S., 303/799–1504 collect from abroad* ⊕ *www.dinersclub.com.* **Discover** ☎ *800/347–2683 in the U.S., 801/902–3100 collect from abroad* ⊕ *www.discovercard.com.* **MasterCard** ☎ *800/622–7747 in the U.S., 636/722–7111 collect from abroad* ⊕ *www.mastercard.com.* **Visa** ☎ *800/847–2911 in the U.S., 410/581–9994 collect from abroad* ⊕ *www.visa.com.*

TRAVELER'S CHECKS

Some consider this the currency of the caveman, and it's true that fewer establishments accept traveler's checks these days. Nevertheless, they're a cheap and secure way to carry extra money, particularly on trips to urban areas. Both Citibank (under the Visa brand) and American Express issue traveler's checks in the United States, but Amex is better known and more widely accepted; you can also avoid hefty surcharges by cashing Amex checks at Amex offices. Whatever you do, keep track of all the serial numbers in case the checks are lost or stolen.

LOCAL DO'S AND TABOOS

GREETINGS

Hawaii is a very friendly place and this is reflected in the day-to-day encounters between friends, family, and even business associates. Women will often hug and kiss one another on the cheek and men will shake hands and sometimes combine that with a friendly hug. Children often refer to elders as "aunty" or "uncle," even if they aren't related, which reflects the strong sense of family.

When you disembark from a long flight, perhaps a bit groggy and stiff, nothing quite compares with a Hawaiian lei greeting. This charming custom ranks as one of the fastest ways to make the transition from the worries of home to the joys of being on holiday.

If you've booked a vacation with a wholesaler or tour company, a lei greeting might be included in your package, so check before you leave. If not, it's easy to arrange a lei greeting for yourself or for your companions before you arrive. Contact Aloha Reservations Lei Greetings if you're arriving at Kona International Airport. A plumeria or dendrobium orchid lei are considered standard and cost about $22 per person. Hilo International Airport does not allow companies to provide lei greeting services, but there are lei vendors at the airport should you wish to purchase one upon arrival.

INFORMATION

Aloha Reservations Lei Greetings ⊕ *www. alohaleigreetings.com.*

LANGUAGE

Hawaii was admitted to the Union in 1959, so residents can be sensitive when visitors state their own hometowns are "back in the States." When in Hawaii, refer to the contiguous 48 states as "the mainland" and not as the United States. When you do, you won't appear to be such a *malahini* (newcomer).

English is the primary language on the Islands. Making the effort to learn some Hawaiian words can be rewarding, however. Despite the length of many Hawaiian words, the Hawaiian alphabet is actually one of the world's shortest, with only 12 letters: the five vowels, *a, e, i, o, u,* and seven consonants, *h, k, l, m, n, p, w.* Hawaiian words you're most likely to encounter during your visit to the Islands are *aloha, mahalo* (thank you), *keiki* (child), *haole* (Caucasian or foreigner), *mauka* (toward the mountains), *makai* (toward the ocean), and *pau* (finished, all done).

Hawaiian history includes waves of immigrants, each bringing their own languages. To communicate with each other, they developed a sort of slang known as "pidgin." If you listen closely, you'll know what is being said by the inflections and by the extensive use of body language. For example, when you know what you want to say but don't know how to say it, just say "you know, da kine." For an informative and sometimes hilarious view of things Hawaiian, check out Jerry Hopkins's series of books titled *Pidgin to the Max* and *Fax to the Max,* available on most local bookshelves in the Hawaiiana sections.

▍PACKING

Hawaii is casual: sandals, bathing suits, and comfortable, informal clothing are the norm. In summer, synthetic slacks and shirts, although easy to care for, can be uncomfortably warm.

One of the most important things to tuck into your suitcase is sunscreen. Hats and sunglasses offer important sun protection, too. Both are easy to find in island shops, but if you already have a favorite packable hat or sun visor, bring it with you. All major hotels in Hawaii provide beach towels.

As for clothing in the Hawaiian Islands, there's a saying that when a man wears a suit during the day, he's either going for a loan or he's a lawyer trying a case. Only a few upscale restaurants require a jacket for dinner. The *aloha* shirt is accepted dress in Hawaii for business and most social occasions. Shorts are acceptable daytime attire, along with a T-shirt or polo shirt. There's no need to buy expensive sandals on the mainland— here you can get flip-flops (called "slippers" by locals) for under $5. Golfers should remember that many courses have dress codes requiring a collared shirt; call courses you're interested in for details. If you're not prepared, you can pick up appropriate clothing at resort pro shops. If you're visiting in winter, bring a sweater or light- to medium-weight jacket. A polar fleece pullover is ideal, and makes a great impromptu pillow.

If your vacation plans include Hilo, you'll want to pack a folding umbrella and a light poncho. And if you'll be exploring Hawaii Volcanoes National Park, make sure you pack appropriately as weather ranges from hot and dry along the shore to chilly, foggy, and rainy at the summit. Sturdy boots are recommended if you'll be hiking or camping in the park.

▍SAFETY

Hawaii is generally a safe tourist destination, but it's still wise to stick to the same commonsense safety precautions you would normally follow in your own hometown. Hotel and visitor-center staff can provide information should you decide to head out on your own to more remote areas. Because their models and colors are obvious, rental cars are magnets for break-ins, so don't leave any valuables in them, not even in a locked trunk. Avoid poorly lighted areas, beach parks, and isolated areas after dark as a precaution. When hiking, stay on marked trails, no matter how alluring the temptation might be to stray. Weather conditions can cause landscapes to become muddy, slippery, and tenuous, so staying on marked trails lessens the possibility of a fall or getting lost. This is especially true on the wetter, windward side.

Ocean safety is of the utmost importance when visiting an island destination. Don't swim alone, and follow the international signage posted at beaches, which alerts swimmers to strong currents, man-of-war or box jellyfish, sharp coral, high surf, sharks, and dangerous shore breaks. At coastal lookouts along cliff tops, heed the signs indicating that waves can climb over the ledges. Check with lifeguards at each beach for current conditions, and if the red flags are up, indicating swimming and surfing are not allowed, don't go in. Waters that look calm on the surface can harbor strong currents and undertows, and not a few people who were "just wading" have been dragged out to sea. When in doubt, don't go out!

Women traveling alone are generally safe on the Islands, but always follow the same safety precautions you would use in any major destination. When booking hotels, request rooms closest to the elevator, and always keep your hotel-room door and balcony doors locked. Stay away from isolated areas after dark. If you stay out late at a nightclub or bar, use caution when exiting and returning to your car or lodging; most establishments will be glad to give you an escort to your car.

▌ TAXES

Businesses on Hawaii Island collect a 4.167% general excise tax on all purchases, including food and services. A hotel room tax of 9.25%, combined with the excise tax, equals a 13.417% rate added to your room bill. Even vacation rentals and B&Bs are required to collect this tax. A $3-per-day road tax is also assessed on each rental vehicle.

▌ TIME

Hawaii is on Hawaiian Standard Time, 5 hours behind New York, 2 hours behind Los Angeles, and 10 hours behind London.

When the U.S. mainland switches to daylight saving time, Hawaii does not, so add an extra hour of time difference between the Islands and U.S. mainland destinations.

▌ TIPPING

Hawaii is a major vacation destination and many of the people who work at the hotels and resorts rely on tips to supplement their wages, so tipping is expected. Tip cabdrivers 15% of the fare. Standard tips at restaurants and spas run from 15% to 20% of the bill, depending on the quality of service; bartenders expect about $1 per drink. Bellhops at hotels usually receive $1 per bag, more if you have bulky items like bicycles or surfboards. Tip the hotel maid $1 per night, paid daily. Tip doormen $1 to $5 for assistance with taxis, bags, or golf clubs; tips for concierges vary depending on the service.

▌ TOURS

GENERAL-INTEREST TOURS

Globus has three Hawaii itineraries that include the Big Island, one of which is an escorted cruise on Norwegian Cruise Lines' *Pride of America* that includes one day each in Kona and Hilo. Tauck Travel and Trafalgar offer several land-based Hawaii itineraries that include two to three nights on the Big Island, depending on the tour. Both companies offer similar itineraries. In all cases, visits to Hawaii Volcanoes National Park are included.

Recommended Companies Globus ☎ 866/755–8581 ⊕ www.globusjourneys.com. **Tauck Travel** ☎ 800/788–7885 ⊕ www.tauck. com. **Trafalgar** ☎ 866/544–4434 ⊕ www. trafalgar.com.

SPECIAL-INTEREST TOURS

ADVENTURE STUDY

A tour of Kilauea Volcano—the most active volcano on earth— is even better with an actual geologist. With tours tailored to small groups, Volcano Discovery Tours offers detailed information about such geologic features as lava tubes, vents, and fumaroles. Big Island Volcano Tours offers an Evening Eco Tour that includes stops at the Kilauea Iki overlook, black-sand beaches, and the Jagger Museum. Seeing lava flows cannot always be guaranteed.

Contacts Big Island Volcano Tours ☎ 808/690–9054 ⊕ www. bigislandvolcanotours.com. **Volcano Discovery Tours** ⊕ www.volcanodiscovery.com.

ART

Whether you want to learn about Hawaiian arts, history, and culture; astronomy, ecology, or botany; or the geology of the Hawaiian volcanoes, Volcano Art Center can design a program for your group that utilizes the talents of local artists, scientists, performers, historians, park rangers, storytellers, and guides. The staff arranges transportation, accommodations, meals, classes, and lectures.

Volcano Art Center ☎ *866/967-7565* ⊕ *www. volcanoartcenter.org.*

BIKING

If you're a bicycling enthusiast, you've got exciting options on the Big Island. Bicycle Adventures has a seven-day Hawaii tour that costs $3,395 per person and includes biking, hiking, snorkeling, sailing, and whale-watching. A six-day budget tour is priced at about $2,695 per person. Both include accommodations, meals, and park admissions.

WomanTours has a seven-night bike tour that circumnavigates the entire island. Included in the $3,390 per person price are accommodations, some meals, and guides.

■ **TIP→** Most airlines accommodate bikes as luggage, provided they're dismantled and boxed.

Contacts Bicycle Adventures ☎ *800/443–6060* ⊕ *www.bicycleadventures.com.* **Woman-Tours** ☎ *800/247-1444* ⊕ *www.womantours. com.*

BIRD-WATCHING

More than 150 species of birds live in the Hawaiian Islands. Field Guides has a three-island, 11-day guided bird-watching trip that focuses on endemic land birds and specialty seabirds. While on the Big Island, birders try to spot forest birds including the Hawaiian hawk, Hawaiian thrush, Hawaiian goose, and the Hawaii creeper. Participants might also get a glimpse of the rare *palila*, the only finch-like Hawaiian honeycreeper that remains on the main islands. The trip costs $4,575 per person and includes accommodations, meals, ground transportation, interisland flights, and guided excursions.

Victor Emanuel Nature Tours has multi-day trips that include the Big Island. The guide for both tours is Bob Sundstrom, who has been leading birding tours in Hawaii and other destinations since 1989. Birders see such indigenous birds as the *amakihi, apapane, elepaio,* and the comical scarlet *iiwi,* as well as endemic birds such as the *omao, palila,* and *akepa* honeycreepers.

Contacts Field Guides ☎ *800/728-4953* ⊕ *www.fieldguides.com.* **Victor Emanuel Nature Tours** ☎ *800/328-8368* ⊕ *www. ventbird.com.*

CULTURE

Road Scholar, a nonprofit organization that leads all-inclusive learning adventures, offers several cultural and educational tours of Hawaii. A 14-night tour of the Big Island, presented by experts on local culture, includes lectures, excursions, and performances. Coordinated by Lyman House and Mission House, the tour includes excursions to Hawaii Volcanoes National Park, visits to Hilo, and walks around the quaint seaside village of Kailua-Kona. Prices start at $3,498.

Road Scholar ☎ *800/454-5766* ⊕ *www. roadscholar.org.*

ECO TOURS

Locally owned and operated, Hawaii Forest & Trail, in business since 1993, seeks to educate, inspire, and entertain visitors. The company showcases the island's amazing diversity with adventures to waterfalls, rain forests, and nature preserves. With access to thousands of acres of private land, the company offers truly off-the-beaten-path adventures. Trips include tours of coffee plantations, sunset views of volcanic eruptions, and explorations of the dazzling night sky. Expertise is a point of pride. Prices vary depending on activity and size of group.

Hawaiian Walkways, run by longtime hiker Hugh Montgomery, offers eco-friendly tours of the Waipio Valley, Kilauea Volcano, and other destinations. Personalized tours can be arranged for small groups. Sierra Club Outings offers tours that can include a service-project component, such as restoring critical bird habitat.

Contacts Hawaiian Walkways ☎ *800/457-7759* ⊕ *www.hawaiianwalkways.com.* **Hawaii**

Forest & Trail ☎ 800/464–1993 ⊕ www. hawaii-forest.com.

Sierra Club Outings ☎ 415/977–5522 ⊕ www.sierraclub.org/outings.

HIKING

Timberline Adventures has an eight-day tour combining Kauai and the Big Island. It includes visits to Hawaii Volcanoes National Park and the Kona Coast. The package costs $3,095 per person and includes accommodations, meals, ground transportation, and activities.

CONTACTS

Timberline Adventures ☎ 800/417–2453 ⊕ www.timbertours.com.

▮ VISITOR INFORMATION

Before you go, contact the Big Island Visitors Bureau to request a free official vacation planner with information on accommodations, transportation, sports and activities, dining, arts and entertainment, and culture. A virtual visit on the bureau website can be helpful, and it includes a calendar section that shows what local events coincide with your visit.

The Hawaii Island Chamber of Commerce has links to dozens of museums, attractions, bed-and-breakfasts, and parks on its website. The Kona-Kohala Chamber of Commerce lists local activities. The Volcano Art Center offers a host of activities at Kilauea, including classes and workshops; music, dance, and theater performances; art shows; and volcano runs.

Contacts Big Island Visitors Bureau ☎ 808/961–5797, 800/648–2441 ⊕ www. bigisland.org. **Hawaii Island Chamber of Commerce** ☎ 808/935–7178 ⊕ www.hicc. biz. **Kona-Kohala Chamber of Commerce** ☎ 808/329–1758 ⊕ www.kona-kohala.com. **Volcano Art Center** ☎ 866/967–7565, 808/967–7565 ⊕ www.volcanoartcenter.org.

INDEX

PHOTO CREDITS

Front cover: Frans Lanting/Corbis [Description: Lava overflowing caldera of Pu'u 'O'o, Hawaii Volcanoes National Park]. 1, Shane Myers Photography/Shutterstock. 2, Fremme/Shutterstock. 5, Polynesian Cultural Center. Chapter 1: Experience the Big Island: 8-9, Pacific Stock/SuperStock. 10 and 11 (all), Big Island Visitors Bureau. 13 (left), Photodisc.13 (right), WaterFrame/Alamy. 16 (top left), Photo Resource Hawaii/Alamy. 16 (bottom left), Corn-forth Images/Alamy. 16 (top center), Photo Resource Hawaii/Alamy. 16 (bottom center), Waterframe/Alamy. 16 (right), Douglas Peebles Photography/Alamy. 17 (left), Big Island Visitors Bureau. 17 (top center), Andre Seale/age fotostock. 17 (bottom center), Hemis/Alamy. 17 (top right), Photo Resource Hawaii/Alamy. 17 (bottom right), Stephen Frink Collection/Alamy. 19 (left), SuperStock/age fotostock. 19 (right), PhotoResource Hawaii/Alamy. 21, Katja Govorushchenko/iStockphoto. 23, iStockphoto. 25, Jay Spooner/iStockphoto. 26, Hilton Hawaii. 27 (left), Photo Resource Hawaii/Alamy. 27 (right), Stephanie Horrocks/iStockphoto. 29, iStockphoto. 31, Photo Resource Hawaii/Alamy. 33 (left), Douglas Peebles/age fotostock. 33 (right), Castle Resorts & Hotels. 37 (both), Hilton Hawaii. 38, Bryan Lowry/Alamy. Chapter 2: Exploring the Big Island: 39, Douglas Peebles/eStock Photo. 40, George Burba/Shutterstock. 41, Big Island Visitors Bureau. 51, Big Island Visitors Bureau. 53 and 56, Pacific Stock/SuperStock. 59, Greg Vaughn/Alamy. 60, Pacific Stock/SuperStock. 65, Pacific Stock/SuperStock. 66, Photo Resource Hawaii/Alamy. 73, Russ Bishop/Alamy. 74, Cornforth Images/Alamy. 80, SuperStock/age fotostock. 88, Big Island Visitors Bureau. 89, Russ Bishop/age fotostock. 91, Photo Resource Hawaii/Alamy. 92, Cornforth Images/Alamy. 93 (top), Pacific Stock/SuperStock. 93 (bottom), Linda Robshaw/Alamy. 94, Interfoto Pressebildagentur/Alamy. Chapter 3: Beaches: 99, Preferred Hotels & Resorts Worldwide. 100, Kushch Dmitry/Shutterstock. 103, Luis Castanedox/agefotostock. 107, Pacific Stock/SuperStock. 109, Cornforth Images/Alamy. 112, Douglas Peebles/eStock Photo. Chapter 4: Water Activities & Tours: 115, WaterFrame/Alamy. 116, Hawaii Tourism Authority (HTA) / Tor Johnson. 117, Russ Bishop/Alamy. 119, Blaine Harrington III/Alamy. 125, Ron Dahlquist/HVCB. 126, SuperStock/age fotostock. 128 (top), SPrada/iStockphoto. 128 (bottom), Gert Vrey/iStockphoto. 129, sweetlifephotos/iStockphoto. 133, Andre Seale/Alamy. 135, David Fleetham/Alamy. 138, Stephen Frink Collection/Alamy. Chapter 5: Golf, Hiking & Outdoor Activities: 139, HTJ. 140, Kushch Dmitry/Shutterstock.141, Douglas Peebles/eStock Photo. 147, Pacific Stock/SuperStock. 149, Pacific Stock/SuperStock. 151, Luca Tettoni/viestiphoto. com. 152, Kaua'I Visitors Bureau. 153 (bottom), Jack Jeffrey. 155, Photo Resource Hawaii/Alamy. Chapter 6: Shops & Spas: 159, Hilton Hawaii. 160, Fairmont Hotel & Resorts, 169 (top), Linda Ching/HVCB. 169 (bottom), Sri Maiava Rusden/HVCB. 170, Michael Soo/Alamy. 171 (top), leisofhawaii.com. 171 (2nd from top), kellyalexanderphotography. com. 171 (3rd, 4th,and 5th from top), leisofhawaii.com. 171 (bottom), kellyalexanderphotography. com. Chapter 7: Entertainment& Nightlife: 179, Hilton Hawaii. 180, Hawaii Tourism Authority (HTA)/ Tor Johnson. 186, Hawaii Visitors & Convention Bureau. 187, Thinkstock LLC. 189, Hawaii Visitors & Convention Bureau. Chapter 8: Where to Eat: 191, Four Seasons Hotels & Resorts, 192, Don Riddle Images/Four Seasons Hotels & Resorts. 213, Polynesian Cultural Center. 214 (top), Douglas Peebles Photography. 214 (top center), Douglas Peebles Photography/Alamy. 214 (center), Dana Edmunds/Polynesian Cultural Center. 214 (bottom center), Douglas Peebles Photography/Alamy. 214 (bottom), Purcell Team/Alamy. 215 (top, top center, and bottom center), HTJ/HVCB. 215 (bottom), Oahu Visitors Bureau. Chapter 9: Where to Stay: 223, Waianuhea. 224, DANA EDMUNDS/Fairmont Hotels & Resorts. Back cover (from left to right); lauraslens/Shutterstock; Four Seasons Hotels & Resorts; Castle Resorts & Hotels. Spine: aquatic creature/Shutterstock.

NOTES

NOTES

NOTES

ABOUT OUR WRITERS

Karen Anderson is a Kona resident who enjoys horseback riding in the hills of the Big Island. She is the managing editor of *At Home, Living with Style in West Hawaii* and has written for a variety of publications including *West Hawaii Today, Big Island Weekly, Hawaii* magazine and the Kona-Kohala Chamber of Commerce. She's also the best-selling author of *The Hawaii Home Book, Practical Tips for Tropical Living*, which received an award excellence from the Hawaii Book Publishers Association. Her monthly editor's column and chef/restaurant profiles are known throughout West Hawaii. For this edition, Karen updated the Shops and Spas, Entertainment and Nightlife, Where to Eat, and Where to Stay chapters.

Kristina Anderson has been writing professionally for more than 25 years. After working as an advertising copywriter and creative director in Southern California for more than a decade, she moved to Hawaii in 1992, freelancing copy and broadcast for Hawaii agencies. Since 2006, she's written for national and regional publications, most notably for *At Home in West Hawaii* magazine, which profiles a variety of homes—from coffee shacks to resort mansions—and for USAToday.com Travel Tips. She also fills in here and there as a substitute teacher, which keeps her busy, as does being a single mom to two teenage boys. When there's time, she paddles outrigger canoes competitively and plays tennis very noncompetitively. For this book, Kristina updated the Experience; Golf, Hiking, and Outdoor Activities; and Travel Smart chapters.